D1342190

When London Calls

The Expatriation of Australian Creative Artists to Britain

For thousands of young Australians the tearful dockside farewell was a rite of passage as they boarded ships bound for London. For some the journey was an extended holiday, but for many actors, painters, musicians, writers and journalists, leaving Australia seemed to be the only path to personal and professional fulfilment. This book is a collective biography of those people who found themselves categorised as expatriates – people such as Leo McKern, Dame Joan Sutherland, Sir Sidney Nolan, Barry Tuckwell, Don Banks, Phillip Knightley, John Pilger, Peter Porter, Richard Neville, Jill Neville and 'megastars' Barry Humphries, Germaine Greer and Clive James. The book tells of choices they made about career and country, yet it is also a cultural history that traces shifts in the complex relationship between Australia and Britain, as the supposed colonial backwater began to develop its own cultural identity.

Stephen Alomes is a Senior Lecturer in Australian Studies at Deakin University. A Harold White Fellow at the National Library of Australia in 1991, he is the author and co-editor of several books. His publications include *A Nation at Last? The Changing Character of Australian Nationalism* (1988), *Australian Nationalism: A Documentary History* (1991), and *High Mark: Australian Football and Australian Culture* (1998). In 1983 he was co-founder of the Australian Studies Association.

For Kate, Rosemary, Murray and Alan

When London Calls

The Expatriation of Australian Creative Artists to Britain

Stephen Alomes
Deakin University

CAMBRIDGE
UNIVERSITY PRESS

PUBLISHED BY THE PRESS SYNDICATE OF THE UNIVERSITY OF CAMBRIDGE
The Pitt Building, Trumpington Street, Cambridge, United Kingdom

CAMBRIDGE UNIVERSITY PRESS
The Edinburgh Building, Cambridge CB2 2RU, UK http://www.cup.cam.ac.uk
40 West 20th Street, New York, NY 10011–4211, USA http://www.cup.org
10 Stamford Road, Oakleigh, 3166, Australia

First published 1999

Printed in Australia by Brown Prior Anderson

Typeface Adobe New Aster 9/12 pt.   *System* QuarkXPress® [BC]

A catalogue record for this book is available from the British Library

National Library of Australia Cataloguing in Publication data
Alomes, Stephen.
When London calls: the expatriation of Australian creative
artists to Britain.
ISBN 0 521 62031 7.
ISBN 0 521 62978 0 (pbk.).
1. Expatriate artists–England–London–Biography.
2. Artists–Australia–Biography. 3. Australia–Relations–
Great Britain. 4. Great Britain–Relations–Australia.
700.92294

ISBN 0 521 62031 7 hardback
ISBN 0 521 62978 0 paperback

Contents

Abbreviations

AAA	Australian Artists Association
ABC	Australian Broadcasting Commission (later Corporation)
AETT	Australian Elizabethan Theatre Trust
AIF	Australian Imperial Forces
AMA	Australian Musical Association
AMFL	Australian Musical Foundation in London
ANU	Australian National University
ANZAC	Australian and New Zealand Army Corps
ASIO	Australian Security Intelligence Organisation
B&B	bed and breakfast
BBC	British Broadcasting Corporation
CIA	Central Intelligence Agency (USA)
CIS	Commonwealth Investigation Service
Con	New South Wales Conservatorium of Music (later Sydney Conservatorium)
CSIRO	Commonwealth Scientific and Industrial Research Organisation
FBI	Federal Bureau of Investigation (USA)
JCW	J. C. Williamson's Ltd
MP	Member of Parliament
MSO	Melbourne Symphony Orchestra
MTC	Melbourne Theatre Company
NIDA	National Institute of Dramatic Art
P&O	Peninsular and Oriental Steam Navigation Company
POW	prisoner of war
QSO	Queensland Symphony Orchestra

R&R	rest and recreation
RADA	Royal Academy of Dramatic Art (UK)
RSL	Returned Services League
semi	semi-detached house
SAW	Society of Australian Writers
SSO	Sydney Symphony Orchestra
TSO	Tasmanian Symphony Orchestra
UTRC	Union Theatre Repertory Company (Melbourne)

When London Calls

They leave us – artists, singers, all –
    When London calls aloud,
Commanding to her Festival
    The gifted crowd.

She sits beside the ship-choked Thames,
    Sad, weary, cruel, grand;
Her crown imperial gleams with gems
    From many a land

From overseas, and far away,
    Come crowded ships and ships –
Grim-faced she gazes on them; yea,
    With scornful lips.

      ès

The student of wild human ways
    In wild new lands; the sage
With new great thoughts; the bard whose lays
    Bring youth to age;

The painter young whose pictures shine
    With colours magical;
The singer with the voice divine –
    She lures them all.

      From Victor Daley 'When London Calls'

Preface

When I sat down with the Australian actor Alan White and a tape recorder on a greyish London day in 1982, I thought that I was beginning a short piece of research about Australian actors and writers who had gone to London in the 1950s and stayed. It was something which might complement my other research on how the British press viewed Australia. Geoff Bolton, then head of the Australian Studies Centre at the University of London, had given me the original idea while I was attached to the Centre on study leave. Over the next few months the small project began to expand; it continued to expand for many years.

After I had returned to Australia it began to be clear to me that the subject of expatriation spoke to many other Australian experiences. It also took me back to earlier personal events: to my own 'big trip', departing on the Chandris Lines ship *Australis*, and then 'Greyhounding' around North America, hitchhiking Western Europe, and working for £20 a week plus luncheon vouchers in an office just off Charing Cross Road, while living in deepest Muswell Hill; then to Bangkok, Singapore and the Nullarbor Plain by air, sea and land on the way home. Although coming from a Tasmanian family which goes back to the first colonial settlement, the research called to mind an earlier sense of Tasmanian expatriates on the mainland – from footballers to artists and public servants – and then my own experience in becoming one of them. I looked back to my father's 'big trip', from 1939 to 1945 with the Sixth Division AIF, to the Middle East, North Africa, Greece, Britain and New Guinea. And forward, to an overpowering fascination with my own changing society, one conceived in international and comparative terms. Perhaps Australians, or some Australians, are, as Charmian Clift wrote, like the albatross, natural fliers who often 'wander further ... dare higher ... accept risk and hazard as part of the exhilaration of getting off the ground'.[1]

In 1989, as interest in Australia grew in Britain and Europe, at a Commonwealth literature conference in Barcelona I shared a platform with the poet Peter Porter. The conference theme was 'A Passage to Somewhere Else', and I was introduced as the one who had not gone away, in contrast to the distinguished expatriate writer of an earlier generation.[2] By then I was seeing this project as both a group biography and a cultural history. The subject was not only the experiences of the expatriates, but the nature and history of the society they left. Of course this did not make the completion of the work easier. As it expanded, both in scope and in the number of subjects, as interviewees recommended that I talk to other expatriates, gave me their friends' phone numbers and suggested new approaches and extra subjects, the complications inherent in writing about the professional and personal lives of several groups of people over a period of years became more and more apparent. Sometimes it seemed that there was no effective way to understand the phenomenon, particularly across professions or periods, or that someone else 'must' be on my list. The demands of several other books called, some related and some not, including studies of contemporary Australian popular culture, Australian nationalism and contemporary France and French nuclear testing.

In the end I decided that the way to analyse the phenomenon was to tell the stories. This I have done, through my own lens, using the stories of the expatriates to explain Australian cultural history, and analysing Australian society from the 1940s on in explaining their experiences. These diverse individual stories are of compelling interest, both on their own and as they help reveal the complexities of expatriation and of Australian cultural history. Narrative or story – in theatre or opera, in fiction or in journalism, that other storytelling craft – is a wonderful vehicle for analysis. It has helped me to understand the shape and parameters of the cultural history of Australia and, to an extent, London, the great world city of the Sixties. This book also has something to say about the choices everyone makes in life – about jobs, people and places – even the choices we make by default, such as 'staying' in a place or a job. As reflected in the interviews drawn on in this study and in the many published sources cited, many of the expatriates made active choices, not all about country or city. Their decisions often included a choice to be freelancers. Many chose to work in a semi-independent relationship with cultural and professional institutions.

The stories of the expatriates introduced in this book are like the stories of many people in many fields of endeavour. In an era of globalisation (or, as the French term it, *uniformisation*) the human story matters all the more, despite attempts to replace it with statistical analysis or hyperconceptualisation. This story is a beginning, a door which might ideally lead to many other accounts of creative Australians – at home or away. Such stories might be told in many different ways – in biographies and autobiographies, or in studies of particular creative professions or individual works. This contribution seeks to sketch those stories, and the changing views and experiences of expatriates over half a century, while placing them in the context of Australian cultural history. Individual actions, which have their own subjective and personal validity, might also be seen as part of larger patterns, such as the epic story of the changing cultural relations between Australia and Britain, particularly London, over time.

Often, when people asked me that recurring question 'What are you doing at the moment?', I answered by mentioning the book about Australian expatriates in London. Their immediate response was 'Oh, you mean Germaine Greer, Barry Humphries and Clive James'. (Some added John Pilger.) In a sense they were right, as these larger-than-life characters figure prominently in any such study. But this book is also about many other people besides this high-profile trio or quartet.

This book is about the experience of being an expatriate in London in the creative and performing arts. It focuses on several clusters of expatriates – in writing and journalism, the stage and music. As a result, other individuals – in politics and business, in law and medicine and in the universities – are not part of it. Even within the arts it would be no more possible to tell the story of every expatriate than it would be to tell the story of every Italian or every Briton who came to Australia.

This study does not concentrate solely on the many high achievers, the most well-known Australians, although their prominence makes them crucial in the story. Nor does it guillotine the period of expatriation. 'Length of stay' is not the sole criterion. Expatriates are those who think of themselves as expatriates rather than immigrants, those who keep up their relationship with the country from which they departed. That often public relationship self-selects them as expatriates for this study. The expatriate experience could be felt very intensely by some who only stayed briefly or became 'serial commuters' between London and Australia. Others, who became integrated into British society, rather like the British newcomers who settled into Australia, the 'immigrants', are generally outside my scope, even if the line between expatriate and immigrant is sometimes a fine one. Since this study is contemporary, those who gave their time and thoughts with generosity are more prominent than those who said 'No' – the publisher who was impossible to deal with (even by phone), and the conservative intellectual and the novelist living in the country, who both emphatically declared that they had no interest in the subject. One group, artists, figure only briefly in this study. Artists travelled often and widely across the world and Australia, but were rarely expatriates in London, despite significant major exceptions such as Sidney Nolan and Arthur Boyd.

Many other Australians form part of this story, but as a backdrop and a chorus, such as the poetry, music and/or lager lovers of Earls Court to Fulham, at the Down Under Club and its successors, and those from even more respectable society. Just off stage are the Australians who made major contributions to important British institutions. Several served the Court of St James: Frederick Fox as Royal Milliner and Stuart Devlin, designer of Australia's decimal coinage, as the Royal goldsmith jeweller. Sir William Heseltine, as press secretary and then private secretary to the Queen, began the necessary process of the 'democratisation' of the monarchy in the 1960s, which would later, in a very different era, have unexpected and unfortunate results. Another rather detached and distant chorus resulted from institutional links between Australian 'colonial' elites and British society: rural and urban upper middle classes travelled to London and the Home Counties for 'the Season'; young Australian girls went to Swiss finishing schools, while other Australians, mainly male, were sent to do a first degree at Oxford or Cambridge. Intermarriage between pastoral wealth and English blue blood was one traditional imperial–colonial result of these patterns. Some later prominent individuals went to Britain to study or live. Malcolm Fraser was sent to Oxford, as was Rupert Murdoch, the son of the Australian press baron, Sir Keith Murdoch, while amongst several Australians who had moved into English society through marriage was Lady Dale Tryon, a fashion designer known as 'Kanga' and friend of Prince Charles.[3] Other diverse Australian involvements in British life, from education to politics, while important, are outside the frames of reference of this study.[4]

In its own way the book pursues, in Lawson's words, 'the tracks we travel', but not usually those of the bush nor those along George Street or Collins Street. They are those of London. Along the Strand, up Charing Cross Road and Shaftesbury Avenue, down Fleet Street and Grays Inn Road (and stopping to drink cold lager at the Surrey Hotel opposite Australia House), performing at Covent Garden and Wigmore Hall, living in Notting Hill Gate, Holland Park, and sometimes Earls Court or Soho, around Russell Square and Kings Cross, and arriving at Tilbury, Waterloo or on the Piccadilly tube line from Heathrow.

I want to thank a number of people. First, the people I interviewed in the course of researching this book, Australian and English, for their participation and assistance, and also the many very helpful English people in London. The following people deserve extra thanks – Kate Jones, in particular, Paul Strangio, and my publisher Phillipa McGuinness, whose visionary enthusiasm has been a stimulus to many authors. Finally, the many people who have commented on chapters, or offered bibliographical and other suggestions: Rosemary Auchmuty, Despina Babbage, Geoffrey Bolton, Godwin Bradbeer, Tim Brown, Jean Callaghan, Frank Campbell, Rosemary Clark, Bruce Davidson, Jim Davidson, Peter Fitzpatrick, Christine Hubert, John Hurst, Patrick Hutchings, Doug Kirsner, Bella Lesman, Bernadette

Lingham, Tom Millar, Dave Nadel, Algerine Neri, Richard Nile, Terry Norris, Wenche Ommundsen, Michael Provis, Michael Roe, Hazel Rowley, Murray Sayle, John Small, Terry Smith, Jim Walter, Carol Williams, Cathy and Bruno at Kensington Fruit and Vegies, and anyone inadvertently left out.

I am grateful to Deakin University for conference and research leave grants, to the Sir Robert Menzies Centre for Australian Studies, which hosted much of this research, and to the conferences of the International Australian Studies Association, the British Australian Studies Association and the European Association for the Study of Australia. Along with innovative courses at Deakin, and students deeply interested in Australian culture and its contexts, they furnished further stimuli for the study of Australian culture in a wider world. I am also grateful to numerous libraries, from Geelong and Moonee Valley to London, and to the National Library of Australia in Canberra for a Harold White Fellowship, which facilitated this research. The reference services of the State Library of Victoria were invaluable. I would particularly like to thank Judy Barber and the changing staff at Deakin who laboured over the transcription of interviews. Finally, I have to thank Don Walker and J. S. Bach for inspiration and that great Australian institution, long service leave, for the time to finish this book.

The following copyright owners have given permission for the reproduction of photographs: Australian Broadcasting Corporation (Jane Holland, Charles Mackerras, Sidney Nolan, Madge Ryan); Australian Music Centre (Don Banks); Douglas Copeland (Geoffrey Parsons); Rolf Harris Productions Pty Ltd (Rolf Harris); David Moore (George Johnston); National Library of Australia (Richard Beynon, Charmian Clift, Peter Finch, Francis Lymburner photographed by Geoff Hawkshaw, Clive James photographed by Virginia Wallace-Crabbe, Leo McKern, Rupert Murdoch, Peter Porter photographed by Peter Coleman); National Press Club (Germaine Greer); John Pilger (John Pilger): Qantas Historical Collection (QANTAS 707); Alan Seymour (Alan Seymour); Heide Smith (Barry Humphries); State Library of New South Wales (*Otranto*); Joan Sutherland (Joan Sutherland); Belinda Webster (David Lumsdaine); View Films (Leo McKern and Julia Blake); Greg Weight (Arthur Boyd, Martin Sharp); Alan White (Alan White). Other photos were taken by the author. I am also grateful for permission to quote from textual sources: to A. D. Hope and Curtis Brown for the poem 'Australia'; to Ray Lawler for excerpts from *The Piccadilly Bushman* (London: Angus & Robertson 1961, revised edition Sydney: Currency Press, 1998); and to Peter Porter for his clerihew, reproduced in Chapter 6.

Every effort has been made to obtain permission to use copyright material reproduced in this book. The publishers would be pleased to hear from copyright holders they have not been able to contact.

Chapter 1

Introduction - Going Away

In the Australian spring of 1946 the ocean liner *Orbita* left Sydney carrying a variety of travellers. A small number were setting out on the grand tour of what remained of Europe. Some were English people returning home. Others were young Australians in search of adventure or a career. One of them was the 26-year-old Reginald Leo McKern. An amateur actor at May Hollingworth's Metropolitan theatre in Sydney, he had also had a professional role in a J. C. Williamson theatres performance of the play *Uncle Harry*. Behind lay other short-lived vocations: an adolescent career in engineering which had looked less promising since he had lost an eye in an industrial accident at the age of 15; an unhappy army experience; an unsuccessful marriage to a Sydney painter which had only lasted 18 months; and a minor career in radio serials and soaps. When Leo McKern arrived in Liverpool with two pounds and ten shillings in his pocket, enough for a train ticket to London (he had spent 325 pounds on the boat fare), he was not only beginning an early stage in his theatrical trajectory, he was also embarking on a journey beyond the geographical one he had already made.[1]

Like many young Australians, he had not made this big move solely in search of a career. Nor had he scraped together the fare just for the romance of Britain and Europe or the call of adventure or the London stage. Like many others in the war-swept 1940s, he pursued love. The actress Jane Holland, whom he had worked with at the Metropolitan theatre in Sydney, had left on an earlier ship, the *Stirling Castle*. McKern followed her in a variation on that other continuing Australian saga, 'For Love Alone'. They would soon be married in a registry office in the outer suburb of Bromley. Along with other young couples in the 1940s, in Britain and Australia, they began their life together living in a single room – first one in Goldhawk Road, Shepherds Bush, then another in Hampstead. They were ready, as much as circumstances allowed, to spread their wings.

That voyage of over 12 000 miles (or 20 000 kilometres) would become an increasingly common one in postwar Australia. Many young Australians made it, with or without the Onkaparinga long johns which McKern's parents had foisted on him, rightly it turned out, given the freezing winter of 1946–47. Their voyages were at the beginning of a rising wave of postwar movement to Britain, a strange and smaller reverse mirror of the even larger human flows south. However, McKern and Holland, and those who followed, continued an older tradition of expatriation.

Expatriation meant, for most Australians, a return to the British Isles. Ever since convicts had been transported for the term of their natural life, and settlers, soldiers and merchants had crossed the seas, the return to Britain had been culturally important. It was almost a natural inversion of the original banishment of convict exile or even just of colonial separation. For the earliest generations of settlers (but not for the Aboriginal people whose continent they had invaded), the islands of England, or its Celtic periphery, were home. The filial aspect of that link would be strengthened by continuing migration from Britain, still predominant in the era of the great European migration of the 1950s, as it had been over a century before.

The links across the world were maintained by sea. The 'Mother Country' and its distant settlements drew nearer in the era of the steamship, particularly after the opening of the Suez Canal in 1867, and the telegraph connection in 1872. In the period of worsening international conflict around the turn of the century, also the era of the height of the romantic mythology of the British Empire, the ties became even closer.

The growing 'Australianist' sentiment amongst the native-born in the years leading up to Federation in 1901 might have arrested this 'imperial' tide. However, at the same time, with the era of the new imperialism, Britain was increasingly romanticised as 'Home'. British popular culture and imperial sentiment reinforced the emotional attachment to the imperial capital, London. Popular song and story, imperial rhetoric and display in schools celebrated the Union Jack, the heroes of Empire (Wolfe of Canada, Clive of India and Gordon of Khartoum), and a world mapped in imperial pink. The blood spilt in the Boer War of 1899–1902 and the Great European War (as it was sometimes then known) of 1914–18, and the rituals of Empire Day on May 24 and royal visits (1901, 1920) further tightened the bonds of the British Empire, as they would do for generations.[2]

In the twentieth century, more sophisticated Australian institutions, based on British models, British ideas and branches of British industry (in publishing as well as manufacturing) tightened the tie. The link, reinforced by the export of Australian primary products to Britain, was now stronger than in the second half of the previous century, when Australians had looked more to the 'Bush' for their influences.

This tradition, slightly changed in character, reached its peak in the period from the 1940s to the 1960s. The ending of World War II allowed people to travel once again, and growing prosperity brought such travel within the reach of more of the population. Even during that peak, the character of 'returns' began to change. Despite strong ties with Britain, and their continuing status as 'British subjects', Australians felt a keener sense of identity, of their own, Australian nationality. In the era of transition, of the last and largest waves of expatriates, more and more of the returnees felt not British, nor British-Australian, but Australian, Australians living overseas. Others felt their identity was divided – they were Australian citizens but their passports designated them as 'British subjects'.

The significance of the expatriate myth in Australian culture, the story of Australians feeling the need to undertake an odyssey or 'return', has been explored in literature. It was a theme in Henry Handel Richardson's novel trilogy *The Fortunes of Richard Mahony* (1930) and in several auto-biographical and fictional accounts, including those of Stella Bowen and Christina Stead. The subject has recently attracted scholarly interest, at a time when the world and travel have become even more diverse. K. S. Inglis explored it in 'Going Home: Australians in England, 1870–1900' while Ros Pesman, in *Duty Free: Australian Women Abroad* (1996), addressed the broader subject of travel by women.[3] Several recent academic studies, novels and short stories have pursued Australians as travellers and tourists and the Australian expatriate experience from Paris to Tuscany.[4] Jim Davidson's *Lyrebird Rising* and *Kathleen O'Connor: Artist in Exile* by Patrick Hutchings and Julie Lewis tell, respectively, the stories of two Parisian careers: those of Louise Hanson-Dyer, who created the Oiseau-Lyre (or Lyrebird) record label, and Kathleen O'Connor, the Western Australian artist, on the other side of the Channel as well as the world. *An Antipodean Collection* (1993) brings together a more recent connection – with Tuscany – which has been important for a diversity of creative individuals including the painter Jeffrey Smart, and the writers David Malouf and Germaine Greer.[5]

A rich popular literature tells biographical, autobiographical and oral tales of expatriation. It includes Garry Kinnane's biography of George Johnston (1986), Charmian Clift's stories of the Johnston–Clift family life in Greece in the 1950s and 1960s; and Alister Kershaw's reminiscences of postwar Paris. Two collections – Clyde Packer's *No Return Ticket* (1984) by expatriates in North America and Europe, and several expatriate tales in Russell Braddon's anthology *Australia Fair?* (1984) – take the story forward. So do plays such as Hannie Rayson's *Hotel Sorrento* (1990), which later became a popular film, and Jack Hibberd's *Malarky Barks* (1983).[6]

Two books have addressed the most high-profile expatriates of the recent era. Christine Wallace's lively biography, *Greer: Untamed Shrew* (1997), captures Germaine Greer, while Ian Britain's *Once an Australian* (1997) paints a series of portraits of, by one reckoning, four talented 'Tall Poppies' or, by another, four 'professional Australians' on the larger stages of London and New York – Germaine Greer, Barry Humphries, Clive James and Robert Hughes. Both studies pursue the relationship between the individual experiences and the oeuvre of these talented media celebrities, performers and writers.

Despite this recent interest in the expatriate experience, absences are still more noticeable than presences. Distinguished Australian expatriates often do not appear in Australian biographical dictionaries, apparently 'written out' of Australian society. Nor has the Australian cultural history of the second half of the twentieth century yet been written. Geoffrey Serle's overview, *From Deserts the Prophets Come* (1973, 1987), charts the outline of the cultural coast. Several specialist studies in music, theatre, literature and art, as well as supporting symposia and reference books, pursue aspects of other areas. Biographical and critical studies are strong in some, but not all, fields. Australian cultural history is no longer a version of *terra Australis incognita* (an unknown great south land), and the myth of *terra nullius* has been refuted regarding culture (as it has long been refuted regarding culture in Australia before 1788). However, the map of the Australian cultural landscape from which the expatriates departed in the 1940s to the 1960s is still more one of outline than of detail.[7]

Filling in the gaps requires several maps. One might focus more closely on a particular artistic profession or movement, or on an individual creator or performer. Another might focus on the act of relocation itself, as demonstrated by the inhabitants of Australia, the most isolated and the most modern of all societies: deracinated, transplanted, immigrant, technological and urbanised. It might pursue the whole gamut of Australian travel and expatriation, from backpackers and group tourists to adventurers and settlers, to Europe, to North America and to Asia and beyond.

However, as an English-speaking society 'founded' by Britain, the relationship between former colony and former imperial centre is fundamental. It has long shaped Australian social institutions and ideology, cultural traditions and practices. In the postwar years 'cultured' Australians, like many American artists and intellectuals in the nineteenth and early twentieth century, often looked to Britain and Europe as the fount of their traditions.[8] As fundamentally different as Australian society is from that of England (or from the other parts of the British Isles), the influences and ideas derived from Britain have been powerful. Many are still important today.

Too often the cultural history of a society or the career of a talented individual is seen in simple terms. In Australia, dualism dominates. Two opposed sets of terms describe the cultural history of the new world society and of the relationship of its leading creative talents to it, particularly the expatriates. On the one hand, different bodies and individuals look for an 'Australian identity' expressed in the arts – an 'Australian sound' or 'sounds Australian' in music, an 'Australian look' in television. Like the earlier bush or beach images of idealised Australia, such aspirations can involve a romantic conception of a national culture, or even a national essence.[9]

It is as if, since the cultural efflorescence of the 1970s, the ideal of the title of Geoffrey Serle's cultural history of Australia, *From Deserts the Prophets Come*, has been realised. A deeper and more sophisticated national culture had been created, although very different to the old 'Australian Legend' bush ideal. Serle's title draws on A. D. Hope's poem 'Australia', written in 1938, the year of the sesquicentenary of the landing of the First Fleet. In it the poet reflected on his country and its future:

> Hoping, if still from deserts the prophets come,
> Such savage and scarlet as no green hills dare
> Springs in this waste . . .

Yet, despite the important redefinitions of Australian culture and identity by the original Australians, the indigenous Aboriginal people, and by elements of the pluralist settler society, and despite the influence of postmodernist ideas of play supplanting meaning in a world of shifting identities, the dream remains strong. It has become all the more compelling in times of incessant change, in a world which is international and global as well as national and local. It is not, however, as the expatriates well know, the entire story.

The other story, an opposite or even antithetical tale, is equally romantic. It is the story of the talented individual and loner, a creative outsider, an Odysseus only able to realise his or her talents through their wandering. This romantic tale, informed by the Byronic adventurer myth and then the twentieth-century ideal of the artist as different, was reflected in the infatuation with the Bloomsbury group in some cultural milieux in the 1950s–60s. In the Australian context, the romantic story is often one of *from deserts the prophets escape*. From a land of provincialism and mediocrity, of materialism and even egalitarian repression of the different and the talented, the artists flee. Would time and experience reconcile these two essentialised ideals of artist and nation?

The life of a country and its culture and the careers of expatriate artists are more complex than such romantic simplifications will allow. It is the common role of creative artists and performers, those who leave and those who stay, to explore (often at a personal cost) moral, aesthetic and social questions. Many of those who stayed, as well as those who went, were committed to their society, even as they were tortured by its contradictions. 'Nugget' Coombs, patron of the arts in Australia and the architect of government support for the arts from the 1940s to the 1970s, declared himself, in the words of the poet James McAuley, 'fitted to that land as the soul is to the body', even while he worked to reshape some aspects of Australian society.[10]

Expatriation increased the contradictions experienced by artists in general, and expatriates were often torn by their longing and their divided cultural and social selves. In the romantic tradition, their lives and their self-knowledge were won sometimes by suffering which could include the pangs of longing or even angst regarding their own identity. Sometimes love was expressed as frustration or even anger at the imperfections of the loved one – their country of origin.

These two romantic dualities, of national essence and artistic wanderers, have popular versions as well. In one version, the expatriates went to London because of an Australian colonial cultural cringe which inevitably assumed that the best was found overseas and that the Australian was inferior. In a variant of this theme, the cringe was *about* culture. Australia was a land of sport, leisure, agriculture, not artistic creativity. The colonial tradition associated Britain, especially London, with the mind and 'culture', Australia with matter and 'nature'. In the other version, the expatriates, whether viewed from positive or negative positions, were 'tall poppies'. They might be either talented individuals, deserving of recognition, who had had to leave the country to get it, or merely self-important 'ex-patriots' who had 'got too big for their boots' and 'needed to be cut down to size'.[11]

This book will show that, however appealing the romantic polarities, the complex truth of being an Australian and an Australian expatriate in the twentieth century was more interesting and more profound than either idealised position. Reality was much more difficult than simple images associating Europe with standards and culture, and Australia with body and sun.

Expatriation ... An Australian Story

An ocean-going liner had long been a visual motif in Australian life, especially from the 1940s to the 1960s. Dramatic emotional scenes would occur as the great liners arrived and departed. Arriving, they carried a human cargo of immigrants who had just had their first sight of their new land. Departing, they took not only travellers and some returning immigrants, but thousands of young Australians who were setting out to 'see the world' or to pursue a career beyond what they saw as provincial Australia. The paper streamers, which joined the passengers to the shore crowds until the ship sailed away and then cut them 'like a hundred umbilical cords' (as Jill Neville recalled), the farewell parties, the last hugs and kisses and the exchange of letters and addresses with those who had gone ahead were rituals of Australian adulthood. For many Australians, the overseas odyssey was central to their own coming of age. At the same time, the continued absence of so many talented young people would frustrate the nation's social, cultural and political development or, as some observers called it, Australia's 'Coming of Age'.[12] In the arts and intellectual life, was London's gain Australia's loss?

The great wave of expatriation to London and Europe after World War II, which this study focuses on, occurred during the last important stage of imperial–colonial relations. Although no longer a colony, Australia still seemed provincial, unable to appreciate the arts or to sustain full-time careers in them. Writers, artists, musicians and actors set out on a journey in search of new opportunities, while also following in the tracks of their predecessors. Their distinguished number had included the writer Henry Lawson, the painter Arthur Streeton and the singer Nellie Melba. The origins of the journey to the imperial centre and the old world lay in the derivative character of Australian culture and in the dependent colonial relationship of the Australian settler societies to Britain.

The Australian experience after 1788 was not just that of six colonies of Great Britain. The colonies were also part of a larger entity – the greatest empire the world had seen. Improved communications led to colonial dependency in the arts and the loss of talent to the imperial centre becoming the norm. I have argued elsewhere that a key period in Australian history is that of 'Dominion Culture' from the late nineteenth century to World War II. In these years, named for Australia's formal status as an 'autonomous' 'Dominion' within the British Empire (a concept defined in 1926 and formally acquired through the Statute of Westminster in 1931), provincial orientation to the 'Mother Country' severely qualified the seeming national independence of Federation in 1901. (Australia did not ratify the statute until 1942, in the dark days of World War II.) Steamships, telegraph cables and later radio strengthened the colonial bonds of 'Empire'. Just as Australia produced wheat and wool, soldiers and sportsmen for 'export', in the arts 'the export of talent' to London had become commonplace.[13]

The Colonial Cultural Cringe

'Colonial' meant more than the division of artistic labour and capital between the imperial centre and the colonies, the latter providing audiences and young talent, but few career opportunities, except in popular variety. The word also carried the association of status inferiority which followed from it. Colonial often meant inferior, second rate, provincial and even crude. In the formal 'colonial' era, before Federation, critics found colonial beer insipid, colonial wine undrinkable and colonial speech uncultured. In 1869, an observer remarked that 'the word "colonial" is often used to express disparagement; "colonial manners", for instance, is now and then employed as a synonym for roughness'.[14] Nor did such views disappear entirely in the mid-twentieth century. In the 1950s, the linguist A. G. Mitchell suggested that Australia was the only Anglo-Saxon community which was ashamed of having its own way of pronouncing the English language.[15] Even later in the century, Australians arriving in Britain were still being received as 'colonials', a term at best a form of amused condescension, at worst an expression of politely masked social and cultural contempt. In 1998, Kathy Lette, the ever outspoken Australian novelist and performer in London, remarked that Australians were still seen by the English as 'the Irish of the Pacific ... with some sort of recessive gene'.[16]

Australian social, cultural and professional institutions placed the English and British originals at the apex of the pyramid of status in the Dominion Culture. First, British training and development, later British and imperial honours, capped Australian achievements. Cultural industries were centralised in the metropolis of London, at the expense of the small capitals of the less populous colonial societies. This concentration frustrated and impeded the elaboration of cultural institutions in Australia – professional theatre companies and orchestras, book and music publishers. Cultural centralisation seemed to confirm that Australia was a frontier or bush society, oriented towards the pioneering emphasis on the physical, valuing material over cultural achievement. Expatriates were pulled to London by career possibilities in writing, music, theatre and journalism. Simultaneously, they were pushed away from Australia by the lack of such professional opportunities, by the unsophisticated level of development, and by the absence of an appreciative audience in Sydney or Melbourne, Brisbane or Perth, Hobart or Adelaide. A British elite view, shared by many Australians in the arts and the professions, was that the Australian cities were as much provincial extensions of London as were Bristol or Birmingham.

The colonial theme of intellectual frustration in Australia, of alienation from the country, is often central in the expatriate story. Distaste for Australia or alienation recurs often in Australian intellectual history, in part because of English children's books which taught a love of England and its country gardens. Shirley Hazzard, the expatriate novelist who chose European and American routes, recalled her 1930s–40s schooling in which literature 'had placed Australia in perpetual, flagrant violation of reality'. In suburban schools in Australian cities, girls were taught about Kew gardens, 'Come down to Kew in lilac time (it isn't far from London!)'. In opposition to the rich colour of English history, 'Australian history, given once a week only', was 'easily contained in a small book, dun-coloured as the scenes described'. In contrast, 'History itself proceeded, gorgeous, spiritualised, without a downward glance at Australia'.[17]

Implicit was a rejection of the wild beauties and subtle nuances of the 'Bush'. It often went deeper than the teaching of English flora rather than the beauties of the gum tree. Despite Dorothea Mackellar's expression in 1908 of poetic love for her 'sunburnt country', many colonial settlers had not come to terms with their land or with themselves. Henry Lawson sketched a disgruntled Australian in New Zealand who declared that Australia is 'only a mongrel desert . . . The worst dried-up, God-forsaken country I was ever in . . . I was born there. That's the main thing I've got against the darned country'.[18]

Like other 'colonials' around the world, Australian intellectuals felt the frustrations of being inferiors, far from the centre with which they sought to identify. Like 'educated' Africans and Indians in the era of the British Empire, like some Americans until the early twentieth century, they also dreamed of the mists and mystique of London, or, less often, Paris. Frantz Fanon's theory of the 'colonised' has partial applicability to the settler colonials of Australia and their cultural–social relationship to London and Britain. Fanon's analysis, with the word 'colonial' substituted for 'jungle' in the last sentence, may help explain the hesitancy of Australian cultural development:

> Every colonised people – in other words, every people in whose soul an inferiority cultural complex has been created by the death and burial of its local cultural originality – finds itself face to face with the language of the civilising nation; that is, with the culture of the mother country. The colonised is elevated above his jungle status in proportion to his adoption of the mother country's cultural standards.

The qualification that Australia as a settler society was derived from the 'Mother Country', unlike the subject Aboriginal people whom the settlers had subjugated, is essential. Within a century and a half, however, 'white' Australia had acquired its own accent, and its own voice, if not a different language. Here the hierarchical relationship of imperial–colonial superiority and inferiority merges into a metropolitan–provincial relationship. 'There is the city, there is the country. There is the capital, there is the province', Fanon continues, noting that the Lyonnais in Paris has a similar problem.[19] Many Australians learned a colonial cultural cringe which demanded that they distance themselves from the uncultured tones of their Australian selves. Arthur Phillips' famous article, which introduced the term into Australian intellectual debate in the 1940s and 1950s, intensified awareness of an already familiar problem.[20] This habit of 'culturally cringing' associated status and significance with 'overseas', particularly with London achievement, influencing both the psychology of expatriation and of Australian cultural activity.

The problem for Australian creators and performers was partly structural. However, often their artistic frustration was emotionally expressed by expatriates as a tale of rejection, or of indifference, on the part of an uncultured or uncaring country and its people. This was the economic cringe. Structures of production, or the lack of them, in the form of professional arts institutions offering training and employment, were the first problem. A parallel problem was that the dominant structures of prestige placed the highest status value, and therefore also monetary value, on imported performers and writers. To understand these two structural constraints, and the smaller market available to those creating at the periphery rather than the centre, it is necessary to look beyond simple views. The simple national maturation or 'coming of age' model, itself an inevitably colonial concept, is inadequate. Nor does a depiction of an uncultured, uninterested Australia adequately describe the reality. The continuing situation was one of under-development. (Geoffrey Serle utilises the more neutral 'delayed development' regarding the 1950s–60s.) Only over time would home-grown structures of production and prestige emerge. A larger question was that of how they would contend with the economies of scale, the celebrity status mechanisms and world markets in the subsequent eras of internationalisation and globalisation.

A recognition of these structural factors does not deny the often bitter historical reality. The relationship between the writer and the country had always reflected the inevitable ambivalence about Australia and London. Henry Lawson simultaneously looked down on 'the surplus little men of London journalism' who edited Sydney journals while having 'an ignorant contempt for Australia and all that was Australian', and yet sought London himself. He asked for assistance from the literary patron, the Governor Earl Beauchamp, to make the trip: 'The position of purely Australian literature is altogether hopeless in Australia – there is no market. The oldest and wealthiest Daily in Australia fills its columns with matter clipped from English and American magazines … Nothing "goes" well here that does not come from or through England'.[21] Often the very attempt to fit into English mores led to a divided self, to being torn between a London style and an Australian persona, whether expressed in accent or speech, dress or manners. For expatriate artists, outward renunciation of their own country, which did not offer a career in their chosen profession, was one way of attempting to resolve the inner division. Lawson's London episode from 1900 to 1902 had mixed results. He wrote the impressive 'Joe Wilson' stories about the bush while there, and received good reviews. However, after his return to Australia only two years later his ongoing decline continued, partly due to personal difficulties, including a failing marriage.

The very term 'expatriate' and the related term 'exile' express these contra-dictions. Many later, post-World War II, expatriates felt themselves refugees from Australian culture and society, and sometimes from the conservative politics of the Cold War and the Vietnam War eras in general. However, most were cultural expatriates who departed voluntarily, despite the enforced separation that distance, length of journey and cost entailed in the era of sea travel. Only a few political exiles were driven from their land by legal banishment.[22] They comprised two groups. Several physics research students, who were also Communists, protested outside Australia House in London during the 1949 coal strike. They knew that their job prospects in Australia would be poor.[23] A second less visible group comprised those young men who left Australia in the 1960s to avoid possible conscription for the Vietnam War. Expatriation was by choice rather than legal necessity, however strong the emotional imperative to escape or depart. An expatriate by choice, sometimes through work and love, could over time become an immigrant, blending into the scenery and becoming fully integrated into their new society. Some actors, writers and musicians would eventually carry a British passport or, at least become more widely known in Britain than in Australia.

Many others remained self-consciously expatriates, Australians in Britain. The actor Alan White carried his nationality in legal form – in an Australian passport, which required more visas than a British passport. Other expatriates maintained their links with Australia, whether by occasional return, or through letters and friends. For actors, this was usually a private rather than a professional persona. To be an Australian on stage, a role played by Bill Kerr, could confine an actor to few or minor roles, a colonial cousin variant on the country yokel. It was not much in demand.

A small minority of Australians in Britain comprised a very different type, the *émigré*. Some members of the elite families, such as the Baillieus and Boyds, felt that they were a kind of *émigré*, returning to Britain as well as leaving behind the uncultured society of Australia. The expatriates sometimes felt outside Australian culture and society. They no longer fitted in. However, most did not feel part of somewhere else – where they also didn't quite fit. In contrast, the wealthier *émigrés* left as much because they felt themselves to be part of Britain as because they felt themselves to be not completely part of Australia. This complex theme, which is another story, ran through the culture of Melbourne's Boyd family and is explored in the novels of Martin Boyd.[24] In Rome, he found a personal solution. There, he was free of being either colonial upper class in Australia or still a 'colonial' in Britain.

An Old Tradition

Expatriation was an old custom which grew over time. In one of the cruel ironies of colonialism, the first large exodus of expatriates occurred at the very time Australia was moving towards the nationhood expressed in Federation in 1901. The 1890s Depression drove artists and writers away in search of a livable income. The actor and playwright Haddon Chambers, and the vaudeville and music hall star Florrie Forde, were amongst several Australian performers who went to Britain in the late nineteenth century. In the early 1900s, many artists put together the boat fare and followed. In this era, Victor Daley lamented that 'When London Calls', Australian artists and writers answer:

> They leave us – artists, singers, all –
> When London calls aloud,
> Commanding to her Festival
> The gifted crowd.

For the artist the allure was often deceptive. While 'Her crown imperial gleams with gems/From many a land', for painters, students and storytellers from 'the Empire's rim' her welcoming smiles were 'death to him'.[25]

This first generation of expatriates – artists and writers, singers and musicians – which appeared between the 1890s and the Great War, provoked bitter debate even then. The painter George Lambert declared that 'an artist belongs to no one country; it's a provincial outlook to think so'. The occasional traveller and writer, artist and cartoonist Norman Lindsay had a different view. He dismissed the species: 'an expatriate is only half a person'.[26] Expatriation – for shorter or longer – had varying results. While Henry Lawson had written some of his best stories in London, the 1880s–90s artists achieved less. In Bernard Smith's summation of the early 1900s, 'it was in the Chelsea Arts Club that the Heidelberg School established its last and least distinguished camp'. Smith discerned a significant pattern in these phases of Australian cultural history. When the Genesis of the Heidelberg School had given way to Exodus, there was a loss for art as well as for Australian culture. The Leviticus, which saw the return and the honouring by established society of such artists as Sir Arthur Streeton, whose work had now lost its freshness, was also a problematical moment for Australian culture.[27]

In the 1920s, although not on the scale of the American expatriation to Paris, London continued to attract the colonial sons and daughters of the Empire who sometimes had family as well as cultural links with Britain. Some, like the freelance writer Jack Lindsay, would remain in Britain for decades or even forever. The onset of the Great Depression in 1929 meant that for a decade and a half (till the end of the war in 1945), the journey became less common. Even then, several performers sought opportunities in London. They included the ballet dancer Robert Helpmann, who had added the European second 'n' to his name, the pianist Eileen Joyce, who had left to study in Europe in 1927, and the singer and broadcaster Wilfrid Thomas.

In the years after World War II, travel to Britain and Europe took on a new character. Travel changed, as did society in the old and the new world. The poverty which had sent immigrants south in their thousands had its opposite in postwar economic growth in Australia, which provided the wherewithal to travel for a last generation of expatriates. Paradoxically, that same growth was, very slowly, strengthening support for cultural activities in Australia. But mass expatriation was on the verge of turning into mass travel. Just at the time when more and more people could contemplate expatriation, this Australian phenomenon was under pressure. The odyssey of several years would eventually give way to the short trip of a year, a few months or even a few weeks. By 1972, with the coming of the Boeing 747 jumbo jet and cheap air travel, Qantas introduced a round-trip economy-class return fare to London of $750, or around eight weeks' pay for the average Australian male. In 1946, Leo McKern's £325 one-way fare by ship was equivalent to more than the average male pay for a year.[28] In an increasingly international world, from the late 1960s young travellers would head off on shorter or longer journeys to Europe, North America and Asia as well as to the UK.

The changes in Australia were not a simple progression from colonial dependency to maturity. There were costs, both for the society and for individuals. Some of the expatriates had felt confined to Australia by the war of 1939 to 1945. Others escaped a 1950s and early 1960s Australia which they saw as combining suburban materialism with the repression of difference and of dissent. The material affluence which drew the immigrants simultaneously repelled sensitive young Australians, while providing the money to support their overseas journeys. The voyagers went mainly to London, the mecca of the English-speaking world, where Australians could also legally work. As they pursued their off-beat adventures and their careers in Britain, Australia, which had seemed on the verge of a cultural maturation in the 1940s, temporarily stalled. The lack of professional cultural opportunities, that is employment in the arts, had forced them to leave. In turn, the departures of so many talented people inevitably exacerbated the limitations of Australian cultural activity. In a circular way, the process seemed to confirm that if you wanted to pursue a cultural vocation, Australia was 'A good country to get out of!' Completing the circle, as a Senate committee on Australian television noted in 1963, the absence of so many of the best writers, directors, actors and designers made it hard to develop Australian drama in the new medium.[29]

Almost as the new waves of expatriates were departing in the early 1960s, immigrants from Europe and their children were beginning to contribute to Australian cultural and intellectual life (after the difficult early days of the battle for economic improvement). Similarly, from the late 1960s, the baby boomers began to make their cultural–political impact. Many travelled, but soon returned from overseas. Having grown up in a suburban Australia, with limited links to the imperial past and diminishing connections with British culture, they were reshaping Australian culture in original ways.

In Australia's divided culture, the best and brightest were encouraged to go away, and a number stayed away. In the arts, the universities, the press and medicine and law, it was assumed that 'overseas' (which usually meant

Britain) was a desirable step on the career ladder. For the artistic individuals, the Ulysses who set off north on their personal odysseys, the journey was a complicated one. In many ways it was even more complex than the voyage of the immigrants who sailed south, forsaking their homelands to seek economic success and a new life in Australia.

Yet in some respects it was also an easy and obvious move. Young Australians had grown up in a society which, socially and visually, was influenced by institutions on the English model.[30] Imperial pink marked the familiar parts of world maps, red telephone and letter boxes, even school doormats, were branded, first with 'GR' (George Rex) and then with 'ER' (Elizabeth Regina). Government mail was 'OHMS' (On His/Her Majesty's Service) and Australians were 'British subjects' who carried passports with the term 'British Passport' on the outside cover only, except for a brief period in the late 1940s when the Chifley Labor government created an Australian passport. In some social circles the formal English accents on the ABC, the English repertory theatre voices and the drawing room comedies on Australian stages seemed to confirm that Australia was like England, or Britain, with more sun. As the historian Jim Davidson has observed, for many expatriates at this time 'there was no particular wrench involved in getting up and going to London; it was merely a move to the other end of the spectrum'.[31]

The World They Made

The postwar experience of expatriation to London is a chapter in Australian cultural history. It tells the story of the tensions and difficulties of creators, performers and writers who felt intense ambivalence about Australia and about Britain and about being, in the words of the journalist Murray Sayle, that 'other nationality' – an Australian expatriate.[32] It is also the tale of an Australia between colonial cultural dependency and vitality; of a culture between the tradition of looking to Britain for institutions, opportunities and excellence and the creation of an autonomous locally centred culture, one which did not look automatically to London for status or standards. Self-confident Australian institutions, still within Western artistic traditions and within the Anglo-Saxon cultures of publishing and the stage, neither provincially parochial nor mechanically deferential, were an inevitable natural outcome. But this would take time. A dispersed population, the lack of a single metropolitan centre providing large audiences for performances, and a relatively small market (which was also open to the trade winds of British and American culture because of the common language) all frustrated Australian cultural development.

In the 1950s and 1960s, expatriates often felt themselves to be in 'no man's land' – both alienated and loving critics of Australia. In Britain, they were sometimes seen as 'pushy colonials' or 'aggressive Australians'. In Australia, they could be viewed as traitors, as 'ex-patriots', as the newspapers often spelled the word. At a simple level, the expatriate was seen as a traitor for leaving his or her own native land. In more precise ways, expatriate critics of Australia, including Barry Humphries, Germaine Greer and the very different John Pilger, were welcomed and dismissed in the 1970s, 1980s and 1990s. They were *either* seen as perceptive observers, saying what could not be said within the country, *or* viewed as out-of-touch expatriates with no right to comment, who caricatured a past Australia as the present. From the 1970s era of national self-assertiveness onwards, such criticism intensified.

At the same time, several successful expatriates were welcomed back as 'tall poppies', Australians who had 'made their mark' on the world stage. Two examples of this were the Joan Sutherland return of 1965, and the popular embrace of Barry Humphries in the late 1960s and early 1970s. Like the private and public rituals of departure, the return of the successful performer was an Australian social institution. In particular, the Sutherland opera tour, which echoed the Dame Nellie Melba seasons of earlier in the century, seemed to suggest that little had changed in Australian culture.

In the creative and performing arts, a number of expatriates remained in Britain for varying periods, including 'forever'. They are central in this study. In classical music, amongst the many prominent expatriates were the composers Don Banks, Malcolm Williamson and David Lumsdaine, the singers Joan Sutherland, Yvonne Minton and Geoffrey Chard and the musicians Charles Mackerras, Barry Tuckwell, Geoffrey Parsons and John Williams. In theatre, the cast included Peter Finch (who went to Hollywood), Leo McKern, Keith Michell, Alan White, Madge Ryan, Michael Blakemore, Alan Seymour and Richard Beynon. In other fields, the earlier traveller, the dancer and performer-at-large Robert Helpmann, the designers Loudon Sainthill, Jocelyn Rickards, and later Luciana Arrighi, and the painters Arthur Boyd and Sidney Nolan found audiences for their work in Britain as much as Australia.

The 1950s was the last great decade of attraction of writers to London. However, the legacy left on the strand of the Thames included the novelist Jill Neville and the poet Peter Porter. Working at their typewriters around Fleet Street were the feature writers Phillip Knightley, Murray Sayle and John Pilger, as well as, for a time, the media magnate Rupert Murdoch. Hundreds of journalists spent time in London, either on working holidays or working for the London bureaus of the Australian papers, although the US and Canada and later Hong Kong also attracted a few scribes.

The highest expatriate profile came in two very different forms. One was the brief discovery of 'Swinging London' in the 1960s by a peaceful army of travellers including Richard Neville, Martin Sharp, Marsha Rowe and the other *OZ* magazine enthusiasts. Another, ongoing, phenomenon provided the public and media face of expatriation for the rest of the century: from the late

1950s onwards, four 'stereotype Australians' – Barry Humphries, Clive James and Germaine Greer and their brush-wielding and wobble-boarding confrère, Rolf Harris – built media careers in Britain, and also performed in Australia. An even larger contingent of travelling young Australians were associated with Earls Court or 'Kangaroo Valley', even though most Australians were dispersed around London's myriad suburbs. The former were apotheosised in Humphries' caricature, 'Bazza McKenzie', the innocent beer-drinker abroad, renowned for 'holding his own'. The stereotype also confirmed the strongest of British prejudices about their uncouth Antipodean cousins.[33]

The British Story, the London Story ... and Australia

The Australian expatriate saga is also a window into the changing history of Britain, especially London. In the half-century after 1945 Australian expatriate artists made their careers in a Britain which was changing socially and economically, culturally and politically. The young Australians participated in the revival of postwar cultural activity in a Britain experiencing the austerity of rationing and housing shortages. They then lived through several social, cultural and political eras. The 1951 Festival of Britain and the 1953 Coronation raised hopes of renewal; confirmed in part by London's rise as a world musical centre, at a time when Europe was still coping with the devastation of war. Then came the magic of Sixties London, when the post-imperial capital became the 'international city', followed by the economic difficulties and social/political conflicts of the 1970s–1980s, and their concomitant cultural stringencies. Finally, in the last decade of the century, persistent older themes were complemented by the hopes of a European 'New Britain'.

The story is also one of the often parallel, but often different, Australian developments. The postwar lack of opportunities slowly gave way over subsequent decades to the elaboration of professional institutions. Change continued. The social/cultural/political conflicts of the 1960s led to the 1970s hopes and cultural nationalism of the Whitlam era. Then followed the political/economic and social/cultural redefinitions of the Fraser, Hawke and Keating political eras. Finally, in Britain and Australia, the 1990s saw a new diversity of cultural forms and opportunities, the pressures of economic stringency and the penetration of global culture. The cultural relationship between Australia and London and the roles of the expatriates were often central to Australian cultural history during these years.

Over time, as Britain and London changed, and Australian institutions and society evolved, generations of Australian expatriates had to make personal and professional decisions about their lives and about where their own futures lay – in London or Australia. Those decisions, like their original decision to voyage to London, would have great significance for them, for Britain and for Australia. Questions of a cultural career or an ordinary everyday career, of whether 'to go or not to go', were pressing. Individuals had to choose between the often exciting, but frustrating, Australian stages, concert halls and newspapers of the 1940s and early 1950s, and the journey to the traditional imperial capital of London. It is with these decisions that this story begins.

Chapter 2

An Australian Theatre or A Career on the Stage?[1]

The greatest drama of all, World War II, shaped Australian society and culture in the 1940s. After a decade of economic depression, the threat of war to national survival engendered cultural as well as military responses. In new small theatre companies original Australian plays and European classics contributed to questions of national culture as well as to popular entertainment and polite civilisation. Refugee ballet dancers, visiting American musicians in the military, returned servicemen from the army entertainment units, as well as from less entertaining units, were contributing to Australian cultural life. The republication in 1944 of Joseph Furphy's novel *Such is Life* and the wartime rediscovery of the 'Legend of the Nineties' – the 1890s cultural efflorescence of Henry Lawson, the young *Bulletin* and the Heidelberg painters – confirmed that there was an Australian tradition. Charles Chauvel's film masterpiece, *Forty Thousand Horsemen* (1940), celebrated the Light Horse Brigade of World War I. Films by the English Ealing company, such as *The Overlanders* (1946), which were set in Australia and told Australian stories, also brought Australian themes before Australian audiences.[2]

The idea of a national theatre became a subject of widespread interest and debate in the 1940s, with numerous individuals and organisations making proposals to the Commonwealth government, although the idea also suggested the contradictions of the time. The Australian debate reflected similar proposals in Britain, but it raised two quite different questions: one, developing Australian traditions on the stage; and two, providing professional opportunities for Australian actors. This combination was exemplified in a submission made in 1948 by the Theatre Council of Western Australia.[3]

It proposed a touring company (rather than merely a Sydney or Melbourne company) which 'should consist mainly of Australians' and seek:

(i)   continually to raise the standard of Australian productions
(ii) to provide a vehicle for the best Australian producers, actors, artists and playwrights
(iii) to develop a discriminating Australian audience.

The problem was not just the social and economic one of creating a professional theatre which was popular and financially viable. It was also a cultural one. As the Army Education pamphlet 'Drama in Our Lives' observed, theatre organisations mainly presented 'overseas plays which have recently been smash-hits'. The resultant theatrical habit of mind was suspicion regarding 'plays about our own life', which the audience now shared. They tended 'to think a play is only "real" when it deals with Mayfair, Brooklyn or Ruritania'.[4]

The national theatre debate culminated in a report, commissioned by the Chifley government a few months before its demise in 1949, from the visiting British actor-director Tyrone Guthrie. The underlying question, then and later, was whether Australia would develop an Australian stage or whether actors and playwrights who wanted to work full-time at their profession would have to go overseas, mainly to London, to pursue their chosen vocation.

The prospect of an Australian theatre had been emerging for some time. The proliferation of little theatre companies during the depression and war had shown that adversity could nurture opportunity. New companies in the 1930s had included Doris Fitton's Independent in Sydney, the radical New Theatres in Sydney and Melbourne and the National Theatre Movement in Melbourne. In the 1940s the productions of the Mercury and the Metropolitan theatre companies in Sydney were further evidence of a more established theatrical life. Original Australian plays, including Sumner Locke Elliott's frank drama of army life, *Rusty Bugles*, and Douglas Stewart's verse play, *Ned Kelly*, suggested that an Australian theatrical culture was emerging. The Playwrights Advisory Board's annual competitions and Leslie Rees' work in developing ABC radio plays seemed to confirm the positive signs.[5]

The 1940s also offered more practical advances, especially for actors. The war had allowed some performers the unusual opportunity of several years paid work on the stage, entertaining troops. Meanwhile the new union, Actors and Announcers Equity (later Actors Equity), successfully campaigned for a closed shop and better wages and allowances. Combined with the possibility of regular, if theatrically menial, work in the new radio soap opera industry, this made it possible to make a kind of living as an actor.

Other off-stage events raised the hopes of young Australian actors as well. Australian cultural paradoxes were at their most intense in the darkest years of the war. The very threat posed by German submarines and Japanese aircraft carriers offered a practical, if perverse, stimulation to Australian cultural activity as well as to Australian manufacturing industry. When the usual overseas stars of stage and concert hall could not get to Australia, Australian performers grabbed the hitherto missing opportunity to play the lead roles on stage or as soloists with orchestras. That old colonial principle, enunciated by the entrepreneur James Cassius Williamson, that 'Australians won't have Australians', and practised by 'the Firm' (J. C. Williamson's) that still bore his name, was under challenge. The colonial cultural cringe assumption that real stars came from overseas was, perforce, rejected. Lloyd Lamble became not only president of the industrially militant Actors Equity but a leading man of the Australian stage, including the world of 'JCW's'. Audiences began to realise that yesterday's visiting 'stars', who had had their names up in lights, were nothing of the kind; they had either been fading stars or lesser lights who suddenly became 'stars' when presented to unknowing Australian theatregoers. The experience of being thrown in the deep end enhanced Australian actors' development more effectively than any conventional apprenticeship could have done.

Could it be that Australia was at last coming of age in the performing arts? Or even, as the comedian 'Mo McCaughey' (Roy Rene) and the compere Jack Davey were demonstrating at the Tivoli and on radio, older traditions of popular theatrical entertainment were now alive again? Positively, the 1940s was an era of indigenous and international influences. The de Basil ballet company of the Ballet Russes, stranded in Australia by the war, the Borovansky Ballet formed in Melbourne from 1940, and the visiting American conductor Eugene Ormandy were early stimuli.[6] An underlying paradox was that often the local, if not necessarily indigenous, was stimulated by the foreign. Developments that suggested a new vigour in the performing arts included the appointment of the conductor Eugene Goossens to the Sydney Conservatorium of Music, the enlarged Sydney Symphony Orchestra, the Olivier/Leigh 'Old Vic' Company tour of 1948, and the gathering movement for a national theatre.

The cultural excitement of the 1940s attracted new talent. Among the legion of actors recruited to the stage were Keith Michell from Adelaide, Richard Beynon from Melbourne, and Peter Finch, Lloyd Lamble, Michael Blakemore, Leo McKern and Alan White from Sydney. Nor were Australian cities without their bohemian groups. In Sydney they gathered in cafes, pubs and clubs in the city and at Kings Cross. Further up the hill in Edgecliff, at parties at the bohemian artists' grand house, 'Merioola', actors, designers, writers and painters created their own stage. Its stars included the painter Jocelyn Rickards and her friend the photographer Alec Murray, the designer Loudon Sainthill and his friend Harry Tatlock Miller. Actors, journalists, drinkers and would-be philosophers could also be found with Peter Finch at

Kings Cross parties or at the Saturday night 'dos' at the Bondi flat of the journalist couple George Johnston and Charmian Clift.[7]

Mercurial Dreams, Theatrical Hopes

The prospects and frustrations of an Australian stage were apparent in the history of the Mercury theatre company in Sydney and in the careers of its principals, who included Peter Finch and Alan White. The Mercury theatre company, in which the actors pooled their small box office, grew partly out of the improvisations and mateship of the Australian Army Entertainment Unit. In the spirit of the times, a number of returned soldier actors, including Peter Finch and Allan Ashbolt, had taken things into their own hands.[8] Swept up with contemporary nationalism and internationalism simultaneously, they championed the creativity of drama over the destructive force of war. Peace offered both increased cultural opportunities in Australia and personal possibilities beyond its shores. A chance meeting between Peter Finch and the Hungarian refugee Sydney John Kay in a cafe in the Cross led to the creation of the Mercury company, supported by the 'capital' of the army back pay of Finch and his fellow returnees White, Ashbolt and Michael Pate. Amidst the contemporary ferment of ideas, dreams of a national theatre coalesced with the international influences of Gogol, Ibsen, Molière and Strindberg, and the dramatic ideas of Louis Jouvet and Stanislavsky. The approach to breathing of Gertrud Bodenwieser, the refugee from Austria who was to become the founder of modern dance in Australia, was a further influence. Mercury's local aspirations reflected the idealism of the times. As the Australian Co-operative Theatre, Mercury's first object was 'the establishment of a professional theatre as a Community Enterprise'. The Mercury played first at the Conservatorium theatre, then at the modernist Minerva theatre. Later it took plays to lunching factory workers through the Mercury Mobile Players.[9]

Peter Finch's theatrical abilities had been apparent at North Sydney Boys High. Later, when his schoolmate Paul Brickhill had found him a job as a copy-boy at the Sydney *Sun*, with characteristic cheek he did character impersonations of editors. Although he had moved to more conventional stages and studios by 1939, the Australian Army Entertainment Unit offered him opportunities to create new audiences. He had also found a special forum, 'a wonderful place' – Kings Cross. In the 1950s Finch reflected that this first bohemia offered people and ideas more interesting than those he encountered in London and New York.[10]

Already a radio star before the war, Gunner Finch (NX26035) was discovering new stages. One was that of the Ballet Russes dancers, also deposited in Australia by the European turmoil. For Finch, they were personified by the dancer Tamara Tchinarova of the Melbourne-based

Borovansky Ballet, whom he married on 21 April 1943. Another stage was the all-night Journalists Club in Phillip Street, a predominantly male club where those who worked into the night could have a beer, throw a steak on the grill or enjoy nocturnal talk. Actors, musicians, writers and bar performers and visiting celebrities, as well as those on the daily newspaper rounds, found it congenial. The club and all-night parties appealed to Finch, especially as Tamara was often away on tour. His club friends were journalists and writers, including the Melbourne 'expatriates' George Johnston and Charmian Clift.

National Dreams, Individual Talent

In the 1940s, the three fundamental problems of Australian theatre – the lack of professional companies performing at the highest level, the absence of opportunities which allowed actors to reach their fullest development in Australia, and the absence of a stage for Australian playwrights to create a national theatrical tradition – looked as if they might be soluble. A national theatre might stem the expatriate flood by providing opportunities in Australia. Postwar excitement about the idea culminated in the Tyrone Guthrie report, already mentioned. Unfortunately, Guthrie's proposals said more about the problems of the Australian cultural situation than their solution. He argued perceptively that Australia should be more than 'dominantly a "primary producing" appendage of Great Britain' and that a 'growing national consciousness and national self-respect' demanded 'further means of expression'. He also condemned the lack of 'national self-confidence' expressed in the middle-class anxiety about the Australian accent.

His solutions, though, were much more traditional. He proposed an 'export-import' scheme in which he advocated 'the import of a planned series of theatrical productions of the very first class'. To be performed over a three-year period by distinguished visiting companies, predominantly from Britain, these would educate the audience, significantly improve local standards and not lose money. The other side of the scheme endorsed the pattern of expatriation, although seeking to turn it to Australia's advantage. The export of colonial talent to the imperial centre via a scholarship scheme would allow talented actors, producers, designers and technicians to work in London, and learn their craft. Then the best would come together to form a company in London. Having won English acceptance, public approval in Australia for what would become a national touring company would follow. As such, Guthrie's scheme was more likely to reinforce than break the existing imperial–colonial mould.[11]

Visiting stars and returned Australian performers were asked for or offered their views on what made for a national theatre. Sir Laurence Olivier was one who dismissed the Guthrie proposal. He believed that the roots of a national theatrical tradition were spiritual, and that they would be found 'not in a building' but in an Australian voice in Australian plays. Later the entrepreneur who brought an Australian play to London, he answered the question of what he would do to develop the Australian theatre with: 'Nothing until you produce a playwright of your own'.[12]

The Minerva theatre director, Kathleen Robinson, who had spent some time acting in England, offered a practical analysis of the limitations of the Guthrie scheme:

> What is the good of our actors and actresses saving their pennies and going overseas? If they make good, there's no incentive for them to come back – and they don't. If they don't break in, they come back little better off than they went. This is where they should be encouraged and have the opportunity to work – right here.

In the same issue of the union journal *Equity*, the visiting actor Robert Morley warned that Australia was 'breeding a race of "supporting actors" who revolve in the background around imported players'.[13]

With the idea of a national theatre in the air, Peter Finch lectured on the history of Australian theatre at the Mercury theatre school. He also taught the techniques of Louis Jouvet, which he had learnt through film. However, the possibilities in Australia were limited. Although Finch was asked to play a strong Australian bushman in Harry Watt's Ealing Studios film of the Eureka Stockade, this was a provincial role.[14] The stereotype would be passed on, over four decades, from Chips Rafferty to Bryan Brown, who would play the role taken by Finch in the television mini-series re-make of the 1956 film, *A Town Like Alice*. The 'colonial' leading man in a film for English or American companies which relied on its 'exotic' setting was a limited vehicle for an actor of real power.

Despite the Mercury's high artistic aspirations, the fruits were limited. The critical success of Mercury productions did not translate into a large box office, and the Mercury theatre school only produced a modest income. Even when the Mercury took its plays to audiences in factories and workplaces, the brave venture remained financially precarious.

Peter Finch's personal prospects were brighter. During a performance of Molière at O'Brien's glass factory, Finch's theatrical and personal charms caught the eye of Sir Laurence Olivier, and were even more appealing to Vivien Leigh. He answered their call to stardom on the wider stages of London and beyond. Two and a half months later Peter Finch and Tamara left for London on the P&O liner *Esperance Bay*, full of hope. As he departed, optimism about his prospects in London was mixed with anxiety about the future of the Mercury theatre ideal.[15] Although Finch had many egalitarian Australian attitudes (he had humped his swag around the country, travelled for two months with Aborigines in Arnhem Land during the making of a documentary film, and drunk too well at the Journalists Club), he also knew that theatrical fame came only from overseas.

Actors for Export

As the dream of a national theatre faded in the postwar years, the Australian stage began to look like an informal mirror of the Guthrie 'export-import' scheme. Australian actors took to the boats in increasing numbers, following earlier travellers or recruited by visiting English theatrical proconsuls such as Olivier and Morley. Meanwhile star status went to visiting English companies, including Anthony Quayle's Shakespeare Memorial Company in 1948–9 and his 1953 Stratford company. (These companies often included expatriate Australians.) At the same time, directors who had come from overseas (for example John Sumner, to the Union Theatre Repertory Company in Melbourne in 1953, and Hugh Hunt, to the Australian Elizabethan Theatre Trust in Sydney in 1955) were one manifestation of Guthrie's proposals for importing talent and skill.

'London calling' was a siren song as well as a radio title for actors in the 1940s and 1950s, a period which produced more actors than Australia could sustain. Some with young families, such as Allan Ashbolt, found alternative careers in radio broadcasting. Others stayed with the regular income from radio soaps. When the Mercury theatre idea disappeared like a mirage in the early 1950s, the Australian scene seemed to offer little. For many expatriation was the only recourse, and for most actors the call was to London and the West End.

The rollcall of the departed over the two decades from 1945 was a long one. The Sydney list included Leo McKern and Jane Holland (1946), Peter Finch (1948), Bill Kerr (1947), Lloyd Lamble (1950), Alan White (1954), Ron Haddrick (who came originally from Adelaide, and left Sydney in 1954), Ray Barrett (originally from Brisbane, 1958), Walter Brown (who had come to Australia from New Zealand, and left for London in the late 1950s), John Meillon and June Salter (1959), and John Bell and Richard Wherrett, who both left during 1965. Among the painters and designers were Loudon Sainthill (1948) and Jocelyn Rickards (1948–49). Michael Blakemore (1949–50) would pursue a career as an actor and director. The early escapee Robin Eakin (1945) would, much later as Robin Dalton, become an agent and then a film producer.

Melbourne sent off Richard Beynon in 1947, the young refugee actor John Bluthal in 1949, the larger-than-life Frank Thring (who went to Stratford and then to the Hollywood of *Ben-Hur*) in 1953, Charles 'Bud' Tingwell in 1957 and Peter O'Shaughnessy in 1959. Zoe Caldwell left in 1958, working in Britain and then the United States. Others, who directly or indirectly followed the path of Dame Judith Anderson to the United States, included the writer Sumner Locke Elliott (1948) and the actors Michael Pate (who had worked in the Australian Army Entertainment Unit and left in 1950), Rod Taylor (early 1950s), and Ron Randell (1947). These talented performers were only part of a much larger cast of departing actors.

A Hard Row to Hoe

This pattern of expatriation, partly a product of the times, also had historical precedents. Before the turn of the century the playwright Haddon Chambers and the actor Oscar Asche had made the voyage to Europe. In the 1940s London called again. When the hopes raised by the cultural renaissance were dashed, young performers realised the impossibility of a professional career in Australia. However, expatriation also had its roots in the actors' different personal influences, and the experience of expatriation varied despite the underlying similarities. A family, personal or professional link in the chain could draw the individual to London, as could Australian connections and theatrical references and contacts in London. Often there were early difficulties in basement or attic bedsit flats, and adjustments to the weather and to the style of the English stage. Australian links – both with other Australians in London and with those at home – were inevitably diluted over time.

Peter Finch's lot was not the common one of difficulty and hard slog. For him, the transition was simpler. Finch departed for London with Tamara in October 1948. When they arrived at Southampton on 17 November with an introduction from Harry Watt, director of the film *Eureka Stockade*, and an invitation from Sir Laurence Olivier to contact him, things looked promising. Even so, work in theatre or film did not come immediately, although unlike many others, Finch was able to secure some work with BBC radio in December 1948, within a month of his arrival. When the call did come from the Oliviers, it was an invitation to drinks – with a dozen others. Then suddenly things happened for Finch: a film test and the film *Train of Events* (1949), an introduction through Olivier to the prominent agent Cecil Tennant, who ran the Myron Selznick agency and gave him a role in an American hit comedy, *Daphne Laureola*, which he was producing at Wyndham's Theatre in the West End. Playing the part of a young Pole, Finch, in the words of the *Daily Telegraph* reviewer, made 'a name in a night'. He entered a five-year contract with the increasingly entrepreneurial Olivier, and the unstoppable Finch career was on its way. Soon he and Tamara moved up in the world as well, from a bedsit in Notting Hill Gate and an attic flat in St Martin's Lane to the modern comforts of Dolphin Square.[16]

London's Many Parts

While the theatres of the West End and the great companies beckoned young actors, making it in London was never easy. Even aside from the difficulties of keeping alive there were other, deeper, transitions. For Leo McKern expatriation was a fundamental breach:

> I sailed for England down the beautiful harbour and out through the Heads in 1946. As we passed Rose Bay, I heard across the water the sound I recall so vividly – the warning bell of a tram heralding its presence, bringing the familiar picture of the driver stamping on the knob in the floor of his cabin, that rang it. Then out into the Tasman Sea, the Heads fading then vanishing – and with them my childhood and youth in the Sunburnt Country.

The London to which Leo McKern and Jane Holland had come was simultaneously welcoming and difficult. For McKern, who as a young boy had been delighted at being able to pronounce 'London', it was excitement beyond belief. He had come to London with 'a heart full of hopes ... convinced that this was where it was all happening'. Leo and Jane had a mixed reception from 'the natives: condescension, tolerant amusement, resentment, great friendliness'. Sometimes the English flinched at the Australian accent. McKern realised he needed to change his to improve his chances of working on the stage.[17] Having grown up hearing people talk of England as 'Home', learning at school of Britain, Great Britain and the British Empire, the cultural transition was not all that difficult. In practical terms it was hard. This was the London of food rationing, of cold winters (especially the horror winter of 1946–47), of sometimes riding a bicycle to work through the snow. McKern's main concern was to keep body and soul together.

In practice this meant performing in theatres other than those of the West End – as a cinema slide drawer, a soft-goods salesman in Camden Town, a jeweller's assistant at Marble Arch and, first and foremost, a meat porter at Sainsbury's Temple Fortune grocery. Meanwhile Jane Holland brought in an income as a copy-typist as they shared the problems of nearly everyone in Britain. They lived with daily food rationing and sudden power cuts, at first in a cold bare-boarded room (and the second-hand gas heater had to be sold in a bad week to buy food). Such difficulties were illuminating even for a Depression child. McKern's appreciation of the British people, who had already suffered the sacrifices and deprivations of the war itself, was deepened by his experiences in these early years.

The struggle to survive and the battle to find professional work were biting into him. In the face of difficulties and discouragements, his wife's long-standing determination to develop her career in England, and her savings, made staying possible. 'Her sedulously preserved return fare to Australia, in case of utter failure, was untouched; for to return home, defeated, was as yet unthinkable.'[18] Nor did the young actor find that the doors of London opened to him like a colonial Dick Whittington. His entrée card was in the form of the 'five precious letters of introduction' which he carried with care. One woman agent received them without enthusiasm. She tore up and dropped into the wastepaper basket a reference from her former lover, an Englishman now in Australia, and asked 'Why do you Australians come over here trying to take the bread out of English actors' mouths?'[19]

The door opened first for Jane Holland, who had a reputation as an actress of talent in Sydney. Opportunity came in the form of a role in a play touring Germany with a Combined Services Entertainment Unit; through her contacts Leo obtained an assistant stage management position on a similar tour. These young Australians saw, as did the travelling artist Albert Tucker and the musician Charles Mackerras, devastated cities which scarified their spirits. It was an education in horror which stayed with McKern, reinforcing both a certain conservatism and a stubborn dissidence towards ruling conventions.

The young McKern had disadvantages as well as determination. Short in stature, one-eyed and already with a slightly bulbous visage, he could never be a conventional tall and handsome leading man in the fashionable drawing room comedies of the West End. Persistence, skill and luck provided opportunities. The expanding theatrical stage of the emerging companies, the Old Vic and the new Stratford Shakespearean company, part of the postwar revival of serious theatre, furnished roles for young actors. So too did working with the proposer of the 'export-import' scheme for the Australian stage, Tyrone Guthrie, who had directed McKern in an Arts Council tour of Molière's *The Miser*. After three years in London, the entrée Guthrie provided to the Old Vic was McKern's breakthrough. It seemed that he had more than 'rocketed to fame': 'not only was I appearing in the West End of London, the very heart of the theatre world, but I was a member of one of the great companies'.[20] Directed by Guthrie and by Hugh Hunt, and working with Michael Redgrave, who was then at the height of his powers, Leo McKern the actor had come home. For the individual actor, for McKern, it seemed the ideal tale of expatriate success in the performing arts. But for Jane Holland and for the theatrical culture he had left behind, the picture was less rosy.

Though Leo McKern's expatriation to London was in many ways typical, like the independently minded and literally one-eyed actor himself, it was also atypical. In this respect his experience was like that of many other Australian actors whose move to 'the centre of the theatrical world' was, simultaneously, something they shared with their peers and a unique adventure.

Other actors, performers and designers, from varying social backgrounds and different parts of Australia, joined the cast of expatriates in the late 1940s and early 1950s and had varying tales to tell. The experienced Sydney actors

Lloyd Lamble, Alan White and Walter Brown all had long stage and radio experience before they made their departures. Richard Beynon, raised in working-class Melbourne, was at the beginning of his career, while John Bluthal, also from Melbourne, had come from a refugee family which had escaped Europe just in time. In contrast, Keith Michell grew up in rural South Australia and the industrial town of Port Pirie. In the Eastern Suburbs of Sydney, Michael Blakemore turned his back on the professional career his father planned for him to make a career on the stage. Their different stories reflect both the individual variations of expatriation and the recurring patterns in the creative professions – both the forces which drove many of the talented away from the limited opportunities in Australia, and the factors which drew them to the cultural metropolis of London. Nearly all had been affected by the impact of the Great Depression in which, with very high rates of unemployment, Australians suffered more than most Western peoples. In some cases, difficult childhoods deepened the appeal of getting away. The seeds of Leo McKern's peripatetic life were sown in 1930s Sydney; his parents, like so many others during the Depression, never owned their own home and often had to move on.[21]

Richard Beynon grew up in the 'down' world of the industrial inner suburbs of Prahran and Carlton. The respectable well-spoken boy from a struggling working-class home was an outsider in the tough and blighting atmosphere of the schoolyard, seen as a 'Pom' and a 'sissy' in a culture which, except for Australian Rules Football, was not his. Keith Michell's world was also different. In his parents' shop and at school at Bordertown in the South Australian wheatbelt, the young Keith Michell was a dreamer, a reader and a painter. Later, in the lead smelter town of Port Pirie, he found his escape in school plays. So too had Alan White, the boy from the inner-western Sydney suburb of Five Dock, when a student at Sydney's famous Fort Street selective high school.

The call of the theatre was powerful, easing the difficulties and dis-orientations of leaving home and family for an unknown future across the world. Richard Beynon, who had been an energetic reader of plays and an amateur actor while working as a junior clerk in a Melbourne office, was in his element in London. Although he arrived in the worst winter for 87 years, he was more than content. 'Living in a basement [and] loving it', he could not have been happier, as he was doing 'exactly what I wanted to do' – acting. When he came seven years later, Alan White also landed on his feet, becoming a veritable 'spear-carrier to the chief' as a spear-carrying extra for six weeks in Olivier's film of *Richard III*. That initial employment was followed, fortunately for this actor with a wife and children, by a play at the Victoria Palace and then a seven-year film contract with Associated British.

The single John Bluthal found London in some ways more welcoming, although less engaging, returning to Australia only four years later. The transition from the New Theatre in working-class Melbourne to the similarly Left Unity Theatre in London was a natural one. Despite this rapid adjustment, as someone almost born to international travel, Bluthal became one of the first of the postwar travellers back and forth, starting with that initial return to Australia. When first in London he worked with Warren Mitchell, who helped him to get his first professional job, in a pantomime in Worthing. A versatile performer, he would work in fields as diverse as the political plays of the Unity Theatre, concert party tours in the provinces and in that Christmas staple of theatrical income, the panto. Bluthal was fascinated by accents, and did not share his friend Leo McKern's problem of eliminating an Australian accent (which in McKern's case would eventually lead to his distinctive 'Rumpolean' burr).

The transition to London, like any process of migration, was complex in its practical and emotional details. Its elements included the initial connection (with either an earlier voyager or a recruiting officer), the decision, the voyage and arrival, accommodation and a source of income, references, contacts and the search for work, and the getting of an agent. Very often on the almost vice-regal tours of visiting companies, such as that of Olivier and Vivien Leigh in 1948, these imperial proconsuls of the theatre also worked as talent scouts, picking up young talent from the colonies. Sometimes this came in the form of the almost direct call, such as that of Olivier to Finch, or the Young Vic theatre school audition of a Michell, or through agents such as Elsie Beyer, who beckoned Alan White to London several times before he finally went. At a meeting at the Lema coffee bar in Bligh Street, Beyer discussed with him what he was doing next and asked 'why didn't he come to Britain?' She gave the question a practical dimension, providing letters of introduction to Olivier and Gielgud, getting White out of his contract and booking tickets for him and his family. After just ten days he was on his way. Later, with the first disorienting months in London long forgotten, he remarked 'the most important things in life just happen like that'.

Looking for work in London could be complicated as both McKern and Beynon found to their cost. Beynon's problem, which arose some years later, was not with prejudice. His obstacle was the actors' lifeline – the agent. Playing the lead – the juvenile lead as befitted his age – in a West End play, he was signed exclusively by an agent whose select list of 12 actors included the stars Greer Garson, Wilfrid Hyde-White and Margaret Lockwood. Thinking 'Boy, this is it!' he sat back and waited for work, fruitlessly. Eventually he realised that he was being stupid, that he himself needed to secure the work, leaving the agent to talk money. Such serious reversals threatened the fragile ego of young actors who had pulled up their roots by crossing the world to pursue a career. 'It nearly killed me' Beynon recalled of that time spent relying on the agent to get him work:

> I was in a terrible nervous state about it all, so I had to think of the only thing, the biggest most impossible thing I could do to restore my self-esteem, and that was to walk to Australia, and that's what I did.

Leo McKern, like most expatriates, found that the personal and the professional interacted with each other in complex ways. Social pressures – and probable unfortunate consequences – were there too:

> 'Stay away for three years and you'll never come back!' was the dire warning delivered to me by compatriots, who believed that this somehow revelationary period would result in my becoming 'pommyfied', seduced and traduced from the sunburnt country by the sybaritic refinements of the civilization of England. I dare say there is some small truth in this generalization, but I have been back several times; and God willing, barring accidents, I hope to die in my own country.[22]

The forces which moved the young postwar actors across the sea were themselves dramatic. Several of them felt at a crossroads in their personal and professional lives. Alan White, summoned by Elsie Beyer, recalled that 'somebody offered me, a door opened ... at 30, I really needed to move on altogether. I'd seen all of Australia, I'd been in the war'. Nor did he look forward to another 13 months of touring *Dial M for Murder*. English parents (from Portsmouth) also gave England a particular fascination. Peter Finch, who had a strong sense of Australian culture, had been born in England. The South Australian Keith Michell later reflected that he had made the 'right decision' in two respects. The first was his decision to choose to be an actor rather than an artist. At a time when 'everything said you've got to go to England', he believed that he had also made the right decision to go. When accused, accurately he believed, of being a deserter, he reflected on the term: 'Deserted what? I mean, it wasn't the theatre ... there was no theatre to work in'. He had, as he later advised young actors to do, followed his nose.

For Richard Beynon, Australia was cut off by distance and size. Beynon also feared small and probably declining theatre audiences in the suburban late 1940s and 1950s. Australian society had a short history by comparison with Great Britain and, as in the case of other colonial societies, little sense of historical memory. Beynon, White and McKern sensed the call of what they had been taught of as 'The Old Country'. The difficulties were also a stimulus, as Beynon recognised. Because Australia was 'cut off', 'I worked harder at my profession in Australia than I did here because I was being denied and not just my profession but knowledge of literature and everything'.

That very frustration also prompted departure. Cumulatively, if not individually, the losses further denied opportunities for growth. Beynon recalled that the last review of his performance in George Bernard Shaw's *You Never Can Tell* before he departed had said that 'Beynon would have a great future as an actor if Australia had a National Theatre of standing'. His intention was to go to Britain to get as much experience as possible and then return to 'get in on the ground floor of the National Theatre'. The idea of a national theatre company travelling the Australian capitals was a contemporary dream which enthralled many actors of the time, while its failure to materialise contributed to their decision to leave. John Bluthal would rhapsodise about it decades after it had become clear that it was never to be more than a dream.

Double Bay to Bohemia (and Beyond) – A Better Class of Expatriate

Although there had been earlier artistic expatriates, the journey to London and Europe was not available to most Australians – all the more so during the depressed 1930s and the wartime 1940s. However, the trip to Europe had long been an essential part of the life of better society, facilitated by their greater opportunities to travel. The 'London season' beckoned in the northern summer, fuelled by aspirations to meet royalty, or at least aristocracy, at Ascot and Wimbledon and to win the status conferred by having visited the cultural sites of Europe. In Sydney the upper middle-class society of the Eastern Suburbs and the upper North Shore was linked – financially and professionally, socially and culturally – to England. From their ranks came several expatriates in the theatre, in music and in art and design. The future conductor Charles Mackerras from Rose Bay, the later theatrical agent and film producer Robin Eakin (later Dalton), the actor Michael Blakemore and several young musicians were part of an exodus from the more salubrious society of the Eastern Suburbs.

The life of Robin Eakin, the daughter of a Sydney doctor, mixed very different worlds. One was a potentially snobbish 'closed' Eastern Suburbs – the private school with her best friend the governor's daughter, boarding at Frensham, and the prospect of a Swiss finishing school. Her other world, however, was that of Kings Cross, where her father practised, and which had a diversity of culture and cafes, refugees and red-light establishments. Young Robin's life at the Cross, where everybody knew her father, as well as her time at boarding school in the country and summer holidays at Palm Beach, just north of Sydney, was later captured in her memoir, *Aunts up the Cross*. Eakin's early reading and English family links strengthened the call of

Europe. In 1945, that call acquired a note of urgency. She fell in love with a Royal Navy officer and managed to hitchhike to the northern hemisphere on a converted bomber.[23]

Growing up in a comfortable and lively large household (with servants and many long-term 'guests'), Robin Eakin felt that 'all Sydney was an extension of the security of the house'. It was an augury perhaps of the good luck, as well as good management, of so much of her later life. She reflected that her 'home life' was 'not peculiarly Australian' except perhaps for 'the informality and wholehearted participation of all friends and attendants in our family affairs [which] would have been impossible in a stricter culture'. Yet Australian casualness ('everybody joined in') was coupled with Eastern Suburbs comfort, as she remembered with a hint of literary exaggeration:

> Now the city abounds in restaurants and night-clubs, but then there were only two really smart ones, Romano's and Prince's, and it was in one of these two that I spent almost every evening ...
>
> We, in our teens, led a more sophisticated life than English or European adolescents: freer, and at the same time, simpler. We lived in or on the sea all summer, danced half the night, and raced our parents' cars up and down the perilous coastal roads. These were the years just before the war and we were conscious of nothing but the sun, and the sea, and the wide, warm, free country spilling its splendours about us.[24]

Such freedom and confidence would later help her in varying London roles, as a theatrical agent and film producer.

For Michael Blakemore and Jocelyn Rickards, two shy local children who would themselves make a theatrical impact, opportunities for self-expression seemed far more important than any search for a national voice. The son of a Sydney surgeon, Michael Blakemore also grew up with a degree of wealth, in a Rose Bay house with a harbour view. Sent, unwillingly, to an authoritarian boarding school, he also went for holidays on the coast and had a private club to change in at Bondi Beach.[25] An unwilling medical student at Sydney University, he lived in St Paul's College, at the same time as the older law student and graduate of the Burma Railway, Russell Braddon. Blakemore preferred his true loves, film and theatre, to medicine. He also participated in the life of the student prince, Sydney upper middle-class style: 'drunken college booze-ups ... parties in private houses ... dances in golf clubs and balls at Government House'.

Blakemore's father aspired for him to join the ranks of Sydney professional society, the 'Ideal of Respectable Australia', as typified by

> a well-qualified doctor who had boxed and played rugby at a private school, volunteered for the armed forces in a World War and who

had stood up when a woman came into the room before resuming his conversation with the man he was already talking to.

That culture celebrated the values of 'Gentlemen', a group which 'was very small and mainly British', and sport, from rugby union and boxing to the surf. It was a narrow in-bred society with no tolerance for the 'Fools' and 'Crooks' out there.[26]

Richard Beynon had sought to escape from the narrowness, rigidity and poverty of his working-class environment. Michael Blakemore fled from the confines of his very different milieu. Enraptured by the Sydney surf and by surfing, the young Blakemore had other fantasy worlds. Dance and magic, film and theatre, provided a 'secret life' which he put against the violent and provincial upper middle-class society which seemed his destiny. Although he lost his first major 'battle' with his father over his future in the dining room of the exclusive Royal Sydney Golf Club, and enrolled in medicine, the self-described 'straight poofter', that is the artistic and cultured outsider in a conservative upper middle-class milieu, sought divertissements other than those of the scalpel and of polite 'society'. His acting improved, but his results did not. When Robert Morley gave him a job as 'publicist' on his Australian tour of *Edward, My Son*, Blakemore knew that it was time to go, in his case to study at RADA, the Royal Academy of Dramatic Art, in 1950.[27]

Although a near contemporary at Sydney University, the journalist Murray Sayle believed that the Eastern Suburbs were another world (for him 'sentient minds' stopped at the Cross), the different spheres sometimes met, especially at artists' parties. Symbolically and precariously poised at Edgecliff, the border between the Cross and the Eastern Suburbs, was 'Merioola', the house of culture.[28] Theatre met design and painting – and 'society' and arty bohemia – in the experiences of Jocelyn Rickards and Loudon Sainthill. In the war years the adolescent Jocelyn Rickards had moved from her Eastern Suburbs childhood to the study of art at East Sydney Tech, just off Taylor Square. She found her artistic and theatrical home in 'Merioola', the old mansion occupied by a colony of artists at Edgecliff. Here, Rickards shared pleasure, art and gossip at the 'society' end of artistic bohemian society with a dramatic cast, including her lover, the photographer Alec Murray. The theatrical designer Loudon Sainthill designed the brilliant program for the 1948 Olivier/Leigh 'Old Vic' tour and, adventurously, mounted an exhibition, 'A History of Costume Design from 4000 BC to 1945 AD'. Other roles were played by his lover, the writer, art critic and later curator of the Redfern Gallery in London, Harry Tatlock Miller, the artist and character Donald Friend and the chatelaine of the house, Chica Edgeworth Lowe. Later, often unsympathetic, critics used the term 'Merioola group' as shorthand for the Sydney 'charm school' of painting. Jocelyn Rickards remarked that the newspapers saw the house as 'Sydney's pet cultural zoo'. 'We were feted, shown off, indulged, and reams of rubbish were written about us daily in the proliferating gossip columns'. One newspaper cartoon pictured Alec Murray in white tie and tails and Jocelyn Rickards in a long gown dancing at Prince's on Victory Night. Parties were held for the Ballet Rambert, for the six Dior models who introduced the New Look to Australia in 1948, or for their own sake. Alec Murray was, to Jocelyn Rickards' chagrin, particularly interested in Carole, the most beautiful of the Dior girls. These spirited performances of the 'Merioola' company were as colourfully transcendent as Sainthill's exotic theatrical designs.[29]

While many expatriates left behind – or escaped from – family and every-day society, with varying degrees of difficulty, 'Merioola' was like a rocket range, a Woomera, inevitably a launching pad for travels to somewhere else. By the end of the decade Alec Murray and Jocelyn Rickards, Loudon Sainthill and Harry Tatlock Miller had all departed for London, sharing a house at Clareville Grove, SW7. As Robin Dalton later recalled, many of them – Peter Finch, Diane Cilento and the young actor Michael Blakemore – knocked on her London door.[30] After the heyday of 'Merioola', the elevated centre of Sydney's respectable bohemia, several painters also departed for other scenes: Donald Friend to Italy and London, and, later, Justin O'Brien to Europe and Francis Lymburner to London and beyond.

Openings and Closings

Ambition and the seduction of new fields were not the only reasons for leaving Australia. The cultural opportunities of the 1940s were under threat well before the end of the decade. A transition from innocence to experience had occurred as war, the threat of invasion (and the actual 'invasion' of half a million American servicemen) shook Australian society to its foundations. Responses varied. One was a recognition of the avant-garde and an openness to the realities probed by the scalpel of modernism in art and literature, particularly in the painting of Arthur Boyd, Albert Tucker, Sidney Nolan and Russell Drysdale. Another tendency was the very opposite, a desire to shut the shutters of suburban respectability to keep out the darker forces recognised in this era of Freudianism and modernism, expressionism and surrealism; to keep young Australia happy, healthy and wholesome, ideally free of foreign evils, foreigners and foreign invaders. This latter urge took different forms. One was the active repression of the new and artistically dangerous. Another was a passive indifference towards culture, manifested in a lack of public support for the arts. Several dramatic episodes of repression during the 1940s and into the 1950s era of suburban materialism and the Cold War made it clear that provincial Australia did not welcome the artistic adventurer.

The rollcall of artists on trial was long and honourable. In 1944 William Dobell faced a court action arguing that his modernist portrait of Joshua

Smith could not win the 1943 Archibald Prize, as it was not, in the most traditional sense, a portrait. Max Harris, editor of *Angry Penguins* magazine, was charged with obscenity before the Adelaide Police Court for publishing poems by the pseudonymous poet 'Ern Malley' in the Autumn 1944 issue. This led to a fine of £5. The depictions of army life in Lawson Glassop's novel of Tobruk, *We Were the Rats* (which often used the word 'bloody'), and in Sumner Locke Elliott's play *Rusty Bugles* (which captured the equally 'bloody' boredom of army routine in the Northern Territory), attracted the ire of the New South Wales Chief Secretary. Glassop's publishers were fined £10 in 1946. As a result of the massive free publicity generated by the banning of *Rusty Bugles*, it won an audience of over 100 000 people in a few years, at the artistic cost of 'cleaning up' its language. The jailing of the novelist Robert Close for the 'obscenity' of his frank novel *Love Me Sailor* was indicative of the time.[31]

In the wash-up of this provincial repression, escape seemed the only realistic option. William Dobell had won his case but suffered a breakdown which left him unable to paint for a year. Sumner Locke Elliott had already left for New York when the *Rusty Bugles* drama was exploding in the press, and Robert Close would find French readers even more interested in his novel than the Melbourne courts. In the act of departure, they echoed Albert Tucker's declaration, made on the wharf at Port Melbourne in 1947 – 'I am a refugee from Australian culture'.[32]

In the theatre, the repression was political as well as moral. The small Australian stage also fell victim to the Cold War. The role of Communist Party members in building up Actors Equity as a union with teeth made the theatrical profession a target for McCarthyism. Actors Equity was no longer a tame company union, with offices provided by theatrical managements. Instead it fought for actors, working conditions, including wages, for a closed shop and for Australian content on radio. As a result, the theatre would be one of several creative fields – others were literature and science, as well as religion, sport and the universities – which were diminished by political repression.

Newly militant, Actors Equity believed that the old Australian convention of deferring to visiting 'stars', who had often only 'played the lead in Birmingham', and of paying Australian supporting actors a pittance had to be fought. In 1944, a successful national strike directed against J. C. Williamson's non-union performers, such as Gladys Moncrieff, led to one hundred per cent Equity membership in professional productions.[33] In the 1940s the Commonwealth Investigation Service and the Victorian Lowe Royal Commission into Communism both became interested in the union. The Australian Security Intelligence Organisation (ASIO), which had been founded by Chifley in 1949, maintained the interest, sharpening its Cold War fangs under Menzies in the 1950s. 'Communists in Actors' Equity of

Australia', the subject of the NSW regional director's minute, was a stirring theme. Amongst those listed were Peter Finch (partly due to his wife Tamara Tchinarova's Russian origins), Lloyd Lamble, Chips Rafferty and Michael Pate.[34]

The attentions of ASIO had practical consequences which went beyond becoming the subject of a public service file. The New Zealand-born actor and for a short time waterside worker, Walter Brown, had worked in 1950 with the Maritime Industries Theatre for the Communist Waterside Workers' Federation. He recalled the appearance of two strange Americans around the theatrical scene and the subsequent closing off of his employment opportunities in radio. Brown, a committed Leftist rather than a Communist, was 'fingered' by their local assistant, dubbed 'the smiling axeman', whose job was to identify all 'dubious' actors. Suddenly radio studios were unwelcoming, perhaps due to the American advertising money which underpinned so many soaps and Sunday night specials. Along with over a dozen other actors, Brown was barred from 2GB in Phillip Street – three doors away from the house where he lived. Brown looked south to Melbourne for work, before finally heading overseas later in the decade. He had been part of an Actors Equity case against J. C. Williamson's in the Arbitration Commission in which actors sought holiday pay, like other workers. After the case, Walter Brown felt out in the cold again, this time with J. C. Williamson's, so he chose to try his luck in the UK in 1958, which he recalled as the year of the killer fog. In the small transplanted world of the era, he later found a flat in Elgin Crescent, Ladbroke Grove for his fellow thespian Barry Humphries, who arrived with a collection of fans painted by the artist Charles Conder.

Lloyd Lamble had a high profile, both as one of Australia's leading men and as president of Actors and Announcers Equity (as it then was) in several of its great struggles against the managements. Suddenly Lamble found the stage door closed to him. Even when he sought to use his name to create a production to tour New Zealand, halls and theatres became mysteriously unavailable. When only two independent studios continued to use him – Crawfords in Melbourne and Morris West in Sydney – and dates were suddenly double-booked (or simply cancelled by JCW-owned theatres) for his own touring show, the writing was on the wall. Paradoxically, this known dissident had played, as had Alan White, such defenders of the status quo as the All-American radio superhero 'The Shadow'. Lamble left for the better working conditions he had been fighting for in Australia in his six years as president of Actors Equity. The philosophy of the theatres' managements – 'let's get rid of these characters' – was driven by the employers' anti-union self-interest, McCarthyism providing a means and justification. The result for a fed-up Lamble was the decision to 'get the hell out' of Australia.[35]

Lloyd Lamble found success as an actor in the early 1930s and also as a unionist in the 1940s. Professionally, he had starred in many JCW shows, played opposite Neva Carr Glynn in *The Man Who Came to Dinner* on a New Zealand tour, appeared with Robert Morley in *Edward, My Son* and starred in *Pygmalion* and in many Lux and Macquarie Radio Theatre plays. Although he produced wartime propaganda for the government, to the emerging security services – the Commonwealth Police, the Commonwealth Investigation Service, and the Australian Security Intelligence Organisation – he was a different character. Along with other executive members of Actors Equity and habitués of its 236 Pitt Street offices and the Actors Club (an address which one citizen believed was 'a hotbed of Communistic propaganda'), Lamble's 'loyalty' was in doubt.[36]

A February 1949 Commonwealth Investigation Service report on the cast of Communists and fellow travellers gave this Actors Equity president star billing:

> Lloyd Lamble: Currently reported as a definite Communist. It is alleged that he is an atheist and that when a friend died some time ago he would not go to the church service but later read his own oration.

In fact, at the burial service for the comedian George Blackshaw, who did not want a Christian funeral, Lamble, as both Actors Equity president and an old friend, was asked to deliver a valedictory oration. Although it was reported that he had been at Communist Party of Australia fund-raising functions (for War Loans!), it was never factually demonstrated that he was a party member.[37] Most of the large cast of 20 or more Actors Equity associates attracted the attention of the Commonwealth Investigation Service. Their files were marked 'Reported to be a Communist' or, in the case of Peter Finch who was already overseas, 'Regarded as a Communist' and 'on record in this office in regard to his Communist connexions' (perhaps a reference to Tamara).

As the Cold War deepened, ASIO added to its lists of potential intriguers and subversive actors. An ASIO minute of October 1953 described three categories on the managements' 'black lists':

> (a) DEFINITE ... members of the Communist Party of Australia.
> (b) VERY DOUBTFUL ... almost certain that the persons are members of the Communist Party of Australia but the managements have not yet completely satisfied themselves on the matter.
> (c) DOUBTFUL. This means that the persons named are being closely watched for obvious reasons.
> DEFINITE
> ... Lloyd Lamble
> Leslie [sic] Jackson

VERY DOUBTFUL.
... Leonard Theile [sic]
DOUBTFUL
... Michael Pate.[38]

Perhaps it was their 'Communism' that would lead Michael Pate to play American Indians in Hollywood and, on the side of the underdog, Leonard Teale (not 'Theile') to play Superman on radio and later a police detective on television. It was not clear whether ASIO gave Lesley Jackson star billing in her own right, or because she was married to Lamble.

Whether the problem was the security services, JCWs, the radio companies or even the new monster of television, an actor's life seemed less and less promising in 1950s Australia. Suburban living, TV and the political blacklist all put live theatre and radio on the endangered list. A dead film industry, with only a few British and American films with overseas stars shot in Australia for local colour (such as *The Sundowners*, 1960, and the tale of the end of the world, *On the Beach*, 1959), didn't help either. Most actors had two real choices: a day job or evacuation to more hospitable theatrical climates. While a few, including Leonard Teale and Ruth Cracknell, battled on, expatriation seemed to be almost the norm. The success of Peter Finch, and the return to Australia of Keith Michell and Leo McKern with visiting British companies, confirmed that the expatriates had made the right decision. The vision of a national theatre had, like the departing expatriates, disappeared from the horizon. In Australia and in London, though, a few brave souls believed that a new Australian drama was waiting in the wings for its chance on the stage.

Chapter 3

Sydney or Fleet Street[1]

One profession in which travel for work and experience often led to expatriation was journalism. In this trade and craft as well as profession the parochial and, to a lesser extent, the international shaped the journalistic ethos. The culture of Australian newspapers was predominantly that of suburban career values (the regular job as a 'hack'), partly varied by the related, but different male culture of the inner-city pub with its brand of beery cynicism. But there were other sides. Journalists met everyone, from politicians to police, from prostitutes to theatrical performers, in their work and in the daytime and nocturnal societies of the inner city. Meeting travellers and artists, they were stimulated by other possibilities. Overseas often called those who wanted to escape the daily grind. Literary aspirations also appealed to some individuals. In Sydney, the diverse ranks of the scribes included would-be novelists and putative poets as well as established ones such as the editor and published novelist Brian Penton and the poet Kenneth Slessor.[2]

Some journalists sought to expand their physical and intellectual spheres. As they made the intellectual move from everyday reporting to challenging and re-interpreting the news, they also looked overseas to further their careers and expand their horizons. Meanwhile in reporting and subs rooms, and at newspaper pubs, dedicated and cynical journalists, raconteurs and frustrated novelists rubbed shoulders. In the bar they saw their horizons expand through talk, enlarging their hopes and swallowing their frustrations through a schooner, a middy or a pot of beer.

Their dreams often involved other papers, other towns, other editors and other stories. Australian journalists had long been peripatetic, working around the six capitals and the larger provincial towns. Some had spread their wings even further, to New Zealand and to the sub-imperial South Pacific of Papua New Guinea and Fiji. It was only one further step to the bigger trip, whether that meant Fleet Street and international events, Hong Kong, or sometimes even Canada and the US. Given the lack of Australian overseas bureaus, London was often the launching pad for other destinations.

Australian journalists also had a long tradition of heading to where the action was. International events varied: the 1900 Boxer Rebellion in China pursued by 'Morrison of Peking'; Wilfred Burchett as the first Western journalist at Hiroshima after the bomb, or, later, Richard Hughes in Hong Kong; or the European theatres of war reported by Alan Moorehead and Chester Wilmot. In any event, they found professional platforms outside Australia.[3] The London newspapers, from the cheapest tabloids to the quality broadsheets, were seen as the height of the profession. Unlike Australian newspapers, which were produced on the smell of an oily rag for small capital city and state markets, these had national circulations which meant that they also paid well. Of almost equal significance, a journalist blessed by experience in Fleet Street sometimes found it easier to climb the career ladder back home, particularly at the august *Sydney Morning Herald* and the Melbourne *Age* and *Argus*.

In the 1950s, for a generation born during the Depression and the first years of war, the postwar world offered not only affluence which allowed the less-than-rich to travel, but also the boredom which could be the result of suburban living. Journalism itself was a mixed world. In still-provincial Australia access to tertiary education and opportunities for careers in the embryonic cultural industries were limited. Journalism offered a step up the career ladder and an income for many who had just left school. Having entered the door as a copy-boy (or for women, a copy-typist), a journalism cadetship could furnish an income and a semi-professional career. It offered upward mobility for working-class and lower middle-class boys and career choices for a few determined girls in an era of limited career possibilities. The cadetship provided an income for those who could not afford to go to university in the days when scholarships were rare. Cadetships had another advantage over university for aspiring journalists. Many newspapers from the Melbourne *Herald* and *Sun* to the Sydney *Daily Telegraph* did not take graduates as cadets.

Journalism also provided vicarious adventures as reporters reported on real dramas and gossiped about others in that world where boozy male Sydney met the bohemianism of Kings Cross and later that of the Push. At the Journalists Club, up the Cross, in city pubs and at parties, journalists could either stick together or could also meet the actors, broadcasters, musicians and the painters of inner Sydney.[4]

The tabloid journalism of Frank Packer's *Daily Telegraph*, or its competitor the *Daily Mirror*, and the career cycle of journalism, could be frustrating.

A job at 16–17 (or 20–21 if you'd finished university), a grading at 20, top jobs and/or fights with editors, sub-editors and chiefs-of-staff at 22–24 could mean that a plateau was reached at an early age. If not settled down with a family and a mortgage, or a flat and too great a liking for Tooheys, the mid-20s was a time to get a move on, before decay and decline. Long nights and long sessions at the pub could lead to an early death, or just the repetition of the daily round of commuting and the paper.

'Overseas'

In the 1940s and 1950s the magic word 'overseas' meant Fleet Street for Australian journalists, as much as it meant 'London' for travellers. And journalism in Australia was a nomadic profession as careers were made – and sometimes resumed after a fight with the editor or chief-of-staff – by moving on to another paper in another city. For journalists, curious and migratory by nature, the step onto a liner towards other theatres of human performance was easier than for many more home and family-oriented people. The call of the next big story could have its own career logic, like that of the next good role for actors.

In Britain too in the 1940s and 1950s, journalism joined class and career mobility with geographical movement. Working-class and lower middle-class boys and girls came to London from the English provinces, Scotland, Wales and Ireland in search of opportunity. Journalism and travel offered – whether in Sydney's Kings Cross or London's Notting Hill Gate – new experiences of postwar freedom, away from the parental and neighbourly eyes of suburban streets. In practical terms, Fleet Street viewed Australian grading as equivalent to the provincial experience it demanded from British recruits. For Australians the compulsory stint in the provinces before Fleet Street was unnecessary.

When Australian Associated Press and the New Zealand Press Association joined the owners of Reuters in March 1947, this opened up positions for Australians in London, besides those in the London bureaus. Approaches varied. The Melbourne *Herald* sent and brought back staff, while Frank Packer's Australian Consolidated Press paper, the *Daily Telegraph*, saved money by hiring them on the spot. One of those travellers was a young Sydney University arts graduate Glen Renfrew, who, after running short of money in Italy, joined Reuters on a salary of £4 a week as a trainee in 1952. Characterised by administrative skill, he rose in later decades to be the managing director. Sometimes, in journalism and publishing, Australians' practical skills and low-cost approaches were in demand.[5] Many other newly arrived journalists, whether passing through or aspiring to higher things, also found work at Reuters over the next few decades, often as casual sub-editors. London was a world news city and Reuters was one of its most important nuclei. By the mid-1960s, Reuters news services were reaching nearly 6500 daily newspapers in over 100 cities, with an aggregate circulation of 276 million.[6]

The travelling journalists and writers were diverse in experience. They included the already London-based Alan Moorehead, the other European war correspondents Chester Wilmot and Sam White, the ex-POW Paul Brickhill, and the former Pacific war correspondent George Johnston.[7] A number of younger journalists, some of whose by-lines would become well-known, included Murray Sayle, Phillip Knightley, Donald Horne, Liz Hickson, Ed Morrisby and their travelling Sydney 'Push' friend, Bill Harcourt.

Journeys north varied in character. The older journalist-writers, George Johnston and his new partner Charmian Clift, who had earlier uprooted themselves from Melbourne to Sydney, had a smooth and comfortable transition. Johnston was sent in February 1951 to head the office of Associated Newspapers, publishers of the Sydney *Sun*, in London. First-class travel, a chauffeured car to meet the ship and a Bayswater apartment were not the usual lot of journalistic voyagers. However, Johnston and Clift too went to see Paris within two weeks of their arrival.[8]

George Johnston was a symbol of the opportunities for journalists and writers at the time. A 'golden boy' of Australian journalism, reporting New Guinea and the Pacific during the war, he published several novels during the 1940s and held senior editorial jobs in Melbourne and Sydney. His legend was added to by his 'bohemian' relationship with the beautiful and talented Charmian Clift. In July 1946 he resigned from the editorship of the *Australasian* weekly after she had been sacked for being involved with him, a married man, something deeply shocking to conventional opinion. The reputation would later grow to legend. After four and a half years in Sydney, including the daily column in the *Sun*, the 'Sydney Diary', and nearly four years as the very well-paid head of the *Sun's* London bureau, they made a different break. Johnston and Clift decamped with their children to the Greek islands of Kalymnos and Hydra to write novels. Their mythic status as artists and travellers was comparable with that of Peter Finch – 'Finchy' was already on his way to becoming a legendary actor, star and Hollywood hell-raiser. Both stories fused Australian tales of success and bohemianism with creative pursuits and expatriate adventure.

Like many expatriate stories, their tale was intertwined with another history. The broadcaster Wilfrid Thomas and his actress wife Bettina Dixon had known Johnston and Clift since Sydney when she had performed in an ABC broadcast of a Clift radio play. In London, Wilfrid Thomas was making radio programs on refugees and displaced persons who wanted to migrate to Australia. These included the sponge-divers of Kalymnos who could replace Japanese pearl-divers in Australia's north-west. A chance meeting with Thomas in Regent Street would send George Johnston to the Greek islands in pursuit of the book he wanted to write. The commitment would also offer an escape from regular journalistic employment.[9] Over time, through her short stories and newspaper columns, Charmian Clift would share the limelight with this author of a different story of national archetypes, *My Brother Jack* (1964), which also dealt with the escape from suburban bliss. Tragedy would also become as much part of the Johnston–Clift myth as 'freedom'. Their Greek idyll was troubled by marital and financial problems, and both would die prematurely after their return to Australia. However, for generations they remained beacons, or sirens, calling young Australians to the overseas odyssey.[10]

Beyond Canterbury Boys High – Murray Sayle and Phillip Knightley

Expatriation came in many forms, not all as dramatic or as eventful as the Johnston–Clift and Finch stories. In journalism, as in the arts, the war period produced a coming generation ready to jump the normal life of career, house and family which so characterised 1950s Australia. The young Murray Sayle, who had grown up in the lower middle-class suburb of Earlwood, discovered the high drama of war as reported in the newspapers and presented in department store window displays of the battle of El Alamein. Both suggested an exciting world beyond conventional suburban life. Sayle and the younger Phillip Knightley both attended the selective Canterbury Boys High School. For them, the discovery of cultures beyond everyday Australia came early. Even as youngsters, they were tantalised by a society already more complex than the simplistic 'decent Australian', '98% British' rhetoric of the day.

The personal was even more important than the national. Sayle's success in youth radio debates suggested abilities and aspirations. Other would-be stars of those debates were destined for different arenas; they included the boy from working-class Balmain and later premier Neville Wran, and the Russian Jewish refugee and later Australian National University academic Eugene Kamenka. Their challenges provided suitable confirmation for the ego of the young Sayle. The Andersonian atmosphere of Sydney University in the 1940s reinforced his inquisitive tendencies. Central to this was the professor of philosophy, John Anderson, the Trotskyist turned Cold War sceptic, whose strength and weakness was his critical, dismissive even, approach to ideas and ideals. This influence stimulated a university otherwise characterised by the staid sobriety of Anglican respectability. In reaction against it, an intoxicated period of related sub-cultures emerged. Ranging from pure Andersonian 'Free Thought' to bohemian libertarianism, their scenes included pubs and parties around nearby Broadway, in the city and up the Cross.[11]

Opportunities for young journalists came early due to the number of men away at the war – Sayle, for example, was editor of the student newspaper *Honi Soit* at 17. Already on the fringe of the daily newspapers, he was also developing his theatrical abilities. When ringing his contributor 'Dimity Sprigg', who, as Liz Hickson, had another life as a Fairfax or *Sydney Morning Herald* journalist, 'Slabs O'Mulligan' (Sayle) was beginning that search for different personas; such social skills would later prove invaluable for the investigative journalist. Liz Hickson did not lack initiative. Energetic and independent, in 1948 she 'hitched' a ride on a plane to Rome which was destined to pick up migrants bound for a new life in Australia. She had already expressed her independence in other ways. After a dispute with the *Sydney Morning Herald* women's editor, the formidable Constance Robertson, she had picked up her typewriter and taken it down to the men's area.

Sayle's happy knack of being on the spot when things were happening manifested early. In April 1944, when the Minister for Information, Arthur Calwell, banned articles in the *Daily Telegraph* under wartime censorship provisions, Sayle printed some of the censored articles in *Honi Soit*. In the same turbulent year, fact and fiction inflamed Australian cultural politics. 'Ern Malley', a self-effacing poet from the suburbs of Melbourne, had apparently been discovered by Max Harris, editor of the Adelaide modernist review *Angry Penguins*. Harris took up O'Malley's cause, seeing him as an unsung (and indeed unknown) hero of modern poetry. Sayle, the young student editor-cum-journalist and detective, was one of the first to expose the 'Ern Malley' affair as a great 'everyman poet' literary hoax perpetrated by the Sydney poets Harold Stewart and James McAuley.[12]

Sayle's Sydney watering holes went beyond the pub. They included the fashionable Repin's Coffee House in George Street and the cheap Italian restaurant, the Florentino, in Park Street near the *Daily Telegraph* office. The high-fashion haunts of Romano's and Prince's, pivotal institutions in the social world of Robin Eakin before her departure, were, however, foreign to him. Socially, Sayle's world had long transcended everyday Anglo-Saxon Australia. He had met Greek students from Newtown at Erskineville school 'opportunity classes', and been introduced to a new palate of cultural experience when taken to Dixon Street, the heart of Sydney's Chinatown. Raised on lamb and two vegetables, he ate a bowl of fried rice. He was suddenly overcome by the revelation that food could actually taste good, taste more interesting than roast lamb, lamingtons and rock cakes. Later Asian interests were being anticipated over a restaurant table.

Sayle's formal journalistic career began after he had dropped out of Sydney University, despite topping first year Psychology. He rose rapidly. Travelling north to work as a sub-editor on the *Cairns Post* at 21, he eventually started a column as 'Sydney Mann' on the front page of the *Daily Mirror*. At 22, the pay of a super 'A' grade and a flat at the Cross, in sight of the 'gracious living' of the

Eastern Suburbs, inevitably posed the question of 'where to next' for the precocious 'boy about 12', as the young columnist was known by his cheekier colleagues. Libertarian parties and drunken debate, between times dropping in an occasional load of washing on his mother in Earlwood, inevitably offered only a short-term solution.

A brief marriage to a soprano was not the answer. Eventually other musically romantic imperatives took over. In 1952, at the age of 26, and in pursuit of the folk singer Shirley Abicair, he took the ship. More prosaic realities were also present. Landing at Tilbury docks, he took a cab from the East End all the way to Lancaster Mews, where the postwar pioneer Liz Hickson lived. Arriving at her door in search of a roof over his head, he asked with plaintive charm, 'Liz, will you pay the cab?'

Sayle's mission in pursuit of this early 'grand passion', Shirley Abicair, did not succeed, although the friendship of these two castaways endured over time. She would have her moment of fame in Britain as the zither-playing folk singer over the next decade. Other paths were opening up quickly, not least as he immediately broadened his horizons with a short trip to Paris, which exhausted his remaining financial resources. Accompanying him on the ship was his friend, the artist Francis Lymburner, with whom he would share a flat, and the initial discovery of Paris.

The age at departure also varied, from the itchy footed 18-year-olds to others who at 30 reached a 'now or never' stage. Phillip Knightley left at the age of 26 in 1954, the year of the Royal Tour and a Cold War election campaign. Knightley had begun as a copy-boy on the *Daily Telegraph* and increasingly entertained himself in the Cross, while sleeping in the family home in the Southern Suburbs. Over time he slowly changed. Simultaneously, he became aware of the limitations of Sydney journalism and fascinated by the exotic. The latter began with the Hungarian, Viennese and Russian refugees who ran the cafes up the Cross.

Journalists returning from Europe, whether the distinguished war correspondent Sam White, or the younger Paul Brickhill, experienced the more repressive side of Sydney newspapers. Sam White, who threatened everyday values by wearing suede desert boots, which Knightley thought were the first ever seen in Sydney, was put in his place by being given the suburban courts round. His 'stuff this for a lark' response was to leave after about six weeks, offering further inspiration for the young copy-boy Knightley. In Knightley's view, Sydney journalism then was reflected in this attempt 'to give the overseas returned man a deliberately humiliating job', 'to deliberately take a bit of the pride away to get them used to working in Australia again'. Their colleagues would let them 'know very quickly that they weren't interested in what their views were of all the places they'd been and the life they had experienced abroad – "you know, don't give me all that overseas just returned bullshit sort of stuff" '.[13]

The case of a returned Melbourne *Herald* reporter who had been banished to the shipping rounds (which at least offered the consolation of interviewing the famous who were about to land on Australian shores) led Phillip Knightley to reflect on the social responsibility of journalism. Knightley condemned the Australian view that journalism was 'a trade in which you do the minimum in order to earn whatever salary you want and not think of it as anything more than that'. That is, it was not about 'changing society or drawing people's attention to injustices or anything like that'. Journalism was too often measured 'in so many words, so many columns, good story, poor story'.

Perversely, such attitudes sometimes encouraged returned journalists to talk at length in the pub about their times overseas as a 'real journalist', to tell tales which inspired those who experienced frustration, along with itchy feet. In the colonial circularity of Australian culture, the response was not always generous; parochial prejudices were often intensified as a result. In the bush, a valid colonial distaste had developed towards the Pom 'new chum' who came out as a bookish expert without necessary local knowledge. Now, less justifiably, the returned 'old chum' could encourage the Colonial Cultural Cringe Inverted, the view of some 'hacks' that 'overseas' had nothing to teach.

Freedom vs Repression?

Vacillating between security and adventure, Knightley's final departure came in 1954, after short periods in Melbourne, Fiji and New Zealand. Political events sparked off his decision to go to London. When political change did not come in the 1954 federal elections – after Menzies played the three cards of conservatism, the Royal Tour and the Cold War bonus card of the Petrov spy case, Knightley sailed away. He left Australia's provincial and repressive politics, wondering later if he should have stayed and fought, rather than fleeing. While covering the Evatt Labor election campaign, he had gained from the former president of the United Nations a sense of international affairs. At the same time he watched Evatt's assistants suffer at the hands of the Petrov Commission.[14]

Moral, not political, repression provided another stimulus for departure. In a Sydney Central Criminal Court case, an anthropologist was charged with obscene libel for bringing into Australia a Papuan woodcarving which depicted a man's penis entering his mouth. When the anthropologist was sent to jail, Knightley decided to leave this stultifying society for a more open one. In the 1960s Knightley would form a friendship with another victim of repression, the fellow exile who lived at times in Paris and London and later in Majorca, the writer Robert 'Bob' Close.

Close, the former sailor, vacuum cleaner salesman and *Truth* journalist, had left for France in October 1950. He had been sentenced in 1946 to three months in Pentridge Jail and fined £100 because of the 'obscene libel' of his critically and popularly successful novel, *Love Me Sailor*. The novel recounted the amorous adventures, tensions and language of a ship's crew. The first edition sold out in a few weeks. Close was handcuffed and taken to Pentridge in a Black Maria. Although he was bailed, and the jail sentence was later quashed on appeal, a bruised Close departed for fresher pastures, to France where his book, *Prends-moi, Matelot* or 'Take me, Sailor', had had an enthusiastic reception. The writer's distaste with humdrum routines and everyday values, beginning with 'my discontent at having to waste time on a job to earn enough to support my suburban home', was compounded by his political–legal difficulties. His feelings of being 'tired of living in an atmosphere of parochial suburbanism' were shared by many others who had not come into conflict so dramatically with ruling values. Living with a woman out of wedlock ('living in sin') was perceived as threatening the very foundations of national life, as Close and George Johnston and Charmian Clift, frequent visitors to his Sorrento abode, had found.

The Crown's desire to prosecute Close was apparently politically motivated. Although not a Communist himself, the ex-seaman had many friends who were. Political repression as well as wowserism drove Close away. His 'burning and ruthless urge to grow as a writer, to earn a place in Australia's literature' continued, but in a different form and in different places (Paris, London, Majorca). Despite his continuing contact with expatriate Australians in London, literary nationalism played a diminishing role in his aspirations. The *Love Me Sailor* trial experience had led to his continuing 'self-imposed exile from [his] native land'.[15]

The process of prosecution took more than two years, extending from March 1946 to the second trial, which involved a jury irregularity, and then to the appeal in June 1948. For that period Close, who had already spent a weekend in Pentridge Jail between the conviction and the sentence, and was on £50 bail, had a cloud hanging over his head. The perpetrator of what Judge Martin considered to be a 'gross assault on the morals of the community' understandably felt little confidence in Australia as a place for a writer.[16]

Outsiders

Murray Sayle felt similar frustrations. Of the feelings of alienation which underlaid his own departure, he later wrote:

> I sailed from Sydney, my birthplace, aboard the old R.M.S. *Otranto* on August 8, 1952. I left a good job which, alarmingly, looked like

getting better: I felt the Australian emptiness closing in on me and I had to get out. There was a business about a girl to trigger me, but I had planned to come to London for years, and anyway she'd gone there, too.

It was, as he noted, 'easy to join a mass movement':

> We had aboard a couple of young architects headed for the LCC [London County Council], two or three dentists who'd heard about the National Health bonanza, a gaggle of typists looking for Rex Harrison-type English husbands, academics, advertising men, schoolteachers, nurses, pianists, poets, painters – a section of the young artistic and professional group making the customary pilgrimage to London, and every ship from Australia brings another. Like all migrants, we were looking for something we couldn't find at home, and we weren't coming back without it.[17]

The journalists formed something of a ghetto, with other Australians they knew from the smaller worlds of the capital cities and with other newcomers from around the world. Young graduate researchers, such as the politics student Ken Minogue (who would stay in London), or just travellers who thought that 1950s Australia 'was so dull you just had to get out', were part of a changing inner-city London. This was the London of migrants to the 'big smoke' (or sometimes, in the years before the 1956 Clean Air Act had an impact, of deadly smog). The new Londoners came from around Britain and the Commonwealth, and also from Eastern Europe and around the globe.

Other characters in the society of Sydney journalists included Bill Harcourt (at Australia House at Aldwych) and Ed 'Shoulders' Morrisby. The nickname, suggesting 'Head and Shoulders' above the others, was interchanged in a ritual of camaraderie (as Murray Sayle and Phillip Knightley, two seasick sailors, would later fax each other across the world as 'Cap'). In the small world of inter-war New South Wales, a very young Murray Sayle, aged 3, had first met Ed when his family holidayed next door in Newcastle. An older Morrisby would later take over the 'Sydney Mann' column from Sayle in 1952. Other worlds were wider. Ed Morrisby knew Loudon Sainthill, the theatrical designer of 'Merioola', and the art student Jocelyn Rickards. Sayle, a 'personable chap' as well as a gossip columnist, knew a variety of people in Sydney: the classical composer David Lumsdaine; the actors John Cazabon and Alan White; the young violinist Patti Tuckwell, and the typist and aspiring writer, Jill Neville.

Sayle's friendship with Francis Lymburner would be strengthened during the voyage on the *Otranto*. Sharing a flat at 27 Croftdown Road, Parliament Hill Fields, NW8, they also shared the discovery of Paris. Murray Sayle moved about, living for a time near South Kensington station, then moving to 44 Palace Gardens Terrace in 1953. They both had a 'thin time' in 1950s London. They were supported by girlfriends and occasional mundane work, Lymburner as a framer and Sayle as a sub-editor. The writer reduced to an editor and the painter sent to the margins of framing suggested the difficulty of realising the colonial dream of making it in London; the road to London success had many deep potholes. Drying canvases by gas fires, and unable to sell a painting, Lymburner also found consolation in a glass. On one occasion the writer Peter Porter, who was working in a paint company, provided a can of paint to brighten up a bare abode. At different times Lymburner stayed with Sayle and with another expatriate, Barry Humphries. Similarly, Robert Close would later stay at Sayle's place in London when the journalist was off covering stories in distant places, particularly Vietnam.

In the spring of 1961, after Sayle's career had hit an unusual brick wall, Lymburner and Sayle both sought respite. Temporary salvation came in an unlikely form: working at a salmon-fishery at Porton on the South Wales side of the estuary of the Severn, between Newport and Chepstow. Ye Olde Tippling Philosophers, a nearby riverside pub, offered an eccentrically appropriate solace for these two cultural wanderers.[18]

Notting Hill Gate Bohemia – Cosy in a Basement?

Sometimes this generation of expatriates lived, in their work and private life, in a peninsular extension of Australia. Phillip Knightley, for example, worked for the Sydney *Daily Mirror* London bureau. But there were also explorations. Relationships without a wedding, a ring and a suburban home, but with new sexual opportunities, stimulated and troubled these refugees from the suburbs. Despite the Andersonian belief in free thought and the libertarian ideal of free love, which some shared, freedom was more complex; in practice it came with angst. Parties at which the women were, in Phillip Knightley's recollections, Italian and Indian or occasionally Australian supply (or relief) teachers, were part of their Australian/international and generally un-English world. The male world of the Surrey, the journalists' pub just across from Australia House, could also be a meeting point for Australian and English journalists within the freemasonry of the trade. It had extra appeal for Australians, even for those from outside Victoria – unusually for the time, it had Australian beer (Fosters) on tap.

This mid-1950s world of parties and pubs was a semi-bohemia, a world of making their own fun when career opportunities either didn't exist or were mundane. When Sayle returned from working in Paris, one focus of social action was the flat at 44 Palace Gardens Terrace in Notting Hill Gate/ Kensington. A body on the floor in a sleeping bag was often the latest journalist or friend just off the boat at Tilbury or Southampton. At parties, Murray Sayle was even more leader of the pack than he had been in Sydney. Tall and thin, and towering over conversational partners, he cut a figure as powerful as it was eccentric. Enhanced by a prominent proboscis and an artist's short pointed beard, he freely offered Andersonian, or perhaps 'Saylean', cross-examination of different opinions.

In a way, in these inner London circles, the Australian journalists were experimenting unselfconsciously with their own bohemia. Their social and sexual discoveries came decades after those of the Americans in Paris in the 1920s but before those of London in the 1960s. At times, however, it was depressing and frustrating. Murray Sayle's Zanzibarian friend, Babu (more fully, Abdulrahmann Mohammed Babu), recalled that they felt excluded by the English. They were looked down on as 'colonials', at a time when some English people already felt that they themselves were being pushed out by newcomers.

For these outsiders, the life of partying was not exactly the life of Riley. It was, however, brightened by exciting moments. On one such occasion a piano fell out of the Sayle flat into the grounds of the Russian embassy and an attempt was made to hoist it back – an episode which would provide useful contacts for a journalist during the Cold War. Sayle, the performer, was capable of different roles as well as the one-man show; for example, the theatrical performance of journalist-turned-city man, in pin-stripes and bowler, heading off to Fleet Street in search of employment. On another occasion, in appreciation of Liz Hickson's 'really gracious living', he took her out for coffee and an explanation of the atom bomb. Sayle's characteristic opening 'Let's talk about this . . .' had unintended consequences. A cigarette butt which fell into a box of 78 records before they left brought flames and fire engines to greet them on their return.

Behind these stories were also less exciting moments. Anxiety was one of the leitmotifs of the age. Sayle and Knightley shared it with another group of travelling writers of the time, mainly from other Commonwealth countries and colonies. Dan Jacobson from South Africa, Doris Lessing from Rhodesia, and the American J. P. (Mike) Donleavy, who had been in Ireland, and the Australian writers Jill Neville and Peter Porter were amongst those who had felt impelled to leave their homes for London. In the late 1950s the expatriate Irish publisher Timothy O'Keefe brought together their reflections on discontent, with their own countries and with Britain, under a title reflecting contemporary angst, *Alienation* (1960). In his essay Murray Sayle, always the searcher after either larger patterns or immediate dramatic events, saw Australia's early convict settlement and tough land as having formed a limited society. 'Underneath the spectacular Australian success, from semi-desert to gracious living in four generations' he discerned 'a deep consciousness of failure'. For him, Australians had exchanged the choice of a New Jerusalem 'for two-car garages and outdoor barbecues'.[19] It was a society limited by its economically secondary character and now by its mass media stars and sporting heroes. Exploring the alienation of the Angry Young Men/Beat/Ban the Bomb era of the late 1950s and early 1960s, he picked up the tradition of Australian intellectual alienation. At one pole he critiqued the suburban working-class 'Alf', the personification of materialism and anti-cultural attitudes, of 'militant ignorance'. Nor was he enthused by another type, the 'Roy', who saw himself as the opposite of the 'Alf', but in practice was the enshrinement of provincial middle-class cultural taste. Sayle gave currency to the idea of the 'Alf'. So would the playwright Alan Seymour in *The One Day of the Year* (1960), and *OZ* magazine, and later, through his 'Ocker' characters, the performer Barry Humphries. It was a theme which other critics of suburban Australia would soon take up.

In expatriate self-justification Sayle argued that for the sensitive Australian 'the only refuge from the infantile self-congratulation he hears around him is exile, internal or external'. His critique also embodied a sceptical Andersonian version of another national pastime, 'knocking'. Only departure, he argued, would save the cultural creator from the 'new-nation clamour' of the prison of nationalism and the ruinous 'adulation given even to little fish in little ponds'.[20]

Knightley and the former Melbourne journalist Graeme Edwards wrote an unperformed television play, *Cosy in a Basement*. It dramatically presents the cultural and national tensions of Australian expatriate London.[21] Its two major Australian expatriate male characters, Colin and Ray, are variants on the 'Roy' and the 'Alf' stereotypes. Colin Harrison, the sensitive expatriate librarian with an Indian girlfriend, Gala, finds the racism of the Australian and South African-run 'Welcome Visitors Club' grossly offensive. His mate Ray Prentice is the cocky salesman who jumps off the boat to run up against English culture, and finds he doesn't like it – 'little mug Pommy' taxi drivers demanding tips, the politeness which evaded straight answers: 'We'll be writing to you, Mr Prentice'. 'Please keep in touch with us, Mr Prentice.'

The dreamer Colin, a thin librarian, is an unusually sensitive 'Roy'. He likes a society in which career doesn't matter so he can 'avoid the pitfalls of getting ahead, and of making major decisions'. In contrast Ray is a hustler and an Alf, preferring, almost, the 'best bloody place in the world' with its innovations, such as drive-in bottleshops, to a slow Britain:

> queueing for buses and cinemas . . . Tipping – particularly taxis. You can't get a decent shower. The service in the shops is lousy. And in the restaurants too . . . unless you want to spend a fortune . . . And the bloody beer's not cold.

Although the English girl Judy likes his directness and endorses his freedom from 'good form and good taste and all those trappings of a stagnant society', Ray isn't Colin's cup of tea. In fact, remarks Gala, Colin has left home 'to get away from people like Ray'. With his matey talk to men and women (to Judy, 'Hello, pet. How's tricks? Gotta cuppa for a neighbour?'), and his hustling ways, Ray is an embarrassment, even a threat, to the more sensitive soul trying to fit in with the politesse of English manners. At the same time Ray affirms a warmth and breezy no-nonsense directness free of the repressions of little England. He is also concerned to see that his mate doesn't become 'a real no-hoper', that he isn't going downhill at the age of 35 with his stagnant career and interest in books, films and a silly boat.

The opposite to Colin's 'rut' was Ray's get-a-foot-in-the-door salesman version of the contemporary working-class desire to get ahead. Wearing his Joe Lampton 'Room at the Top' hat, Ray resembles one contemporary English type, the working-class young man 'on the make'. Ray is 'going to the top because that's where all the sweet things in life are'. He 'could only put up with this place' (London/England) if he 'had plenty of money'. Nor did Australia, which lacked theatres and thought and had a White Australia policy, appeal to Colin. Not that prejudice and discrimination were entirely lacking in Britain and in the India from which his girlfriend Gala came.

To the Englishman named Derek Sloane, the Australians who came to London were contradictory in the extreme. Many endorsed Ray's views about the English, declaring 'you couldn't manage a country out-house'. Like him, though, they wouldn't go home, perhaps sharing his desire to 'make my mark first'. Sloane finds Ray's attitudes typical:

> You come over here with a chip on your shoulder because you come from the end of the earth. Then you criticize and whine but none of you want to go home ... Sometimes I think you come here to get your own back on us for transporting your ancestors.

As the temperature rises, he develops, angrily, the case for the prosecution:

> The trouble with most of your sort is that you're hypocrites. You accuse us of being arrogant and class-conscious, and all the time you're the same yourselves. You say you hate our pretence, yet the moment you land in Britain you parade your nationality. You plaster yourselves and your cars with patriotic symbols – kangaroos and kiwis and badges – and wait for everyone to fall on your necks. I've met some decent types, but the lot who come here are loud-mouthed, ill-mannered boors ... or, in your own slang ... a pack of wingers [sic].

In the way of late 1950s naturalism, the dramatic result is a battle of wills which soon becomes a battle of blows: English cunning and imperious style versus Australian direct aggression. Neither wins. Nor can Ray, whose un-English heavy selling of encyclopaedias leads to the sack. But he can't 'go back a failure', a 'has-been', a basement-dweller to be laughed at.

A sales opportunity with an American company in Britain saves Ray from his trough. Business becomes more important than ethics regarding racial prejudice when it comes to meeting the American boss. For this expatriate the choice is between money or conscience. Many people in a changing Australia would face a similar choice. Others, in London and Australia, would have to choose between the calls of fame and art, or between fame and social/political commitment.

'A feeling of impermanence' would be an even more fundamental part of the expatriate burden for Murray Sayle. It was a product of the 'colonial' legacy. Although attached to his part of the earth, he had grown up with Christopher Robin, roast dinners and at school a literary English language of 'brook' and 'dale'. The sense of deracination, of, unlike the Aborigines, not feeling part of the earth was, for him, compounded by an interest in the influence of a larger past in a society which talked always of the future. In 1960 he argued that Britain was 'part of greater Australia'. Living in London, he was not 'adopting a new nationality – on the contrary, I am getting to grips with an important part of my own'. Proof lay in the Australian view that success for Australians still depended on being acclaimed in Britain. 'I won't say that this had nothing to do with my coming here, either.' Neither English nor quite a tourist, he already sensed that to be an Australian expatriate was almost an entirely different nationality. Unimpressed by British snobbery (despite occasional role-playing), he discerned a 'pervading phoniness' in Britain as well. However, contemporary Britain offered the Australian expatriate a freedom not possessed by the English, the Scots or the Welsh of whatever class. These unplaceable Australians had a freedom 'to move from group to group', coupled with a familiarity and comfort which softened 'the harshness of exile'.[22]

Expatriate intentions and justifications varied dramatically. The journalist Anthony Delano, whose journalist father had worked around Australia during the Great Depression, aimed to leave and never go back. Feeling that Australia was very distant from what was happening in the rest of the world, he headed off to London. He followed two beacons – one was love (he was pursuing a woman), the other was journalistic passion. On the evening on which he arrived in London he traced out Fleet Street on the map, caught a bus there and put his ear against the walls of the *Daily Telegraph* to hear the presses start at 11 p.m. He would, over the next few decades, return only twice to Australia, when his parents died and for the 1954 Royal Tour. In 1956, a *Daily Mirror* executive assumed that with a name like Delano he could speak Italian. With characteristic expatriate adroitness, he didn't disabuse him of the idea and went off to the exciting Rome of Gina Lollobrigida and the Catholic Church before Vatican II. (He developed a liking for Italianate coats and hats such that, even some years later, he at least looked the part.) He was then posted to Paris in the era of the Algerian war and the assassination attempts on President de Gaulle. This journalistic performer as well as reporter was, in journalistic terms, where the action was.

Women journalists were still few in Australia and Britain and were still mainly confined to the women's room or area, although there were exceptions, more commonly at the *Daily Telegraph* than at the *Sydney Morning Herald*. Individuals such as Constance Robertson had worked in Fleet Street and as overseas correspondents in the 1930s and 1940s, but this was unusual. Sometimes discrimination in Fleet Street was a dual discrimination, against an Australian as well as a woman. While Constance Robertson brought news from Britain and France of 1940s fashions and of rationing to her readers, at Fairfax she ruled over her staff with an iron rod. Like the blunt Brian Penton at the *Daily Telegraph* and the forbidding Rupert Henderson at the *Herald*, she was part of the old authoritarian tradition of the press.

There were always exceptions. Some women journalists escaped to the women's magazines, while the rebellious Liz Hickson found an exciting if uneven world overseas. Liz Hickson's wanderlust would take her from the London *Daily Mirror* to the United States in the mid-1950s. During the 1950s and 1960s she worked on the *Daily Mirror*, the *Daily Sketch*, the *Despatch* and the *Daily Mail*. Journalistically, she lived through and reported the dramas of the death of the king (1952), the Burgess and Maclean spy scandal (1951) and the sex and espionage tale of the Profumo affair (1963). She experienced many milieux until, in the late 1960s, independence was overwhelmed by contemporary social realities. Her husband, who had just signed a contract with the ABC, dragged her 'kicking and screaming' back home to Sydney. Other women would later follow her trail north, many of them in eras in which women, as well as men, would be prominent war correspondents and foreign correspondents.[23]

Parisian Escapes – Sayle's Travails

As Sayle's second wife Tessa Sayle later reflected, wearing her hat as a tough-minded literary agent, whether the expatriates stayed 'depended on how well they did' in London. To many of them London was the 'big time', as there was no Australian 'big time' then. Murray Sayle's mercurial career reflected, but also went beyond, that truism. After a couple of years as a successful Fleet Street vice exposer, and having lost Shirley Abicair, who had 'given [him] the boot' in 1954, he headed off for the romantic city of Paris. He worked for the World Veterans Federation publication *Nouvelle Ere* in the mid-1950s, and also pursued his other activities, collecting people as well as knowledge, taking in as well as giving out through informal lectures and dialogues.

Roland Pullen had already come to post-liberation, late 1940s Paris, and in the 1950s Sam White was discovering the journalistic opportunities of the bar of Le Crillon, on the Place de la Concorde near the British and American chanceries. Sayle's milieu was more on the Left Bank. There, the adventurer, scribbler and larrikin intellectual met other expatriates: the black American writer Richard Wright, the Australian painter Roy Dalgarno and his wife Betty. In their replay of the earlier eras of Fitzgerald and Hemingway, the expatriates lived in cheap hotels, drank into the early morning in bars and brasseries and hung around George Whitman's Shakespeare and Co bookshop.

In this Paris, still a congeries of local *quartiers* not yet swamped by the mass commuter and tourist city, also lived other groups of wanderers. Alister Kershaw, poet and bohemian, conservative libertarian by preference, and occasional journalist to Australia by necessity, had left Australia in 1947. He gathered around him travelling Australians at the de facto 'Hotel Australia' in Montparnasse. But these voyagers, including Geoffrey Dutton (the Oxford student and later writer and publisher), Sidney J. Baker (the student of Australian English), Alannah Coleman (the artist and curator) and David Strachan (the painter), were not really a beachhead for a larger invasion. Instead most, except for the artists, came on R&R from the Anglo-Saxon sobriety of the UK or even from the wowserism of 1950s Australia itself.

The great achievement for the self-taught Murray Sayle was a personal one. This Sydney University non-graduate was blessed with more than a hint of old Australian working-class style as well as intelligence and a talent for languages. Living and working in Paris, and learning the French language, his loquacious charm brought him a stylish European catch. He successfully wooed this glamorous Austrian lady, Tessa, herself a 'refugee' from Austrian aristocratic society. When he lost his job in Paris, London offered a respite in the northern autumn of 1956. Building on his successful earlier career with the Fleet Street tabloid *The People*, he continued working on the project which would launch Sayle, the writer, rather than Sayle, the mere journalist. The result, the novel *A Crooked Sixpence*, appeared in 1960. In this tale of vice, brothels and gangsters, an Australian journalist explored and experienced London vice. The book would not become a film or make Sayle the new F. Scott Fitzgerald, as he had hoped. It led instead to a law suit for libel from a minor character in the novel, an aristocrat, and the withdrawal of the novel by the publisher.

Sayle, Sydney columnist, Fleet Street tabloid journalist and would-be novelist, fell into a slough of despond from which he was sometimes rescued by the support of a still self-effacing Tessa, or by the theatrical escape of parties with expatriates and writers. By the early 1960s, when Tessa, an extremely tidy woman, had left Murray, an extremely untidy man, for the charms of J. P. (Mike) Donleavy, the odyssey was paling. However, beyond the rocks of marriage, new possibilities appeared. A second stint in Paris, with Agence France Presse, meant both an escape from his London trough and a return to everyday news bureau journalism, although he never felt quite happy with that side of the trade. Paris, not Australia, offered the bolthole he wanted. Then, serendipity, in the form of his Kensington postman, Babu, brought new life to this would-be writer, wanderer and adventurer in the changing Sixties. Babu was also a London School of Economics student and, more importantly, an African revolutionary, whom Sayle followed to the Zanzibarian revolution and later to Cuba. The revolutionary postman offered a taste of politics and culture beyond Sydney *and* London.

Phillip Knightley's wandering career also had its moments. Ever attracted to the 'East' in all its forms (from the Pacific to India, from Austria to Russia), he jumped between the exotic and the secure. In 1947, as an 18-year-old intoxicated by Joseph Conrad and Somerset Maugham, he had worked for the *Fiji Times*. It was in a Suva which seemed to come out of *Lord Jim* that his taste for the international and the exotic grew. So too did a distaste for the class and race society of which he had been on the top rung in Fiji. In London though, he was becalmed, not in paradise but on the London bureau desk of the Sydney *Mirror* for over seven years, clipping and rewriting the United Kingdom news for Australian readers – 'scissors and paste' work 'absolutely boring, mind-numbing beyond belief'. Although the offices were in Fleet Street, this Australian environment was almost without connections to London journalism. Those 'wasted years' were 'one of the great regrets' of his life. Knightley's stagnation was mirrored by others who found work in London at the bureaus of the *Daily Mirror*, the *Telegraph* or the *Truth* and *Sportsman*, or even at Reuters, as a means of paying the rent and feeding the gas meter.

Old Vienna on the Kings Road

Knightley's independent bent was more personal and entrepreneurial than physical. His October 1954 marriage to Eva Hajek, which allowed her to stay in the United Kingdom, was deliberately brief. A business idea offered a potential escape from drudgery. In 1959, after returning from Murray and Tessa Sayle's grand wedding in Vienna, he bought the lease on an old coffee shop in the Kings Road. Grandly, and pretentiously, he renamed it the 'Old Vienna'. Less fruitfully, having failed to engage an Austrian chef, he took on a Pole who had an unfortunate taste for alcohol. His Austrian venture, at the wrong end of Kings Road, met with less than modest success. Having known refugees up the Cross was not the best qualification for being the owner of an 'Austrian' restaurant in Chelsea. Nor did Sayle, Knightley's newly wed carpenter, do too well out of it. Having helped create the Austrian, rather than

Australian, facade, he was promised coffee for life – it did have a Gaggia espresso machine after all! It turned out only to be for the short life of London's first Austrian restaurant.[24]

Knightley was developing his own quiet theatricality. A dapper style of dress and Litrico suits contrasted with his democratic values, his liking for a sociable beer and for gossip, which could take him to hard information. However, his career progress was limited. Returning to Australia in the early 1960s he worked for the ABC (just before it escaped the government broadcasting straitjacket of uncritical respectability), and for Sydney newspapers. But he also made other unusual escapes. One was editing the magazine *Imprint* in Bombay, which specialised in children's books. This was an unwitting association with espionage, as he later found out – *Imprint* was a CIA-sponsored publication which ran tales of 'good' and 'evil', including Cold War stories of escaping Russia and finding freedom in the US. Its parent company was also a cover for visiting CIA intelligence men. (He also met his second wife, Yvonne, an air hostess, in Bombay when he was travelling overland towards Australia.)

What would the future hold for this restless journalist? As the Australian print and electronic media broadened their horizons, and the country embraced a new liberality, this 'Colin'-like character might find a place in Sydney. A career might be possible at the ABC or at Rupert Murdoch's new liberal broadsheet, the *Australian*, the first national newspaper. At the time Australia was beginning to liberalise its longstanding racial immigration policy as well. Or, at least, a new chapter was beginning. Would Phillip Knightley, a more determined 'Colin', meet up again with his old sparring partner, 'Ray', overseas, or in Sydney? With Murray Sayle, who had something of the 'Ray' persona, though more an intellectual than a huckster, with just a hint of Ray's salesmanlike bravado?

Chapter 4

Musical Directions[1]

On a humid Sydney night, early in 1940, the four young musicians had to decide what to do next. Patricia Tuckwell the young and pretty violin student, Richard Farrell the New Zealander and piano student, Lois Simpson who was studying the cello and the even younger Charles Mackerras considered several alternatives. These included visiting what they called the 'Seduction Room' of the 'Con' (the New South Wales Conservatorium of Music on the edge of Sydney's Botanic Gardens), going to their favourite cafe in Castle-reagh Street nearby, or having a meal at one of the Viennese cafes in Macleay Street, Kings Cross. For these four young musicians Sydney in the 1940s offered every opportunity of making their own music.

The artistic choices available to young musicians were, however, about more than how to spend an evening. Australia's evolving musical culture and the effects of world war on a distant and provincial society were coming together to create new possibilities. Their other performing stages were many. Richard Farrell worked as a ballet pianist for the Hélène Kirsova Company, and Charles Mackerras played the piano with the orchestra at the State Theatre, Sydney's most ornate inter-war picture theatre. At 16, Mackerras moved into the limelight as a pianist, oboist and then arranger with the new Colgate-Palmolive Radio Unit, working on such shows as *Calling the Stars* with the famous host of the day, Jack Davey.

At a time when the war meant that many orchestra scores were not available in Australia, the teenage Charles Mackerras busied himself tran-scribing from records. He also wrote a ballet score for Hélène Kirsova based on 'Waltzing Matilda'. Although the ballet was never choreographed, the *Waltzing Matilda Fugue* which ended it would be played by the Sydney

Symphony Orchestra (SSO) under the visiting American conductor, Eugene Ormandy.[2]

The changing relationship between musical composition and performance in Australia and overseas was complex. It would shape both the destinies of talented young Australians and the Australian music scene during the war years, and in subsequent decades. Focusing on several musicians, particularly Charles Mackerras, Barry Tuckwell, Joan Sutherland, Geoffrey Parsons and Geoffrey Chard, and the composers Malcolm Williamson, Don Banks and David Lumsdaine, this chapter explores the story of that first postwar wave. Over time their unfolding relationships – with music, with Britain and with Australia, and beyond – would reflect the times as well as their own talent, hard work and success, and the opportunities available to them. Those opportunities would pull many of them in different directions – between different places, particularly London and Australia, and between different forms of work, from permanent positions to the opportunities and pressures of freelance work. Some people were denied that full range of opportunities, including Richard Farrell, who would die prematurely. Others chose Australian rather than expatriate roads, Lois Simpson performing as a principal cellist with the SSO and, much later, as a soloist with the Australian Chamber Orchestra. Patricia Tuckwell, who was the model 'Bambi' as well as a violinist, moved to Melbourne in 1948 after marrying the Melbourne photographer, Athol Shmith.

In this emerging musical society, opportunities came from the institutional bases established earlier in the century. The conservatoriums in the larger capitals trained musicians and the Australian Broadcasting Commission (ABC) orchestras had been formed during the previous decade. In Sydney, the SSO had increased to between 72 and 82 players by 1945, more than double the 35 of ten years before.[3] A temporary stimulus, providing work for young musicians and high levels of responsibility at an early age, was the absence of so many musicians at the war. Patricia Tuckwell's younger brother Barry, who had started to learn the horn at 13, had his first professional dates at 14 and his first full-time job with the Melbourne Symphony Orchestra at 15. At a time when musical genres were already diverse, the children of Charles Tuckwell, the popular theatre organist, were performing musicians at a young age. In Melbourne in the late 1940s, where the young performer and composer Don Banks was admixing his classical interests with jazz, in the form of the Donny Banks Boptet, the same efflorescence of musical culture – classical, jazz and popular – was also found.

Musical elaboration continued in the postwar years. Eugene Goossens arrived as the Director of the NSW State Conservatorium of Music and the conductor of the further enlarged SSO, on a salary greater than that of the prime minister. The Musica Viva chamber orchestra was formed in 1945 by the Austrian Jewish refugee Richard Goldner. Both developments suggested a higher level in the classical music culture of Sydney. Postwar refugees and returned soldiers who had discovered cultural interests due to the stimulus of war and through army education, might also augment concert audiences. Would the musical culture of postwar Australia end, or at least modify, the colonialist tradition which sent a tide of performers, most famously Dame Nellie Melba, overseas? Would Australian concert halls no longer remain half-empty, except when visiting 'celebrity' performers starred, supported by local musicians?

Classical Music's Origins: Concert Hall to *Corroboree*

Historical and personal factors and contemporary cultural and economic logics would still take many of the talented young performers across the seas to the 'old world' from which most classical music had come. Over forty years after his own departure, Sir Charles Mackerras argued that Australians still needed to go to Europe to achieve musical excellence. 'It is actually where all the composers came from who provide us with the great repertoire of classical music.'[4] The postwar waves to Britain were part of an older tradition of expatriation to London and Europe which had sent hundreds of young Australian musicians abroad to study and to perform and then to live. The long rollcall of names who had gone before included the singers Nellie Mitchell (Dame Nellie Melba), Florence Austral, Strella Wilson, John Brownlee, Joan Hammond and Peter Dawson, and the composer Percy Grainger and the pianist Eileen Joyce.

Ever since the early white settlers' ships had brought pianos and other instruments along with their human and animal cargoes, the six Australian colonies had been colonial inheritors of British and European musical traditions. Despite an increasing, if still minor, interest in Australian folk music during the war years, and the Jindyworobak poets' fascination with the land and their conception of Aboriginal culture, Australians still looked to Europe when it came to classical music. John Antill's *Corroboree*, performed by Goossens in 1946 and played as ballet music in 1950, was, however, a breakthrough. But it was not clear whether it would be a watershed, marking the beginning of a new phase in Australian music, or become the landmark exception, which proved the rule of the dominance of the derivative tradition.[5]

In the contemporary context, the call was strongest from the European centre of the Allied war effort, London. In music, as in other spheres, Australians were attracted to the imperial capital, rather than to war-ravaged, partly 'enemy' and later 'Communist', Europe. Benefiting also from the exodus of European refugees, London was beginning, bombed buildings and shortages notwithstanding, to enter one of its most significant eras as a centre of musical and operatic performance.

A Colonial Condition

Australia's colonial inheritance also created cultural and economic factors that encouraged departure. The absence of rich patrons in this new world country, limited wages and other musical opportunities, and small audiences, ensured that many musicians remained part-timers. Nor did the cultural milieu of classical music-making augur well for local performers, however talented. In the 1930s, under Charles Moses and with the musical advice of Bernard Heinze, the ABC decided that to make its concerts successful it needed two status devices. One was the imported performer, dubbed a 'celebrity' – thus the 'ABC Celebrity Concerts'. The second was ensuring the patronage of 'society'. The colonial class cringe and the colonial cultural cringe came together in this 'ideal'. If vice-regal patronage could be obtained, with the governor's wife as patron, along with the support of a few 'leading lights' in each capital, the rest of the audience would follow. 'Heinze believed the patronage of the social elite was very important to successful concert-giving and that the Ladies' Committees should be taken very seriously', recalled the later ABC Director of Music, Harold Hort. These cultural and social cringes had been institutionalised in the years before World War II.[6] Paradoxically, the appeal to 'society' reinforced the popular twentieth-century assumption that classical music was for 'stuffed shirts' and 'longhairs', not for ordinary people. In the long run, it limited audiences rather than guaranteeing them as intended.

In the assessment of Phillip Sametz, 'the cult of the international Celebrity ... was undoubtedly bad for local music-making. It reinforced our sense of cultural second-rateness all too well'. 'Triumph of Celebrities', the *Sydney Morning Herald*'s review of 1939, declared: 'Local singers and instrumentalists were able to give solo recitals only on the smallest scale. Even then their concerts were a losing proposition. The plain fact is that the public has lost confidence in the resident musicians'. 'Australian conductors, in particular, were unpopular', recalled a subscriber at the time. 'You had to be a visitor to be any good.' During the war, when the visiting soloists and conductors were unable to come, conductors and audiences were often surprised at the quality of the local musicians. Antal Dorati, the visiting conductor stranded in Australia by the war, remarked on the local musicians' lack of self-confidence:

> The spirit to combat in the players is a certain inferiority complex, even in your major orchestras ... very good results came from the method of merely persuading them, in the first place, that they *are* able to do the job.

Bernard Heinze also reflected on how the local performers had risen to the occasion when opportunity finally came, despite the fact that 'they had simply not been taken seriously as soloists before'.[7]

The Export of Talent

The formative influences on the young musicians were diverse – imported and local and contemporary – despite the lack of a recognised original Australian musical tradition. As classical music lost popularity in the twentieth century, in face of the popular music of the jazz age – swing and then rock and pop – the appeal of 'overseas' grew for singers, musicians and composers, despite the more solid institutional foundations provided by the conservatoriums and the ABC orchestras. In composition, the lack of music publishing houses and recording companies, the difficulty of getting works performed and the generally low status of Australian music drove composers overseas, following earlier travellers such as Percy Grainger and Peggy Glanville-Hicks.

From the postwar years until the end of the century, the experiences of the conductor Charles Mackerras and the horn player Barry Tuckwell, the composers Don Banks, Malcolm Williamson and David Lumsdaine, the singers Joan Sutherland and Geoffrey Chard and the accompanist Geoffrey Parsons mirrored the changing character of Australian music and its relation-ships with London and Europe. Personal lives, professional life cycles and creative employment would shape their destinies over the next half-century. They, and others of their time, would in turn prepare the way for succeeding generations, including the guitarist John Williams and the pianists Roger Woodward, Geoffrey Tozer and later Piers Lane, who would have closer and more continuing relationships with their home country.

The meteoric rise of Charles (or, more fully, Alan Charles MacLaurin) Mackerras reflected both the character of the times and the legacy of a talented and complex family. Mackerras inherited one of the oldest of settler Australian traditions, as a descendant of Isaac Nathan, sometimes known as 'The Father of Australian Music'. Nathan, who arrived in Sydney in 1841, was the composer of the first opera written in Australia, *Don John of Austria* (1848). Despite the derivative theme and title of that work, he was amongst the first to try to set down the indigenous music of the Aborigines. Paradoxically Mackerras was culturally nurtured, like many artists, by a deep gulf in his family. His mother Catherine's European artistic interests were often in conflict with the Anglo-Saxon respectability and solid commercial values of his father Alan Mackerras and his maternal grandfather Charles MacLaurin. Born in New York State in 1925, where his father was working as an engineer, he had an Eastern Suburbs childhood in Vaucluse. In 1933, the family built a house in Turramurra, across the new Harbour Bridge in the respectable WASP society of the upper North Shore. Young Charles embodied the contradictions of his family, deeper ones than were the norm in respect-able society. The conversion of his mother, Catherine, to Catholicism in 1928 led both to a deep divide in the family and to the musical stimulation of Charles by the Jesuits of St Aloysius College. The expected balance would come back, momentarily, when Charles was a boarder at the Protestant Kings School at Parramatta, 16 miles from Sydney. The scales would jump even more wildly when he was expelled. He reacted against the uniform, the military-style discipline, the emphasis on games and the isolation from the city. He ran away several times until Kings gave him his final marching orders.[8]

The repressiveness of upper middle-class Sydney – in some respects worse than the English public school and professional model on which it was based – was not the only fare on the table, especially in the city and up the Cross. Both his parents fostered his musical talent. Childhood play was also imaginative, including family creations of marionette versions of theatre and opera, from *Snow White* to Wagner's *Ring Cycle*. His mother's European interests and his father's Anglo-Saxon scientific materialism would help form Charles' interests and the worlds he would enter in later life. Perhaps that stimulating fusion, genetic and cultural, shaped one of Australia's most talented families. It included Colin Mackerras, the distinguished Sinologist, Alastair Mackerras who became headmaster of Sydney Grammar School, Malcolm Mackerras, the 'bookie' of the electoral polls and academic and media psephologist, and Neil Mackerras, a barrister. All made their mark in Australia.

The improvisatory musical culture of wartime Sydney, various 'unsuitable friends' and commercial musical opportunities helped prepare Charles Mackerras for the voyages of a future career. He often missed the last train to Turramurra and stayed with friends up the Cross; in his late teens he moved briefly to a flat at the Cross itself. Although drawn back to the upper North Shore by parental hopes and fears, the possibility of a musical career emerged when he was offered a job as second oboe in the ABC Sydney Orchestra. The family, with the aspirations of their class and time, had seen music as additional to a normal professional career as a doctor or lawyer. They now accepted the path he chose for himself. However, they had reservations about his already visible pattern of trying to do too much – adopting roles from instrumentalist to radio pianist to ballet arranger.[9]

The question of what role Charles would play and on which stages was still to be answered. He had already composed, arranged and transcribed scores from records, and played piano and oboe. Where would he make his contribution? To the musical culture of Australia, inspired by the strains of his *Waltzing Matilda Fugue*? Or on other stages and to other performing traditions?

Charles Mackerras was not the only musician formed by the times. They also influenced Barry Tuckwell, and his sister Patricia, who came from a very different background. The Tuckwells came to Sydney from Melbourne. Their father Charles Tuckwell found a career as a popular pianist and theatre organist – 'Charles Tuckwell at the Mighty Wurlitzer' – when permanent work in classical music was not possible. Charles Tuckwell, like many other performers, actors and others struggling through the Depression, worked around Australia and New Zealand. He was a musician at the cost of being on the financial edge, something of which the young children were unaware till later. For the young Barry, the musical world was his oyster. He could read music before he learned to read, and then learned the violin, piano and organ. When he entered adolescence his sister was a violinist in the Sydney Symphony Orchestra and he was introduced to the society of a 'group of "single" musicians', including Charles Mackerras and Richard Farrell.

Learning the horn in 1944 at the age of 13, he found a satisfying musical environment. It contrasted with the family's wandering around Australia and around the suburbs of Sydney, from industrial Botany Bay to suburban North Strathfield and genteel Rose Bay. Professional dates came within a year for the young Barry Tuckwell. He had his first full-time job with the Melbourne Symphony Orchestra at the age of 15. In 1947 he returned to Sydney to join the Sydney Symphony Orchestra. His second horn teacher, Alan Mann, taught him about 'the big wide world' as well as about his instrument. The Sydney music scene, ranging from symphonic music to jazz, stimulated him, particularly 'as a lot of things happened after the war. The dam had sort of been held back'. The return of many surprisingly mature 19 or 20-year-old musicians from the war in 1945–46 was a new stimulus. A second powerful impact came from the influence of Eugene Goossens, who was a visiting conductor in 1946 and SSO conductor and director of the Con from 1947. Tuckwell would play with the SSO in the first exciting years under Goossens, at the same time developing his confidence and his political and industrial awareness, including an appreciation of how poorly most musicians in Australia were paid.

Young composers were becoming even more aware of the dangers of chill penury than performers. Another of the postwar brigade, Malcolm Williamson, started at the Sydney Con in 1942 at the young age of 11, studying piano, French horn and composition. Stimulated by the family's piano and by his father's Anglican ministry, he also reacted against the bush as he knew it, the hot-as-Hell plains west of Sydney where his father had a parish at St Marys. Nor did he find creative inspiration in the sprawling suburbia of Sydney, which would, much later, engulf these western plains. Stimulation aplenty came at the Con, where his fellow students included Tuckwell and Mackerras, and later Richard Bonynge, Joan Sutherland and Geoffrey Chard. With the rhetorical fullness of the musician, he later described the Sydney and Melbourne Cons in the 1940s and 1950s as 'the finest in the world'. Special postgraduate composition lessons from Goossens and from his piano teacher Alexander Sverjensky, who would later teach Roger Woodward, supported such a contention.[10]

An Australian Musical Culture?

An emerging operatic scene complemented the excitement of the Con under Goossens, and of the SSO (in Barry Tuckwell's words, 'we played wonderful music at a high level'). Central were two returned singers, Clarice Lorenz and Gertrude Johnson, and Goossens, the recruited teacher and conductor. Goossens staged operas at the Con and beyond, while opera also flourished through Clarice Lorenz's National Opera in Sydney and the operas of Gertrude Johnson's National Theatre Movement in Melbourne. In the 1951 performance of Goossens' own work, *Judith*, the principal was the young soprano Joan Sutherland and the cast included the young baritone Geoffrey Chard. Joan Sutherland, like her fellow students, realised then the importance of Goossens. From 1946, he had been strengthening and deepening that vigorous musical culture which had been emerging during the decade.[11]

The new vitality of classical music and the support of the ABC suggested that a professional life in music might be possible in Australia. Only six years into the next decade a new cultural organisation, the Australian Elizabethan Theatre Trust, would create an opera company which toured an all-Mozart season on the occasion of the 200th anniversary of the composer's birth (as well as the year of the Melbourne Olympic Games). On stage, the Borovansky Ballet kept the tradition of classical dance alive. Within a few years, despite intermittent financial difficulties, the Australian Opera and the Australian Ballet would emerge, at first supported by the Trust, and later as separate national companies.

Yet there was a lack of confidence about the depth of the musical culture and particularly about the audiences, both their size and their character. For 'Neil Smith, butcher', who became 'Neil Warren-Smith, opera singer', it seemed that the audiences were mainly, in the vernacular of the day, 'reffos' and the 'blue rinse set' of upper middle-class wealth. And neither would have much truck with anything new or different, preferring the confirmation of the respectable and traditional. For him it was a case of 'thank God' for 'the reffos' and 'their social and cultural impact on Australia'. In a pioneering country, which was only slowly adjusting to 'foreigners', professional cultural activity still seemed odd and even unnatural. Smith's social life had been uncomplicated as a butcher in the days when 'opera in Australia was something that concerned only arties and reffos'. But, as he tried to make a career as a singer, he was 'confronted by faces that went strangely blank' when he revealed how 'I spent my time'. Eventually, the inevitable question was asked – 'But what do you do for a *living*?'[12]

Individual Journeys ... Cultural Patterns

Neil Warren-Smith kept his day job in the early years, leading to useful publicity shots, and then was able to continue a local career. This was unusual. In singing, the ideal route was to win a major quest which offered a large cash prize, such as the *Sun* Aria or the Mobil Quest. This allowed the young performer to go overseas for study and ideally success. This tradition of the travelling scholarship in music, and in painting, was as old as the other traditions of visiting companies, 'international' celebrities and returning expatriates' tours.

Making a career as a professional musician, and aspiring to the highest levels, was often a complicated story in itself. It could involve choices between different teachers, between permanent and freelance work, between Britain and overseas. It was often even more complicated for the Australian expatriates of the late 1940s and the early 1950s. Australia was still a society dominated by small capital cities inadequately linked by sea, by slow rail services and, now, by air. As a result in some fields there was limited professional movement. After nearly two decades of depression and war, opportunities remained limited for many artists and performers. Expatriation in search of a professional career could also involve emotional questions about independence, personal and financial, for those brave enough to cross the world. Some expatriates arrived in London with one of their parents. Either family affluence or protective parents – or both – kept them under the parental wing, even when away from home. Others found a way of locating themselves in a different land through new relationships, often leading to marriage at an early age. For different reasons, perhaps, they did what they might have done at home, even had they pursued a career as a lawyer, an accountant or a stenographer.

Other professional patterns also recurred: letters of introduction from Eugene Goossens to prospective teachers; links to other Australian friends who had gone earlier, softening the landing in London; difficult personal adjustments to everyday privations; early opportunities as London orchestras increased their activities after the war. When building careers during the 1950s, most expatriates could afford neither the money nor the time, the several months for a return boat trip, required for returning home. Finally, in the late 1950s or early 1960s, success in London often furnished the resources, and the opportunities, for personal and professional visits to Australia.

In the careers of some of those who went north from 1947 to 1951 and one who stayed, not leaving until the end of the decade, the patterns and the variations can be discerned. The musical voyagers did not all leave at once. The conductor Charles Mackerras departed in 1947, the composers Don Banks, from Melbourne, and Malcolm Williamson, from Sydney, both left in 1950, the soprano Joan Sutherland in 1951, the French horn player Barry Tuckwell in 1950, and the accompanist Geoffrey Parsons in 1950. Parsons' contemporary, the baritone Geoffrey Chard, did not leave until the end of the decade.

Joan Sutherland won the Mobil Quest, worth £1000, in 1950, following her earlier *Sun* Aria victory. Now, for her, the road to the great opera houses of the world seemed open. Although she left behind her typewriter, used at the Council for Scientific and Industrial Research and at a rural supplies firm, she retained a practical sense.[13] Although she did not depart until 1951, the imperative to go overseas had already sent off many of her contemporaries. Barry Tuckwell followed the tradition that 'you had to go overseas. You had to go away and then when you came back you had to be good because you had given a Wigmore Hall Concert'. This was a matter of colonial economics and the colonial cultural cringe to overseas, as well as deference to the international artistic milieux of music and London's increasing role as a musical centre. Tuckwell, who would become a strong advocate for musicians' conditions and wages, knew that, with only the SSO, the ABC's two dance bands and commercial radio orchestras, the variety of opportunities for professional work was limited. When he did leave on his overseas trip, not intending to stay, he began to enjoy concerts and travel. However, when it became necessary to get a job or return, letters soliciting work eventually landed him a job playing the horn in the Hallé Orchestra in Manchester. A new path was, out of circumstances, evolving.

Other paths led also to Britain. While Malcolm Williamson was taken to Britain by his parents, and Joan Sutherland was accompanied by her mother, others went alone. Charles Mackerras had chosen Britain over New York partly because of its proximity to Europe and his growing interest in European music. Equipped by his mother with warm clothing and the promise of a supply of food parcels, he left Australia on the *Rangitiki* in early February 1947, the ship still fitted out in the dormitory style of wartime. Fortunately, he had relatives to stay with in Highgate and he had planned to share a flat with his journalist friend Roland Pullen, who had also travelled on the ship. He carried letters of introduction to Goossens' brother Leon, the oboist, and to Adrian Boult and Malcolm Sargent, two of the leading conductors of the day, whom he had met in Sydney, and he did not meet resentment from his English competitors for work. However, with his usual independence, he did not accept Sargent's call to the Liverpool Philharmonic, as he was too busy to give Mackerras lessons in conducting. Freelance jobs, then second oboe and repetiteur for a Sadler's Wells opera company tour meant a sudden entry onto the London musical stage.[14]

Canterbury (NSW) to London

The paths of instrumental musicians and singers were equally diverse. Another contemporary in that great 1940s generation at the Con was Geoffrey Parsons who, along with Geoffrey Chard, grew up in Sydney's southern suburbs and attended Canterbury Boys High School. It was an era more dedicated to cricket and tennis than music, in the last years of Don Bradman and the time of Frank Sedgman. Out of that suburban world, which included the young local tennis player Ken Rosewall, came two boys with considerable musical talent. In an Australia which had a strong sense of the war and of the Anzac tradition, Geoffrey Chard first sang in public in a choir at a Remembrance Day concert, with Parsons accompanying. He also performed for the Sydney Opera Group, under the direction of the young theatrical writer and director who had come originally from Perth, Alan Seymour. While Chard mixed the practical advantages of an accounting course with part-time studies at the Con, juggling tennis and singing in his leisure hours, Parsons was a full-time student there. When Goossens came to hear Chard singing in *Tosca* at the Rockdale Town Hall, his encouragement suggested the prospect of a career in music, even though Goossens' worlds, including the demi-monde of Kings Cross, remained distant for a suburban boy from Hurstville with a fine voice and a good serve.

In the socially and culturally stratified society of the time, there was also a gap between the 'serious' culture of classical music and the popular musicals of J. C. Williamson's, despite the popularity of Gilbert and Sullivan and of operetta in the respectable suburbs and beyond. Contemplating a career in serious music, Chard said an emphatic no to an offer from J. C. Williamson's to play in *The Song of Norway*. A travelling show with a wage of £15 a week was not enough to persuade him it was worth risking the possibility of becoming 'doomed' as a serious musician. Instead, Chard found his opportunities in Clarice Lorenz's National Opera in the early 1950s, still associating singing with pleasure rather than a career. He pursued the postwar dream of a job, a home and a family, marrying the soprano Marjorie Connolly, who shared his musical interests. They both sang in the Trust's 1956 Mozart season.

His contemporary, the single Geoffrey Parsons, who had won the 1947 ABC Concerto and Vocal Competition, took a more direct route overseas. Touring Australia as an accompanist for Essie Ackland in 1948, he would later leave for London. He began his career in the year of his arrival, accompanying an earlier-generation expatriate, the great popular as well as operatic singer Peter Dawson.

The discovery of self through career and travel and the separation from parents took unexpected paths for Geoffrey Chard. In reaction against the childhood insecurities of the 1930s, he and his wife chose the conventional route of security. At first, with a young child, David, and a mortgage, Geoff Chard retained his job as a company secretary, which he hated. Although they put aside touring for some time, a cruel twist of fate would bring a total change of direction. After winning the Mobil Quest, Marjorie set off on the tour of Queensland in 1959 but suddenly suffered a brain haemorrhage and died. Now the family assumption that the 'good honest process of buying a block of land and putting a house on it', and 'everything was right' as long as you 'obeyed the rules', no longer made sense. It seemed absurd. Suddenly becoming a male single parent, circumstances and contemporary social values drew him closer to his own original family. Chard felt like an adult sent back to school to see the headmaster, and immediately becoming a school kid again; his father had resumed his role as head of the house.

Under immense pressure, he turned adversity into brave necessity, spending the proceeds from the sale of a house on a trip to London in late 1960, at a time when several other friends were going to join the Sadler's Wells Company. That trip provided opportunities as well as reconnaissance. He returned in 1962 for a summer festival with the SSO and the MSO, conducted by Charles Mackerras on a return visit as a modestly successful expatriate conductor. Chard then gathered up his belongings and took his young son to a new life on the other side of the world. He was now already embarked on a London career, despite the difficulties of being a singer and a single parent in a foreign land. He found a suitable house in outer suburban Harrow, allowing him to pick up the Jubilee line to Trafalgar Square (Charing Cross Station), itself just down from the stage door of the Coliseum. Aided by a live-in housekeeper, an elderly widow, he was slowly getting on top of things. Freelance singing, from the opera stage to summer cruise liners to America, made for a lively musical life and kept the wolf from the door.

The musicians' sense of adventure, and even desire to escape, had been great after Australia had been cut off from the rest of the world by war for over half of a decade. A recurring expatriate story, of being on one of the first passenger ships to leave Australia, was told by Nancy Phelan regarding Charles Mackerras' departure.[15] Australian performers arriving in London came into an expanding musical scene, which often presented opportunities. Mackerras' connections in the UK and his level of experience, unusual for a young performer, meant that, along with Barry Tuckwell and others, he landed on his feet. Geoffrey Parsons' work with Peter Dawson helped give his skills as an accompanist a higher profile. Barry Tuckwell, like many new arrivals, worked in the provinces – with the Hallé in Manchester (1951–53), the Scottish National Orchestra (1953–54) and then, further south, with the Bournemouth orchestra (1954–55). Eventually, in 1955, his desire for a job in London, if he was to stay in the 'lousy climate' of Britain, was realised when he became first horn of the London Symphony Orchestra. His first progression, through three phases, from the SSO to the English provincial orchestras and then to London was fairly typical, except that he felt that he 'had left [in Sydney] an orchestra better than the one I was playing in'.

Music, Travel and Marriage

For the young soprano Joan Sutherland, the common experience of further study preceded the development of her career. The personal and the professional came together in several ways. Having had the courage to give up her job to embark on this odyssey, she found her mother intent on protecting her from the dangers of London. Mrs Sutherland, a very powerful personality, accompanied the 'young' Joan, by then aged 24, to London in 1951 on a voyage supported by her Quest wins and by £1000 provided by a generous cousin. Life in bedsits at Notting Hill Gate with her mother and a not very good £14 piano, climbing five flights of stairs and sharing bathrooms with other tenants was not exactly fun, despite the possibility of winning the Pools. However, slowly learning the stagecraft of opera, going to concerts and plays (usually in the cheap seats) with her friend Richard Bonynge, who was studying at the Royal College of Music, leavened this bare everyday life with music and hope. She was supported by a letter of recommendation from Sir Eugene Goossens to David Webster, the administrator of the Royal Opera House, Covent Garden. (She had fundamentally changed her vocal technique, on Richard Bonynge's advice extending her upper range, as she moved from dramatic to coloratura soprano.) She was chosen in 1952 to join the prestigious company (as later would be Margreta Elkins, one of her competitors in the Mobil Quest). 'Aussie', as the Covent Garden fruit market porters called Joan Sutherland, was now one of the four sopranos at one of the great opera companies.

Music and life meshed in several ways, which included Richard's contribution to her technique and the conflict engendered with Mrs Sutherland. After several years in London Mrs Sutherland caught the boat home in 1954. Joan had leased a house at 20 Aubrey Walk in familiar Notting Hill Gate. Richard was staying over so often that they decided they should do the respectable thing. At a very small gathering, with only one bunch of flowers, a bouquet of red carnations, they were married. A cable to Colombo where her mother's boat was due advised Mrs Sutherland of events beyond her control. She cabled back 'You naughty children. Watch yourselves. Love Mum'.[16]

Charles Mackerras was another practitioner of the art of sudden marriage. This occurred much earlier in his British–European career, as things tended to happen with the impatient and in-a-hurry Charles. When working with the BBC Scottish Orchestra as second oboe in May 1947, a few months after his arrival (he had no time for freezing in garrets or washing dishes, although he did join the postwar pioneers of Notting Hill Gate), he was much taken by the English clarinettist Judy Wilkins. In the summer of 1947, he knew that he would be leaving in September to study in Prague on a British Council scholarship. He proposed and they were married in August, news which he communicated, nervously, by letter to his mother Catherine. Despite the hurried arrangements, they had a church wedding. Her family and friends were present and the bride 'carried a small bouquet of carnations'. Even given the inevitable fears that Charles might have acted in haste, his family in Sydney was reconciled to the match.[17]

Marriage and family had varying implications for other expatriates, particularly as partners and children often gave them personal as well as musical/professional roots in England. The 1953 marriage of the composer Don Banks to the New Zealand-born social worker Valerie Miller provided both the benefits and economic costs of a family of three children. There were also some practical benefits for a young composer without real income. Though they lived in simple flats in which second-hand pianos had to be winched up (and often left when they departed – buying a new one was cheaper than removal fees), Valerie's work with the London County Council children's department as a social worker allowed them to make ends meet, just, and gave Banks time to compose.

Freelance Freedoms and Costs

The economic and personal commitment of marriage was often counter-pointed by a different professional decision, to choose freedom at some cost. By choice or necessity many of the expatriate musicians were freelancers. Yet they all sensed the need to make a decent income, as well as the difficulty of ensuring that. It was something they had learned early in Australia. Free flight was implicit in the work of composers such as Don Banks and Malcolm Williamson, as they moved from piece to piece, from commission to commission. From the beginning they needed other work to supplement the meagre payments for original classical compositions in a musical world which too often believed that significance demanded being long gone from the earth. Although the situation in Britain was better than in Australia, where the ABC was only compelled to play Australian compositions as a minute 2.5% quota of its musical offerings, they had not chosen a lucrative profession. Malcolm Williamson played a mixture of jazz and Cuban piano in nightclubs in the 1950s to keep his head above water, an experience which would influence his work as well as improve his relationship with his bank manager. (There, he met Colin MacInnes, the unusual Australian expatriate who 'discovered' London's emerging black 'underground'.) Don Banks, luckily perhaps, discovered a financially rewarding area of composition. Able to write to tight deadlines and within strict constraints, he composed numerous film and television scores from the late 1950s, while still actively working on his own compositions.[18]

David Lumsdaine, from Sydney, was another struggling composer of that generation educated in music both by the Con and by jazz. Arriving in London in 1953, he endured an era of 'bohemian poverty' in which 'a lot of the time I wasn't buttering my bread', although he found occasional work as a supply (or relief) teacher. At first he socialised with other expat. Australians. He met Peter Porter and Jill Neville, whom he had also known in Sydney, at parties at Murray Sayle's place in South Kensington, an abode which he remembered as being characterised by its dirty socks. Although he later moved out of Australian circles, he shared a place on the other side of town in Belsize Park Gardens with Peter Porter. A decade later, in 1964, he set Porter's poem 'Annotations of Auschwitz' to music. Lumsdaine had left Australia during the Cold War 1950s, seeking 'fresh air, socially, musically' as he sought to escape Australia's 'stultifying social morality'. He would admix music and a personal political commitment, being active in the early years of the Campaign for Nuclear Disarmament, as were many 1950s expatriates from around the Commonwealth.

Charles Mackerras and Barry Tuckwell were two strong-willed as well as talented individuals who at different stages chose independent paths. Charles Mackerras began with the Australian assumption that it was not possible to make a living as a freelancer. In a country with a small, dispersed market, little private patronage or record income and a classical music industry dominated by one employer, the ABC, independent roads were rare. After a short time in London, he realised that there the reverse was true. The early years with the BBC orchestras involved the opportunity of working with up-and-coming performers such as Joan Sutherland and a variety of jobs, not all of them satisfying. Freelancing at first also demanded some hack work. As the young Mackerras had been versatile and busy, he remained so. In Nancy Phelan's summary, 'he was over-working because he was afraid that if he refused an offer he would not be asked again'. It was a pattern of work and speed, which he would, perhaps unfortunately, never lose. The irons that he kept in the fire included, for good and bad: arrangements and orchestrations, film scores and occasional music for plays as well as conducting and his continuing personal research into the original scores and performances of Mozart, Handel and Haydn.[19]

Along with various jobs came a willingness to travel, which had begun with his original journey from Australia and his studies in Prague. A young musician's eyes could be blinkered by the demands of study and practice and/or opened by travel and the experience of the city's nocturnal arts culture. Charles Mackerras' large eyes were opened to the horror of recent world events even more dramatically than for most expatriates who suffered shortages in postwar London. Like Leo McKern and the artist Albert Tucker, he saw the ravages and destruction of World War II in Europe itself.

On Wednesday, 24 September 1948 at 9.20 in the morning Charles Mackerras and the now Judy Mackerras were on a train which left Victoria Station for Prague, the capital of Czechoslovakia. After a brief stop to see the sights of Paris and to visit Roland Pullen, now working as a sub-editor on the *Continental Daily Mail*, they headed further east. The train took a circuitous route through Germany and Austria, allowing them to see the material destruction. Charles Mackerras was 'completely devastated' by what the war had done to Czechoslovakia and to Austria. Vienna looked as if it had been razed to the ground. He recalled the 'Viennese or Budapestean atmosphere' which the 'continental restaurateurs' had given to the Cross, an attraction for artists and performers. In contrast he saw destruction and poverty. He 'hadn't realised that the war would completely destroy all the things that I had come to expect from European culture'. Food parcels from Sydney, cigarettes from England and the coffee and tea brought from London helped the thinning young Charles and Judy survive in a time of almost no dairy products and a general tendency to malnutrition.

Few Australians studied on the Continent. Almost none studied in a Communist country, which Czechoslovakia had become after the *coup d'état* of early 1948. However, over time, musicians, like artists, did travel. Their work was not confined by language, as was the work of writers, journalists and actors. In the 1940s and 1950s travel most often meant work around Britain. Charles was again different. International travel would become one leitmotif of Mackerras' professional life, embraced by him even more than the role required. However, after Europe came 'settling down' into a semi in suburban Finchley, a young family and several years as a repetiteur, and then assistant conductor, at Sadler's Wells, and a shorter period as the first full-time conductor of the BBC Concert Orchestra. In 1955, he resigned from the constrictions of the BBC to take to the more adventurous road of the freelance conductor. Working in Europe, at British festivals and in Cape Town (1958), where he was visited by Catherine, as well as at Sadler's Wells and with the BBC, he was combining music and travel.[20]

Geoffrey Parsons would also become a travelling musician, touring as an accompanist with Elisabeth Schwarzkopf, Victoria de los Angeles and many other eminent singers. In contrast to most other expatriate Australian musicians, the accompanist to 'celebrity' singers would be able to return to Australia to work for ABC concerts as often as every second year over the next few decades.

Barry Tuckwell developed a career repertoire of skills and personas, as well as later becoming perhaps the most renowned French horn player of his era. When playing with the London Symphony Orchestra, which had musicians on the board, Tuckwell, by his own account 'a bit of a rebel', led the revolt of the younger players and found himself ('muggins') elected. The outspoken Australian accepted a political role, later becoming chairman of the board for six years. These skills and his assertiveness would continue to serve him well.

These luminaries of the postwar generation of musical expatriate musicians, including Mackerras, Tuckwell, Sutherland, Parsons and Chard, had made an impact by the early 1960s. Expatriate composers, including Don

Banks, Malcolm Williamson and David Lumsdaine, were also making their way, even if it was less brilliantly lit than the musical paths of the public performers. Over time their roots in London had grown deeper. It remained an open question as to what part Australia would play in the lives and careers of these rising stars, and in those of many talented compatriots living and working in London, during the following decades.

Chapter 5
Patterns of Discovery: Artists[1]

In several fields of professional endeavour the call of London was associated with institutions, with places of performances, from theatres and concert halls to law courts and hospitals. English language was the second factor making London the preferred location for actors, playwrights and journalists. A complementary factor for them was the ease of obtaining working rights. In two other fields, painting and writing, neither theatres of performance, nor language, nor legal working rights, were so constricting. Artists and writers had less need of being in a traditional metropolitan location for the creation and sale of their work, although they needed galleries and publishers. It is possible to write or paint anywhere in the world, free of the constraints facing other professions. As a result, these two artistic professions were even more peripatetic than some other fields. In the era of faster and cheaper travel, these patterns – of diversity of location and of travel – would become even more common. The painter Sidney Nolan, for example, painted in nearly every continent (including Antarctica), while the novelist Thomas Keneally has written on European, American, 'international', Irish and Australian subjects, and has lived in Australia, in Britain and in North America.

A second difference regarding expatriation was that both professions had long existed in Australia, winning a degree of recognition for their best talents greater than that of classical music or of serious theatre. Since the time of the colonial painters, John Glover and Eugene von Guerard, and 1890s Heidelberg School impressionists (Arthur Streeton, Tom Roberts, Frederick McCubbin and Charles Conder), art had a public standing in Australian life, despite the contemporary anxieties of conservatives about modernism. In similar terms, the nineteenth-century short story writers and even the inter-war novelists gave Australian literature a degree of public acknowledgment.

Despite this, in both art and writing, the subjects of the next two chapters, expatriation remained significant. In the conservative 1950s the market for Australian art was weak, and a private gallery market in the major capitals was only beginning to evolve. As painters continued to discover the creative possibilities of their own country and of other parts of the world, this London domination was not immutable, though the imperial cultural metropolis remained very important in the 1950s and early 1960s. As before in Australian cultural history, London still offered socio-economic benefits, the status of overseas success and the income furnished by the larger market. It would continue to be important for many of those who left in the postwar years, and stayed, particularly the artists Sidney Nolan and Arthur Boyd.

The first two decades after World War II, especially the late 1950s and early 1960s, saw the re-emergence of Australian artistic groupings and more diffuse literary clusterings in London. In this period groups and institutions were either offshore replications of Australian support organisations or pre-cursors of official and unofficial Australian organisations. The Australian Artists Association, along with the Australian Musical Association and the Society of Australian Writers, would 'fly the flag' for Australian talent in Britain during the 1950s when the postwar waves of expatriation reached their first peak.

Significantly, this period would see an emerging Australian awareness of Australian achievement in the arts. That rediscovery in a more sophisticated (and populous) Australia was confirmed by a related event, the British re-discovery of Australia, particularly in the arts. Significant moments included the 1958 staging in London of the Ray Lawler play, *Summer of the Seventeenth Doll*, and Joan Sutherland's 1959 *Lucia di Lammermoor* at Covent Garden. The performances of the Australian Ballet and the Sydney Symphony Orchestra at the 1965 Commonwealth Arts Festival, and the works of the writers and artists, confirmed the validity of Australian culture. The Society of Australian Writers' 1953 book, *The Sunburnt Country*, was one of the first postwar profiles of this faraway land. Several major exhibitions, including the Whitechapel and Tate exhibitions of 1961 and 1963, presented the visual aspect of Australian light, nature and experience. As the art critic Kenneth Clark remarked to the painter (and former cyclist) Sidney Nolan, after seeing the *Doll* in London, 'You were right, Sidney, you Australians are certainly pedalling along quite well'.[2] In the 1960s that artistic recognition would be reinforced – and also qualified – by the popular media's growing fascination with 'sunny Australia', which was also the focus of British migration campaigns at a time of a burgeoning cult of sun-worship.

Artists at Home and Abroad

Since many Australians still habitually looked to London for artistic stand-ards, the British discovery of Australian art would help certify the validity of Australian achievement in Australia, particularly in the early 1960s. At the same time Australian institutions were evolving, including the state, regional and private galleries, and the magazine *Art and Australia*. The result, as Bernard Smith noted, was the appearance of two markets for Australian painting: one in England and one in Australia.[3] In the familiar contexts of Australian arts, in the structures of production and of prestige, expatriation would involve positives as well as negatives, even though individual experience would vary dramatically.

This discussion explores the London experiences of several artists and their relationships with Australia, particularly the prominent Melbourne ex-patriates Sidney Nolan and Arthur Boyd, and the shorter expatriations of two Queenslanders, Francis Lymburner and Charles Blackman, who had already spent time in the southern capitals. Their stories of expatriation are as much about social and personal experience as about artistic talent and fashion.

Several artistic waves went to London in the postwar years, following the artists of the 'Sydney Group', or 'Merioola' or, less kindly, the 'charm school', who left for overseas from the late 1940s. Other artists, of a more 'Antipodean', or nationalist/figurative expressionist bent, also departed over the next decade.[4] One 'pull' factor of London and Europe was the opportunity to see the originals of great works in the Western tradition. It was reinforced by a 'push' factor, the social and political conservatism apparent in the court cases concerning the Joshua Smith Archibald Prize, 'Ern Malley' and Robert Close's *Love Me Sailor*. Another 'push' influence was that lack of art institu-tions in Australia, noted earlier. At the same time as that infrastructure was beginning to evolve, travelling scholarships, overseas training and exhibitions were also integral to an artist's career. However, some awards, such as the Helena Rubinstein scholarship, worth £1300, echoed something of Tyrone Guthrie's 'export-import' plan for the arts: the terms of the award required the traveller to return.[5]

In some ways, the postwar departures continued a tradition interrupted by the war. An older generation, including William Dobell and Russell Drysdale, had studied in London before World War II. The postwar names and numbers were both significant. Albert Tucker, who went to Japan, Germany and France, and as noted earlier declared himself a 'refugee from Australian culture' in 1947, although his reasons for leaving were as much personal as national. Kenneth Clark, who had visited Australia in 1949, attracted Sidney Nolan, who went in 1950 but travelled back and forth, and Russell Drysdale, who made several trips overseas. The 36-year-old Francis Lymburner, originally from Brisbane, was one of the Sydney Group escapees, leaving with his friend Murray Sayle on the *Otranto* in August 1952.[6] The greatest congregation of Australian artists in London since the turn of the century occurred around the late 1950s and early 1960s. The new arrivals, several of them scholarship winners, came at the time of new interest in Australian art. Arthur Boyd, at the age of 39, left Melbourne for London with his family in November 1959, two months after the death of his own father, Merric Boyd. Charles Blackman and Brett Whiteley arrived in 1960, and Leonard French and then Colin Lanceley came later.[7]

It was an open question as to the benefits and costs, for individuals and Australian art, of the London experience. Would they be spurned as mere colonials, without a 'reputation' in the larger pond of British art? How much would what interested British gallery directors, critics and audiences influence Australian art? The artists might gain from British training and example. At worst, there would be a replication of the processes of the 1890s–1900s–1920s. In that transition, for the Heidelberg painters, Australian Genesis was succeeded by Exodus and then a final return to a Leviticus, a formal dominance of the tired older men of the artistic tribe.[8] Even the Melbourne modernists, the expressionist artists of the 1940s 'Angry Penguins' era, including Nolan, Boyd and Albert Tucker, might relive, like an endless cycle, that experience: public indifference and conservatism leading to escape, then a final return of the important man of society as well as arts. Or, would the process resemble the maturation of an adolescent? The celebrations might be like a 'coming of age', offering the key to the future, celebrations blessed by the 'imperial' parent as a necessary prelude to the independence and self-confidence which would follow. An adult assertiveness and creativity were waiting to appear. Like the butterfly in the chrysalis, the 'adolescent' artists were almost ready to fly.

In art, as in literature and music, it could be argued that the transition, from provincial deference to the imperial centre to a metropolitan sense of self, involved a series of processes. It required preliminary stages. While most of these occurred in Australia, a parallel stage was the elaboration of an Australian cultural colony in London and the social groups and the institutions of artists, writers and musicians.

Paradoxically, the least institutional of activities, painting, offered the highest profile in Britain itself. Art, like film and tourism, introduced the exotic Australia which most interested a largely ignorant British public. In these years, art presented Australia to Britain. The Australian Artists Association had several shows in the mid-1950s, its 1953 show exhibiting 38 of the 90 Australian artists said to be working in Britain. In these and other exhibitions, including Nolan's 1957 show at the Whitechapel Gallery, the 1961 Whitechapel exhibition and the 1963 Tate exhibition, Britain discovered that

Australia had a culture.[9] Although a few alert individuals were already aware of this reality, others needed to be shocked out of their imperial condescension towards the colonies.

The Cycles of Artistic Fashion and Expatriation

Expatriate artists' experiences varied. Some artists would find limited benefit in their transition to London. Two lyricists who came originally from Queensland, Francis Lymburner and Charles Blackman, would find interesting social circles but discover that the wheels of artistic fashion did not always generate an audience for their work. Francis Lymburner was 'a real country boy', as Murray Sayle recalled, who 'was attracted by the glamour and sophistication he associated with big cities – first Brisbane when he was growing up, then Sydney. Always an aesthete and a dandy, he identified with a romanticised Georgian London roughly contemporaneous with the colonisation of Australia, as if he wanted to run the national history in reverse'.[10] Having left a wife and child in Sydney when he chose London and his career, he found himself poor, staying with, or sometimes 'bludging on' friends for long periods, including Murray Sayle at his places in South Kensington and Notting Hill Gate, and later a basement flat of Barry Humphries'. Lymburner, the 'languid dandified figure in a black velvet jacket, a jaunty red neckerchief and always a cigarette and a glass of wine', as Barry Humphries described him, did not realise his potential. Too often 'Lymmie's' dreams foundered in the bottle.[11] Although he exhibited during the 1950s he was also not the fashion of the day. Unlike Jocelyn Rickards and Loudon Sainthill, and the Melbourne designer Kenneth Rowell, who found opportunities in theatre design (as did Sidney Nolan and Arthur Boyd), Lymburner did not find another metier. At last, in the early 1960s, he had successful shows in Australia as well as London. It was Bernard Smith's review of his 1963 Melbourne show that attracted him back to Australia. Here too, Dame Fortune was unkind. The 'Two Decades of American Art' exhibition in 1967 reflected the artistic fashions of the day, in what Bernard Smith had seen as 'Sydney's provincial scramble to be up-to-date'.[12] As a result, Lymburner was only intermittently appreciated in Australia as well. He did not look after his health. Already infirm, he died in 1972 at the age of 56, when lunching at his favourite restaurant at Whale Beach.

'Gum Trees on the Heath': Artists' Groups North of the Thames

Charles Blackman similarly found London's offerings very mixed. Although he exhibited three paintings in the Whitechapel exhibition, his schoolgirl silhouette paintings differed from the intense landscapes, bright colours and mythic themes which were associated in English eyes with Australian art. Blackman did find other consolations. Along with his energetic poet wife, Barbara, he was part of the Australian expatriate artists' new camp, north of the Thames at Highgate and Hampstead. Around the Blackmans, as Barbara tells it, evolved a large, if changing, Australian creative society. It reproduced the cross-cultural links which flourished in the smaller artistic societies of the Australian capitals. It began with a very simple urban expression of 'mateship' – the need to find a place to stay (to 'doss' or later to 'crash') when you arrived. The artists' circles offered sociability and professional contacts. The very nature of art also influenced this society. In the most solitary of professions, artists would break out from their studios for drinks and company. A different long-term cycle saw successful artists go from early poverty, which made 'bohemian' group living a necessity as much as a choice, to economic as well as artistic success. Economic success was significant as it facilitated travel between Australia and the rest of the world, especially in the era of the jet. That initial community of poverty, however, created a larger sociability, all the more so when living in a distant and foreign city.

Barbara Blackman's autobiography, *Glass by Glass* (1997), and the catalogue *Charles Blackman: Schoolgirls and Angels* (1993), give a detailed account of that Australian artists' society around this time. The Blackman family arrived in London in February 1961, staying first with Arthur and Yvonne Boyd at Highgate Hill and then moving into a furnished house near Highgate Woods at 27a Jackson's Lane. The peripatetic Blackmans, who had lived in Sydney, Brisbane and Melbourne, had reunions with the Queenslander Charles Osborne, now working on *London Magazine*, the Melburnian actors Barry Humphries and Peter O'Shaughnessy, the jeweller Rod Edwards, the painter Francis Lymburner, the newspaper editor J. D. Pringle and the writers Jill Neville and Ray Mathew, and another new arrival, Brett Whiteley, among others. Charles Blackman met English artists through the energetic Whitechapel curator Bryan Robertson, while other Australian artists, including Leonard French and Fred Williams, passed through.[13] As Barry Humphries recalled, he went off for a Paris weekend with Arthur Boyd and Charles Blackman to see Braque and Goya exhibitions. Around this time Humphries, his second wife Rosalind and his young family were living in Grove Terrace, Highgate Road.[14] Not all artistic circles were bohemian. In 1962, Charles Blackman met the Queen at the opening of the exhibition, *Commonwealth Art Today*. Barbara Blackman writes expansively of how 'the John Perceval and David Boyd families and photographers Axel and Roslyn Poignant join[ed] the swelling Blackman circle'. These networks were by then not just artists or Australians. They also included writers, publishers and performers, including the poets Al Alvarez and Ted Hughes, and the English satirist Peter Cook.

The Wellington, just along from Charles' Archway Road studio, was the centre of the regular Sunday night pub scene, at which on one occasion Charles Blackman and Barry Humphries did a two-man routine. For the Melburnians, including the Blackmans, who had lived there for most of the 1950s, the pub and the artists' colony might have been an extension of the Swanston Family Hotel and the groups who gathered at Eltham, Heide and Murrumbeena. The Blackmans' apartment was also 'alive with parties planned and spontaneous soup and cheese nights after the pub on Sunday nights'. Later, when the Blackmans moved to a mansion flat overlooking Regents Park, Robert Hughes and Colin Lanceley took adjacent apartments.[15]

The London expatriate cluster of artists was more a hive than a ghetto, a gathering of creative individuals, many at the height of their abilities, for art and for invigorating conversation and fun. It would have varying results. One was creative and multi-disciplinary collaboration, a kind of cross-fertilisation. The artists exhilarated Barry Humphries, Al Alvarez' BBC interview with Charles Blackman was lauded as 1965's 'Interview of the Year', Ray Mathew wrote the text for the book, *Charles Blackman* (1965), and Colin MacInnes had contributed 'The Search for an Australian Myth in Painting' to the 1961 volume, *Nolan*. Artists' work became popular as cover illustrations for several books by Australian authors. Nolan's works adorned the jackets of books by Colin MacInnes, Alan Moorehead, Patrick White (who had returned to Australia over a decade earlier) and George Johnston, with whom Nolan had stayed on the Greek island of Hydra. Cross-fertilisation amongst the Australians fused mediums, as in Nolan's sets for Robert Helpmann's ballet *The Display* (1962), and Arthur Boyd's sets and costumes for Helpmann's *Electra* (1963, 1966).

The stimulus of the society of the small pond, of Australian cultural life, came together with that of lively metropolitan society in the early Sixties. The expatriate artists' London had a vitality which Sydney and Melbourne were in danger of losing in the dour Cold War 1950s and before the artistic excitement and drama of the Sixties had arrived.[16]

Antipodeans – Artists and Exotics

Two cultural patterns are significant here. One is the impact of the exhibitions of these Australian artists, in Britain and Australia. The second is the social and cultural stimuli which they gave to, and received from, other Australian creators in London. For the towering figures of Arthur Boyd and Sidney Nolan, there was also a complex relationship between Australia and Britain and an interaction between landscape and myth and tradition and family over several decades. It was these years of excitement, particularly from 1959 to 1964, which put contemporary Australian art on the map – in Australia as well as in Britain.

This high point of Australian art in London in the early 1960s was prepared over time. Nolan and Drysdale had both exhibited in 1951 (at Harry Tatlock Miller's Redfern Gallery), and Nolan's 1957 show at the Whitechapel Gallery was the beginning of a British discovery of his mythic force, energy and lyricism. Australian art would be gradually taken up by some British critics and audiences. It could seem like a new exotic in the avant-garde of the day, the work of the wild men from the colonial bush. Critics pursued the British perception of Australian art first expressed in Joseph Burke's 1951 mono-graph on Drysdale, with its images of 'an epic struggle with nature' and 'an elemental landscape', 'primitive, timeless and without remorse'. It was as if these painters were untutored colonial minds, rough-hewn frontier indi-vidualists expressing the spirit of a *jardin exotique* without the benefit of European influences.[17] In fact, their work was the product of the meeting of modernism with national myth and the landscape of the interior. However, for some British audiences of a more traditional bent, the dominance of figurative expressionism could make the Australian oeuvre an attractive alternative to American hard-edged abstraction and action painting, although Bryan Robertson, the curator of significant Australian exhibitions, had also introduced Pollock to Britain. London also called the Australians of the 'Antipodean' school, with their commitment to figure and nation. They were drawn by Nolan's early success, and in some cases pushed away by the rising interest in American non-figurative work in Sydney in particular.

In the late 1950s and early 1960s, the colour and diversity of the Aus-tralians appealed in London. Nolan's warmth, colour and mythical elements suggested that figurative art had something left to give, while Boyd's allegories, the drawing skills evident in Blackman's figures and the line and colour of the young and radical Whiteley all attracted interest. Australian art became a popular as well as specialist sensation. Bryan Robertson recalled the crowds and the media coverage of the 1957 Nolan exhibition, including the support in the *Observer* of J. D. Pringle, a British journalist with a develop-ing Australian connection. Nolan's 'Leda and the Swan' series, exhibited at Mathiessen Gallery in June 1960, created public interest, while his 'Gallipoli' works took up the theme of this national myth, itself the subject of the expatriate writer Alan Moorehead's major book *Gallipoli* (1956).

Bryan Robertson was one of the reasons why, in Barry Humphries' words, 'London was a Mecca for Australian painters and Australian art was "hot"'.[18] Robertson's 1961 Whitechapel exhibition, 'Recent Australian Painting', cap-tured the power of Nolan, Boyd, Blackman and Whiteley. It happened before the Tate Gallery exhibition, planned for 1962. That would be held in 1963, and despite the influence of the Whitechapel exhibition, this government-approved retrospective of Australian art did not avoid the conventional rut of presenting Australian art over time as a pastoral celebration of healthy Australia – a better place for migrants and tourists than for artists. The

Australian artists in London mounted a response. In 1963, the theatrical and entrepreneurial Alannah Coleman, an unsung hero of Australian arts in Britain, made a dramatic contribution. She staged the exhibition 'Australian Painters and Sculptors in Europe Today' at a modernist gallery in Folkestone, under the patronage of Kenneth Clark, who described it as 'the most impressive group show of Australian art ever in Britain'. It was later taken up by the German government and exhibited at Frankfurt, where it was enthusiastically received.[19]

Despite the fact that Boyd, Whiteley and Blackman took Australian art beyond the Antipodean myth, it was that 'colonial exotic' which captured British interest. Clark's interpretation had led to Nolan's work coming 'to be accepted in its own right as painting rather than as exotica'. In Clark's summary, 'though [Nolan] has drawn his strength from a locality he is able to transcend it, the local becoming universal'.[20] However, the British interest in these wild men of the frontier, and their celebration of the 'primitive', the 'natural' and the 'wild', meant that, with exceptions such as Nolan and Boyd, the Australian moment would be like a passing comet in the artistic skies of the era. Unlike the appreciation of Australian art in Australia, fantasy about the colonies would disappear almost as fast as it had come.

The recognition of the intensity of Australian art – from the 'Angry Penguins' to the Antipodeans – would encourage a depiction of the Australian combination of 'landscape with figures' as expressing a national myth rooted in the experience of a harsh land. A British metropolitan view, with debts to D. H. Lawrence, depicted the 'sunburnt country' as an antipodal land of extremes and conflicts, as also expressed in those other mythical Australian tales – the legend of the ANZACs at Gallipoli and Patrick White's troubled explorer in the desert, Voss. These frontier and war bravery clichés, and the related metropolitan views of a *terre sauvage* of untutored wild men, were limited, though British approval would initially help encourage the new popular interest in Australian art in Australia.

A Blackman Transition

Not all Australian artists fitted this 'colonial' or frontier ideal, however. Charles Blackman's artistic, if not personal, story resembled that of Lymburner. In travelling to London he was 'staking out his ground as a lyrical painter against the emerging trend among English artists towards hard-edged abstraction and Op art'. Although he exhibited with other artists, by the mid-1960s, as he was painting for his anticipated large Whitechapel one-man show, similar forces of change were at work in Britain. The exhibition did not eventuate in 1965, 'due largely to [the] rise of [a] new generation of British painters', including David Hockney and Francis Bacon. This 'bitter blow . . . sharpened his awareness of his expatriate status'.[21]

The artistic patterns of the 1960s which appealed to Martin Sharp of *OZ* magazine and Colin Lanceley, the Annandale Imitation Realist, made London no longer Blackman's artistic centre. Now, his lyricism was appreciated less than it had been in earlier years. Yet the metropolis still had a hold. Leaving for home in January 1966, the Blackmans travelled from the London snow to century heat in Perth, and on to Melbourne. They had felt the lack of a beach in England, and were eventually drawn, after Brisbane, to Woollahra in 1967 and to a different romantic ideal – access to Bondi Beach. However, Blackman cut his London links slowly. He had given up the lease on the London flat in 1966 but not until 1968 did he '[terminate] London life by shipping back possessions to Sydney'.[22]

Blackman's brief expatriation found a travelling artist's conclusion, if one with a contemporary dimension. Instead of returning to a single city, he decided in 1966 'to treat Australia as one city', travelling to paint and exhibit widely. At the same time he continued travelling overseas. At last, he had some works in a small exhibition at the Leicester Galleries in 1968 and also went to Italy and New York. There, he met Ray Mathew and the up-and-coming Brett Whiteley. In New York art circles he found 'little interest in unknown Australians unless they [were] prepared to live there'.[23]

Blackman's 'one city' Australia offered an alternative to the metropolitan expatriate dream. In contrast, when the most distinguished of the younger generation of artists, Brett Whiteley, came back, like most expatriates he returned to a particular 'home' city, in his case Sydney. There, he carried on a tradition which owed much to place – as well as to the psychedelic and international times of the Sixties – in several works which captured the blues of Sydney Harbour.

Landscape with Figures: Sidney Nolan and Arthur Boyd

London still attracted other artists. Colin Lanceley, who had left Australia on a travelling scholarship, stayed in London, also working in Europe, until 1981. However, it was the public figures of Sidney Nolan and Arthur Boyd who would continue to demonstrate the significance of a British connection in Australian art and art markets. Both would forge major careers in the UK and Australia and work on specifically Australian landscapes and themes, as well as on other subjects within the Western tradition. In some ways these were tales of two visions, as well as of two countries. Nolan looked out on the Thames from Putney and later Whitehall, while painting Australia, and Boyd painted the Shoalhaven River landscapes of the South Coast of New South Wales in rural Suffolk. The work of the two painters demonstrated that Australian painting, like all the Australian arts, was a product of two worlds, derived European influences meeting indigenous Australian experiences, both of nature and society.

In the early 1960s it was already becoming apparent that for Sidney Nolan there was a third element. In the era of the Beatles and the Stones, Jean Shrimpton and *Blow-Up*, the new *Sunday Times* colour magazine and Carnaby Street, the media were becoming important. So too were continuing artistic tensions, which could take on a colonial–imperial, as well as a class, character. Nolan, the son of a Melbourne tram driver, became an international artist, a knight of the British Empire, the creator of a popular Australian visual icon, in his Ned Kelly images, painted in the 1940s. After a long period overseas, mainly in Britain, some critics were quick to suggest that he had 'sold-out' on Australia.[24]

The Sydney artist John Olsen criticised Nolan's 1961 Sydney show of the 'Leda and the Swan' series of paintings as 'contaminated with the over-ripe atmosphere of Bond Street'.[25] Nolan no doubt felt ambivalent when he received such criticism from Australia at the same time as he was being taken up as the next big thing in British arts. Nolan rode the wave of popularity of the new and the Australian. As Brian Adams wrote in the authorised biography:

> With Leda and the Swan a good seller, Nolan was riding high again after a lengthy absence from what he called 'the English art game'. He was approached by the editor of *Queen* magazine to contribute a series of articles because in fashionable circles Nolan and Francis Bacon were seen as likely to be the dominant painters in Britain during the 1960s.

Lilian Somerville of the Arts Council championed Nolan, suggesting that he might even have a show at the Venice Biennale as a British artist. As Adams put it, 'All that was needed was to drop the Australianisms, which he had done with Leda, and change his passport'.[26] Nolan did not change his nationality, although he did, despite several warnings, encourage the use of the new medium of television to present his art, and himself, to a larger audience.

Nolan's career over the next three decades would be both British and Australian and would involve painting around the world as well as in Australia and Britain. As the McCullochs note, 'much of Nolan's later career involved travelling, being photographed, interviewed, written about and filmed'. Nolan would rise in stature in the UK and beyond. It was as if, in popular media and in some art circles, Kenneth Clark's simplistic 1947 grab, describing Nolan as Australia's 'only real painter', would anticipate the future. The emerging art and media reality was that Nolan would be seen as, in the McCullochs' summary, 'Australia's most internationally celebrated painter'.[27]

Was this perception a product of his considerable talent? Or was it the result of a combination of talent for painting and for marketing, and a continuing degree of British ignorance about Australian art. The known painter was clearly the greatest painter, an assessment which those who knew the work of Albert Tucker, John Brack, and John Olsen, and later Fred Williams, Brett Whiteley, Jeffrey Smart, Imants Tillers and the new Aboriginal artists, might challenge. Perhaps Nolan appealed to the British view that there were only a few 'artistic Calibans' coming from the 'colonies', exceptions that proved the rule about the uncultured Antipodes. It was a formulation which would recur in other spheres.[28]

This conundrum also raises the question of why Nolan chose to live mainly abroad, returning to Australia for regular trips, to recharge his artistic batteries and for exhibition openings. Regular injections of Australian light and Australian natural forms remained important to him and to Arthur Boyd. While they saw better from a distance, they were aware of the danger of losing touch with part of their visual inspiration.

Since Nolan's fame in Australia remained even greater than that in England, distance allowed him to get on with his work, free of the constant demands of the media and far from the disputes of the Australian art world. This 'tall poppy' might also have felt that he was too big for the Australian scene or that other critical scythes might threaten to bring him down to size. Nolan, who did not feel financially secure until he was in his 40s, became happily placed in London. Nolan, 'something of a loner' when a boy, would be a 'loner in art'.[29] He would also, like some other returning expatriates, have disputes with institutions in Australia, including new performing arts centres in Perth and Melbourne. In 1984, after the success of his Paradise Garden paintings at the Victorian Arts Centre Concert Hall (which opened in 1982), a second commission for his work to decorate part of the foyer of the new Victorian State Theatre had a less favourable outcome. His paintings were not hung, and there was no explanation. Nolan described the experience as 'another Melbourne situation in which nobody comes clean'. Nolan felt ambivalent towards Melbourne, finding it simultaneously beautiful and depressing:

> There's an unresolved part of me that cannot relate to Melbourne, and most likely never will. I have to say I don't think Australians are very fair fighters, but must add I don't consider myself one either. That means we're well matched.[30]

Like the scoreboard in a Michael Leunig cartoon of an Australian Rules Football match, the sport which Nolan so loved as a boy, the expatriate contest for Nolan was between 'Us and Them' or even between 'Me and Them'.[31]

Sir Sidney Nolan also played the public role of the famous expatriate, the great painter, who was much celebrated upon his returns. He received four honorary doctorates (from universities in York, London, Canberra and

Sydney) and other awards, including a knighthood in 1983 and a Companion of the Order of Australia in 1988. He was one of the only 24 recipients of the Queen's Order of Merit. The story of his rise was differently reflected in his *Who's Who in Australia* entry of 1991. Unusually, it recorded some of his earliest jobs, as 'a cleaner and a factory hand'. The initial recognition of the Kelly paintings in London and Paris, rather than Melbourne or Sydney, may also have reinforced his evolving feeling that it was 'overseas' which mattered in art markets and art criticism, not Australia.

Arthur Boyd was different. He was not only of a different class, but he was a member of the Boyd family. In a country which has no aristocracy – although some graziers and knights had pretended they were part of one – the Boyds were the nearest Australia, or at least Victoria, came to an artistic elite. The family had continuing English social connections and, more significantly, an abiding sense of a European cultural inheritance. Over several generations and in disparate fields (Robin Boyd in architecture, Penleigh, Arthur, Merric and Guy Boyd in painting and pottery and Martin Boyd in literature) the Boyds have made an unparalleled contribution to Australian artistic and intellectual life.

Arthur Boyd was also shy and, like many artists, primarily concerned to get on with his work. Unlike Nolan who became a national icon through the Ned Kelly series and the attendant publicity, Boyd became a reluctant icon. Australian of the Year in 1995, an 'Australian Legend' stamp was issued in his honour for Australia Day 1999, following the more typical sporting predecessors, such as Sir Donald Bradman, Shirley Strickland and Dawn Fraser. More often, however, in the rural calm of Suffolk or of the Shoalhaven, or on a cargo boat to and from Australia, he was safely away from the glare of TV cameras and of photographers' flashbulbs.

Innocence and Experience

Nolan and Boyd shared the fact that their art originated in innocence and experience, and in perceptions of landscape and society. In Nolan's painting his naïve images such as Ned Kelly, arising from an Australian landscape and sky, carry a heavy weight of meaning. Boyd's different work in landscape and myth had its origins in childhood and adolescence. The painter of the coastal region of New South Wales recalled his 'sentimental attachment to the pictures I did in Rosebud as a teenager when I lived with my grandfather'. That 'tranquil time' and the 'sheer, limpid clarity of the landscapes around the bay triggered a lot of landscapes', both then and much later.

Nolan was influenced by the European symbolist poets of the late nineteenth century, particularly Paul Verlaine and Arthur Rimbaud, as well as by Australian landscape and myth. Boyd has worked in a parallel vein in his landscapes, with allegorical figures carrying a symbolic weight. In a sense their work, like their under-appreciated fellow Melbourne expressionist, Albert Tucker, had its roots in World War II. Artistic imaginings were stimulated by the 'images of modern evil' which Tucker discerned amongst the nightlife of St Kilda, and by the surrealist, Freudian and moral lenses through which they perceived the extremes of human life. Boyd's interest in human horror, the association between love and tragedy, pervaded his scenes with figures, including 'Love, Marriage and the Death of a Half-Caste' (his 'Bride' series of the late 1950s). At Port Melbourne and St Kilda, he had seen the 'unfamiliar' images of 'people in fairly dire circumstances, cripples, very poor people'. Later, he was shocked by his first contact with the Aborigines of Central Australia in the 1950s and then by the horrors of Vietnam, coming back to the West – demonstrations in which 'there were people immolating themselves on Hampstead Heath'. Along with the darker forces of his father's iron will, he approached these horrors, and his sense of 'utter desolation, a nasty, vicious thing eating into your soul' indirectly – through Biblical myth.[32]

Boyd addressed moral questions and human evil, which he explored through Judaeo-Christian and Greco-Roman traditions. He collaborated with the poet Peter Porter in pictures and text in *Narcissus* (1984) and *Mars* (1988), following his earlier collaboration with T. R. S. Boase in recording the Old Testament story of the fall from grace of the greatest king of Babylon, *Nebuchadnezzar* (1972), and his banishment into the wilderness. It was partly those traditions, and his sense of a European inheritance, which kept him in the northern hemisphere, although Australia and the Australian arts were themselves shaped by Western tradition.

After Nolan and Boyd returned to Canberra on ANU Creative Arts Fellowships in 1965 and 1971–2 respectively, they would both be attracted to this new centre of artistic stimulus. Boyd was increasingly drawn to the Shoalhaven. He first bought land at Riversdale on the Shoalhaven two years after his Canberra stint, and subsequently bought nearby Bundanon, with its Georgian house, in 1979–80. He was making his own rediscovery of the Australian landscape, the softer Australia of the coastal bush and its rivers.

The Nolans would eventually follow Boyd, in 1985 buying the adjacent property on the river. Later in 1993, in a generous gesture, the Boyds and Nolans would jointly donate the land to the national estate, as a gift to the nation. Nolan, however, would remain predominantly the expatriate in Britain despite frequent trips to Australia to paint, to design for the Australian Opera and for exhibition openings.

Partly it was absence and tradition which allowed Boyd to 'rediscover my Australianism' through the river. The Australian who had been away for most of the 1960s and 1970s saw that aspect of the river which was in some ways 'overwhelming, difficult and alien', as the nineteenth-century painters of the picturesque had embraced the wildness of Australian nature. However, he also captured the calm, beauty and light of coastal Australia, the slightly different nature of coastal New South Wales. In a sense, as he discovered the regenerative nature of the river, he was also returning, albeit indirectly, to the Port Phillip Bay and littoral of his Melburnian childhood.[33]

The Nolan and Boyd stories became intertwined, not just as artists and expatriates. They formed an unlikely duo as the two most prominent and most continuing expatriates in Britain at a time when the tendency was in decline. Boyd, the retiring son of an elite family with English links, and Nolan, the outwardly confident media performer and the Irish-Australian son of the working-class inner suburbs, were an odd couple. Decades after the Melbourne art scenes of Murrumbeena and Heide in the 1940s, they came together through a kind of dynastic alliance in the art world. After the death by suicide of Cynthia Nolan in 1976, Sidney Nolan married Mary Perceval, Arthur Boyd's sister. Nolan had known her first at Heide in the 1940s, then around Hampstead in the 1960s, and met her again when she came to live in Britain in the early 1970s after the breakdown of her marriage to John Perceval. Arthur and Yvonne were witnesses at the February 1978 wedding, as Sidney Nolan had been a witness at their wedding 34 years earlier. Nolan joked that it must look like 'an in-house job'.[34] The marriage would also lead to a bitter rift between Patrick White and Nolan, on whose behalf Nolan had gone to Stockholm to collect his 1973 Nobel Prize for literature. White believed that the artist had recoupled with indecent haste.

The Boyds and Nolans had come even closer together at the Shoalhaven. However, despite the familial, personal and historic links and their shared expatriation, they were very different. Sir Sidney Nolan was, perhaps forever, the successful expatriate artist who had 'made it' in the art world and in society. In this period of personal affluence and jet travel he believed it was possible to 'pop back home any time I fancy because Australia's not so far away any more'. In contrast, Arthur Boyd, while later nearly always financially comfortable, could not handle plane travel, making his one and only plane journey between London and Paris to see a Picasso exhibition in 1966. Like Leo McKern, his many voyages south were made by ship, increasingly the slow boat of the cargo ship, as the passenger liner routes disappeared during the 1970s.

Why hadn't Nolan and Boyd returned to stay? Nolan, born in Carlton in 1917, died in London in 1992. Boyd, born three years later, continued his life of 'two worlds' connected by the sea. Nolan may have endorsed the view of a younger character in the 1990 play of expatriation, *Hotel Sorrento*. When asked 'why I didn't come home', the prize-winning London writer, Meg, remarks that 'I used to say it was because the artist has no status in this country. Why make art when you can make money?' Ten years later Meg still saw Australia as a country in which 'the real cultural heroes are good blokes who make a lot of money, don't take themselves too seriously and have no pretensions whatsoever about their intellect'.[35]

In fine art, the art versus money dichotomy was no longer valid. For Blackman and Lymburner and other Australian artists who had not won London fame, the emerging art market meant that Australia now called. Back home, rather than in London, Blackman in particular would be recognised at last. For Nolan and Boyd, artistic success offered financial success, unlike their earlier years of economic exigency. However, by the 1980s, two decades after Arthur Boyd had gone to Britain with a young family, his children and then his grandchildren were nearly all in the UK. They kept the Boyds at this other antipodes – over 20 000 kilometres away by sea from the Australian aspect of Arthur's artistic inspiration. Despite this, Boyd came back to visit the Shoalhaven often. After the long voyage home in early 1999, he would die, aged 78, in his original city of Melbourne on 24 April 1999. Nolan, who had spent most of the second half of the century overseas, lived mainly in London but also in Ireland (partly in search of his familial roots) and in Herefordshire. His predominantly British location was the legacy of history – imperial and personal as well as national. Perhaps, Sid Nolan, who became Sir Sidney Nolan with a British career (which, however, did not entail painting British subjects), could 'never go back'.

At the same time as Boyd and Nolan were making their increasingly triumphal progress, Australian art was becoming more 'international' and more diverse. While in the Sixties some critics feared that artistic Sydney was becoming a south-western suburb of San Francisco, or an outer borough of Manhattan, by the 1990s a larger pluralism was apparent. The achievements of the 'Angry Penguins', including the force of Albert Tucker as well as of Nolan and Boyd, were revisited and lauded, in Britain as well as Australia. Individual life retrospectives also acknowledged the achievement of Blackman and Lymburner. While Australian artists would always travel, and the Australia Council had nearly a dozen overseas studios, including Paris, London, Rome, New York, Los Angeles and Tokyo, now times had changed. The artists' situation had similarities with that described in a study of artists in another field – Irish writing. No longer was the story one of 'exile' and 'departure', which 'suggested an out-dated degree of permanency'. Australian artists, too, 'no longer go into exile, they simply commute'.[36] The experience of a generation of Australian writers was, however, slightly more difficult.

Chapter 6

Patterns of Exploration: Writers[1]

Writing was one of the few artistic mediums which had expressed an Australian voice since the formally colonial era. From the late nineteenth century onwards, in the short stories of Henry Lawson and later through the novel, a tradition of a kind had existed. Despite Lawson's authentic tones, the economics and the social position of writing in Australia made it an even riskier activity than marginal farming on the dry lands of the interior. Australian literature, ignored by the universities and poorly served by low standards of criticism in the newspapers, remained a colonial inferior. The first major history of Australian literature was not published until 1961, and the first Australian dictionary, the Macquarie, only appeared in 1981, nearly 200 years after European settlement.[2]

The impossibility of being a writer in Australia was a recurring theme in the first half of the twentieth century. The Western Australian novelist Katharine Susannah Prichard had been told that 'You're better dead' than being a writer in Australia. In the period between 1935–40, the novelist Eleanor Dark had an average weekly income from four novels of half that of a junior journalist. Perhaps it was this sort of economic situation which led to the distinguished writer Miles Franklin, author of nine published novels, describing her occupation in 1938 as 'home duties'.[3]

Paradoxically, as in music, the isolation of war improved things during the 1940s. Australian books were important for national morale while the influx of metropolitan literature was stemmed by the threat of Japanese warships. During the war decade, for the first time, Australian publishers published more Australian novels in Australia than their London counterparts. That change in the number of fiction works published was continuing, rather than momentary; there was a two to one ratio of Australian-published Australian novels to London-published Australian novels in the period from 1954 to 1965.[4]

Even if, in the postwar years, 'Australian literature' was no longer a contradiction in terms, as the critic Dorothy Green had once been told, the economics of publishing still pushed Australian authors to London. Australian-published books with print-runs of 1500 or 2000 did not furnish a living for a writer. That continuing theme of 'London calling' would shape the lives of Australian writers who left for the imperial metropolis and the English-language publishing capital. It had already become an abiding theme in Australian culture and carried the weight of colonial deference to the imperial centre. Even into the 1960s, many books with Australian subject matter were published in London. The Australian branches of British publishers mainly functioned as sales and distribution outlets for their parent companies, and few Australian publishers existed.

At a time when the experience of war and the last days of Empire strengthened the ties between Australia and Britain, the London magnet would shape the lives and careers of several writers, including the war writer and biographer Russell Braddon, the young would-be novelist Jill Neville, the Brisbane poet Peter Porter and the very different Brisbane actor, critic, administrator and performer, Charles Osborne.

Advice to Writers: 'Seek London, Yankeeland, or Timbuctoo . . .'

The voyage to London remained one of the strongest imperatives in Australian literary culture in the 1940s and early 1950s. Escape seemed preferable to many writers to more morbid conceptions of what the aspiring young scribbler should do. Henry Lawson had bitterly suggested such a choice when he was intent on seeking the stamp of the great city. In 1900, when he had begged the assistance of Earl Beauchamp, the Governor of New South Wales, so that he could undertake the necessary journey to London, he advised the talented young Australian writer to

> go steerage, stow away, swim, and seek London, Yankeeland, or Timbuctoo – rather than stay in Australia till his genius turned to gall, or beer. Or, failing this . . . to study elementary anatomy, especially as applies to the cranium, and then shoot himself carefully with the aid of a looking-glass.[5]

Many distinguished writers have followed in Lawson's tracks. Over half a century later, as Morris West, then a writer and an independent radio producer, reflected, 'if you wanted to become a professional novelist . . . you had to go abroad'.[6] Writing of Australia in the 1940s, the writer-journalist Donald Horne remarked that 'we all knew that there were no real markets in Australia for serious work, nor any good publishers, but there was more than that to it – there seemed something so dull about Australia that it might not be possible to write well while living in it'.[7]

Between the wars, the appearance of the novel from those 'exiles at home' – Kylie Tennant, Eleanor Dark and Katharine Susannah Prichard, Marjorie Barnard and Flora Eldershaw – and the emergence of several enthusiasts for Australian literature, ranging from Vance and Nettie Palmer to P. R. Stephensen – suggested change. However, expatriation to the 'real world' of London still seemed necessary to escape the colonial unreality of provincial Australia. 'Real writers' were found in London or Europe, where Henry Handel Richardson and Frederic Manning had gone before, followed in the inter-war years by Christina Stead, Jack Lindsay, Alan Moorehead, and a dozen more. In Moorehead's words:

> to go abroad – that was the thing. That was the way to make your name. To stay at home was to condemn yourself to non-entity. Success depended on an imprimatur from London ... to be really someone in Australian eyes you first had to make your mark or win your degree on the other side of the world.[8]

At this time, the rich sent their children to Oxford and Cambridge to get a 'real' degree, and the best students went off to Oxford on a Rhodes scholarship, one third never to return in the years to 1939.[9] Australia was condemned as inferior, as false, as lacking validity. Only in Europe did the writers feel 'real'. Alan Moorehead dated his life from the moment his ship entered Toulon Harbour: 'I had come home. This was where I wanted to be'. For Graham McInnes' generation 'the real challenge, the real excitement, the real possibility of success, lay 12 000 miles away in England. "Home" in fact'.[10] Despite the fillip given to Australian letters by wartime publishing of Australian classics, and the appearance of the cultural quarterly *Meanjin* in 1940, the urge to go overseas to make a living as a writer was strengthened by the new possibilities. George Johnston had sought to escape from the everyday life of the suburbs, as pictured in the Beverley Grove of *My Brother Jack*. After the war, he wanted to leave behind an Australia 'dominated by Randwick, Bradman and the White Australia Policy'.[11] The postwar exodus of writers, like that of actors and musicians, was a product of that great paradox of the era: wartime imperatives and increased opportunities, followed by the inability of the Australian cultural infrastructure to sustain them, particularly at a time when Angus & Robertson was still languishing. As with wool and minerals, the primary products or 'raw materials' would be Australian, and the 'value-added' process would occur overseas. Colonial dependence continued. Even in the 1950s, booksellers and librarians too often heard their customers and patrons remark 'if it's Australian, I don't want it'.[12]

The Last Days of Empire, War Memories and Literary Economics

The postwar years saw a revived interest in the British connection despite economic growth and growing American political and commercial influence on Australian life. In the last days of Empire the British connection had symbolic and emotional appeal. The great celebratory moments of the end of the war in Europe and then in the Pacific, the 1951 Festival of Britain, the 1953 coronation of the young Queen Elizabeth (which encouraged dreams of Britain entering 'a new Elizabethan age') and the 1954 Royal Tour of Australia reinforced the British tie, which was also being strengthened by British immigration to Australia. At this time the exodus of Australian writers was dramatic and continuing. Paul Brickhill and Russell Braddon had begun their careers as London writers even earlier, Braddon in 1949. When the Society of Australian Writers was founded in London on 14 May 1952, its membership attested to the extent of the exodus. It was as if in writing something akin to the Tyrone Guthrie 'export-import' plan for a National Theatre in Australia was being enacted. The talent was assembled in London, and their skills honed (Guthrie's first 'export' phase). Later, as in Guthrie's second 'import' phase, most would return to Australia. The isolated nature of the writing life notwithstanding, it would have been possible to select not just a cricket XI but an Australian Rules Football team of 20 from the complement of writers, playwrights and journalists with literary aspirations.[13]

War's Literary Legacy

Some travels were influenced by the impact of world events on individuals. The war correspondents Alan Moorehead, Chester Wilmot and Sam White returned to the European theatre of international events. Russell Braddon and Paul Brickhill had both been shaped by their prisoner-of-war experiences on both sides of the world during World War II.[14] Subsequently, they would make their lives and fortunes as the writers of war books. Brickhill, an escaped POW, carried the manuscript of *Escape to Danger* through the snows of wartime Germany; it would finally be published in 1946. Braddon's account of Changi prison camp and the Burma railway, *The Naked Island*, appeared in 1952. Like many other soldiers, they both found it hard to adjust to 'civvy street'. Repatriated to Australia, Brickhill had found the daily grind of journalism at the Sydney *Sun* was not for him, and eventually returned to London in April 1949.

Turmoil would engulf Russell Braddon. He had experienced most of the war as a prisoner of the Japanese, 16 000 kilometres farther south than Brickhill. This searing experience of the war left a complex legacy. The son of an old Australian family, he had grown up in comfortable North Shore Sydney and went to Sydney Grammar School. After returning from the war he continued Arts and Law at Sydney University, living at St Paul's College at the same time as the 'conscripted' medical student and volunteer actor Michael Blakemore. After his wartime horrors, Braddon, aged 27, could not settle down to everyday life. Having 'failed everything ... failed as a soldier, failed as a student', afflicted by recurring malaria and depressed by the drugs to control it, he took an overdose in his room at St Paul's. Five months later he was in Brisbane, with nothing to do except play tennis, and a lack of partners during the day. After three weeks he counted his £340 deferred pay and said to his family, 'I'm going to London'. His escape north – to travel, to pick fruit in France and then return – was his response to that boredom. It was also because he suffered 'from that lovely dream that all Australians had who hadn't been there of seeing London, seeing Europe, seeing all those things'. He had 'an excuse to go'; in his case the monetary 'excuse' was his deferred pay. He had also got to know a number of English, Scottish and Welsh soldiers during his imprisonment. He was not to know that the post-war voyage would provide him with a career and also 'cure me of hatred'. Strongly Australian, he would also grow to appreciate Britain, 'the country that would heal me'.[15]

The writing came after, by chance and by connections from the old school of Changi. The unexpected hand on his shoulder at Waterloo Station was that of Sidney Piddington, his Changi comrade, whose mother had cabled him of Braddon's arrival. Piddington had just been commissioned to do eight light entertainment broadcasts with the BBC, and he asked Braddon to do the scripts, knowing his talents from the particularly small theatre of war in which they had suffered together. More immediately, Ronald Searle, the English cartoonist and Changi caricaturist, gave him a place to sleep in his studio. Braddon, who had not wanted to follow in the family tradition of law, was already beginning to write in 1949. His radio work was followed by a successful stage show, which would lead to a popular book on the Piddingtons' story from Changi to the Palladium. *The Naked Island* went through many editions, selling over a million copies during the 1950s and became a play and a film. Most importantly, it gave Braddon an income and a high profile in both Britain and Australia.[16] He went on to write biographies of an unusual expatriate, the Australian hero of the resistance in France, Nancy Wake (1956), of Joan Sutherland (1962), and the British airman, Leonard Cheshire, VC (1954).

Paul Brickhill's books, *The Great Escape* (1950) and *The Dam Busters* (1951), both sold in the millions, were translated into 20 languages and became popular films. Later, John Laffin, a returned soldier from the New

Guinea campaign, continued the tradition of British-based Australian writers of war books. His books included *Digger: The Story of the Australian Soldier* (1959).[17] Another colonial incongruity mirrored the country's celebration of expeditionary nationalism, that is, the national myth of ANZAC valour based on fighting 'loyally' in 'other people's wars'. The resultant Australian appetite for the romance of war was fed by the work of expatriate authors living in London. The celebration of the Empire at war by 'colonials' offered a cultural mirror of the role of Australians as loyal soldiers, often fighting in the regional wars of the Empire, and then of another 'Great Power', the USA.

The Braddon-Brickhill war stories phenomenon was a postwar literary phase comparable with the political fashion in Australia of seeking former generals for governors and governors-general, or in other countries, such as the US, as national leaders. The pre and postwar movement of other writers to London would have varying results. Some writers would return after a few years. Rex and Thea Rienits pioneered TV drama, including, at the beginning of the 1960s, *Stormy Petrel*, an account of Captain Bligh's conflicts as a governor of early New South Wales. Dal Stivens came back around the same period, according to the socialist patrician Geoffrey Dutton, 'affecting a surprising English accent and manner'.[18]

London in the Fifties: A Colonial Writer's Marketplace

The success which Russell Braddon won was not just the result of talent, a popular interest in war stories and his connections from the 'playing fields' of Changi. It came because London was a writers' marketplace. London had agents, publishers, markets, and the opportunity to supplement income from book royalties with reviews, criticism and radio work. In some ways, the Australian artistic colonies in London were a last colonial aberration, at the time of the retreat of the formal British Empire. In a related view, they prefigured the cultural groupings of a more self-confident, more self-referring and self-sufficient national or 'metropolitan' culture in Australia, one which arose with increased population and sophistication and government support during the 1970s. It is drawing a rather long bow to see the Society of Australian Writers as a rehearsal for an Australian writers' professional body, or as an unofficial anticipation of the official support for writing furnished by the Literature and Drama Boards of the Australia Council. However, the colonial lack of confidence of Australian letters in the 1950s provides some support for that interpretation. At minimum, the Society arose out of the frustrations of trying to 'make it', or at least 'make a living', as an Australian writer – in London and in Australia. The London-based and London-published Australian writer was particularly conscious that they suffered from 'colonial' royalties: books on Australian subjects, which sold well in Australia, generated lower rates of royalties from their 'colonial editions'.

The Society of Australian Writers was also the product of a particular time and place. This very specific space was Dolphin Square by the Thames in Pimlico. Europe's largest complex of modern apartment flats, which had central heating and a swimming pool, appealed to Sydney expatriates such as Peter Finch, Russell Braddon and Ian Bevan, and to various travelling sportsmen and politicians. Out of this 'very comfortable Changi', as Braddon termed it, came not a swimming or squash club, but a writers' society. In the English spring of 1952, Ian Bevan and Paul Brickhill got in touch with a number of playwrights, actors and writers. The first included Alan Stranks, later a successful writer for television, and Hugh Hastings, whose play *Seagulls over Sorrento* would be the first television drama produced by the Crawfords – Hector and Dorothy Crawford – in 1960. Actors included Peter Finch (described by Russell Braddon as 'the worst dressed man in Dolphin Square') and Lloyd Lamble, former president of Actors Equity. (Peter Finch and his wife Tamara, Charmian Clift, Robert Helpmann and a young Rolf Harris – supported by a stuffed kangaroo – were also amongst the 'talent' at the Australia House basement party which launched the Australian Artists Association.)

The Society of Australian Writers (SAW) became mainly a writers' association, despite early suggestions of alternative titles, including the 'Australian Literary and Drama Association'. It sought 'to further the cause of Australian writers and writing wherever possible, and to act as a spokesman and advice and information centre for Australian writers in the United Kingdom'.[19] Oriented to professionals, rather than amateurs and enthusiasts, it offered full membership to any professionally published Australian writer, playwright or scriptwriter. Associate membership, for those not so qualified, and corporate membership were also available. Australian High Commissioners, who supported the Society from the beginning, included Sir Thomas White, who had been soldier, author and book censor as Minister for Customs in the 1930s, and later Sir Alexander Downer. Downer, an Anglophile and an Adelaide Establishment man, had also been Russell Braddon's resident elocution teacher in Changi.[20]

The Society's principals were diverse in age, literary mode and time of arrival in the UK. The playwright Betty Roland had arrived in 1952, and would stay for a decade. Others such as Mary Elwyn Patchett, the author of over 40 books for children, which would soon include *The Brumby* (1958), had come before the war. Wilfrid Thomas, the longtime ABC and BBC broadcaster of travels and observations in Britain, Europe and later North Africa, was a continuing link with Australia. A former singer, he was later on the committee of the SAW's sister organisation, the Australian Musical Association (AMA).[21]

In those last days of the British Empire ideal, the collection *The Sunburnt Country: Profile of Australia* (1953), published prior to the forthcoming Royal

Tour of Australia, was the high point of the young Society's activities. In this book, edited by Ian Bevan, literary activity, Queen and country came together. It presented a number of Australian writers to English and Australian audiences, and to the young Queen Elizabeth, through essays on different aspects of Australian life. 'Their Books' by Dal Stivens happily noted that books by Australian authors had sold upwards of a million copies in the last year. In other chapters, Colin MacInnes reflected on art, Eric Partridge on language, Martin Boyd on links with Britain, George Johnston on the way of life of writers, and Alan Wood on their achievements abroad. Chester Wilmot wrote on Australia's expanding horizon, Paul Brickhill, Colin Wills, Jack McLaren and Mary Elwyn Patchett on the landscape, Judy Fallon on the Australian woman, and Russell Braddon on the Australian serviceman. The endpapers were designed by Loudon Sainthill.[22]

The Sunburnt Country was well received, selling 23 000 copies in Britain and Australia by May 1954, despite fears that the critics in Australia

> might crab the book. You know the cry that can be raised about ex-patriots [sic]. But aside from one or two waspish comments made before the book was released in Australia, reviews have been uniformly favourable and in many cases enthusiastic.[23]

The professional activities of the young Society included regular monthly lectures, with audiences ranging from 40 to 130 people, displays of Australian books, often designed by Robin Lovejoy, occasional play readings, and poetry readings at Australia House. The Society gave £50 towards the campaign for a chair in Australian Literature at Sydney University, and it held an annual lecture on Australian arts. The first, given by Alan Moorehead, was appropriately titled 'The Struggle for Tradition'. A play-reading panel assessed playscripts to help Australian plays reach the London stage. At a time when there was a weak public sense of Australian literary tradition, in Australia as well as in London, the Society also offered support for a literary plaque on the house at 90 Regent's Park Road, NW1 in which Henry Handel Richardson had lived when writing *The Fortunes of Richard Mahony*. A 1953 ABC radio discussion between Catherine Gaskin, Ian Bevan and Ralph Peterson (who later returned to write the pioneering TV comedy *My Name's McGooley, What's Yours?*) addressed the subject of trying to break into 'the London market'; it might have helped some writers in Australia who were thinking of coming over.[24]

Although there were tensions within the Society about different conceptions of literature ('popular' and more 'serious'), and between professionals and amateurs, it had remarkable energy in its early years. Less than a decade later, one of its early enthusiasts, the writer and editor Dal Stivens, would be the moving force behind the creation of the Australian Society of

Authors in 1963. While literary tradition in Australia was not a *tabula rasa* or blank slate, in some ways the SAW, like the AMA, was a precursor of the rediscovery of Australian cultural creativity by Australians from the late 1960s.[25] 'Offshore', Australian creators gathered, waiting either for the chance to make it in London or to find opportunities at home. By the late 1960s, the belated burgeoning of Australian literature and screenwriting led to conflicts between Australian resident and expatriate writers. In late 1967, Russell Braddon protested vociferously on behalf of the SAW and of Australian screenwriters in London at the Australian Writers' Guild's policy that 60% of Australian television series 'must be written by financial members of the Guild, who are also resident in Australia'.[26] By that time, when writers more often just passed through London, and others returned to Australia, the Society of Australian Writers' activities had retreated; it became mainly a vehicle for screening Australian films. The films attracted audiences of up to 200, including many Australians in London (amongst them the scriptwriter Alan Seymour), and even prospective immigrants. In contrast, literary readings often attracted less than 50 people. Writing is one of the more solitary of creative professions and most established writers who remained in Britain had drifted off to their own activities. That earlier London experience would, however, shape the destinies of several young Australians who had landed on the Strand of the great city during the postwar era.

Three Artistic Journeys: Jill Neville, Peter Porter and Charles Osborne

Leaving Sydney for Britain, on the liner *Otranto* in January 1951 were three young Australians: a shy would-be poet from Brisbane, Peter Porter, aged 21; his painter friend Brian Carne; and a nervous but effervescent 18-year-old typist and would-be writer from Sydney, Jill Neville. On the boat, Neville and Porter discovered each other as they shared a romantic sense of anticipation created by the journey and by their destination, London. Two and a half years later, Charles Osborne, the Brisbane actor, writer and poet, set out from Melbourne on the voyage north, accompanied by the actor Peter Kerr.[27] Their different journeys through life and their London and literary experiences would involve problems as well as creations. Negotiating a way through the shoals and sharks of life's seas – including relationships with others, with London and with Australia – would require industry and luck as well as talent.

Jill Neville's experiences had many similarities to those of the narrator-heroine of her 1966 novel of expatriation and 1950s London, *Fall-Girl*. In one scene, on a hot summer night by the harbour, a girlfriend says to the central character 'I really think we *are* going to go. And you're going to stay there and *never* come back'.[28] Jill Neville's decision to cross the world at such a young age was a brave one. But what would Sydney have offered a young woman in that era of suburban domesticity – a house, a husband, a Holden car and kids? She later reflected that, with neither money nor connections, only 'a weird eccentric bit of talent', 'there really wouldn't have been anything for me in the Fifties if I'd stayed in Sydney'.

Jill Neville's talent was the product of nature and nurture. Nature came in the form of the beauty of the Blue Mountains, between Sydney and the Great Dividing Range, where she spent some of her early years and later many school holidays. Nurture came from the stimulus of very different parents. Her 'boring but solid' father was a retired army officer, accountant and later business manager of *Country Life* magazine. He contrasted with her performer mother, a poet and literary conversationalist, a musician wearing a Prince of Wales suit, with a cigarette and a drink beside her piano. As happened with many other creative individuals, that hybrid background energised the young Jill Neville.

In London, even more than Sydney, she made an instant and continuing impact. Murray Sayle has written of the personal magnetism of this young woman with 'hazel eyes and auburn hair'. She was

> the acknowledged beauty and outstanding personality among the first wave of talented young Australians who lit up the British scene in the drab years immediately after World War II. She radiated the qualities Londoners have come to think of as refreshingly Australian: energy, self-reliance, infectious friendliness and an unquenchable, innocent curiosity.[29]

Peter Porter had also been stimulated by his growing up, although more by difficulty than by diversity. Like those other children of the war years, Clive James and Germaine Greer, who each 'lost' a parent, he faced a similar loss, although not due to war. When he was aged nine his mother died from illness. For Porter, one result was an uncertain relationship with his father, which, he later reflected, he wished had been 'more vital and direct'. This was compounded by a traumatic experience of the bullying brutality and dull rigidity at a Brisbane version of an English private school, Brisbane Church of England Grammar. Affectionately known as 'Churchie' by some, it was remembered by Porter as 'Auschwitz by the river'; subsequently he went to a more humane school in Toowoomba on the Darling Downs. An unrewarding year as a cadet journalist with the *Courier-Mail* in Brisbane (he didn't like chasing stories) and working in his father's manchester business did not add to this young boy's confidence in dealing with the world.[30] Like Jill Neville, he had an insatiable appetite for knowledge. His life would intertwine with the Britain and Europe of literature and musical knowledge, as Jill Neville's

Byronic moments would be shaped by passion and by events in Europe and beyond.

Porter's desire to get away involved 'pull' as well as 'push' factors. His actual departure was influenced by the common experience of 'chain migration', or chain expatriation. Roger Covell, who had lived up the road from him in Brisbane and had fallen on his feet as an actor (and as a publicist for the Festival of Britain!), wrote suggesting that he come. He was 'discontented with the place ... and with my own efforts', with the limitations of working in his father's business and with his own writing. He left, despite originally 'not having any particular intentions of leaving Australia' and being 'un-adventurous'. An unstated lack of stimulus and opportunity was another cause. Porter later recalled that, for a poet, practice and support were not available:

> Now in Australia today, you could get that, but, in my time it seemed hopeless ... there seemed to be no colleagues doing it, or at least it seemed so in Brisbane. There was no supportive atmos-phere. When I came to London, for instance, and discovered by talking to other Australians in England the utterly different experi-ence they'd had in Sydney, I realised what I'd been deprived of.

The young Porter had not known the Sydney of Finch and the Cross, of Sayle and Neville, of Mackerras and Tuckwell. In his family tradition it was just a place to go for holidays with relatives at Woolwich rather than a city to take seriously in cultural terms.

Porter would increasingly gravitate, in the way of a self-taught colonial, to European culture. But it was to its ideas, music and history rather than their physical and visual expressions. They too could be weighty. He took 'more than three hundredweight of gramophone records and books' with him on the ship,[31] but did not set foot on the 'Continent' for ten years, just living in London. Porter was a product of his era, one of postwar and Royal Tour Britishness in Australia, with a sense of shared nationality which would eventually fade:

> In the early '50s there was very little sense that to be Australian was to be different from an Englishman. It is all a good deal dif-ferent today since there is a burgeoning increase in national self-consciousness which has coincided with a greatly increased activity and self-reliance in Australia itself. In my time in Australia there was theatre and there were books but somehow they didn't seem at the centre of national intelligence or national consciousness.[32]

Charles Osborne, in contrast, seemed unrestrained by Brisbane. Even at an early age, when he edited a school magazine with the pretentious title

Intelligentsia, he declared his rebellious spirit against a society which preferred, and demanded, conformity. He co-founded the *Barjai* magazine and poets group and was a co-owner of the Ballad Bookshop, an alternative literary, and largely gay milieu in which Peter Porter did not feel comfortable. 'I didn't have the courage', Porter later said of his shy, adolescent self.[33]

Charles Osborne's 'dauntingly sophisticated' style, as the more reticent Porter saw it, and his theatrical flair were first manifested in the cultural assertiveness of the Barjai group.[34] This small band of poets included Barrett Reid, the writer Laurie Collinson and the poet Barbara Patterson (later Barbara Blackman). Or perhaps Osborne's creative and dramatic spark – in strident opposition to Brisbane and the provincial respectability of the times – could be discerned in his appreciation of the under-appreciated Laurel and Hardy.

Osborne, thespian and stirrer, was already strutting his stuff on different stages. The adversarial style of this cheeky chappie got him into trouble. He was harassed by Brisbane's finest, or 'a carful of thuggish detectives' as he later termed them, for unseemly behaviour – this 'longhair' was wearing a colourful shirt while walking across the Victoria Bridge. A complaint to higher authority became the real problem. In an era when colourful shirts and longish hair were associated with 'pansies' and 'poofs', the police on the beat always reminded him that they would remember him.[35]

Osborne was not a one-city person. He visited Sydney and spent a year working in radio and plays in Melbourne in 1946. In 1951, he followed his fellow Barjai group member and later literary editor Barrett (Barrie) Reid to Melbourne, and escaped more permanently to this southern city. A thousand miles south of Brisbane, he acted with John Bluthal in Hugh Hastings' *Touch of the Sun*, and plays by Christopher Fry. This departure was, more importantly, the 'first stage in my plan to leave Australia':

> By this time, I cordially loathed my native town and hoped never to see it again. I did see it again, of course, for even after I had begun to live in London I returned occasionally to see my ageing parents. But I did not really come to terms with the city of my birth until my 1979 visit, after the death of my parents, when somehow the burden of my past was lifted from my shoulders.[36]

Osborne liked the limelight of the stage. He had already met a visiting parade of theatrical and musical stars, including Laurence Olivier in 1948 and Otto Klemperer in 1950. He also met Sidney Nolan in Melbourne, and again in London, and later became a friend of Barry Humphries. Osborne proclaimed himself 'not a modest person', declaring in his self-confessed search for a moment of immortality in a dictionary of quotations, 'Modesty is the fig leaf of mediocrity'. He added that 'my detestation of mediocrity is the natural obverse of my admiration of excellence'.[37]

More immediately, he found that the Globe Theatre Players' claim to be 'Australia's First Professional Theatre Company' was severely qualified by its difficulty in paying the actors. Finally, in July 1953, in his mid-twenties, it was now or never. He left on the *Oceania*, which was bound for Genoa and Europe.[38] Whatever the practical imperatives, Osborne later justified his decision to depart in a language of seriousness and purpose:

> I had already decided that it was essential for me to leave Australia because, with the exception of books, most of the things I cared about were not to be found there.[39]

Exiles Away: London in the 1950s

Charles Osborne had to go, before 'it would be too late', to where he could see 'operas, *real* plays, *real* operettas for that matter and to look at paintings and baroque churches, and even see some *real* modern architecture' (italics added). Thus his Australian cultural experience was a pre-history. In a recurring expatriate metaphor, it was 'a preview of life. I am travelling to Europe to be born. Australia had been a sort of womb'. Carrying with him Laurence Olivier's autograph, obtained in Brisbane in 1948, he was voyaging to a new world.[40] Later expatriates would use similar rhetoric. The writer and critic, Peter Conrad, who journeyed from Hobart to Oxford and beyond in 1968, would declare later that 'I can remember the exact moment of my birth. It happened on Westminster Bridge'. Now he was completely free of his Tasmanian-Australian past. As his ship passed through the heads of Sydney Harbour, Clive James would also dream dreams of reincarnation in the real world over there.[41]

Osborne, and many other expatriates, found that the gleaming pearl they imagined London to be would be less bright in reality. It was dimly perceived through a London fog, or seen through eyes tired from mundane jobs; felt through skins cold from unheated flats; and tasted by palates jaded from the boozy vacuity of expatriate or Soho semi-bohemia. Osborne shared a flat in suburban Muswell Hill with other Australian musicians, including the music student Peter Andry, and then stayed near Victoria Station, in Ebury Street, SW1, where Mozart and Patrick White had lived. (The musician Geoffrey Parsons helped him move in.) Life was often difficult, and unfulfilled creative dreams made the vista even drabber. It was an experience Jill Neville and Peter Porter shared.

Arriving at Tilbury on the day the weekly meat ration fell to ten pennyworth of meat and two ounces of butter per person, Porter's and Neville's often grey 1950s experience of London was typical.[42] In her autobiographical novel, *Fall-Girl*, Jill Neville tells the story of a young Australian girl meeting the poet, Seth, on the boat, and her subsequent London activities, several of them shared with him. These include concerts, play readings, snacks in Lyons tea-houses, and her life in a houseboat on the Thames, several flats in South Kensington, Notting Hill Gate, and in Belsize Park Gardens and Hampstead. Jill Neville herself lived in an attic flat in Glenmore Road, while Porter shared basement flats and bedsits with Brian Carne, with his friend from the Brisbane *Courier-Mail*, Roger Covell, and with David Lumsdaine in South Kensington, Notting Hill Gate and later at 23A Belsize Park Gardens.[43]

In the London of the 1950s they found a variety of white-collar jobs. Peter Porter worked as a clerk in International Paints for £6 a week, as a bookseller, and in advertising. Jill Neville was employed as a typist at the BBC and else-where, and also later worked in advertising. This was a time of self-discovery and sexual growth for the young couple. There was also a small Austra-lian camaraderie around the bedsits and attic and basement flats and Jill Neville's Chelsea houseboat. Jill Neville had already met the composer David Lumsdaine and Murray Sayle in Sydney. In this goldfish bowl of the expatriate society of the recently arrived, they inevitably became closer.

The consolations of nationality and fellow feeling didn't really ameliorate their difficult situation, however. Seth the poet, the sad 'old lag . . . looked wretched':

That's what we'll be like after ten years in this bloody dump of a town. All the life beaten out of us. You'll have gone off and married one of these smart young men in charcoal grey suits, and I'll still be a clerk.

Transported to London, the Australians found solace amongst their own kind, away from England and its class system, of which Seth, after Orwell, remarked 'A man is branded on his tongue in this fucking country'.[44] The displaced Australians escaped from the rationing, the cramped spaces, and the social distance many of them felt from the English, in their own cele-brations, often held when a food parcel arrived from Australia.

At the Sayle New Year's Eve 'dos' in South Kensington and Notting Hill Gate, or on the Chelsea houseboat, the expatriates, mainly from Sydney, brightened up the struggle that was their life in London. (If all else failed, they escaped on a brief voyage to the romance of Paris.) Although Jill learned of the ways of the English from her flatmate, Mary Tuck, it was in the often macho society of the journalists that she felt at home.

Love and nationality came climactically together at one party on her houseboat in a cold London spring. Affairs of the heart, of masculinity and nation together, unleashed powerful energies. At the party, as fictionalised in *Fall-Girl*, 'the last to arrive was a well-known Australian journalist', a Murray Sayle-like character with 'a profile like a Roman emperor', who was ever ready to pronounce on thought, life and love. His subjects, this night, included a young boy, Reg. 'Reg has got it bad about you' he informs the girl. In Jill Neville's fictional account, a jealous Seth (Peter Porter) saw her and the young Englishman, Reg (Ralph Barrington Howard), dancing together and displaying an interest in each other. Anger was his response. Shoving her out of the cabin, he pushed her into the Thames. Murray, the wit, recalled shouting to the wet heroine, 'Come on Jill, you can do it, you can do it. I can't come and save you because of the state of my underwear'. In real life, Jill swam back to the boat and was hauled out by Murray. As if in a scene from a Chelsea Western, Peter and Ralph fought over the girl. Bedraggled and without shoes and earrings, she and Ralph ran along the Chelsea embankment, pursued by the antipodean furies, the friends of Peter.[45] Very fortunately a taxi took their cold, wet bodies away to the warmth of Ralph's Russell Square flat. Circumstances and a Bronteish chemistry shocked them into each other's arms. Her former – although already 18 months past – intimacy with Porter was now as dead as a 'dead marine', a bottle floating in the Thames.[46]

Porter's life was becoming even more difficult. That first great passionate relationship with Jill had ended. After Roger Covell's return to Brisbane to marry, he was very down and undernourished, living in the solitary and unheated flat. Twice in 1953 he turned on the gas in unsuccessful attempts at suicide. A brief return to Brisbane in December 1953 was a different attempt to escape from the futility of his life in London; in his biographer's words, 'to retreat from the maelstrom'. He also sought to come to terms with his relationship with his father.[47]

Coming into Their Own

The London sun would eventually shine more brightly for Peter Porter and Jill Neville, as it did for many other expatriate artists and writers. 'Overnight success' was on its way. In 1955, Porter met 'a group of writers just down from Oxford and Cambridge, including Philip Hobsbaum, George MacBeth, Edward Lucie-Smith, Martin Bell, Peter Redgrove and Ted Hughes (later to be called "The Group")'. At last he received very useful responses, of a specifically poetic kind. His first poem was not published until he was 28, and his first book of poems, *Once Bitten Twice Bitten*, did not appear until 1961 when he was 32. He met the Englishwoman Jannice Henry in 1958 and they married in 1960, the same year in which he settled into the first of several rented flats in Cleveland Square, bordering on Paddington, Bayswater and Westbourne Grove. Despite fights over rent and tribunal hearings in the 1980s, this square would remain his home over the following decades. He also made his first trip to Europe when they went to the Amsterdam Arts Festival, an unwitting anticipation of an unexpected later role. Work became more interesting and remunerative, first, at Bumpus Bookshop in Oxford Street and then, from 1959, as a copywriter with Notley's advertising agency.[48] This 'Australian, who writes the kind of tough, aggressive, prize-fighter verse that has become fashionable in the last year or two' was welcomed by the poet and critic Al Alvarez, and others.[49] As in film, television, stage and popular music, in poetry it was a moment of opening up to different regional, class and Commonwealth voices.

Jill Neville's life was often dramatic. Her talents were also recognised in several ways by Alvarez, with whom she had a relationship in the early Sixties. This young woman, with a youthful charm and vitality she would never lose, often would have to live with her own interesting and impulsive decisions. In her achievements, in her professional frustrations and in her sufferings, Jill Neville's literary and 'dramatic' life mirrored that of Porter. She was in London, uncertain in dress and skinny, but with a hint of the femme fatale, and missing the surf. She knew some of the Soho mob, travelled to Paris, 'the shrine of sensory values', and remained long enraptured by the poet even when the relationship was past. In England, as well as Australia, she was a girl who threatened some men because she had 'swallowed the dictionary'.[50]

Life's ups and downs, that is downs, seemed to be the story for Porter and for Jill Neville. Too often, in the words of the prefatory quotation to *Fall-Girl*, she would jump into 'a mess of cactus' because 'it seemed like a good idea at the time'. Her fate, like the narrator in *Fall-Girl*, would often be one of marrying only partly successful men who were not 'just interested in success. A failure would need me'. Jill Neville did fall for interesting men, who left her with young children. Because her father had character, she assumed that all men had it, 'just the way they have noses'. 'I just took character for granted . . . and I went for charm and fascination and they had no character'.[51]

Like many women of a generation before Sixties-style feminism, her independence and assertiveness had an explicitly sensual element: a flirtatious and 'tense, talkative' confidence, which in her case masked her lack of self-confidence. She also preferred the company of men to that of women. The young aspiring writer's three wishes began with those of the *Fall-Girl* herself: 'Money. A house near the sea. A super husband'.[52] In fact, Jill Neville's desires were more complicated, involving an opportunity to write and the complexity of an interesting man, in either order. She was both a stray and a comforter of strays in a dreary, cold city in the postwar 1950s; London was 'cold', despite the camaraderie of friends and flatmates. It was, however, a world in which they made their own fun, unlike the more 'glossy', 'commercialised' 1960s.

Committing 'all my passionate 20s and 30s' to building a circle of networks and people in London, she realised that the odyssey had costs as well as benefits. While her 'definition of paradise is not to be fragmented', over time she became divided. Her literary and artistic self was in London, while her 'physical self and more than physical, idealistic spiritual self' was at home, 'back there' in Sydney. To come to a country when you are 18 and decide to make a career there was to uproot yourself in a dreadful way, 'damning yourself forever to be cut in half'.

Her fate in love and in literature would shape her divisions. Her two marriages to powerful journalists, the South African Peter Duval-Smith of the BBC and the Englishman David Leitch of the *Sunday Times*, did more than take her from the interior 'female' culture of literary salons into the boozy and machismo male journalistic world. Duval-Smith, who had left her when she was pregnant, was later killed in Saigon, when on assignment in Vietnam. Leitch, later author of the autobiographical *God Stand Up for Bastards* and *Family Secrets*, and co-author of several *Sunday Times* Insight books, had a drinking problem.

Her social milieux reflected the meeting of worlds in the villages which made up London. Through the journalistic and 'colonial' world around Sayle and Knightley in the mid-1950s, she met David Lumsdaine, the composer whom she had known in Sydney and introduced to Peter Porter. Lumsdaine and Porter later collaborated on several artistic works. In literary circles she knew Fay Weldon, the Canadian Elizabeth Smart, the 'theatrical' theatre reviewer and entrepreneur, Kenneth Tynan, and Peter Porter's literary friends, including Al Alvarez. In the different society of journalism, a 'predominantly ruggedly male' culture prevailed, in which, as she recalled, war correspondents were viewed as the *crème de la crème*. Here, the worlds of Eros and Thanatos met. The love and death instincts were very close for men who lived dangerously, and for their women, who often defined themselves as 'a man's woman'. From the late 1960s, perhaps escaping her little brother Richard Neville's Swinging London, she was in Paris, enraptured by the events of May 1968, a rebellion on the verge of becoming a revolution.[53] She would be tossed around by international events, public and private, over the next two decades.

'Ex-Patriot' Wars: Sparring with the 'Antipodes'

In the early 1960s, a period in which the successful expatriates encouraged the British discovery of Australia, there was increasing tension in Australia about expatriation and the role of intellectuals in Australian life. While a tired postwar Britain sensed new vigour in the southern civilisation with its 'Bush' roots and traditions, Australian intellectuals intensely debated the character of their society and the phenomenon of expatriation.

As Australian artists were being taken up in London, many writers felt a growing frustration at their continuing inability to make a living in their profession in Australia. Intellectuals lambasted the suburban materialism and anti-intellectualism of 'God's own', soon dubbed 'Godzone', country. The September 1962 issue of *London Magazine*, edited by Charles Osborne and the young Australian playwright Barry Pree, focused on Australia. It gave several expatriates a platform to fire salvoes at a country which had disappointed and alienated them, sending them off in search of true cultural activity in London and Europe. The voices of expatriate critique, and sometimes of frustration and self-justification, were becoming a chorus. Anticipated in an earlier debate over expatriation in 1958, they would be echoed in later condemnations, including an article by John Pilger in *Nova* in the late 1960s, before becoming the stock in trade of later condemnations of 'Ocker' Australia.

The debate had begun in a spirited but polite way in the April 1958 issue of the Adelaide magazine *Australian Letters*. Alister Kershaw's essay 'The Last Expatriate' was responded to by the returned Patrick White in 'The Prodigal Son'. Kershaw, bohemian and bon vivant, poet and wit, had left his own 1940s modernist Melbourne for London and then France. Living around Paris on his wits, and for a time secretary to the exiled English writer Richard Aldington, he was also, as noted earlier, a Parisian focal point for several visiting Australians.[54] He was the expatriate in Europe par excellence, drinking Pernod on the Left Bank. Kershaw celebrated the 'New Europeans', the Australian artists who had discovered new selves but were charged with 'los[ing] your roots', with becoming 'decadent', when in fact rather too many of them were inoculated against foreign infection by their tendency to hang together. Kershaw toasted these last expatriates, sensing that the tide was turning, contrasting them with what he saw as the 'sinister vehemence' and 'grisly consistency in the cult of stay-at-homism'.[55] (Much later, he cheekily asked whose article was livelier, adding 'Shouldn't I have received the Nobel Prize?') White had returned at 36, after nearly 20 years overseas. He declared that he had rejected cosmopolitanism, and belief in the rightness of everything British, and escaped the danger of turning into 'that most sterile of beings, a London intellectual'. He maintained that he had to return to his Australian roots, despite the fact that 'in all directions stretched the Great Australian Emptiness, in which the mind is the least of possessions'. White believed it was possible that his creative work might be helping to 'people a barely inhabited country with a race possessed of understanding'.[56]

Onto that battleground in the early 1960s stepped the young playwright and poet, a refugee from Australian literary cliques, Ray Mathew, who contributed his expatriate's assessment of Australia to the September 1962 'Australian' issue of *London Magazine*. Ray Mathew's departure had been noted in a couple of lines in the *Sydney Morning Herald* in January 1959: 'Did you know we are losing yet another of our writers ... Ray Mathew is off overseas on the *Castel Felice* on January 26. He tells me he will be away indefinitely'.[57] The former country schoolteacher, CSIRO employee and university lecturer was a poet on the outer. He was not of the school of James McAuley and A. D. Hope, and knew he was outside what Max Harris called the contemporary 'prevalence of poetesses'. As a playwright, he was outside the stage naturalism of Ray Lawler's *Summer of the Seventeenth Doll*. On that Australia Day he left for Europe, carrying references from Patrick White. Early success for this outsider came quickly. His play *The Life of the Party* was produced in London, and he received an Arts Council bursary. Despite loathing London, and being unsure of his own abilities, he still retained a 'Lawrentian' distaste for Australia, as well as for its literary cliques and their regimentation and control of what little arts money there was.[58]

The special issue of *London Magazine* included stories by Patrick White and Hal Porter, poems by Randolph Stow and Judith Wright and a piece by Alan Seymour. Ray Mathew pictured an 'Australia [which] has not changed. Nothing has happened to force Australians to reconsider themselves and their values'.[59] What was perceived as Mathew's expatriate spleen aroused the ire of the Australian press and was critiqued by the complex expatriate Jack Lindsay. A freelance scholar and writer, and a Marxist, Lindsay had lived in Britain since the mid-1920s, never physically returning to Australia. Despite his own expatriation, he assailed this expatriate account of Australian intellectual alienation, which he saw as limited by its externality and by its failure to understand contemporary change. He condemned Mathew and other Australian contributors for

> jeering at the Australian scene as though they have no more responsibility to it or for it than if they were superior visitors from Mars making their derisive report. Here we have persons alienated in the simple sense that they feel quite outside the thing they describe; they are cut off and view the idiot scene from the other side of the asylum-wall.[60]

Lindsay discerned a process whereby expatriate alienation was inverted into superiority. He traced its roots to a more fundamental alienation of intellectuals from Australian culture. Brought up on imported culture, they often became spiritual exiles at home before they departed for the 'real world' of Europe. Others, who had tried to find an audience for their works, and an income from that audience in Australia, left impelled by a double frustration, economic as much as spiritual and creative.

Lindsay was conscious of several great paradoxes. First, many of the repressive and materialist attitudes found in Australia were not 'nationally peculiar' and could be found in most Western countries during the Cold War. Second, the assaults were occurring when Australia was beginning to shake off its impediments to cultural growth. Third, the British situation, in an era of 'decayed imperialism', had become uncertain.[61] *Alienation*, the 1960

collection which included pieces by Murray Sayle and the Rhodesian expatriate Doris Lessing, had painted a bleak picture of Britain as well as of the
'colonies' from which the essayists had escaped.

The conflict did not go away. Charles Osborne endorsed Mathew's views.
He had an exciting trip back in 1962, receiving a warm, even hot, welcome
after nearly a decade away. The Brisbane *Courier-Mail* ran a story 'Un-
Australian Activities by Expatriates in London', attacking the Australian issue
of *London Magazine*. In Sydney, Craig McGregor, who had met Osborne
during his London years, offered a 'Portrait of a Pundit' who liked whisky,
which, according to Osborne, the *Sydney Morning Herald* had provided.
Osborne was criticised here (and in a Melbourne TV interview, in which he
was also charged with squatting with Communists in an Aldermaston anti-
bomb protest) for condemning his home town: 'I was born in a concentration
camp called Brisbane ... just like a sleazy frontier town; the Deep South of
Australia. Most of the people are so conformist, so damned dull'.[62]

The 'rabid expatriate-baiters' whom Osborne encountered grew in number
during the 1960s. Or, perhaps, from their point of view, the self-inflated
'just-visiting-from-London' types expanded in number and size; so did the
temptation of 'lesser mortals' to prick such balloons. Osborne later reflected
that 'it took me many months to make peace with my Brisbane friends'. Peter
Porter also ran into similar problems from a few far too casual – or even,
subconsciously, intentional – throwaway lines. When his first book of poems
was well received in London, Porter observed in a *Times* interview that in
Australia he had had 'only a few friends as listeners, but now he perceived the
beginnings of connection with an audience'. As his biographer remarks, 'such
comments, however apposite, would earn him no friends in Australia'.[63]

A frustrating period in London and his unsuccessful return to Brisbane
both strengthened Porter's resolve to succeed as a writer in England. Such
determination distanced him from Australia. This struggle, as well as his
European interests, his metropolitan identification and his sense of an
English literary tradition which gave a prominent place to Shakespeare
(much of which he knew by heart), further increased the distance from
Australia. Porter delineated an adversarial-to-ironic relationship to many
contemporary attitudes and ideologies, including those created by advertising; similarly he defined himself – with divided loyalties – against Australia.
At times this had poetic expression. One poem began with the title first line,
'In the New World happiness is allowed/No, in the New World, happiness is
enforced'.[64] He also wrote a provocative clerihew:

In Australia
(Inter alia)
mediocrities
think they're Socrates.[65]

The colonial cultural cringe in Australia guaranteed a legitimate, and an illegitimate, reaction against the prevailing systems associated with imperial and now merely 'metropolitan' culture. The exaggerated role of London in Australian cultural pecking orders, which the cringe created, ensured a valid and excessive reaction against that metropolitan cachet. Majority deference to London engendered in reaction a minority rejection of the status and authority associated with the great city. This latter response varied. It could express a valid concern for valuing artistic achievement over the formal mechanisms for conferring status, or it could be a merely mechanical 'Cultural Cringe Inverted', as A. A. Phillips termed it. Denying the validity of the extra-Australian, the latter position assumed a chauvinistic preference for the home-grown. The 'refined' product of expatriation was automatically distorted and inferior, losing its 'essential' Australian qualities. In this way the Cringe Inverted was like a photographic negative of mindless deference.

Changing Images, Negotiating Relationships

In the late 1970s Jill Neville exchanged the role of being an Australian 'plant' in the English gardens of literary London, the observer sitting and watching the ecology of the locals interacting, for that of the returned expatriate. After London and Paris, she returned to Sydney after a quarter of a century. She had left Australia as an 18-year-old and now returned in her forties, with her three-year-old son and her 18-year-old daughter (who quickly went back to her English boyfriend). Like some other expatriates, the now single mother scurried home with her tail between her legs, as her relationship with David Leitch declined. She found herself not welcomed, but resented for having gone, for having 'preferred somewhere else to your native land'.

> You have to get punished if you go away and leave Australia ... Instead of staying at home and helping to create a new culture you went away and partook of the old culture. Sometimes I wonder would they be more angry with one if one hadn't gone back to England, which is the rather loathed mother country. If one had gone away and lived in Greece or something – people quite liked George Johnston ...

She would also find herself caught out in little ways. Treading softly and not spruiking about her London novels or about being a *Sunday Times* book reviewer, her English clothes and her language gave her away. Even aside from accent, Australians reacted when zucchinis became 'courgettes' and the stove became a 'cooker'. Her clothes also seemed dowdy to Sydneysiders, who preferred brighter colours. Later, in England, her Australian clothes prompted her English friends to remark that she looked like 'an overripe melon'. To her cost, one culture's style was another's dowdy, or another's gaudy, it seemed.

Her Australian visit, which might have become a return, was unsettling in other ways. Her fortyish pre-feminist liberated self 'strutting [her] stuff' fell between two different stools: the Sydney couples with their houses and material objects, and the feminists, straight and gay, who had no time for traditional flirtatiousness. Neither 'ferocious ball-breaking lesbians', nor repressed housewives, nor the male style of the society of the Sydney Push, appealed. None was her cup of tea. Nor was work easy. Although she had freelance journalism with the *Sydney Morning Herald*, her aspirations for other jobs went unrealised. She felt that her lack of local connections was the major problem. Freelance work, relative poverty, living in a flat at Manly and not really feeling part of things was not fun. Nor was being viewed as the daughter who had gone away, in contrast to her older sister, who stayed. More pleasingly, though, she was able to bring back some of her literary 'trophies' before her mother died.

Like many returning expatriates she rediscovered not Australia's cities or people (she visited Melbourne only once), but its nature: the bush around the family home at the Blue Mountains and Nimbin, the sea and the bush at Byron Bay and Bermagui. Her sense of the Australian landscape became suddenly intense, awakened like a 'thunderclap', as if a black and white film was 'suddenly . . . in colour. And I was drenched. I was in a state of actual ecstasy'. Nature offered a spiritual, as well as physical, sense of Australia. Other responses varied. Disappointed by the knocking down of old central Sydney, she was exhilarated by the city's 'new' migrant population. Her novels *Last Ferry to Manly* (1984) and *The Day We Cut the Lavender* (not published until 1995) were among the results of her Sydney sojourn.

Peter Porter also entered a new relationship with Australia in the 1970s. After alcoholism led to the death of his wife Jannice in late 1974, he returned to Australia. He had also visited, earlier in 1974, to attend the February–March Adelaide Arts Festival. This was over two decades after his unsuccessful visit to his father in Brisbane in 1953. He then returned as a Writer in Residence at Sydney University in 1975. In the new era of the Australia Council and of Porter's rediscovery of Australia, it was the first of several residencies – in Armidale 1977, Melbourne 1983 and Perth 1987 – over the next two decades. He visited Australia nearly every year over that period, also attending arts festivals and academic conferences in Brisbane, Canberra and Melbourne as well as Adelaide. The change for Porter was partly the discovery of his poetry in Australia and the support of the Literature Board of the Australia Council. Several scholars and universities took an interest in this learned, if non-graduate, poet who had a sense of English and Western tradition and also engaged with the 'modern' world.

The change was also more fundamental. It involved his relationships with his past, with Australian society and with the nature of Australia. The newly single parent with two young daughters came to terms with his feelings about his childhood and his relations with his single-parent father, who had done what he believed was best for young Porter, even if that meant sending him off to boarding school. In the words of his biographer, Bruce Bennett, at times during his 'exile' in Britain 'Porter used Australia as a place on his mental map where things went fundamentally "wrong"'.[66] Porter himself later reflected on how his views were changing:

> This is where I've been unfair to Australia and why a lot of Australians are deeply suspicious of me. I tend to associate what was probably a personal and individual experience or fate with the place; I tend to blame the place where it happened. And therefore I'm inclined to think of Australia as a country where everything goes wrong and people are inept, where somehow it's the opposite of Paradise, the left-handed land in a world of right-handed places. This is exactly what it is not today: today it's a prosperous country with booming capitalism, savage nationalism and a total feeling of success and gung-ho; but it wasn't like that when I was young.[67]

The reaffirmation of the country from which he had alienated himself was, as with many expatriates, focused on the land more than on the society. Although he would continue to write in adversarial terms about 'gung-ho' Australia, this conflictual, dialectical stance was part of his poetic relationship with so many subjects in the modern world. It would take a specifically contemporary form when he jousted in the 1980s with Les Murray, who was universally regarded as the greatest living Australian poet. The self-styled peasant mandarin of the New South Wales North Coast and the London metropolitan played against each other – Murray's rural Virgil to Porter's urban Ovid. (In some ways their interaction echoed, almost, the poetic debate between Henry Lawson and Banjo Paterson, expressing pessimistic and optimistic views of the bush, nearly a century before.) Murray reflected on his appreciation of Porter's work, despite Porter's expatriation. Once, Murray had felt a traditional disgust for the expatriate writer who had 'betrayed' his birthright for the blandishments of London:

> How dare he run off and court the supercilious literary circles of London. How dare he look back at Australia with nothing but scorn. I even used to make snide remarks about selling out one's country to curry favour with the metropolitan enemy.[68]

Having encountered both the poetry and the poet, Murray now renounced this earlier condemnation. Mutual respect, as Les retreated to the farm and

Peter metaphorically came to visit, saw Virgil and Ovid reconciled. Jousting had given way to dialogue, to a creative dialectic, an engagement over the character of Australian culture and of their profession. In poetry and prose, this dialectic deepened an understanding of both the imperial–colonial–natural legacy of Australia and of the character of Australian writing, both in the bush and in the 'big smoke', whether London or Sydney or Melbourne.

Porter's visit to Arthur Boyd at his other home – Riversdale on the Shoalhaven on the South Coast of New South Wales – during 1975 brought an intimacy with the Australian bush. Porter was regenerated by the experience, despite his warnings against the limitations of roots. He had earlier, in 1973, remarked on the negative consequences of roots: 'They may be twisted under the surface, and they may hold you there when you should go'. But these were perhaps his familial roots, both immediate and stretching back to Australia in the 1850s. In contrast he did not feel estranged or discontented in London. He was, perhaps, 'an air-plant, without roots', enjoying London as 'an ideally artificial place to live', somewhere he could 'feel at home in all the better for lacking the roots I had in Australia'. Or was this a consoling fantasy? The Shoalhaven led to an affirmation of nature in its Australian form. No longer did he see Australia 'through eyes blurred by personal experience and soured by the traumas of childhood'. In his seven weeks at the Shoalhaven he discovered an 'Arcadian Australia', glimpsed 'the real land, and it was as if a mask had fallen from a handsome face'.[69]

Excited by the Australian cultural revival, Porter had no time for cultural or political chauvinism, for 'blunt nationalism/A long winded emphatic, kelpie yapping/About our land'. Nor did he approve of the isolationist or xenophobic corollaries of national self-confidence, such as the view that 'all the rest of the world is out of step with Australia'.[70] He defended the English at a time when nationalism made criticising the declining imperial mother country a popular sport of the new cultural classes, a kind of inversion of the metropolitan elites' traditional contempt for the colonies.

Porter's return in the mid-1970s, his rediscovery of Australia and his renewed optimism also involved a romantic relationship. His muse, whom he met first at the 1974 Adelaide Festival and again when he returned to Sydney in 1975, the Sydney journalist and writer Sally McInerney, would help bring him back into love with Australia. Life was complicated, however. The tyranny of distance over the next seven years was one pressure, even with visits in both directions and an Italian interlude. McInerney separated from her husband, the poet Geoffrey Lehmann, and there were children involved – her three and Porter's two. His connection with her was part of a 'renewal of life', as well as a renewal of his relationship with Australia. Many expatriates had maintained part of their connection with their own society through partners. Some had travelled with them (Leo McKern and Jane Holland, Lloyd and Lesley Lamble, Sidney and Cynthia Nolan, Arthur and

Left Jane Holland, Australian star. (Australian Broadcasting Corporation)
Right Leo McKern as Ned Kelly. (National Library of Australia)

Otranto – on which sailed Jill Neville, Peter Porter and Murray Sayle.
(State Library of New South Wales)

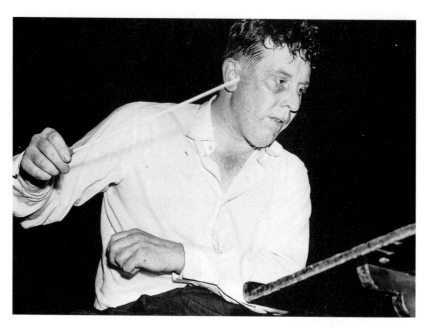

Charles Mackerras hard at work. (Australian Broadcasting Corporation)

Family times – Joan Sutherland, Adam Bonynge and Richard Bonynge.
(Joan Sutherland)

Peter Finch boiling the billy on location. (National Library of Australia)

Swimming pool in Dolphin Square, where Peter Finch, writer Russell Braddon and actor Alan White lived. (Stephen Alomes)

Alister Kershaw, writer and bohemian, *en France* (at home in Sury-en-Vaux, Sancerre). (Stephen Alomes)

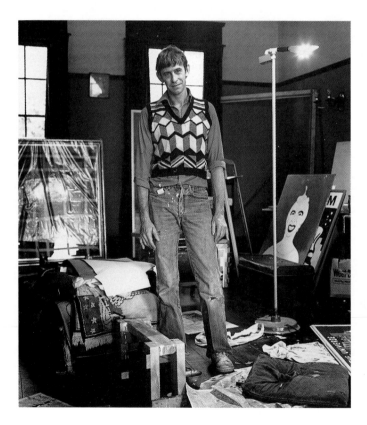

Martin Sharp in his studio. (Greg Weight)

Left Sidney Nolan, artist and designer of *Il Trovatore* for the Australian Opera. (Australian Broadcasting Corporation) *Right* Arthur Boyd, artist. (Greg Weight)

Left David Lumsdaine, composer. (Belinda Webster)
Right Don Banks, composer and Australia Council Music Board enthusiast. (Australian Music Centre)

Phillip Knightley, journalist and writer having coffee in Potts Point.
(Stephen Alomes)

Francis Lymburner in repose. (Geoff Hawkshaw, National Library of Australia)

Yvonne Boyd). Others met them in London (the journalists John Pilger and Scarth Flett) or met on a visit to Australia (Charles Osborne and Ken Thomson). After the tragic death of Porter's wife, this regeneration in Australia was part of a more fundamental renaissance at a time when ancient angsts might have reclaimed him. The complication of his daughters who, having lost their mother, feared that they would lose their familiar world if he went to Australia and took them with him, added to the difficulties.[71] Over time and distance, he would be increasingly drawn back to his London milieux, while still maintaining many of his Australian poetic and personal connections.

Porter's rediscovery of Australia was returned in kind by an Australian appreciation of him and his work. Although some Australian poets and poetry reviewers remained sceptical about what they saw as this London institution, and some English reviewers still felt distant from this 'outsider', Porter was increasingly valued in both countries. However, the critical study *Modern English Poetry* (1986) by the English reviewer John Lucas did not include Porter. Lucas, who admired Porter's work, saw him as separate from the English tradition, possessed of an outsider's vantage point: 'Porter's language ... is truly an international language, quite simply because it isn't the language of any native English poet and because he can do things with it that no English poet can. It's dazzlingly eclectic'. Porter's ability to move through a variety of subjects with ease, his versatility, seemed un-English to this reviewer. Too 'literary' and allusive for some in Australia (and Britain), he was too international for some English ears and eyes. His versatility had several possible sources including tradition. Whether it also came from cross-fertilisation – the Australian in England – or from an expatriate richness of imagination, or even from the everyday stimuli of life (including advertising), Porter's strength placed him outside immediate British and Australian traditions. Interestingly, it was a Scottish poet and reviewer, Douglas Dunn, who recognised the 'personal realignment' and 'recovered respect for his background and nationality' in his mid-1970s work.[72]

The lives of Peter Porter and Jill Neville seemed inextricably intertwined. It was as if the first great passion on the boat would remain with them forever more. Sometimes those furies following them took the most prosaic form – in the proximity of living quarters and other events. In the early 1960s, Jill Neville had a relationship with the poet Al Alvarez. In the 1970s, at the time of the Porter–McInerney connection, Jill Neville was living 'seven miles from Sydney and a thousand miles from care' across the harbour at Manly. McInerney was working in Sydney journalism when Neville, the returned expatriate, missed a position editing the literary pages at the *National Times*. In the early 1990s, Jill lived happily with her husband, the scientist Professor Louis Wolpert, in a garden flat at 63a Belsize Park Gardens, NW3, just a few doors from where Porter had flatted with Roger Covell and David Lumsdaine in the 1950s.

Combat at the Conference: Charles Comes Back

Peter Porter's poetic self-definition, his adversarially intellectual relationship with countries, mores and ideas, was generally controlled and polite, though provocative. Charles Osborne, in contrast, relished an adversarial role, choosing conflict on the stage with the broadsword or the gun over the foil of the poet. He went into battle in 1976 when he returned as a guest of the Adelaide Festival. In the deferential or 'culturally cringing' Australian way, the arts administrator from London was asked to give the opening address at Writers' Week. It was traditional. Keynote speeches in Australia are usually given by English or American, or occasionally European, visitors. In the opposite, anti-deferential, Australian way Porter was given a hard time, both by the editors of quarterly magazines and by writers. The former rejected the expatriate – or to many of them, 'quasi-Pom' – telling them how to suck eggs. After all, the small magazine was an Australian institution which had reached a more developed stage than its less common English equivalent. The writers were even less pleased upon hearing Osborne's suggestion that Literature Board money should subsidise publication and distribution of books, rather than allocating 'large sums' for 'grants to writers' or 'handouts [to authors] to encourage them to write'. The successful London writer wrote about this episode later in his memoirs, without any apparent cognisance of the colonial character and smaller size of the Australian market:

> I could have saved my breath, for the Australia Council continues to fling money indiscriminately at the talented and the untalented. They then frequently have to thrust grants at publishers to coerce them into publishing the books that have been written, which the bookshops fail to sell and which no one even wants to borrow from libraries.[73]

His elaborate conceit concerning the literary process in Australia depicted Antipodean folly in a spirit not too distant from that of his friend Barry Humphries. The problem with the Osborne rhetorical dismissal was twofold. First, Australian novels, like Australian plays, films and television, were becoming popular. Second, despite this change, without assistance many of the talented would not have been published.

Osborne's dismissive tone, as expressed later in his memoirs, suggested the style of his attacks – more bursts from a literary AK47 than strokes of historic broadswords. Such assaults led to expatriates being given a 'hard time' when they returned. Perhaps Osborne was provoked. Another Osborne, John, the once angry young man of English theatre, had a similar experience of conflict. When, with his agent Robin Dalton (Eakin), he was a guest at one of the first national playwrights' conferences in Canberra, a young woman writer 'suddenly attacked' them. 'We don't need you Poms out here', she declared. The visiting 'imperial' expert, and his well-spoken expatriate minder, were more than put in their place. Unfairly or not, they were 'given a hard time of it' in this era of assertive nationalism in the longtime cultural colony.[74]

Changing Times, Growing Ties

Time, circumstances and family tied Peter Porter and Jill Neville to London, and Charles Osborne declared that he would only return if the great opera houses of the world and the Australian continent could be joined together. While, like Russell Braddon, these three London-based writers commuted occasionally, the Australian literary scene was changing. Literature Board fellowships and residencies in universities provided opportunities for Porter and Neville to work in Australia, and Braddon made television documentaries and edited books on the changing Australia of the Bicentennial decade. At the same time, other Australian writers were making their own way in the world.

The changes were more fundamental than merely providing opportunities for expatriate return, as Osborne's testy time in Adelaide suggested. When Russell Braddon sought to interest Australian writers in the British connection during a 1970s television debate, it was clear that he was barking up the wrong tree. Similarly, the Australian Writers' Guild's lack of sympathy for the view that Australian television writers in Britain should be counted as Australian writers for quota purposes was another mirror of the working out of vestigial colonial–imperial tensions, often to the expatriates' cost.[75]

Later generations of writers spent time in London or Britain, but often either as part of the big overseas trip that many young Australians made, or in mid-career. They did not need to travel to London to begin a career as a writer. Even in the mid-1950s, the young Tasmanian writer Christopher Koch worked in Lyons tea-houses and then in an office addressing envelopes, along with the other 'Little People' as he termed them, on his great overseas trip.[76] Despite having a sense of the mystique of the imperial city he also travelled to India and later to the United States and Southeast Asia. From the late 1950s, other waves of writers came to London, but few stayed on. Many travelled, also discovering their own country and other worlds – from Asia to North America. Craig McGregor spent four years in London in the 1960s, returned, and later, in 1969, went to New York on a Harkness Fellowship. The poet and playwright Ray Mathew and the art critic Robert Hughes both went to New York after several years in London.[77] From 1965 to 1973, Morris Lurie spent nearly a decade in Greece, Denmark, Morocco and England, with visits to New York. Thomas Keneally, who came to fiction after leaving the priesthood, journeyed widely. He lived in England in 1970–71 and later spent periods in the USA. David Malouf, then a teacher, spent from 1959 to 1968 in Britain and Europe, teaching in London and then at Birkenhead from the early 1960s. He then returned to Sydney rather than his native Brisbane. When he committed himself fully to writing in the 1980s, his English connections continued. However, he noted that his half-English familial origins would be less fashionable amongst commentators than his Lebanese ancestry or his occasional residence in Tuscany. Morris West lived in Austria, Italy, England and the USA from 1955 to 1980, before settling again in Sydney. His life, like his books, was becoming international, as he explored belief and the contemporary world in a turbulent era.

From the late 1960s an Australian publishing industry emerged, mainly carried on by the Australian extensions of British and later American companies, as well as local companies, including a revived Angus & Robertson. Improved communications also made it possible for a writer to live in Australia, and to live overseas for shorter periods, and to become – like Thomas Keneally, White and West, Peter Carey and Colleen McCullough – international writers, though in differing styles.

The quantitative change was tangible in the era of the new nationalism. Popular interest in Australian works was complemented by funding from the Literature Board of the Australia Council, still necessary given the small Australian market and Australia's exposure to all the works of English-language publishing. In 1972 only 18 novels were published. By 1985, the Literature Board had subsidised 1000 titles (fiction, non-fiction, poetry) and Australian-originated books had increased from 10% to 50% of the total.[78]

The new order was not just an Australian one supplanting a British one. In an international era, Australian authors, such as Keneally and West, also addressed non-Australian subjects. Australia was not immune from the international rationalisation of publishing companies and the rising dominance of accountants and marketers who measured achievement by the bottom line on sales rather than by the quality of their titles. At the same time communications made it possible for the writer in pursuit of a world market to live in Australia and to be published in London or New York. A new era was dawning for the Australian arts, one which would bring its own complications, not totally unlike those of an earlier imperial–colonial era.

Chapter 7

Grander Stages: New Seasons for Australian Playwrights and Actors[1]

In 1956, ten years after the end of World War II, it seemed that Australian actors, including those who had escaped the then depressing Australian stage, might have a career in their own country. Had the moment for an Australian theatre, even a national theatre, come at last? Australian plays, a career for Australian actors in their own country and higher standards – were they now all possible? The critic Geoffrey Hutton's article in the *International Theatre Annual* for 1956 was headed 'Australia 1955–56: A Year of New Hopes'. Depressed by the 'stamp of sterling silver' on so many imported productions with their imported stars in the previous year, Hutton believed that 'the future may be brighter'.[2] New companies and an exciting Australian play augured well at last.

Expatriate actors and writers discerned some positive signs. First, several actors returned to tour Australia: Leo McKern and Keith Michell toured with Anthony Quayle's Shakespearean Stratford upon Avon Memorial Theatre Company in 1952–53. McKern later played the title role in Douglas Stewart's verse play *Ned Kelly* in 1956. Richard Beynon, who toured Australia in 1954, and whose play *The Shifting Heart* won the 1956 Sydney Journalists Club playwriting competition, hoped that a new dawn of Australian theatrical writing had arisen. For Keith Michell, success came in a different way. Combining 'an admired elegance' and an 'Australian dynamism', he found a new vehicle for his talents in the musical *Irma la Douce* in London and on Broadway from 1958 to 1961. Michael Blakemore made a slower progress in repertory companies around Britain.[3] In 1959, however, he appeared in a Shakespeare season at Stratford. Jocelyn Rickards and Loudon Sainthill had moved much faster. Rickards worked as a designer on Marilyn Monroe's

English film, *The Prince and the Showgirl*. Sainthill was in demand at Stratford, the Old Vic, Covent Garden and Sadler's Wells. His sets ranged from an *Antony and Cleopatra* for Robert Helpmann to those of West End musicals.[4] Alan White was working regularly in film, while David Nettheim and Bill Kerr were performing in radio and TV comedy. They were just a few of the soldiers in the invading army of Australian actors, several of whom, including Walter Brown, worked with the Royal Shakespeare Company, which had been formed in 1961.

Despite these encouraging developments, the question of whether the Australian stage would be reborn remained. Would Australia remain a farm for talent, its own stage dominated by visiting stars in West End comedies and American musicals for J. C. Williamson's, and local fare be found only in radio drama and little theatres?

A 'Summer' for Australian Theatre?

As Hutton noted, two disparate but related events returned the prospect of an Australian theatre to centre stage in the mid-1950s. One was the creation of the Australian Elizabethan Theatre Trust as a formal body to support the performing arts in Australia. Even more than most arts organisations, it was linked to polite and even imperial society, particularly given the distaste of its first director, the Englishman Hugh Hunt, for working-class accents and drama set in the backyard. The second event, following the American plays of Tennessee Williams and Arthur Miller and anticipating in their frank speech the English drama of the 'angry young men', was very close to the theatrical realism of the backyard. Ray Lawler's play *Summer of the Seventeenth Doll*, which depicted Queensland canecutters on their annual journey to visit their girlfriends in working-class Carlton, was a long way from the respectable drawing room of West End plays.[5]

The Trust and the *Doll* may at first have seemed an unlikely combination. The Trust had begun its theatrical existence with a Terence Rattigan play starring Dame Sybil Thorndike and Dame Judith Anderson, who had returned from the US to play the title role in *Medea*. However, the Trust took up the new play, the *Doll*, for a national tour. It was first performed by the Union Theatre Repertory Company (UTRC) in Melbourne for a season of a fortnight, opening on 28 November 1955. Then, Sir Laurence Olivier bought the rights for performances in Britain and New York. Would an Australian play, performed by Australian actors, speaking in Australian accents, be the beginning of an Australian native drama? Would, as Ray Lawler hoped, those 'people back home ... devoted to the overseas theatre (which means the English)' now take a 'real interest in their own country' and in the work of Australian dramatists?[6]

The messages sent out by the *Doll* were contradictory, however. Most were positive. The *Doll* introduced Australian culture to an English audience at the time of an English discovery of Australia. The Royal Visit of 1954, the Olympic Games of 1956 and the increasing profile of Australian performers, writers and artists in Britain engendered a new receptiveness. A *Times* reviewer, writing on the March 1956 Imperial Institute exhibition of Australian contemporary painting, observed:

> A mere 20 years ago, the name 'Australia' might have excited only, in many a languid mind, a casual, and even patronising, attention. But now all has changed; and if Australia, to-day, is a continent that excites a new respect and curiosity, one reason may be the influx of so many gifted Australian artists – singers, dancers, actors, writers and, especially, painters – here among us.[7]

Coming to London in 1957, in the wake of the 'angry young man' plays led by John Osborne's *Look Back in Anger*, the *Doll* found a theatrical climate receptive to different experiences as well as to frank speech.

The presentation of the *Doll* in London was not, however, without vestigial elements of the imperial–colonial relationship. These came with the aura of its entrepreneur Sir Laurence Olivier and a first night audience which included Vivien Leigh and Terence Rattigan. Olivier's imprimatur guaranteed the bona fides of the work. Although it came from what some must have thought was 'an obscure company from the colonies', Olivier's role and the critics' approval suggested that it would be the vehicle for legitimising an Australian theatre. At last the prescription of 'Dr' Olivier some years back would be filled. Australia had now produced a playwright of its own.[8]

Sub-editors and some reviewers in the English and Scottish press occasionally succumbed to 'Austcliché' in their enthusiasm. They noted that the play 'crackles like a bushfire' and was 'bonza'. 'This *Doll* is Fair Dinkum, Cobber, Just Fair Dinkum', they said of the *Doll*'s performances in Nottingham, Edinburgh and then London. However, they did sense the significance of this 'Australian native drama'.[9] In interviews in London and New York, Lawler remarked on how overseas success might have a positive impact on the growth of an Australian national theatre. Despite the group of people inclined to reject their own theatre, times might be changing. Now 'our dramatists are beginning to come up'. In New York, he remarked that proper Australians were dismayed at the prospect 'that the English would get the mistaken idea that all Australians were canecutters and barmaids'.[10]

Don Ross, in the *New York Herald Tribune*, portrayed a playwright with a university accent but a blue-collar background, one who loved his native land, and wanted to transcend a derivative culture. He had little time for the 'Mock English Australians [who] come back from London with Savile Row suits and

English accents' – in Lawler's phrase, the 'Piccadilly Bushmen'![11] The *Doll* would be even more paradoxical than Guthrie's unrealised 'national theatre' scheme discussed earlier. As Lawler himself remarked, 'Usually, a play starts on Broadway, goes to London and reaches Australia last. We have made theatrical history by reversing the procedure'. It also came, as Kenneth Tynan noted, at a time of the opening up of London's cultural horizons to social groups from beyond well-spoken Britain. The stage now accepted new voices, whether those of the workers and the provinces or ones from the far-flung reaches of the Commonwealth.

In Australia the success of the *Doll* opened the way for other plays. Richard Beynon's *The Shifting Heart* was toured by the Trust after its initial production in 1957, while in 1959, *The Slaughter of Saint Teresa's Day* introduced another new playwriting talent in Peter Kenna. However, as the young playwright Ray Mathew argued in a 1959 *Current Affairs Bulletin* survey of the state of theatre in Australia, fundamental problems remained. New playwrights lacked dramaturgical skill and there was still no Australian acting style.[12] As a result the summer suggested by the *Doll* did not last. Mathew's plays secured only amateur production in Australia. In 1960, he went to London on an Arts Council of Great Britain bursary, his play *The Life of the Party* having earlier had a short season there. He lived in London until 1968, and then in New York. Peter Kenna went to London after the performance of *The Slaughter of Saint Teresa's Day*. He did not return to Australia until 1971. Other losses occurred without physical expatriation. Oriel Gray's play *The Torrents*, which shared the 1955 Playwrights Advisory Board prize with the *Doll*, was not taken up commercially. Patrick White recoiled against the rejection, by the Governors of the Board of the 1962 Adelaide Festival, of his play *The Ham Funeral*, and the public reaction to his later plays; he left playwriting alone for over a decade.

Neither Australian provincialism (the fear of the new, the controversial and the shocking) nor the colonial cultural cringe, the assumption of the inferiority of Australian indigenous work, had gone away. Perhaps that latter attitude had been encapsulated by Prime Minister Menzies when he bet Dr H. C. Coombs, creator of the Trust and chair of the Commonwealth Bank, five shillings that the *Doll* would not succeed in Britain. Menzies lost the bet but his provincial values and low estimation of Australian work seemed to win the larger argument over the next few years.[13]

One 'Day' ... Many Years

Alan Seymour experienced both the dream of an Australian theatre and the often nightmarish moments of new playwrights. *The One Day of the Year* introduced Seymour all too suddenly into the conflicts which divided

Australian society during the 1950s and 1960s. His drama of generational and class conflict on Anzac Day had been stimulated by the expatriate writer Alan Moorehead's account of Gallipoli as a military blunder of horrific proportions, as well as by childhood awareness of alcoholism and everyday drama. The Board of Governors of the 1960 Adelaide Festival rejected the play as likely to offend the RSL (the powerful Returned Services League), and ex-servicemen, by its depiction of Alf, the drunken ex-digger, and its controversial attack on the national day. It was only performed, and even then in an obscure Adelaide venue, due to the determination of the amateur director Jean Marshall. As with that other approach to Australian military tradition, *Rusty Bugles* of 1948, its banning proved its best publicity. *One Day* would be taken up by the Australian Drama Company of the Trust in Sydney and by the UTRC in Melbourne, which also toured it interstate. It went to London, where its cast was mainly that of the original Sydney production of 1961 (including Ron Haddrick, Nita Pannell, Reg Dye and Patricia Conolly, along with Lewis Fiander, who had arrived in London from Melbourne). It was also filmed for television by GTV9 in Melbourne in 1962.[14] In the same year, Ken Warren and Madge Ryan were amongst the expatriate stars of Seymour's television adaptation of the play for the BBC.

The ABC commissioned Seymour to write a play, *Lean Liberty*, which it then rejected because it was perceived to be too sympathetic to Communism. With his work banned and then suppressed, Seymour left for London. There a commercial television station bought *Lean Liberty* within three weeks for five times the fee offered in Australia. Seymour was already going to London anyway, to prepare for the production of *The One Day of the Year*; the Trust had paid half of his one-way airfare. He 'didn't know then that a full-time return would not happen for 33 years'. At a time when British television was commissioning one-off plays, Seymour fell into work as a writer, and a dozen of his TV plays appeared over the next few years. After being interviewed by the Queensland expatriate Charles Osborne on the BBC, he acquired a second string to his bow as a theatre reviewer, first for *London Magazine* and then the *Observer*. *London Magazine*'s editor was Alan Ross, whose interest in Australian culture followed his cricketing interests. He had recruited Charles Osborne as his assistant editor, and published articles by several Australians, including Ray Mathew and Sidney Nolan, and poetry by Peter Porter. Seymour also completed a novel of *The One Day of the Year*, which was published in 1967.

As a playwright Seymour was both ahead of and behind his times. He came after the new theatrical naturalism in Britain, but several years before the alternative theatre confronted conventional political and social values in Melbourne and Sydney in the late Sixties. He would share a persistent theme with later playwrights – Melbourne's Jack Hibberd and Sydney's Alex Buzo. They were frustrated at the relative lack of interest of the newly established companies such as the Old Tote in Sydney and the UTRC (from 1968 known as the Melbourne Theatre Company – MTC) in developing and staging original Australian plays. This sense of being alienated from their own theatre, of being ostracised, had an extra dimension for Seymour and other expatriates. They were not only frustrated 'indigenes', as Alex Buzo termed himself, they were also alienated expatriates, whose distant voices were easily dismissed or ignored or even condemned. Seymour developed an attitude to Australia that mirrored contemporary conflicts. His rebellion against authority became conflated with an expatriate frustration with Australia. When two of his plays did not reach production he identified himself as an exile, thinking, he later recalled, that he would 'never go back', that he would 'stay away for fucking-ever!'.

Distance, especially cultural distance, played a part in that other great frustration for the scriptwriter, abandoned projects. Seymour was particularly unlucky in being destined to relive history. In the late 1970s, he was working on a filmscript for David Ireland's novel of workplace alienation, *The Unknown Industrial Prisoner*. It had to be abandoned in 1978 when it lost government funding because it had met with the disfavour of the conservative Fraser government and the interference of the minister, Bob Ellicott. Understandably, Alan Seymour couldn't believe he was 'going through all that again'. Australia was a land of tight budgets, as well as provincial repression, as another of Seymour's experiences demonstrated. In this case, a South Australian Film Corporation mini-series, based on Henry Handel Richardson's novel *The Fortunes of Richard Mahony*, was abandoned as too expensive. For Seymour, it had meant 'two years' hard labour' without result.

Alan Seymour analysed one aspect of the problem in his 1977 piece, 'Australian Theatre – Afterword from an Exile'. Effectively, he lamented the continued colonialism of the theatre. English theatre directors, however well-meaning, were like colonial governors. They sought to create provincial repertory companies on English models, for to them Australia was an extension of the provinces, however distant. In Melbourne, Sydney and Brisbane, the English quartet of John Sumner, Hugh Hunt, Alan Edwards and Robert Quentin were the principals of the first major companies and of NIDA, the new National Institute for Dramatic Art which had been established in Sydney during 1958. A variant on Guthrie's 'import' scheme was at work again, in the recruitment of imperial proconsuls to run local companies and institutions, as well as English actors coming in touring companies. Although in Britain he personally had 'more encouragement and greater material and creative help from the English than I ever had from my own countrymen', Seymour lamented the English influence in Australia:

> The baleful influence of the English, the detested and detestable English. Their philistinism. Their crass ignorance. Their muddle.

This influence made it 'so difficult to build a viable and continuing Australian theatre tradition'.[15]

Like Guthrie, who had failed to see an adequate role for Australian talent (the question a teenage Seymour had asked him in Perth), the English directors preferred known ways and known people – English in both cases. Hugh Hunt, of the Trust, was a 'gentle, sensitive, timid soul' not used to 'dealing with loud, aggressive, eager, and ambitious Australians'. The result was 'his penchant for trusting only Englishmen temperamentally like himself'. Seymour believed this was 'the single most inhibiting factor on the development of the Australian theatre in the 1950s'. Alex Buzo was even sharper regarding imported English theatre directors, declaring that 'many Poms can't help lopping fifty points off the IQ of any Australian they meet; it's the way they've been brought up'.[16] In Seymour's analysis, the attempt to develop a style of English acting and the failure to recognise the fringe-like seriousness of some little theatre companies – assuming them to be like the English amateur companies – compounded the problems.

Colonial and Working-Class Accents

In a sense this colonial rejection of the local and the attempt to establish English models was natural. Quentin, Sumner and Hunt came to Australia in the 1940s and 1950s, before the *Doll*. At the time, as Ray Lawler reflected, 'there were no Australian plays as such and there was no place for an Australian actor in an Australian theatre'.[17] In this era the colonial cultural cringe pervaded the values of respectable society. For many educated Australians, as well as for some English people, 'culture' and 'Australia' were antonyms.

Despite the earlier success of the *Doll* and *Rusty Bugles*, this self-denial began with the accent. NIDA, which modelled itself on RADA, the Royal Academy of Dramatic Art, encouraged actors to shed their Australian accents. It carried on a tradition already strong, even in radio drama. Madge Ryan did not recall needing an Australian accent before her role in the *Doll*, and Leonard Teale argued that the only accent you didn't need in radio was the Australian accent. Alan Seymour had had elocution lessons when young and Richard Beynon's parents had encouraged him to speak 'properly'. As noted earlier, the linguist A. G. Mitchell had observed that Australia had a colonial shame at having its own way of pronouncing the English language.[18] It was not until the demand in Australian film, television and even drama for Australian speech became overwhelming later in the 1960s that NIDA abandoned its colonial approach to speech training.

Ray Lawler and Richard Beynon shared early experiences rooted in class and theatrically expressed in accent. Lawler grew up in working-class

Footscray, one of eight children from a labourer's family. He left school at 13 and worked in a foundry for ten years. Living in Britain softened, but did not eliminate, the Australian accent which was known to be an impediment for an actor. Lawler started as an actor knowing that 'yous' was the plural of 'you' ('when there was more than one of yers') until an actress, who had shed her Australian accent, taught him the right way to speak. Even then he acquired a 'funny accent' 'halfway between' how he thought he should speak for the theatre and his 'native accent'. As the cast of the *Doll* had 'never played an Australian play before' they all 'consciously worked at their Australian accent'. Not until several decades later, Lawler believed, did using an Australian accent on stage become natural for most Australian actors.

Lawler later provided his own summation of the normal theatrical trajectory in this era when there was no indigenous Australian theatre:

> The first thing you had to do was get rid of your Australian accent or as much of it as you possibly could, that was the absolute essential. What usually happened was that you worked at that, you saved money and you went to England; that was more or less the pattern of what people did unless you were very fortunate and had a voice that was attractive on radio and you went into a radio career.[19]

Class and colonial culture may have met in the diffidence which Richard Beynon and Ray Lawler shared. Both were unusually modest about their achievements in these two plays. Beynon suggested that he was an actor and a script editor and only an occasional writer, while Lawler says that he only intended the *Doll* to be 'a night's entertainment in the theatre'. He seemed almost embarrassed that it had become a national icon and that this made him a kind of national institution. If, ideally, the Australian theatre had 'grown more, the *Doll* would have been a much smaller peak'.[20] This perceived peak phenomenon, whereby the 'peak' was dissociated from any supporting 'mountain range' of artistic works by others, would be found in several fields.

Seymour, the playwright of conflict who was not averse to a scrap himself, was more confident in such matters. However, he was also critical of how little he had achieved. Having grown up with a Protestant work ethic, he sometimes looked back on certain periods (the 1950s, some of his BBC time, later years in Turkey) as almost 'wasted years'. In the 1950s era of 'Menzies' smugness ... and smarminess', 'what was stifling was not work but LIFE'. Professionally, he had directed opera, learned to write for radio and pioneered the adaptation of novels for television. His Turkish sojourn was also 'one of the richest periods of [his] life', offering an 'experience of a different, "non-Anglo" society', including the 'history ... culture [and] day-to-day living' of the Turkish people.

Class and colonial identity came together in expatriate experience. This was not just an Australian theme of fatalism, rooted in the bush or the convict experience. A colonial theatre which felt uncomfortable with Australian subjects produced Australian playwrights burdened with deep anxiety. The colonial–imperial structure of the theatre, which drew these newly successful writers to the greater opportunities of London, also gave that anxiety new dimensions. Lawler carried a rare burden for an Australian writer – too much money. Success led to an unusual reason for staying away – tax. Yet this quiet man also felt overwhelmed by success and its not always happy consequences: by the success of the *Doll* on the one hand, and the failure of the New York season and of the de-Australianised film of the play on the other.

Some influences and results went beyond the professional to the personal. Many creative people and expatriates were shaped by complex or turbulent experiences when growing up. Ray Lawler, who in the 1960s and 1970s lived for periods in Denmark, England and Ireland, was in some ways an isolate. He had had several years of frequent hospitalisation after being burnt by fire when very young, and did not start school until he was seven. After being away from Australia for 14 years he reflected that he had 'become an exile in the same way … as I became an exile from my family … [as] a child in hospital'. Sometimes a gulf in a family nurtured a young talent. As noted earlier, the musician Charles Mackerras came from a family divided between his engineer father's Protestant and Anglo-Saxon practicality and his artistic mother's Catholicism. For the young Alan Seymour in Perth, the problems, as well as the contradictions, were simpler. He was brought up by his sister from the age of ten after the death of his parents.[21]

The psychological contradictions of growing up, and those of professional success and professional difficulty, mattered. The latter, dominated by the lack of a clear Australian future for their work, made going away easier than staying. This was even aside from the specific reasons which drew Beynon back to Britain, Lawler to the northern hemisphere and Seymour to London. Yet it seemed somehow unfair that when the Australian theatrical scene changed they would lose again, except perhaps for Lawler. Despite the success of the *Doll* trilogy in the 1970s, Lawler was sometimes viewed by the critics as out of touch. He felt he was on 'a cleft stick'. He knew that he couldn't write about modern Australia, and he 'didn't feel I could write about the countries I was living in'. Consequently, he had taken the *Doll* story back to an earlier time with two plays written in the 1970s but set in the past – *Kid Stakes* (1975) and *Other Times* (1976). Beynon also went back in his plays – to his own childhood and to the Anzac myth of Simpson and his donkey.

'The first little waves on the shore', as Lawler saw those late 1950s plays, would become big waves affecting the lives and consciousnesses of their creators.[22] Lawler, who experienced success and failure with the *Doll*, saw his play bastardised in the 1959 Hollywood version. Starring Angela Lansbury and Anne Baxter, with Ernest Borgnine and John Mills as the canecutters, it relocated the action from Melbourne to filmic Sydney, and proved a great flop.

Lawler explored the tensions of the expatriate artist in *The Piccadilly Bushman* (1959), which, significantly perhaps, also dealt with turning an Australian novel into a film. Set in the Sydney Eastern Suburbs harbourside house of the Leggats, a rich couple who entertain celebrities, it deals with deep tensions between an expatriate couple, the actor Alec Ritchie and his wife Meg. The Leggats reflect the cringing anxiety of the Australian upper middle classes. Isabel is beside herself with horror when it is suggested that she has an Australian accent, even a light one. Ever since she was a little girl, she had sought to avoid this badge of barbarity.

The tensions between Alec and Meg concern their relationship as well as identity. Meg condemns Alec for selling his soul. 'You don't belong here any more Alec', she says of this Australian who later spits out his view of his native land: 'I loathe and detest this country with everything that's in me … this is the prison in which I spent my first twenty-four years – the sunlit rock on which I sweated until at last I found a way of escape'.

She sees his rise in the British film world as an Anglicising of himself which transcends 'professional necessity'.

> Meg: That's what I told myself. Tricks of the trade. Like that lizard that can change its colour to suit the wallpaper. But it's what it did to you when you eventually found that you could pass yourself off as an Englishman among Englishmen. 'I didn't tell the producer I was an Australian, darling. I thought it might put him against me.' I knew then that it was more than lizard's stuff and I wanted to say something, but all I could think of was that kid's thing – 'You be careful. If the wind changes, you'll stay that way' – and somehow it didn't seem very appropriate.

Nor did she have time for his other approach – 'Get in there first and slap it before they do, that was the idea. Panic them at parties by reciting "I Love a Sunburnt Country" with a great hayseed accent'. Alec had by then 'become something altogether different' – a 'stranger' to her.[23]

Other complex tensions involve Alec, the English film producer Vincent Franklin, the English scriptwriter Stuart Allingham and the Australian writer Douglas O'Shea, who are collaborating on a film based on O'Shea's book. Fundamentally, the professional tensions are about creative control, culture and identity, especially between Britain and Australia. The Englishmen have no doubts about the cultural pecking order. Vincent, according to Stuart, had 'insisted on the entire film unit being sent out from England' as he would 'never feel easy working with Colonials'. 'When it comes to the point, there's something so awfully second-rate about even the best of them.'

One dramatic question in the play concerns whether the writer of the original book, O'Shea, will work on the film script, a subject Ray Lawler was conscious of after the unsuccessful 'Hollywooding' of the *Doll*. Vincent moves to drop O'Shea who is, in this milieu, unacceptable. Meg can at least take perverse pleasure in describing Alec and others of his nationality-shedding ilk:

> All their little lives they've heard stories of this high and mighty roost, and eventually they've had to make the long trek back to see if they can't fly up there and crow their heart out. And some of them actually make it. Alec, for instance. He crows with the best of them. But for every one that's accepted up on the perch, there's a thousand scratching around at the bottom of it. They'll never be part of the prize flock, but they're all too blind or proud or silly to know it, and somewhere – hemmed in among that mob – that's where you'll find me.

But perhaps Alec, the Piccadilly Bushman, with his English suits and accents, like his English mentors, didn't 'trust [himself] in the bush'.[24]

Class, Colonialism and Culture

The late 1950s playwrights were unlucky. Paradoxically, the Australian theatrical renaissance came at a time when the theatre was set within a middle-class society whose provincial cultural values were shaped by respectability and Anglophilia. The theatre was associated with the society pages and ladies from 'the blue rinse set'. Even if this stereotype is a slight exaggeration, it was no longer a popular theatre; popular audiences had decamped to the cheaper and more accessible pleasures of radio, television and film.

When into that theatre erupted three plays by playwrights of working-class origins, plays which captured the idiom of Australian working-class and popular speech, it was a challenge to the colonial assumption of the theatre that drama came from elsewhere. Theatre administrators and audiences were not used to hearing broad Australian voices on the stage or even seeing plays by Australian authors. Alan Seymour was exceptional in having seen *Rusty Bugles* as a teenager in Perth. Since there was no tradition of serious Australian theatre, there was no perception of the playwright as a canary in a mine, a critical sensor of society's problems.

Theatre ideally meant an English theatrical knight or dame doing Shakespeare or, on the popular stage, an amusing light comedy with stars from the West End or Broadway. When the language and conflicts of the *Doll*, the *Day* and the *Heart* breached the wall of that colonial culture, audiences at first laughed with the 'pleasurable shock of recognition' because they recognised the idiom.[25] This was as true in Melbourne as it was for the Australians who heard familiar voices on the opening night of the *Doll* in London.

The thrill of broad Australian speech was short-lived. Although Alan Seymour believed that audiences wanted Australian characters, the box office for new Australian plays put on by the Trust, the UTRC and the Old Tote suggested that they did not. Often they lost money. In the land of the colonial cultural cringe, 'Culture', like 'Stars', still came from somewhere else. That view had not disappeared entirely several decades later. In 1997 the Adelaide Theatre Company was criticised for its 'gumnut nationalism' by the arts observer Christopher Pearson when it decided on a program of only Australian retrospective plays for the next few years.[26] Earlier in the decade the Sydney Theatre Company's Australia Council grant was under threat, one reason being its lack of Australian plays.

Like the Nigerian colonials who looked up to the 'been tos' ('been to Oxford', 'been to London') in the 1960s, the provincial elites respected those who had been blessed in Britain. In theatre, this meant the graduates of the Young Vic theatre school or those who had performed with the Old Vic, the Shakespeare Memorial Theatre Company (later Royal Shakespeare Company) or the National Theatre. Perhaps, even after several decades, this cringe had not totally disappeared.

Had the plays of Lawler, Beynon and Seymour come a decade later their lives might have been different. The bracing air of the conflicts of the Vietnam era and the new middle class, the children of the baby boom, provided a leaven in Australian theatre. Australian speech and conflicts became the staple of several fledgling companies at a time when the accent was moving from the polarities of 'cultivated' and 'broad' to 'general'. This generation assertively made its cultural declaration of independence by repudiating well-spoken theatre at the same time as it rejected the British monarchy, American imperialism and Australian political and cultural colonialism.

In companies like the Australian Performing Group in Melbourne and the Nimrod in Sydney, but rather less at the Old Tote and the Melbourne Theatre Company, new Australian plays became part of theatregoers' staple diet. Yet, for the expatriates who had grown up with the ruling assumption that theatre came from Britain, Europe and America, expatriation was as logical as had been Australian theatre's denial of its own identity. It was its natural corollary. Having grown up at a time when, in Alan Seymour's words, 'there was virtually no Australian material in the theatre, on television, on film', London called loudly.[27] When Seymour's next play was suppressed, Australia seemed a provincial and repressive society rather than just a cultural colony. Leaving made very good sense.

Later, the expatriates' worst youthful nightmares would return if they received an equivocal welcome back. Australians still salivated over the great from overseas. Was that not the Australian definition of greatness – success in the wider world? However, the Australians from overseas and their nervous attempts to rediscover Australia in their writing were not always favourably received. Was it that they were 'a little out of touch', as Alan Seymour recognised in the 1970s.[28] Or, in the new nationalist Australia of the 1970s, did the 'ex-patriots' – as the word was often spelled – bear the mark of Cain? Having been too early, they were now too late and too far away to be fully part of the theatrical renaissance. Certainly their timing was out.

The failure of Seymour, Lawler and Beynon to continue their careers in Australia also meant a failure to realise their potential. As different as their personalities and experiences were, they reflected the costs and benefits of relocating to London and Europe, and the expatriate artists' theme of frustration – sometimes with country, sometimes with self, sometimes with circumstances.

The *Doll* was not the first landing craft of an Australian cultural invasion. Earlier ships coming to Tilbury and Southampton and planes landing at Heathrow carried Australian actors from a previous generation leaving their country in search of a career. However, the cast of the *Doll* was a major deposit of theatrical talent. After working in the *Doll* in New York, Madge Ryan returned to London to begin a distinguished career on the English stage. Other talented arrivals were June Jago and Ken Warren, among many others. Jago would go on to a successful British career, at the Royal Shakespeare Company, the Royal Court, and in several British films, including playing an Aussie opposite Bill Kerr, the son of Wagga Wagga, in *The Captain's Table* (1959). She later returned to Melbourne to act and to teach. Some cast members 'lived out' their roles in real life. Ken Warren, who played the defeated Roo in the *Doll*, died at an early age. Fenella Maguire, who played 'Bubba' in search of love, found a new stage for her performing skills. Marrying a French millionaire, she hosted functions for Australian and other international tennis players at Monte Carlo, and later settled in Paris. Richard Pratt, who played the new top dog Johnnie Dowd, was called back to Australia when his father had a heart attack, which was a loud cry for him to return to run the family business. Soon he dominated a different sphere, fusing Johnnie's toughness with business acumen, becoming a multi-millionaire in cardboard and recycling and a 'prince', a leading player and patron, in the politics of the arts, business and sport.

Once again Australia produced talent for London rather than for its own theatre. London had long been Australia's other stage, along with those of its state capital cities. Now it seemed to some observers its third stage for performance, after Sydney and Melbourne. The new commercial television stations spent their money on transmission and relay towers, and American sitcoms and Westerns (and then sat back and counted their profits), while the ABC showed British programs. The opportunities for an actor in Australia seemed few. Like Peter Finch a decade earlier, the cast of the *Doll* were beacons calling young actors north.

Richard Beynon's Unshifting Heart

Richard Beynon felt a continuing tension over expatriation and his career choices. *The Shifting Heart* toured Australia for a year from 1957. Olivier presented it at the Duke of York's Theatre in London in 1959, where it was produced by Leo McKern, and Ken Warren, Madge Ryan and David Nettheim were among its cast. It might have launched Beynon into either an Australian or an English playwriting career. In a sense, it did neither.

Chance, in life and work, kept him in England. In the 1950s, after touring *Witness for the Prosecution* in Australia, he hoped for work. When nothing turned up, he offered himself to John Sumner at the UTRC, hoping that this successful tour and his English work might allow him to join the company. Beynon's response to Sumner's reply – 'But I am sorry, Richard, but I have a full complement' – was devastation – 'that really knocked me'. Whatever the cause, and Beynon believed that both he and Sumner were insecure at the time, he felt it left a legacy of resentment; none of his later plays have been done by the Melbourne Theatre Company.

In 1964, he lamented angrily the lack of scriptwriting training in Australia in a letter to the Melbourne *Age*. He was not surprised at the Trust's disappointment at being unable to find new Australian plays through a playwriting competition. He found it was 'understandable, but not altogether unexpected, when one considers what hasn't been done to help aspiring playwrights to learn the craft'. Occasional attempts and work by adult education bodies weren't enough. More impressed by 'the latest idea to commission playwrights', which would be 'at least an acknowledgment that the writer exists', he found the plan to assist one playwright only a rather meagre beginning. What was needed was 'the creation of a playwrights' workshop', an anticipation of developments a decade later.[29]

Beynon's career was also shaped by personal circumstances. The sudden and early death of his wife left him with the responsibility of raising his young children, aged three, six and eight. Continuing work at the BBC as a script editor and producer on the innovative police series, *Z Cars* and *Softly Softly*, was both satisfying and useful for paying the bills. Although living in suburban Barnes, he was never quite the immigrant. He returned to Australia around a dozen times over the next few decades, maintaining the expatriate's umbilical cord to his homeland. He was also unconfident of his abilities as a playwright. Perhaps, like Lawler's modesty, this low self-esteem was the product of colonial cultural relations. The two plays he wrote over the following years were also Australian. One, *Summer Shadows* (1985), concerned his upbringing. The other, *Simpson, J 202* (1989), pursued the national myth of Simpson and the donkey at Gallipoli. When asked why he wrote Australian plays, he replied that he didn't know, 'except that I have no interest in writing English plays'.

Beynon's original work was proof of the principle that drama is grounded in a particular society. He felt moved by the letters he received from children, particularly immigrant children, who were studying *The Shifting Heart* at school. They identified with the immigrants in the play. Beynon had, as one London critic wrote, taken 'the inarticulate and [given] them a voice'. Similarly, 30 years later, the greatest affirmation of *Summer Shadows* was one critic's observation of the expatriate playwright – 'the one thing that he's not forgotten is how to write his own kind'.[30]

Beynon did not have the sense of wasted time that Alan Seymour had, but there was an undercurrent of frustration, of feeling 'regretful'. Perhaps he might have written more had he lived in Australia. Or perhaps he might have put down the playwright's pen entirely. But the sensitive well-spoken boy who was called 'a little Pom' at school had found a welcoming environment in London. At least in a small way he had come back to teach writing, at the Australian Film and Television School in Sydney in the 1980s, as Alan Seymour had in 1979. Similarly, Seymour found the workshops of the first ever playwrights' conference in 1973 to be 'indeed a joyous experience'.

London had offered Richard Beynon training, talented people to work with and an opportunity to work in drama at the BBC for over 20 years. In some ways he still found it a foreign culture, particularly the use of surnames rather than Christian names. Neither British television nor the BBC offered the expatriate writers commissions to write dramas exploring themes in their own society. Expatriation was more difficult for the writer who wanted to speak in his own voice than for the actor who wished to explore many roles from the range of human experience. To the extent that drama was rooted in the community, expatriation dislocated playwrights much more than actors; the latter sought, chameleon-like, many roles, as journalists reported many different events and musicians played a variety of scores. On a later occasion Beynon sought the position of head of drama at Channel Nine. But, as he recalled, his British experience and the more expansive budgets and earnest themes of British programs were seen as a disadvantage; they did not prepare someone for the smell-of-an-oily-rag budgets and ratings-driven world of Australian commercial television.

Sometimes he felt that he was seen as someone who had run off and become 'a small fish in a big pond', an expatriate and an escapee. He believed that it was the other way around – 'Australia let me down', it was 'not me who let Australia down'. He believed that Australians sometimes wanted others 'to fit into a syndrome that they expect'. He detected suspicion – 'the average Australian will feel insecure if you become something more', 'feel vulnerable and threatened'. The same bullying that he had found in the play yard was practised by professional people based on 'a kind of fear' – the possibility that 'they didn't have the talent'. He believed that the returning expatriate was easily cast as 'the whipping boy' to whom those who hadn't gone away threw down the gauntlet, saying 'Show us how good you are'. Perhaps the former nominee for two American television Emmy Awards (for *Madame Bovary* and *Lord Peter Wimsey*), who had a distinguished track record at the BBC, had reason to be chagrined.

Expatriate paradoxes continued to shape his life and thought. On the one hand he found acceptance by the English:

> you were accepted as being almost part of the wallpaper, English, until you said you were Australian – they said 'Oh, yes, we can tell'.

On the other hand there were moments when he wanted to return, for example in winter to watch his beloved Blues, Carlton, during the Australian Rules Football season. At other times, Sydney, which had proven more receptive to his new work, appealed. His relationship with Australia was like that of someone who could not live with their lover but could not live without them: 'I love Australia [but] I don't think I could go back there to live'. Like many expatriates, he wanted both countries. 'I would be very unhappy if I couldn't get back to Australia ... [and] equally unhappy' if he couldn't get back to England.

Seymour's Exile

Alan Seymour had always felt that he 'never would leave Australia', though he 'always felt hemmed in there', but in 1961 he did realise the 'miracle' of escaping from a 'circumscribed life'. 'But that possibly was not just Australia, that was the Fifties', he recalled. In 1960s Britain, Seymour was a lucky man, as were many creative talents then. He was able to live from writing one-off plays for television rather than the series which later became the staple, even in Britain. Theatre reviewing, writing and eight weeks of holidays in Europe every year made life very pleasant and comfortable. He was pleased that this experience allowed him to 'know more about the great big world than just Australia', but was also aware that it carried a cost for his writing.

> I know bloody well that my life would have been much easier as a writer had I stayed in Australia, especially as things started to develop soon afterward ... except that ... I would think I would have had a number of plays done, written and done, and have a more substantial place in this, even the modern Australian canon, than I have now.

Not participating in Australian culture as it was developing in the 1960s and 1970s was both a loss and a problem. When reviewing a new play in 1980, the critics rapped him on the knuckles for being away, arguing that he didn't really know about Australia and what it was like.

To choose expatriation was partly to choose to travel. Richard Beynon travelled to the Mediterranean (living briefly on Hydra around the time George Johnston and Charmian Clift and their family were there) and worked in radio in Luxembourg in the 1950s. He also spent short periods in Italy and Spain. Alan Seymour caught the travel bug in the mid-1960s. He was 'getting very restless' and wanting more than a European jaunt every year. He felt the need to get away from 'media people' of whom he was 'sick to death'. After some time in the Middle East, a summer holiday led to five years in Turkey, in Izmir. Turkey offered a different culture, a different society and a trip to Gallipoli, which prompted him to work on the novel version of *The One Day of the Year*. Yet his writing in this period was often disappointing. 'Writing in a vacuum', he wrote plays and novels, several of which were not published. He would find on his return to London the same problem that bedevilled newcomers to this cultural marketplace, and one which troubled expatriates returning to Australia. The returned writer felt that the groups, the networks, even the cliques, were not exactly open to someone who, after an absence of some years, was unknown to them.

The problem of conflict was also not confined to relations with Australia. The earlier expatriate Michael Blakemore showed an independence of mind, or even a 'colonial' lack of respect for established authority, when he challenged the autocratic structures of the National Theatre in the 1970s, the Peter Hall era. Although he lost the battle, the National would slowly change. He would return to direct for it after a diverse career which included five Tony Award nominations in New York and his film *Country Life* (1994), an Australian work produced by Robin Dalton about a returning expatriate, which drew on Chekhov's *Uncle Vanya*. Unlike the surfing of Biarritz, which the two Sydneysiders pursued, the film had an inland setting.[31]

A Lost Culture

In theatre, in film and in television, the promise of the *Summer of the Seventeenth Doll* and the Elizabethan Theatre Trust had not been realised. In the early 1960s, while Charles 'Bud' Tingwell was working on *Emergency Ward 10*, and even later when Ray Barrett was starring in *The Troubleshooters* in Britain, Australian television (and, as often, film) was in a parlous state.[32] The 1963 Vincent Committee report on Australian television programming was critical, concluding that:

(1) There are insufficient Australian-produced programs – particularly drama.

(2) There is not enough Australian 'indigenous' drama.

(3) There is too much imported drama from the United States of America.

It criticised the excess of 'crime, violence and horror' in imported programs and lamented deficiencies in news, educational, children's and religious programming. There was also a lack of programs 'of special interest to our migrant population' and of those catering for 'minority tastes or special interests'.[33] Looking back in 1968 on ten years of Australian television, Mungo MacCallum reported that only 2.8% of drama on Australian TV was home-grown, compared to 50% in Sweden and Canada and nearly 100% in the US. He concluded, even more pessimistically, that since 1963 the Vincent Report had 'lain as undisturbed as the bones of the Unknown Soldier'.[34]

One theme of the Vincent Report was the pernicious influence of American culture disseminated through American television. Another major concern was the loss of talent overseas since the introduction of television:

> Radio drama declined ... and the anticipated large-scale develop-
> ment of television drama in Australia did not eventuate. It was a
> particularly bad oversight on the part of the responsible authorities.
> Large numbers of Australian actors were unable to find employ-
> ment. They took other types of work or left Australia in very large
> numbers for Britain, America and the Continent. Our actors are still
> leaving Australia because they cannot earn a living in Australia.
> They almost invariably do well overseas. The situation would be
> Gilbertian if it were not so serious. In Australia we have the
> spectacle of a substantial proportion of our theatrical talent going
> overseas to obtain employment. There they assist in the production
> of television programmes which are then purchased for telecasting
> in Australia ... In the last five years [J. C. Williamson Theatres
> Limited] alone has lost 52 actors and 22 actresses. They have left
> Australia and are permanently residing and working overseas.
> Many of them have had considerable success both on stage and
> screen.

Quality was lost as well as quantity. Regarding the loss of Australia's best actors, the report concluded: 'we can hardly expect world quality perform-ances in a country that has been denuded of so many of its finest artists'.

It also discerned 'a similar dismal picture' regarding the Australian drama-tist who was often forced to go overseas. 'We even have the sorry spectacle of Australian dramatists living in Australia, unable to sell their work in Australia either to the Commission or to commercial television, actually making large incomes by selling their scripts to Britain and America.' Emphatically, it concluded that 'Australia cannot afford to continue to lose her best actors and dramatists. Their loss to the Commonwealth has been a sad blow to the healthy development of our culture'.[35]

During the 1960s there was some good news, including the return of John Meillon and June Salter. Meillon and Salter were pioneers in two different television series, he in the richly observed *My Name's McGooley, What's Yours?*, and she in the very different satirical series named after an imaginary character always about to depart for the wider world – *The Mavis Bramston Show*. *Mavis* was a cultural mix: it drew its early stimuli from the Phillip Street revues which had nurtured Australian talent since the mid-1950s, and its commercial legitimacy from the satire boom on British television. The creation of the Australian Film Development Corporation and the Experimental Film and Television Fund in 1970 augured well. So did the return of several actors, including Charles 'Bud' Tingwell, who came back in 1972 to join the cast of Crawford Productions' *Homicide*, one of the few Australian television series.

An Actor's Lot

Nothing could be more variable than an actor's life. There was no neat progression like that through the scenes of a well-made three-act play, and not even a simple career move into one of the great companies. Such roles might come in early, middle or late career. Madge Ryan acted with the National Theatre in the mid-1960s while John Bluthal and Alan White acted with it from the 1980s. The West End actor was, by definition, flexible. This could include doing parts in light plays, voice-overs and commercials, or even long-running plays or musicals. When David Nettheim played Chaucer in the successful musical *The Canterbury Tales*, his bank manager was at last willing to loan him money to buy a house. Similarly, Alan White had a stint in the longest running ever play on the London stage, Agatha Christie's *The Mousetrap*, which helped with the costs of raising a family. Nettheim also added a few pounds to his bank account as the West End reporter on ABC Radio's *The Showman*, which maintained a sense of the cultural links to Britain and kept Australians up to date with the current roles of their expatriate actors and performers.[36]

Similarly, the season of that other play running on the streets of London, an actor's expatriation, was infinitely variable. For some it was brief and for others it was a permanent gig. John Meillon and June Salter had left in 1959 and returned in 1964. For those who left in the 1960s and after, such as John Bell and Anna Volska, it was more often just a few years of study and/or performance. Now there was a professional theatre in Australia to return to, and television and film, and work teaching in drama schools.

A Tale of Two Returns – Leo McKern and Keith Michell

While most actors defined their careers in roles and plays, rather than in terms of themes or countries, some of them did feel strongly about an Australian audience. It was perhaps easiest for the successful to negotiate a return with the major Australian companies (now that there was such a thing) from the 1970s. Two who returned several times, although in different ways, were Leo McKern and Keith Michell.

McKern and Michell both returned early and often. McKern was a short man who would turn smaller anti-hero roles from bit parts to something more. His 1953 Shakespearean Stratford upon Avon Memorial Theatre company trip home, during which he played a powerful Iago in *Othello*, was followed by his 1956 lead role in the UTRC's *Ned Kelly*. The stylish Michell and the plainer McKern had both made their way in the thriving British theatrical and film and television culture of the 1960s. Michell first starred in musicals, co-starring on the London stage in 1964 with the Australian opera singer June Bronhill in *Robert and Elizabeth*, which had music by another Australian, film and television music composer Ron Grainer. Then he was Henry VIII in the elaborate British TV series set in the Elizabethan court. McKern had a supporting role in the Beatles' film *Help*, and in the David Lean film *Ryan's Daughter*. In the cult TV series of control and attempted escape, *The Prisoner*, he was one of the actors who played No. 2, who looked down through Brave New World TV screens at the would-be-escapee, No. 6, played by Patrick McGoohan. Both men also had sensory cravings which sometimes drove them south: Michell enjoyed the Spanish sun, while McKern sailed.

Although both returned in leading roles, their early returns were different in character. One side of McKern wanted to go back to the nature and the society of his own land. In 1970, along with his wife and two daughters, he travelled around Australia in a VW Kombi van, before settling up north. There, John Sumner found him and convinced him to play the lead in Ray Lawler's play *The Man Who Shot the Albatross* (1971).

Although absent from Australia from 1966 for nearly a decade, Michell's returns became more frequent, and from the mid-1970s, increasingly for work; he made six trips between 1975 and 1990. He came home as the distinguished leading man to star in a one-man show in 1975, and to bring the Chichester Theatre Company, of which he was director, in 1978. Yet, although described by the critic Peter Ward as 'this British Australian', he at times claimed that his Australianness was as important as the English courtly roles he had been playing. 'I think everything I do owes a lot to the fact that I am Australian, even if it is a fresh approach to playing Shakespeare', this actor with soft features and a Chesty Bond chin told an Adelaide *Advertiser* journalist in 1982.[37] Wearing his metaphorical digger hat meant a little more than giving interviews in which he declared his love for Australia. In 1981, the first version of *Pete McGinty and the Dreamtime* Australianised Ibsen's *Peer Gynt*. Michell sought a link between metaphysical themes and Australian space, the land and society in which he had been born.

To be returning as a gentleman, if not a knight, of the English stage was not a bad thing. Michell would later be honoured by the naming of a theatre after him in Port Pirie, the town near which he had grown up. He was aware of other aspects of being an expatriate actor. Some Australian attitudes had clearly grated in his early years, particularly before his 1960s success. He later rejected the critical term 'expatriate', declaring 'I'm not an expatriate. I'm a citizen of the world, home is where you hang your hat ... it's where I work'. Yet he would also admit that he was an expatriate – he had left Australia and discovered wider worlds including London – 'my village'. On another occasion, relaxed in New York, he mused on the parts of his identity, his Australian and British selves, when talking to the Australasian journalist Derryn Hinch: 'I suppose I think of myself as an Aussie but I have a nest in Hampstead and in London I think of myself more as British ... But when I'm in America I regard myself as Australian again'.[38]

Other factors made some Australian expatriates feel distant from their homeland. For the aspiring professional there could be a danger in going home. Even with decades of success behind him, Keith Michell 'loved working in Australia and would like to go back there'. The negatives could also be powerful: 'the trouble is, when you go home, everybody says you're on the skids'. In the mid-1970s Michell rejected South Australian Premier Don Dunstan's invitation to return in a theatrically regal role, as director of the Adelaide Festival and the Adelaide Festival Centre, in part because it didn't pay well enough.

In the last years of the repressive Australian Sixties, the end of the era of banned books and shows, Michell shared the distaste of many expatriates who were experiencing the more liberal climes of trendy Britain. Infuriated by the bans on *Oh, Calcutta!*, he believed that 'this guilt complex' (about the human body) applied also to Australia. Keith Michell loved London, acting (and painting) and his family and friends more than anything else. Success, which was also very important, allowed him to travel, including returning to Australia.

Leo McKern would stretch himself between the two worlds. Twice, in the early 1970s and 1980s, he returned to settle and to perform. Twice he returned again to film and television work in Britain. This actor who had become increasingly typecast as the difficult character, the barrister Horace Rumpole, was perhaps becoming like him. Slightly irritable and given to pronouncements on life and politics, in some respects he preferred his known world in London and England. Australian in spirit in several ways, he had become English in culture and society, even as one of his daughters, Harriet, worked in Sydney as a film editor. His other daughter Abigail would join him in the cast of the Rumpole series. McKern, who returned often to work, was different from Alan White who maintained his Australian passport, his visiting Australian friends and his memories, but never returned. McKern also recognised that the Sydney he had left was no longer there. The situation of the expatriate actors would be affected as they grew older by their careers and their personal lives, as well as by how Australia had changed. The experience of several travelling journalists was in some ways even more dramatic.

Chapter 8

Long and Winding Musical Roads: The Careers of Australian Expatriates and Australian Music[1]

Several of the musicians who had left Australia in those first waves of the 1940s and 1950s were coming into their own in musical London in the early 1960s. Charles Mackerras was obtaining freelance work, Barry Tuckwell was principal horn with the London Symphony Orchestra, Geoffrey Parsons had become an established accompanist. In 1959, Joan Sutherland's performance in the title role of *Lucia di Lammermoor* at the Royal Opera House, Covent Garden, made her name in the operatic firmament. Newer waves of talent included John Williams, who had first arrived in London in 1952 as an 11-year-old student of the guitar, and debuted at the Wigmore Hall in 1958, and the pianist Roger Woodward, who had come to London after studying in Poland. Amongst the many singers were Geoffrey Chard and Yvonne Minton, who came to study in 1961.

The hopes and hesitancies of the immediate postwar years for the earlier generation of musicians, and even more for later generations, had given way to a compromise which would embrace a professional life in London, but also allowed an Australian aspect and commitment. The London location appealed for practical, professional and often personal reasons. Their Australian longings were personal, and often intuitive, although as the decades progressed they began to look for professional opportunities where once there had only been desert.

Individual trajectories were sometimes linked to other events. One was the consolidation of the Australian musical colony in London and the organisation, the Australian Musical Association (AMA). A second was the emerging importance of London as a place for international recording. This would acquire an Australian aspect through Peter Andry, who became general manager of the International Classical Division at EMI. He would also, later, form a different and more specialist body, the Australian Musical Foundation in London, which overlapped with the AMA in its aim of encouraging and nurturing talented young Australians who had come to London to pursue a career. A third was the maturation and increasing confidence of Australian musical culture in Australia.

In one way Australian music's new international rather than provincial self-assessment was manifested in 1965. The Sydney Symphony Orchestra made its first international tour, culminating in the Commonwealth Arts Festival in London in September. Individuals who had gone to London earlier or later had to make decisions. Their future might lie in London, in the rebuilt musical cultures of continental Europe or even in the affluent United States, or in Australia. How would they balance their personal and professional commitments? London might remain the centre of their musical work, or just a central location allowing convenient access to performance engagements on both sides of the Atlantic and beyond.

Composing a Life

The musical road for Australian composers in London was less dramatic and sometimes financially more precarious than that of the performers.[2] Opportunities appeared for several composers during the 1960s. In music, as in other fields, London was a fertile garden of new ideas and performances. In quite different ways, Don Banks, David Lumsdaine and Malcolm Williamson emerged onto the musical stage in this era. This 'opening up' in London also came at the same time as the composers Richard Meale, Peter Sculthorpe and Nigel Butterley were beginning to make an impact in Australian music.

Don Banks' multifaceted sides as composer and cultural missionary were already apparent. Banks' London musical milieu was international and contemporary but also organisational. He was involved with several bodies. This contemporary composer had played his first composition at the New Music Society in Melbourne in 1949. Now, he was well established in London, being a member of the London Contemporary Music Centre (which was part of the International Society for Contemporary Music), the Society for the Promotion of New Music and the Composers' Guild in Britain. Later he was a founding member of the British Society for Electronic Music and a patron of the Jazz Centre Society in London. After his first BBC commission, *Four Pieces for Orchestra*, which was performed by the London Philharmonic under Sir Adrian Boult in June 1954, and other works in 1953–54 at Australia House and the Royal Festival Hall, he began to be in demand. In 1962, his *Horn Trio*, commissioned by Lord Harewood and the Edinburgh Festival Society, and written for his compatriot Barry Tuckwell, was performed by

Tuckwell and the Australian musicians Maureen Jones, on piano, and Brenton Langbein, the Europe-based violinist.[3] From 1967, in the small personal and professional societies of music, Tuckwell would acquire new family connections through his sister Patricia's second marriage to Lord Harewood.

Banks earned a continuing income through teaching composition at Goldsmith's College at the University of London and work, as well as recognition, from several festival commissions during the 1960s. In *Tirade*, for the Centre de Musique, Paris, he set three poems by Peter Porter to music. The first addressed the 'Antipodean' paradox, 'A northern race living in the south,/ myths in reverse'. Throughout the 1960s, Banks was writing jazz pieces, instrumental and vocal, and also exploring the possibilities of electronic music. *Meeting Place* (commissioned by the London Sinfonietta) brings three traditions together in a piece for jazz group, chamber ensemble and electronic synthesiser.[4]

The Sydney expatriate David Lumsdaine saw his own work as a composer as that of a sensory outsider, saying of music that 'as a Martian ... I hear it from the "outside"'. 'I am equally removed from the natural world and from Western European music and the music of other cultures.' For him expatriation meant being free, 'free of so many identifications, free of the stultifying provincial complacency ... being outside the allegiances of the art ... outside of the professional world of composition'. At the same time the rise of London as a centre of musical creativity in the 1960s excited him. 'It was absolutely marvellous. That obviously kept me there. I never intended to stay in England but I was stimulated by the kind of alliances with performers and fellow composers.' He became 'very close' to Don Banks in this period, the Melbourne expatriate whom he did not meet until 1964, and he worked with other Australian performers, including Barry Tuckwell and Doug Whittaker.

In London's overlapping circles, Lumsdaine met people from different generations, backgrounds and disciplines. Teaching at the University of Durham from 1970, he also established the Manson Room at the Royal Academy of Music, for the study and performance of new music. Annual composers' weekends and a flexible electronic music studio at Durham, all of which he initiated, were aspects of an era of intense activity. His own compositions included *Bach Music* (1965), *Episodes* and *Kelly Ground*, the first of several works acknowledging his Australian roots. Don Banks, with whom he worked in the revitalised Society for New Music, was an important stimulus. He dedicated *Kelly Ground* to Banks. By the late 1960s, Australian themes were becoming more important in his work, including *Mandala I* and *II* (after Patrick White's novel, *The Solid Mandala*), *Kangaroo Hunt* (1971) and *Aria for Edward John Eyre* (1972). His appointment to Durham would give him a new sense of place, of this part of rural England, at the same time as he was musically rediscovering Australia.[5]

Malcolm Williamson, a more traditional composer, also travelled slowly at first. From the late 1950s when his mother had returned to Australia and the young Williamson remained, work in a publishing house, marriage to Dolores Daniel in 1960 and then three children kept him busy. Concerned to associate his music with what he termed the 'slender Australian tradition', he was certain that it was 'characteristically Australian, although I have never tried to make it so'.[6] He later remarked that 'most of my music is Australian in origin'. By this he meant 'not the bush or the deserts but the brashness of the cities, the sort of brashness that makes Australians go through life pushing doors marked pull'.[7] Was this door-opening as much an Australian expatriate trait as an Australian quality? The cultural doors he pushed were also diverse, that diversity being both a characteristic of Australians in London and of a changing London itself, from the 1950s to the more alternative 1960s. His influences included Boulez and Messiaen from his French studies, jazz from Sydney in the 1940s and Cuban jazz from his nightclub work, and Jewish perspectives which came through his wife. Catholicism was a profound influence; following his conversion at the age of 21, this included Catholic literary imaginations – from the English novelist Graham Greene to the Australian poet James McAuley. His resultant eclecticism and 'popularism' was very different to Banks' new music oeuvre. Williamson's success with his first opera *Our Man in Havana*, staged at Sadler's Wells in 1963, attracted him to the musical stage, including chamber opera and children's opera.[8]

In the early 1960s he contributed to a great Australian artistic enterprise, which fused three expatriate talents. He wrote the music to Robert Helpmann's ballet, *The Display*, for which Sidney Nolan did the sets. First presented by the new Australian Ballet at the 1964 Adelaide Arts Festival, it was then staged in London as part of the 1965 Commonwealth Arts Festival. Exploring indigenous Australian mysteries, from the lyrebird to Australian Rules Football, it was one manifestation of a new cultural depth. This fusion suggested the rich cross-fertilisations which arose from both the small ponds of the arts in Australia and, in a different way, from London collaborations.

As different as was the music of Williamson from the new music of Banks and Lumsdaine, all three composers shared a strong sense of their roots while remaining open to myriad influences. For them, to be an Australian in this time, or perhaps in this place – London – was to be 'international' as well as Australian.

An Island in the Strand

International, British and Australian music would come together in several ways during the Sixties. One link was a body created a decade before, an organisational manifestation of the growing 'Australian colony' in London, the Australian Musical Association (AMA). This had been formed on 16 February 1952. Don Banks was the primary force behind its creation in this brief period between his studies around Europe. Its first executive brought together several big names (some of whom were passing through London), particularly composers, including interim chairman Arthur Benjamin, Dorian Le Gallienne and Margaret Sutherland, as well as Charles Mackerras, the singer John Cameron and Max Pirani, who was teaching at the Royal College of Music. The Association had been founded, it reflected on its 21st birthday, 'to assist two groups of people – Australian performers and Australian composers, and to put Australian musicians "on the map"'. At its foundation meeting, Mr A. Bellhouse remarked on 'the English attitude to Australian music . . . [a mixture of] great interest and a lack of knowledge of achievement on the cultural scale'.[9]

In the 'social' context of classical music, the Association sought formal status from the beginning. Under the patronage of HRH the Duchess of Gloucester, the inaugural concert was held at Australia House in the presence of the Lord Mayor of London and the Lady Mayoress on Friday 3 October 1952. In the following year, Australia and New Zealand loomed larger in British consciousness due to the forthcoming 1954 Royal Tour. The AMA presented, with the New Zealand Music Society, the Australian–New Zealand Royal Concert at the Royal Festival Hall, which was performed in the presence of Queen Elizabeth and the Duke of Edinburgh 'as a farewell before their departure'.[10] Charles Mackerras conducted the Royal Philharmonic Orchestra in a program which included *Heritage* by Arthur Benjamin. In some ways the AMA was one of the last institutional creations of an older Anglo-Australian society, centred less on the young travellers in Earls Court, Notting Hill Gate or outer suburban Muswell Hill than on Australian polite society. Such an event also appealed to well-to-do visitors who came to London for the 'Season' and to many of the Australians in law, medicine and the universities, as well as in the city.

The concert raised funds to assist music students from Australia and New Zealand travelling to Britain. Most of the Association's activities were in a more practical vein and less high profile. 'Useful' activities included recitals, concerts and operas, often presented in the main hall of Australia House. In all its Edwardian glory, 'with its brilliant chandeliers and marble fittings', the Australian High Commission provided 'an elegant venue'. Annual competitions (which sometimes carried substantial prize money), workshops and master classes were run for young singers and instrumentalists over many years. These were important for talented young Australians in search of a career in music. From the beginning the Association was a sudden success; by 1953 its membership was over 200. It would stay above that figure for the next two decades, reflecting the rising Australian population in cultural London. It also had the support of the Australian High Commission, whose

library agreed to assist with another aim, holding and cataloguing its collection of Australian compositions. The AMA received a grant from the Prime
Minister's Department in 1953, as did its sister societies, the energetic Society
of Australian Writers and the Australian Artists Association.[11]

To performing artists at the top of the tree, both busy and successful,
'associations' were often of limited interest. However, they assisted younger
artists who had arrived in London without connections or a name. Sometimes, successful artists, remembering their own early days, also wanted to
put something back, as in the master classes conducted by the pianists Ruth
Nye, Rafael de Silva and Geoffrey Parsons.[12] Those performers had a strong
sense of their nationality, more often social, cultural and natural than
political. Also having a sense of obligation towards their musically talented
younger compatriots, the associations were important to them. Composers,
some of whom were inspired by their Australian experience, needed them
more, particularly early in their career. Works by Don Banks, and Malcolm
Williamson's opera, *The Growing Castle* (1967), were performed under the
auspices of the AMA. Australian newspapers' London correspondents noted
the expatriate connections. When Geoffrey Chard sang the title role in
another Williamson opera, *Lucky Peter's Journey*, the Sydney *Sun* reported on
this 'Big Night for Sydney's 2 Men of Music'.[13]

The AMA was a voluntary organisation. That inevitably limited its role as
an entrepreneurial and promotional body. At different times its supporters,
over-committed in their own careers, reduced the time spent on its work. Don
Banks, who had several organisational obligations, was conscious of needing
more time to write. Similarly, Geoffrey Parsons made his contribution over a
long period. In the 1960s, Geoffrey Chard, then making a successful operatic
career as a baritone at Sadler's Wells, which became the English National
Opera, devoted hours of his precious time to the Association's committee.[14]

In the early 1970s, the AMA reached a new peak, practical as well as
symbolic. The Captain Cook Bicentenary Commemorative Concert at the
Royal Festival Hall on 13 April 1970 was 'a "grand" Australian occasion'.
Supported by an Arts Council grant, the AMA also financially assisted Australian performers to come to London, sometimes from Europe, for its concerts.[15] The vitality of this small offshore island of Australian culture, which
the Australian musical colony in London had become, was also a sign that
classical performance and composition on the 'Australian mainland' were
prospering. Might there be a place in that more vital musical culture for the
expatriate legions, many of whom were studying and working in London?
The singers at Covent Garden and Sadler's Wells, including Sutherland,
Chard, Donald Smith, June Bronhill, Lauris Elms, Yvonne Minton, Joan
Carden, Margreta Elkins and Ronald Dowd, and the conductor Charles
Mackerras, made a formidable list. Might they, one day, contribute to a revivi-
fied operatic tradition on that Australian 'mainland'?

Almost Triumphal Visits I

The complex musical relationship between Australia and overseas was evolving during the 1960s. Young talent was exported, and some of the 'export quality' talented Australians, who had made a name for themselves in London and Europe, returned. In 1967, the number of top Australian musicians playing overseas was such that one frustrated SSO member remarked that 'a first class orchestra could be formed out of Australians who have gone overseas'.[16] They might have provided the talented principals which, Eugene Ormandy had argued in 1944, Australian music needed. He believed that 'this would inspire a new cultural drive as well as teach the next generation of native-born artists'. As with Tyrone Guthrie's proposed 'export-import' scheme for drama, could a case be made for bringing back home those who had become successful overseas?

A successful return visit was a prerequisite, however. Such returns had historically taken two forms. One was the 'hail the conquering hero' triumphal return, in which the successful international star, the stellar performer, the Australian who had been blessed, if not beatified, in the cathedrals of culture in the old world, lauded in the concert halls and opera houses of its international capitals, from London and Paris to Milan and Vienna, returned to the more prosaic antipodes. The other was either the return of the luminous star on a farewell tour, or the return of a less grand star on the verge of retirement, to perform, to teach and then retire.[17] Dame Nellie Melba played both roles in her many tours, including several farewell tours, as the international grand dame of opera – Richmond's Nellie Mitchell 'made good'. She also displayed the prima donna's artistic hauteur in her assessment of Australia's 'colonial' culture, or at least Australian audiences, when she advised the English singer Clara Butt, who was about to go to Australia, 'Sing 'em muck! It's all they can understand'.[18]

Some day there might be a place for Australian talents to return at the height of their powers, to a position of artistic responsibility, rather than just as a visiting star or the performer about to retire. In 1965 the diva Joan Sutherland returned in the style of Dame Nellie Melba half a century before. Echoing the name of Melba's companies and invoking other past triumphs, the Sutherland-Williamson International Grand Opera was a private commercial venture. J. C. Williamson's was still the most powerful entrepreneurial organisation in Australia. It was, however, with the assistance of the Australian Elizabethan Theatre Trust (AETT), and its nascent operatic company, that Joan Sutherland was brought back. Four years after Sutherland's acclaim for her *Lucia di Lammermoor* at La Scala in 1961, and six years after her Covent Garden debut in the role, she brought it to Australia, supported by the young tenor Luciano Pavarotti.[19] Like the major visiting British actors and theatre companies, Olivier/Leigh and the Old Vic in 1948 and Anthony Quayle's Stratford companies of 1948–49 and 1953, this was a social, as much as a cultural, event. It was a great moment in a country which still associated art with 'society' and equated both social status and artistic excellence with the great from 'overseas'. By increasing public interest in opera, the imported Sutherland-Williamson company also, indirectly, boosted support for the local company which would later become the Australian Opera.

Joan Sutherland's visit would be shaped by its social and cultural context as well as by her performances. In the mid-1960s, the Australian pattern of complex ambivalence towards overseas, particularly Britain – predominantly a cringing deference but occasionally a 'knocking' disdain for the imported – still dominated cultural life. Even in an era when a fading Menzies was laughed out of court over the proposed term 'Royal' for the unit of the new decimal currency, Australians were still oriented towards Britain. This, like the cultural cringe, was true in classical and popular music. In *Facing the Music* Helen Bainton, SSO viola player, writes with awe of the experience in 1965 when the SSO went on its first ever overseas trip to Britain (and Tokyo, Hong Kong and Bombay) for the Commonwealth Festival. The orchestra was well received, and also played Australian compositions – a violin concerto by the expatriate composer Malcolm Williamson and the world premiere of the Australian-based Peter Sculthorpe's *Sun Music I*. However, the colonial excitement felt by some at returning to the British fount of culture was, like all colonial conceptions of the great power, almost childish in its character.[20] On the other side of the coin, Australia welcomed the great from overseas. Popular music and public excitement came together in the Beatles' tour in 1964, a much bigger event than the Royal Tour of 1963. It generated much more hysteria than even the 1954 Royal Tour, the first visit to Australia by a reigning monarch, an event viewed at the time as a landmark in Australian history.

Despite such enthusiasms, Joan Sutherland was worried that her 1965 Sutherland-Williamson tour might elicit the other side of the cringe, a 'knocking' of those who had 'achieved their ambition'. She feared a prevailing attitude, that the successful, the 'tall poppies', must 'be cut down to size, particularly if their success was achieved overseas'. Her fears were not realised. In contrast, this wildly popular tour ended in her last Melbourne concert with a screaming, ecstatic crowd throwing thousands of streamers at the stage, as if a liner was going to Europe. She then obliged, emulating Melba, with a finale of 'Home Sweet Home'.[21]

In popular music, too, young Australians sought success in Britain. Rock groups entered the Battle of the Bands (as opera singers sang in Mobil or *Sun Aria* quests) to win a trip to London. The pop group, The Seekers, worked their way over by playing on an ocean liner. One of the greatest bands of that era, the Easybeats, made their journey in 1966, and had several top-10 records, although winning less recognition than their great talent deserved.

In music, although Britain still called the tune (as it did in theatre and journalism), in this period Australian culture started to matter in London. The 1966 publication of the first issue of the magazine *Australarts* reflected that Australian presence in London's cultural life. Addressed to the Australian cultural colony in London, it also sought to keep them up to date with what was happening back home. It reported on many busy Australians doing well in London, including the designers Loudon Sainthill and Kenneth Rowell, the actors Madge Ryan and Diane Cilento, Lesley Stack (the Queenslander who had become director of the Zwemmer Gallery), the artist Arthur Boyd (one of his paintings was used on the cover), the musicians Malcolm Williamson, Charles Mackerras, Yvonne Minton and Ronald Dowd. In different spheres, it reported on the success of the former Melbourne radio man, Alan Freeman, the pop music guru who was said to be the highest paid disc jockey in the UK, and of Ron Grainer, whose musical *Robert and Elizabeth* was on in the West End, starring Keith Michell and June Bronhill. There would only be one issue of this innovative bi-lateral publication. The London peak, however, would be maintained by the continued achievements of many of those featured in the magazine. However, in a great paradox, this was an ending as well as a beginning. As *Australarts* recognised, when reporting on artistic happenings in Sydney, 'a perceptible change in the climate of opinion is beginning to take place in Sydney theatre circles. The time has come, they are saying, when people are beginning to seek things Australian'.[22] While perhaps ahead of its time, and arguably inaccurate in place (Sydney seemed less interested than Melbourne in Australian works), its anticipation of a time when the centre of gravity of Australian arts was in Australia, not London, and when Australian subjects mattered, was prophetic.

Almost Triumphal Visits II

It was unusual for an expatriate soloist to return to perform. Even less usual in the ABC's 'celebrity' listings were visiting Australian conductors. 'Colonials as conductors' were not the thing in London or Australia. Australian chief conductors seemed a contradiction in terms. The ABC Director of Music, John Hopkins, believed that:

> there are so few Australian conductors because of Australian snob-bishness – and it's more the audience than the players. Australian audiences are reluctant to accept Australian conductors so that it has become the ABC's policy to engage foreign conductors. This is the period of the 'star' conductor and Australian audiences regard foreigners as being more starlike than their own.

Only a long period of proving yourself away from Australia might make an Australian conductor 'accepted in his own country', according to Charles

Buttrose, the ABC's Director of Publicity and Concerts.[23] Although there were resident staff conductors, such as Joseph Post for the SSO, the first Australian-born chief conductor was still decades away.[24] In the 1960s, Charles Mackerras made a number of returns, after over a decade in England and Europe. Now freelancing, Mackerras was asked out several times: a 1960 ABC tour; conducting for the 'Elizabethan Opera' (the Trust) in 1962; and in 1963 another ABC tour.

Nancy Phelan notes that Mackerras, the 'Flying Maestro', was 'the first Australian to be invited to return as a "celebrity" conductor' for the ABC, and that 'his concerts were to be part of a summer festival'. Meeting his family, and touring Queensland in its unbearably hot summer, added up to a demanding visit. In 1962, he conducted the Melbourne Symphony Orchestra, the Sydney Symphony Orchestra, and the Trust Opera in Adelaide and Sydney, with some conducting in East Berlin in between! In 1963, he conducted in Oslo on Friday 1 February before rehearsing the Queensland Symphony Orchestra (QSO) in Brisbane on Tuesday 5 February. Four months of touring around Australia and with the QSO to Queensland country towns followed. Mackerras conducted 57 concerts and recorded music for a television opera. Phelan believes that he was 'vastly overworked and much underpaid, 100 pounds per concert, 50 pounds for school concerts', despite the 'unique compensation' of discovering the Great Barrier Reef and tropical Queensland on a northbound, but very primitive, train journey.[25] That theme of the discovery of Australian nature would be a recurring one for many expatriates who, when they left, had known only their own cities, the beaches and nearby bush. Then, the north, like the 'Red Centre', was a revelation to most Australians. They had mostly grown up with a much stronger sense of imagined English nature and architecture, and of coastal Australia, than of the range of their own continent.

Mackerras had come back wearing the white tie and tails of the distinguished, if relatively young, conductor. In the overall scheme of things he was still – as in the Queensland train with its primus stoves and ice boxes – something of a modern swaggie with his baton case, if not his swag, upon his shoulder. Australian music and Australian expatriate performers were still distant. Three days after his departure from Australia he was rehearsing at Cologne in Germany.[26]

The 'non-return' of Charles Mackerras was arguably even more significant than this return visit. For three years in the early 1960s, the SSO did not have a chief conductor and languished as a result. The young Charles Mackerras was one of the contenders for the position. At the age of 36, with a modest but solid record behind him, he was excited by the prospect, its demands and its opportunities. It would also have costs, limiting the opportunity of a young conductor to acquire an international reputation in the distant music capitals of the world. When Charles Buttrose, as the ABC's Director of Publicity and

Concerts, pushed the Mackerras case with the Commission's General Manager, Charles Moses, he was discouraged. 'Tell him to go away and prove himself. The Sydney Symphony still regards him as a second oboe player.' The colonial cultural cringe view was encapsulated, with or without irony, in the *Sunday Mirror's* observation, 'The boy from Turramurra doesn't qualify'. Phillip Sametz, the historian of the SSO, was less moderate, remarking that 'this spectacular, if unsurprising, example of superciliousness and cultural cringe would cost the orchestra and the ABC dearly'. Mackerras later reflected on the decision. 'I think they felt I wasn't ready. But, as Stuart Challender did later, I think I would have grown with the orchestra. I wanted to stay because it would have given me the chance to take up a position with a good orchestra in my own country. I felt that this was something I could make a real contribution to.' While in some respects 'art has no nationality', Mackerras felt a tie, both to his art and to his place of origin.[27]

A Visual Symbol of Musical Progress: The 'Christening' of the Sydney Opera House

Change was afoot by the 1970s, however. In an era of visual symbols and images, great public and open-air ceremonial moments, the 1973 opening of the Sydney Opera House, one of the great architectural wonders of the modern world, was an important symbolic moment for Australian music. It would have not one, but several, openings. The building was opened by a member of the royal family, in the traditional colonial Australian way (which still had a few years of life in it). Queen Elizabeth herself confirmed the status of the new complex on 20 October 1973. On this occasion, songs of joy were also sung a little earlier in a series of opening concerts in September. On his arrival in 1967, at the *de rigueur* Sydney airport press conference, Malcolm Williamson went in to bat for Australian composers. He declared that 'snob appeal' would bar works by Australian composers from the opening night of the Sydney Opera House, which seemed to be getting closer at last. 'Those tiaraed ladies in their $20 seats would prefer to see a Callas or a Sutherland in a traditional opera.' 'The Australian works can come later.'[28] The result was just a little better than Williamson had predicted. The official 'Royal Opening Concert' featured *Jubugalee*, a musical flourish with an indigenous influence by John Antill, which provided local colour, and Beethoven's 'Choral' Symphony, the Ninth. The Australian Opera performed Prokofiev's *War and Peace*, and a concert hall performance of Wagner featured the Swedish soprano Birgit Nilsson and the SSO, under the baton of the 'home-grown guest hero', Charles Mackerras. Further, Don Banks had been commissioned to write a work to mark the event. *Prospects* was the title of a work inspired by looking at Australia after 20 years away and seeing its possibilities.[29]

After the Queen's opening, the first 'Sunday Night at the Opera House' variety concert demonstrated that in popular culture too, overseas status was important. As the visiting English comedian Jimmy Edwards had closed the 'Tiv', doing the last show at Melbourne's Tivoli theatre, the expatriate Australian entertainer Rolf Harris topped the bill at the new Bennelong Point theatre. The show nearly didn't go ahead when Actors Equity demanded an 'Australian', that is Australian-based, performer. Barry Crocker, fresh from his 'Bazza McKenzie' role, headed the balancing 'Australian' show, while Rolf Harris was shocked at being told 'I wasn't really Australian. God that hurt'.[30] (Crocker and Harris had some things in common. As Rolf had played at the Down Under Club in the 1950s, the new 'ocker' star of the silver screen had lived at Kangaroo House, an annexe of the Overseas Visitors Club in Earls Court in 1964, and sung for his supper, actually his lodgings, at the Club.)

Despite these uncertainties – and despite controversies over the cost, the acoustics and the audience capacity of the building – this *visual* symbol put Australia on the *musical* map. To those people in Europe or North America, and a few in Britain, who assumed that music was something only made in Australia by kangaroos or by 'native peoples', here was concrete evidence that Australia had a musical culture. On the occasion of its own majority – its twenty-first anniversary in 1973 – the AMA's reflections struck a positive note:

> The image of Australia is currently changing in the eyes of the world. Until recently, the picture was one of sport, agriculture and the open-air life; now another side is appearing, the cultural aspect. We have our own writers, poets, artists, actors, dancers and above all musicians whose vital contribution to the world of the arts is at last being recognised throughout the world.

The Association was proud that 'we have played and will continue to play a part in this great cultural upsurge'.[31] At the same time, an age-old air, the composers' lament, continued. Grand institutions and buildings – just like the former celebrity concert series – did not necessarily give composers a concert hall for audiences to hear their work.

Australian Music Comes of Age – in Australia and London?

For composers and musicians in mid-career, the successes of the 1960s posed the professional and personal question of 'where to?' in the 1970s. London offered career consolidation through engagements, recordings and commissions. Australia also called. Several performers and creative artists answered that call, at first to visit, during the decade which coupled Australian new nationalism and artistic revival. Don Banks made music in Australia his life's commitment, complementing his dedication to new music. However, his return involved difficulties as well as achievements. At times it encapsulated both the tensions facing the returning expatriate and those between artistic London and artistic Australia at the time.

Banks had first returned to Australia in 1970, the same year as the Captain Cook Commemorative Concert in London. He then returned to take up an Australian National University (ANU) Creative Arts Fellowship in 1972. ANU Chancellor Dr H. C. Coombs had established these precursors of state arts grants. This was also one of the first attempts to bring expatriates home, even briefly. Several distinguished expatriates returned to the ANU, including Banks, the artists Sidney Nolan (1965) and Arthur Boyd (1971), the writer Christina Stead (1969) (who had earlier been denied a major literary award because she had lived overseas for so long) and later Malcolm Williamson (1975).[32]

Banks' return, which excited him, had its financial costs. A $5000 ANU stipend might have been adequate for a single man, but not for someone with a wife and three children in England to support. (It would be raised, retrospectively, to $7500.) In 1973, when Banks came again to Canberra, he lamented that it was 'impossible for me to work and compose' in the small room at the former Commonwealth hostel, Hotel Acton.[33] Complaint was common among composers in Australia or Britain, for they had chosen the most financially difficult of all paths. Such laments were deeper than either an acquired British habit or an expression of expatriate frustration. Maria Prerauer was concerned that Banks' talent would be lost to Australia again. She wrote in the *Sunday Australian*, during his 1972 visit, that 'Don Banks must not escape again':

> First-rate Australian composer-teachers don't grow on gum trees. We need this year's Australian National University Creative Fellow, Don Banks, more than Don Banks needs us. And not just until the end of 1972 when he is due to return to London ...
>
> The big question everyone should be asking is what, if anything, are we doing to keep this Melbourne-born 49-year-old here for good ...
>
> Don Banks – shame that in his country of birth it seems necessary to spell it out – is a most distinguished expatriate composer; a damn sight more distinguished than some of our resident household words. He is expatriate only because 20 years or so ago when he went abroad there was nothing – repeat nothing – for an Australian prophet to profit in his own country.[34]

Banks was inspired by the professional possibilities in Australia. When directing a young composers' seminar in 1970, he was impressed by the high 'percentage of talent' which seemed even greater than that found in England.[35] He returned to Australia permanently in 1973, to two jobs. His bread and butter, and his influence as a teacher, would come from the position as head of Composition and Electronic Music at the new Canberra School of Music. However, he had left behind a significant London career, both as a composer and as Musical Director of Goldsmith's College at the University of London, even more because of a second job. Banks also returned, at the request of Dr H. C. Coombs, to chair the Music Board of the Australia Council, the Whitlam government's renamed and generously funded successor to the Australian Council for the Arts. 'Nugget' Coombs wore many hats. Earlier, he had created the Australian Elizabethan Theatre Trust. Now, he was the white-collar Canberra 'impresario', the patron, the public servant behind so much of the government, institutional and corporate support for the arts in Australia. He was the Medici of the Gorton and Whitlam eras, although his earthy and ironically prosaic style was more a variant on the dry public servant or the laconic bush Australian than on the Florentine prince. When congratulating Don Banks in 1973 on his fiftieth birthday, Coombs caught the excitement and the paradoxes of the artistic renaissance of the Whitlam years from 1972–75. He expected Banks, and others, to 'help create a renaissance in the musical life of Australia; if one can be re-born when one has so far only struggled to be born'.[36]

Though a quiet man, Don Banks energised so many people, institutions and places. He was behind the formation of the Composers Guild and composed works for the Australian Contemporary Music Ensemble. His return to Australia came at a time of multiple artistic excitements, only one of which was the Whitlam government's enthusiastic support for the arts in Australia. Of parallel significance was the interest in musical fusion as the spirit of the Sixties informed the cultural life of generations which had grown up, as Banks and David Lumsdaine had, in the 1940s, with popular as well as classical music. On the Music Board, he worked, above all, for composers and for new Australian music. His enthusiasms extended to performance, wherever it was found, and to jazz. The Board supported Australian performance from Perth to Townsville; it also assisted several concerts put on by the AMA in London. Banks was himself involved, in setting up the Jazz Action Society and making jazz an important part of the Music Board's brief. His London, and international, experiences confirmed his broad conception of the nature of fine music.

Banks the composer was diverse and accomplished. John Sinclair of the Melbourne *Herald* described a retrospective survey of his works put on in 1970, during his first return, as 'a landmark in Australian creative music'.[37] Even the critics who felt nervous about the new music heard Banks with passion and excitement. He was international as well as Australian. His influences included his London composition teacher, Hungarian Matyas

Seiber, his Florence teacher Luigi Dallapiccola, and Milton Babbitt, with whom he studied at Salzburg. His range was wide: commissioned compositions for major European festivals (Kassel, Cardiff, Cheltenham, Edinburgh and the English Bach Festival); jazz ballads for Cleo Laine; and the scores for many feature-length films, mainly horror films. Regarding 'electronics as another wonderful instrument', his major works included *Intersections* (1969), *Equation III* (1972) and the orchestral work, *Prospects* (1974).[38]

Both Banks and the music critics were aware that a composer's lot in Australia was not an entirely happy one. The composer was without 'the courtesy, status or stature he expects to get overseas'. He looked forward to the future: 'the day the community here will recognise that composers are as important as tennis players ... [with] fine skills developed in different directions'.[39] Banks shared the sense of frustration about time and money which affected so many composers. As the chair of the Music Board of the Australia Council, his commitment to the advancement of Australian music diminished the precious time available for his own work as a composer. Several years of devoting his extra hours to the Music Board and as 'an ambassador for the "new deal" in Australia' made him conscious of the opportunities for his own work. His 1974 resignation from chairing the Board created that possibility: 'I shall now put away the typewriter and thankfully take up a pencil'.[40]

David Lumsdaine later reflected on Banks as cultural missionary, the call to Australia and the tension between musical administration and composition. He had himself visited Australia several times during the 1970s, making an extended return to the University of Adelaide in 1976 and further visits in 1978, including residencies at his own musical training ground, the New South Wales Conservatorium of Music.

Lumsdaine felt increasingly close spiritual ties with the land, if also with the land around Durham. He felt alienated from the urbanisation of the coast, however, as he did from the spread of London. He was also torn between answering Don Banks' 'strong calls' to join his cultural taskforce in 1973, and responding to the call of his own compositions. On the one hand he was inspired, when back, by that most exciting time 'during the Whitlam period when so many things were flowering'. Yet he was divided:

I was so physically moved by being back, but there were warning bells ringing every time, which suggested that I should return to London. This was a personal thing. It upset Don very much and there was almost a rift – at one point it was like being a traitor.

He wondered whether Don Banks the composer, who had given 'so much energy for others [and] not enough for himself', had made the right decision.

Banks died prematurely in 1980 at the age of 57. In that year he had been made a Member of the Order of Australia for his services to Australian music. Later, the Australia Council Don Banks Composer Fellowships would perpetuate his name and his contribution to Australian cultural development. Lumsdaine wondered if the pressures of being a returning expatriate had made Don Banks' life and work more difficult and less effective than it might have been:

> In London we could be unattached and there was no question of building an empire. We had done a lot of work with young composers. Don had wanted to do the same thing when he came back. But as an Australian he was seen as an empire builder. Although we were never charged with the question 'What are you doing here?', many of those who had built up entrenched positions saw Don as a threat. H. C. Coombs wanted him here because he was outside of their positions and because of his moral strength.

It may also have been that transplanted ideas – even from a returning Australian – did not readily take root in the local soil.

David Lumsdaine made his own resolution. He married the English composer, Nicola LeFanu, in 1979, and in 1981 they took up a shared senior lectureship in London, allowing more time for composition. He later reflected on his artistic/personal paradoxes: a studio in London, but his heart in Australia; his karma being composing, but his financial base being in London. Australia, which he visited often, remained important. He had remarked that he felt Australia 'like a lodestone', adding that 'it gives me a sense of direction – this is the way it is. It is a physical thing, not an allegiance or an alliance . . . it just happens'.

For the composer of new music, life went beyond society and place. He had not wanted to return to Australia in the early 1970s when it was still engaged in the Vietnam War. By the 1990s Lumsdaine, the composer as 'outsider', also felt separate from England: 'I have no association any longer with the music or social world in England. I am associated with small groups of friends but otherwise I could be in a monastery composing'. Lumsdaine's alienated retreat was also related to political disillusionment. Despite this, the continuing peace campaigner would demonstrate in the streets against the 1991 Gulf War.

Malcolm Williamson also went in more than one direction in the 1970s. In several respects musical Australia called. After nearly 15 years in Britain, Williamson returned in 1967 for three weeks, at the invitation of the Musica Viva Australia Society, to take part in its Spring Festival in Canberra. Despite the frustrations which faced contemporary composers, the newspapers' welcome was warm, headlines reading 'Top composer here again' and 'Composer is ABC "Guest"', referring to his ABC Guest of Honour talk.

He would return to Australia again in 1975 as an ANU Creative Arts Fellow, in the last year of the cultural activism of the reformist Whitlam government, and then again to the ANU in 1982. For Malcolm Williamson musical events said something about not just his own career but also about musical culture in Australia and Britain. Yet London, and more particularly Buckingham Palace, also called. In October 1975, in the same year as his fellowship in Australia, Williamson was made Master of the Queen's Music.

If Joan Sutherland was known as the diva capable of the 'common touch' in London and Australia, there was something very Australian about Williamson. At home in T-shirt, if not thongs, after a night's work on a new piece, he was not one to stand on ceremony. The 'Elizabethan' demands of his Royal responsibilities and English commissions kept him in London, and later just outside London, but his Australian connections remained. Occasionally, his house became 'a nest of Australians', and he worked on several Australian commissions during the 1970s and 1980s, even though his influences remained as international as ever. And, in a curious kind of balance, this prolific and much-commissioned composer would later keep both Her Majesty and Australian orchestras waiting for commissioned pieces scheduled to be performed on a set date.

His relationships with Australia were not without complications, however. In 1970, in a London lecture, he urged the Commonwealth government to support Australian music and the arts generally. His capacity for creating controversy was expressed in the headline of an Australian report of his talk: 'Neglect of arts disgusts musician'. His specific laments were two: that 'Australia has never had cultural attachés in the major cities of the world' (a theme Robert Helpmann also took up), and that 'Australia has never had publishing houses for serious music'. It seemed that 'this music, if not ephemeral, must await some sort of posthumous discovery'.[41] Was this a fine music variation on the anti-colonialist lament of Australian popular composers – that music in Australia meant 'songs by well-known dead foreigners'?[42] (Or was it an unwitting, but prophetic, anticipation of a later Australian government commitment to presenting Australian arts to a British public?)

The musical press was sometimes kind. W. L. Hoffman of the *Canberra Times* described his children's opera *Moonrakers* as 'A triumph for Williamson'. He was, in reciprocity, less kind to some of his more hostile critics a little later. In January 1976, he attacked Australian critics who 'ripped to ribbons' his opera *The Violins of St Jacques*, declaring that 'the Australian press has abused me constantly, vilified me in a way I am not expected to take from any other corner of the world'. Later, he declared, he found Australian criticism 'hurtful'. Even aside from his royal duties, he could not return to live 'because I'm too easily bruised'; surprisingly, he did not attribute it to the 'tall poppy syndrome'.[43]

Williamson, at his human and creative best, was generous in the extreme. The new generation of composers in Australia, such as Peter Sculthorpe, Richard Meale and Nigel Butterley, made him 'feel thoroughly old-fashioned'. 'Only a few years ago Australia was way behind many countries in Europe, musically speaking', but not now: 'the rapidity with which young composers have leapt ahead is startling'.[44] He could also be a demanding perfectionist who was at his frailest, and most irritable, when racing the clock to complete a commission. He was both lovable and difficult, and attracted love and hostility in the musical media. When he was appointed Master of the Queen's Music in 1975, he was caught in an expatriate gulf which was arguably not of his own making. The British critics commented bitterly on this eclectic Australian's insufficient grounding in British music tradition. In Australia, some muffled voices asked whether this expatriate of nearly 20 years could any longer be called a true Australian. In 1987, in *24 Hours*, S. F. Pearce remarked that 'like many other celebrated Australian artists, composer Malcolm Williamson is far better known and his works more often performed outside his own country'. 'Australians often are not overly kind to expatriates', Pearce concluded.[45]

Characterised by the intense love and sometimes anguished frustration of the passionate musician, Williamson was excited and bewildered by Australia. In the early 1980s the work of the eminent historian of Australia, Manning Clark, with whom he shared an interest in Ibsen, drew him again to the Australian National University. In the mid-1980s he wrote, often in hotel rooms, the world's first transcontinental symphony (No. 6) which was performed in 1986 across Australia by the ABC's eight orchestras. In 1987, he declared his personal love of Australia in an interview, remarking that 'Every time anyone has lifted a finger to invite me I've dropped everything and gone to Australia'.[46] Later, he would be politically aroused by the Aboriginal land rights movement and saddened by the original Australians' difficult struggle for justice in their own land. He expressed hope in *The Dawn is at Hand*, which set to music poems by the Aboriginal poet Oodgeroo of the Noonuccal tribe (formerly Kath Walker), and was performed by the Queensland Symphony Orchestra in October 1989.

Vital or Stranded? The Australian Musical Association in London

The emergence of the Australia Council and the opening of the Sydney Opera House in 1973 seemed to augur well for the Australian Musical Association, in the year of its first birthday. Australia now had an image on the musical map through Joern Utzon's creation in Sydney, while the Music Board of the Australia Council, soon under Don Banks, would support the work of the

Association. Perhaps an 'offshore' organisation could play a continuing role in Australian music as young Australians came to London in search of training and older Australians arrived to perform, many of them returning sooner or later.

In fact, the numbers were diminished, as the tightening of UK immigration regulations in 1971 reduced the number of Australians arriving.[47] So did the increasing opportunities for training and performance in Australia and the cheapness of fares on new air routes which also took Australians to North America and Europe proper. In March 1975, the AMA committee noted a 'high proportion of non-renewals' in its membership. Young Australians were still coming to London, but it was for shorter periods rather than longer, for a few months or a year rather than for several years. At the same time the enthusiasts of the founding era were getting older. Despite the work of W. R. (Bill) Cumming, the cultural officer at Australia House, and of stalwarts including Geoffrey Chard, Dr Morris and Mrs Shirley Barr and the longtime Australian broadcaster in London, Wilfrid Thomas, the Association was no longer advancing.

With Australia Council assistance, new Australian music was still coming to London, including works by George Dreyfus (1969) and Peter Sculthorpe (1972). The AMA put on the works of composers living and studying in Britain, including Alison Bauld, and, in June 1973, Anne Boyd and Martin Wesley-Smith. However, more was happening back home. The September 1973 national composers' conference in Canberra had the theme of 'The Status and Role of the Australian Composer'. It also brought back, on return excursion airfares of $700, the composers Martin Wesley-Smith, Alison Bauld, David Lumsdaine, Haydn Reeder and Anne Boyd.

Don Banks believed in both the national and the international. Replying to a correspondent to the Music Board in 1973, he noted that 'As the Prime Minister has indicated in his Policy Speech that he is concerned with the establishment of an Australian identity in the Arts, then I believe that we should seek ways of ensuring that our best artists are encouraged to appear overseas'. A new musical order might change the traditional terms of trade, ones which Banks regretted: 'the general pattern is that a great many overseas artists visit Australia without any reciprocal movement'.[48]

The future was less rosy for the AMA, as its grant was cut during the 1970s. This happened for a number of reasons. One was practical. In several respects the AMA's opportunities were retreating. Even aside from the inward-looking, semi-private nature of performances held amongst the splendour of the Downer Room at Australia House (although the AMA also mounted concerts in major venues), Australia House was becoming increasingly unwelcoming – to Australians and others. The 'security culture' of the 1970s limited access to the building for concerts, while new charging regimens reduced practical support and increased costs for the AMA. Two other reasons involved the Australia Council. The Council's funds were cut by the first of the government razor-gangs, and the AMA was competing for money with other arts bodies.

Despite embarking on a membership campaign in late 1975, the Association seemed to be running out of steam. Perhaps voluntary arts organisations only have limited roles to play and a limited life span. In the era of a vital musical culture in Australia, an 'offshore' organisation was arguably less important, except for helping newly arrived young talent. Or had other bodies usurped the AMA's roles? The former committee member, Peter Andry, had established the Australian Musical Foundation in London (AMFL) in 1975. In the same year Geoffrey Simon's chamber orchestra, the Strand Ensemble, which had AMA committee members on its board, received substantial Australia Council funding, while the AMA lost its grant. It was later reinstated after much lobbying, but the AMA's principals, including Geoffrey Chard, had every reason to feel bitter.[49]

The AMFL had social patronage. The Patron was the Prince of Wales, the joint life presidents were Joan Sutherland and Richard Bonynge, and the committee included the arts administrator and law lord, Lord Goodman, the former air ace Sir Douglas Bader and Sir Claus Moser. A number of city corporations with Anglo-Australian connections were financial supporters. The Foundation was both more 'Establishment' and more singularly focused. It sought to assist talented young Australians who had come to London to pursue their careers. It made substantial annual awards – in 1981 a grant of £6000 over two years to a young musician.

The AMA had helped lift the once-weak profile of Australian music in London. Now, the AMFL supplanted much of the AMA's role, wounding it mortally despite a last burst of energy over the next few years. 'We were a flourishing organisation' (except perhaps from a composer's point of view – 'contemporary music' was a 'death knell' for audiences), reflected Geoffrey Chard, when suddenly the grants disappeared and Peter Andry's AMFL began to supplant the AMA. 'We were left with very little after all the years we had put in', reflected the dedicated Chard. The Foundation had got 'some money' and had 'some big guns behind them'. In many ways this contrasted with the AMA pulling itself up by its own bootstraps during the 1960s (and those bootstraps had often been Chard's own), and going on to do 'some worthwhile major things'. In some ways this was an organisational or territorial battle and even, for the democrat Chard, a class battle. It was also of wider significance. Whereas the specialist AMFL was oriented to individual talent, the AMA had a social, even national, conception of its role as an 'offshore' voice for Australian music, not just on the Strand but in London and Britain. Was this a romantic idea overwhelmed by the hard realities of the market for musical performers? Was it a traditional, colonial idea which had its roots in an English–Australian connection and an older Anglo-Australian society which was in decline in London, even as more and more Australians passed through this imperial-cum-world city? This Australian musical colony on the Strand was a form of transplanted cultural eucalypt. It was both a cottage plant, of limited significance, and a manifestation of an Australian musical culture which still found much of its life, not in its state capitals, in Sydney or Melbourne, Hobart or Adelaide, Brisbane or Perth, or in Canberra, but in Australia's other 'concert hall', musical London.

To Return or Not To Return?

Australia would become more important for Australian musicians, including Charles Mackerras, Barry Tuckwell, Joan Sutherland and Geoffrey Parsons. All would return for significant, and often extended, periods in the 1970s and early 1980s. This raised the question of whether they would stay in their country of birth or return to London, or other parts of the northern hemisphere. The single Geoffrey Parsons' 'returns' were the most enduring and in a sense the most predictable. Australian accompanists were always in demand for recitals and did not require their own direct 'celebrity' status, especially when, as in Parsons' case, it was acquired indirectly by accompanying Victoria de los Angeles. Underlying his visits, however, was a continuing Australian musical commitment, which mirrored the work he did in London in master classes. He also toured rural towns and cities, sometimes displaying a studied disregard for another hierarchy in Australian music, what 'the bods in Sydney' thought was right for the bush. Of the Sydney ABC managers he remarked, 'they have never been to concerts in Horsham and Hamilton – I have'.[50]

Barry Tuckwell became another frequent flyer musician on the international circuit during the 1970s, with engagements in the 'Far East' (to use the European term), South America (1976), and the USSR (1977). He first returned to play in Australia in 1970. Another return came when he began to take on more conducting roles. He conducted the Tasmanian Symphony Orchestra (TSO) from 1979 to 1983, enjoying Hobart's 'wonderful' climate. To return to Hobart, where he had been conceived during his father's performing travels, was a special kind of expatriate return.

The expatriate musicians' relationship with Australia was ambivalent, whether it was a matter of practicalities (dates, distances, seasons, finances, and institutional politics) or of deeper relationships. Barry Tuckwell remarked on the practical problems after his successful stint with the TSO. One problem was that he had to maintain homes in London and Hobart, which meant that he was 'losing money'. In addition, he wasn't happy with the institutionalised character of music-making in Australia. He painted a not-unusual picture of Australian musical performance as a fleet dominated by three battleships – the ABC, the Australian Opera and Musica Viva – which had 'a stranglehold on all three fields'. To this freelancer with myriad opportunities in Europe and the US, to someone who was constitutionally 'a bit of a rebel', the diplomatic and bureaucratic demands of dealing with the top brass of the ABC were at times grating. (He did not comment on that other phenomenon, at times rife in the ABC, as well as some university music departments, of a 'Pom mafia', as one former ABC staffer termed it. The imported administrators might have been kind to someone known in their old country.)[51]

Nor did he think that standards were continually improving. Perhaps with the nostalgia of middle age, he found that an earlier exciting ABC era had gone; it had been supplanted by an organisation lost in 'a quagmire of mediocrity', having lost its sense of 'destiny'. This successful leading performer and freelancer feared that there were too many people who had obtained a permanent job, stayed in it and 'keep everybody out'. Although this was a common situation 'everywhere ... where there are fewer outlets this becomes more of a problem'.

Part of the problem with the ABC bureaucracy derived from the dedication of the musician and his necessarily obsessive commitment to the highest standards. He reflected that:

> there is a major problem for anybody whose life is basically doing something, whether it is painting or being a musician. If that is your life it comes first and it is very difficult to put the family in a more important position because I always felt that this serves the family, and in any case it is my life and if I don't give everything to it, it ceases to be something that I do well, and that is compulsion perhaps. There is no question that the travelling side of it is a real problem.

This had meant several things for Barry Tuckwell. One was a changing personal life. He would marry three times over the years, partly a consequence of the demanding job – nocturnal, nomadic and pressured. He believed that those pressures and his absences were 'a contributive factor to the breakdown of both marriages'. His origins stimulated but challenged his family. His eldest son resumed the Australian connection, spending three years there in a coming-of-age inversion of his father's original odyssey. Tuckwell's personal situation loosely reflected his movements and connections. His first wife was English, the second a New Zealander and the third American.

Although Christmas at his sister's place, at the Harewood estate near Leeds, offered a certain continuity, the only real constants in his life were music and its seemingly necessary adjunct, travel. His peripatetic life meant his London house had become only 'a base to which I get occasionally'. The travelling musician had moved up, over the years, from cheap digs in Paddington, Bayswater and Kentish Town, to St John's Wood, where other successful musicians and arts people, including the Mackerrases, Robin Dalton and Jocelyn Rickards, lived, and then Chester Place, on the edge of Regents Park. The practical comforts of material success did not, however, come with time to enjoy them. Even when he thought that he would 'get a week off', he was busy with roof repairs and missing tickets, and still lacked time to do the necessary practice. While workmen repaired the centuries-old roof on a grey November day, and he shared coffee and Vegemite on toast with them, he reflected on how rarely he was there. Similarly, the travel which went with the work was 'the best and worst of worlds', especially when things happened – lost tickets to Italy, delayed planes etc. The problems of dealing with travel agents were, however, minimal in contrast to two other necessary evils: 'those wretched agents' who took their percentage and those 'other terrible people in our lives . . . critics'.

Barry Tuckwell built up an ambivalent relationship with Britain over the four decades from 1950. Although England once had a 'special flavour', he became less enamoured of it over time. He particularly disliked the grey cold of an English winter. Despite his reservations about the politics of Australian music institutions and about distance ('from London you can get anywhere; the only place that is difficult to get to is Australia'), in other ways he felt welcomed and contented – 'like putting on an old coat, I feel suddenly more at home'.

Charles Mackerras returned in 1982 as chief conductor to the Sydney Symphony Orchestra, which had rejected him two decades earlier. He had been a conductor on the SSO's 1974 European tour, then worked as a guest conductor in 1981. His three-year appointment as chief conductor also allowed time for his international commitments. Nancy Phelan suggested that Charles wanted the best of both worlds:

> Charles had a foot on each side of the world. His home was in London and his work in the northern hemisphere but his own family were in Australia; he loved Sydney, the harbour, the sailing, he enjoyed working with his old orchestra, he liked the way he was treated when he returned.[52]

Yet, life was complicated. His wife Judy liked coming to Australia but did not want to move to Sydney permanently. Her family, and their children, were on the other side of the world.

Charles Mackerras' period with the SSO from 1982 to 1985 was exciting but demanding. Despite faster planes, the 'flying maestro' of 1962 was now 20 years older. This made performing at both ends of the earth on a regular basis, and with a tight schedule, very demanding. Mackerras recognised the problem, writing to his agent in late 1983:

> I feel that working in two hemispheres every season is beginning to exhaust me to such an extent that I doubt if I can keep it up much longer . . . I love being in Australia, and have enjoyed my association with the SSO so much that I encouraged the ABC to extend my contract up till 1988. However, I don't really think I can continue in the position of Chief Conductor beyond 1985.

Mackerras' replacement in August 1985 was the young Tasmanian-born opera conductor Stuart Challender, who had studied in Europe rather than London, and had joined the Australian Opera in 1980. In a sea-change for Australian music, as well as a break with SSO tradition, Stuart Challender became its first permanent Australian-born conductor in August 1987, after being its principal guest conductor in 1986.[53]

Joan Sutherland's return was more traditional, almost. Made a Dame of the British Empire in 1979, she was treading in well-trodden tracks or at least on historic red carpet. The return of the diva, the honoured tall poppy, later in her career though not on the verge of retirement, echoed Melba's returns. But things were not quite that simple in this era. In the days of the jet plane Sutherland and Bonynge maintained their abode at Chalet Monet in Les Avants, the Swiss village above Lake Geneva (which also had major tax advantages) while she continued to perform in London, Europe and beyond. Sutherland and Bonynge returned at a time when the now 20-year-old Australian Opera was facing a board crisis and financial difficulties, including a million dollar deficit. The Sydney Opera House, despite its architectural majesty and symbolic significance, could not seat a large audience. Government funding was also reduced in the post-Whitlam era, during the post-OPEC oil price rise recession of the mid-1970s.[54]

The 'royal' style of the new Queen of the Australian Opera and her conductor and consort, Richard Bonynge, set tongues wagging in musical Sydney. Since Richard Bonynge himself came as part of the Sutherland package, this fuelled suggestions of a Sutherland clique at the centre of the Australian Opera. However, her fellow Sydney Conservatorium student of the 1940s was emerging from the diva's formidable shadow. He would acquire a reputation in his own right as a conductor who reclaimed several eighteenth and nineteenth-century operas, particularly French romantic operas, for contemporary repertoire. His musicological work, like that of Mackerras, stemmed from that youthful 'colonial' thirst for knowledge of the original sources; that research nurtured by a sense of frustration at being separated in time and place from the European origins of classical music.

Mackerras believed in the romantic route of study and performance in London and Europe for young Australians. This historic orientation towards Europe and the past may have explained why the standing of classical music in a forward-oriented everyday Australian society was limited. Was that why, despite Don Banks' hopes, musicians and composers weren't recognised as being 'as important as tennis players' with their own high level of skill? Classical music as performance was grounded in a tradition which looked back to the past and up to the highest standards of performance. Unlike drama, which at different times stressed the relationship between the play and the audience, it was less grounded in the society around it. While contemporary composers were often in a close relationship with their own physical, social and cultural environment, the market for their art through the music publishers of London, and the stimulus of other composers, called them away from their native land. The composer's imaginative ear may have gained from dislocation, as in the case of Sidney Nolan, who painted Australia better while looking out on the Thames at Putney. Not all composers, however, were inspired primarily by the social and the natural, by time, place and society. Whatever the cause, classical music still looked overseas even more than other art forms. That orientation seemed less and less to Britain, however, as Mackerras lamented. British immigration laws now made it very difficult for Australian artists without patriality (an English parent or grandparent) to work in the UK once they had turned 26. In an increasingly global world, would the Australians ever be central again at Sadler's Wells and Covent Garden? Or, alternatively, would a different Australian, and international, musical culture emerge later in the century?

Chapter 9

The Yellow Brick Road to the
Land of *OZ*... and beyond[1]

On the Road

On a typically hot tropical day in Singapore in mid-1966, two young Australians, the editor Richard Neville and the painter and cartoonist Martin Sharp, checked out of the Raffles Hotel. Symbolically they exchanged their suitcases for rucksacks, and set off on the overland trail north along the Malay peninsula. They had arrived in Singapore by air, no longer following the earlier practice of leaving their familiar world on the dock before a long sea voyage to England or Europe.

Their departure was a reflection both of Australian tradition and of the Sixties – escaping from repressive Australia and travelling to what even *Time* magazine termed 'Swinging London'. It also had a new Asian inflection. In Sydney, as editors of the alternative magazine *OZ*, they had just won a series of trials for indecency, but the Liberal Party's participation as a junior ally of the Americans in Vietnam seemed as enduring as ever.

When a friend, the former student journalist Alex Popov, wrote from London 'Everyone else is here – why aren't you?', they succumbed to an imperative which was more Sixties than traditional.[2] Martin Sharp wanted to go straight to London but Richard Neville persuaded him to travel overland, reflecting the nascent counter-culture's discovery of Asia, on the route which would later be called the 'hippie trail'. They headed overland to Cambodia and Nepal. The trip came with pain as well as the sought after pleasure; Martin Sharp travelled with dysentery from Cambodia to Amsterdam and London.[3] Their journeys, including the trip to Cambodia, reflected Australia's emerging Asian links, even if also mirroring its continued Western provincialism: involvement with a new imperial centre, the US.

In London, their batiks would be coupled with the even softer hues of English corduroy, and they would find creative spaces in Soho and the Kings Road. The centre of the ex-Empire, and now a 'world city', was distinctive, as well as being part of a shrinking globe. For Richard Neville it was firstly a family and female world. Like that of many expatriates and immigrants, his voyage was part of a chain. He had followed his girlfriend Louise Ferrier, whom he had farewelled at Circular Quay in April 1965 when she went off to London on the *Fairsky*, catching the streamers thrown from the dock. He also followed his sister Jill, who had left when he was only ten. Arriving after six months on the overland trail, he completed the journey by hitching from Dover. He knocked on his sister Jill's door at 70 Clarendon Road, Holland Park, at 10 o'clock at night, joining his fellow wanderer, Martin Sharp.[4]

Swinging London Calls

For many young Australians in the Sixties the journey to London was a conscious escape from parochial Australia. For others it realised a desire to see the world, either to go 'OS' (overseas) or, more or less traditionally, to set off on a grand tour, or even a not so grand tour, of Europe. It could also be the first step in a professional career along the avenues for talent offered by the cultural market, the great cultural and commercial stage of the international metropolis. Or it could be more than any one of these three: as escape became its own raison d'être, career aspirations sometimes gave way to more immediate pleasures before the traveller settled down, either after returning home or, occasionally, in London.

In the 1960s the paradoxes multiplied as the number of travellers grew. This was the last age of the long voyage by ship, with its sense of the journey, its long duration (4–5 weeks) and its expense. The coming of age of the children of the postwar baby boom and the beginnings of jet travel, through the Boeing 707 and then 747, inaugurated an era of mass travel. In 1968, there were over 250 000 short-term departures (for less than a year) of Australian residents, with around 50 000 long-term departures, a great increase over the 30 000 short-term and 20 000 long-term departure figures for 1950. In 1975, the growth was even greater: there were over 900 000 short-term departures, 66 000 long-term departures and 10 000 permanent departures.[5] These demographic and communications changes would become turning points in the symbolic relationship between Australia and London.

The price of sea travel was slowly falling as the airlines started to become competitive. Yet in the Sixties most journeys were still made on ocean liners because they were cheaper than planes. Now they were the recycled Greek and Italian liners: Chandris Lines' one-class *Australis*, which, as the *SS America*, had carried Australian troops in World War II, the *Patris*, and the *Ellinis*, the *Galileo Galilei* and the *Guglielmo Marconi* of Lloyd Triestino, and the Sitmar Line's trio, the *Fairsky, Fairstar* and *Fairsea*. For those of a better class or merely with more money or a stronger sense of imperial tradition, the two-class liners of Shaw Savill and the P&O/Orient Line's *Orcades, Orantes* and *Oriana* were the way to travel.[6]

Even at sea change continued. Most earlier voyagers travelled by Colombo and Suez and landed in Europe at Naples or Genoa or in Britain on the Thames at Tilbury, as had generations before them. After the closure of the Suez Canal during the 1967 Arab-Israeli War, the ships would take them to Southampton via the Cape of Good Hope or via the Panama Canal and the US. By the late 'Sixties' (in chronological time the early 1970s) some flew. Others, like Richard Neville and Martin Sharp, travelled the overland route. These journeys, through the exotic cultures of Bali and Java, Thailand and India/Nepal, mattered as much for some travellers as their London or European arrival.[7]

The nature of the European trip was also changing. For the old upper class to upper middle class it still reaffirmed their traditional Anglo-Australian aspirations, but a new breed of young travellers – office workers, nurses, tradesmen and unskilled workers who followed in the tracks of the 1950s escapees – saw it as an adventure, 'a chance to let your hair down', to 'do Europe', to see 'the world'. They went to Britain to find jobs, to travel and then to return to the plentiful employment opportunities available in Australia. For some university graduates, who listened to 3AR or 2FC or 7ZR on the ABC, watched French films and drank strong coffee in espresso bars, dutifully read the *Listener*, the *Times Literary Supplement* or the *New Statesman* (as did their teachers in university common rooms), it was a voyage to the European sources of culture. For others, it was a journey to the more progressive politics and liberal climes of the Britain of the Campaign for Nuclear Disarmament (CND), the satire boom and new Prime Minister Harold Wilson's promise of 'the white heat of technology'. It was an escape from the repression and conflict of Robert Menzies' Australia. Escape from the land of suburban lawn-mowing and car-washing in 'Godzone' (God's own country), the land of censorship and then of conscription for Vietnam.[8]

The cultural refugees, like earlier generations, did not notice that in London suburbs like Finchley and the outer commuter belts such as Guildford, Surrey, life was remarkably similar to that of Australian suburbs. Men enthusiastically mowed lawns, sometimes incongruously clad in shirt and tie, and polished cars. Families watched television variety shows while D. H. Lawrence's *Lady Chatterley's Lover* was censored and plays still had to be licensed for the stage.

'Suburbia', and its values, were seen as Australian phenomena rather than characteristic of most of suburban London and much of Britain. Like most English migrants sailing in the other direction they viewed Australia as synonymous with materialism. For these new cognoscenti only metropolitan inner London mattered. That could mean group houses with other 'colonials' at Earls Court or Fulham, basements in Westbourne Grove or fashionable Chelsea. Or, later, bedsits in Camden or Kentish Town in the working-class and increasingly alternative inner north.

In a pattern which would soon become common in Britain and Australia, the *OZ* travellers were expatriating themselves not from one country to another, but from one state of mind to another. The transplanting of *OZ* magazine to London in 1967 exemplified the new expatriation. Two of its progenitors went not to advance their careers or to learn from the 'Mother Country', but to move to new stages. By chance they took their own invention with them.

'All change, please!', as the London bus conductor said, was the cry of the Sixties. The birds of passage of the mid-1960s also journeyed to the London of 'All We Need is Love', of the Beatles and the Rolling Stones. To the 'Swinging London' of Jean Shrimpton and her mini-skirt, which had so shocked the Melbourne Establishment ladies at the 1965 Melbourne Cup carnival, of Mary Quant fashions, and the Mini-850 car (Jill Neville had one which Richard borrowed).[9] By the late 1960s, journeys to Britain were made in a different world. In the 'international' culture of the Sixties it was a trip to London (with or without hallucinogens), as one of the international underground capitals, along with Amsterdam and San Francisco. Soon, it would also be a trip to Carnaby Street as a tourist site, like Buckingham Palace and the Tower of London; but that was another story.

Getting High with a Little Help from Their Friends

In the culture of experiencing the experience, of the highs of 'Do It', of the transcendent moments of rock and the self-discovery, the self-absorption of the 'Me-Generation', the journey was a distinctive one. Once it had been a rite of passage from the new to the old world and a saga of personal movement: a journey from youth to maturity, from provincial insignificance to the cultural heights of Britain and the European old world. The journey from innocence to experience, from mundanity to meaning and from prosaic everyday life to the odyssey of purpose was the old ideal. Counter-cultural aspirations were different. They were about a liberation from the 'straight' society which enshrouded the young, about experiencing the 'high' of the moment, of the 'trip' of the senses, rather than the more serious stuff of which a *bildungsroman*, a story of education in the ways of age and wisdom, could be told.

The flight from the suburbs was one towards the liberation of the self. No longer was it an historical, social and spatial passage to somewhere else. Now it had become a mental voyage, soaring into the urban international world shared by all Western societies. The aspiration was self-realisation, the self discovered through generational cultural experience rather than through the society, and sometimes the artistic language, of another country. Meaning could be found in pleasure rather than in art, in the contemporary underground of London and California rather than in the historical monuments and statues of British achievement and European culture. If success was to be sought, it was in terms of fame, even Andy Warhol's 15 minutes of fame, rather than older calculuses of significance.[10]

Both expatriation and the Sixties search for liberation were often the product of more repressive contexts from which the 'traveller' sought to escape. Expatriation could be a specific revolt against parental authority and the prosaic expectations which went with it: solid, sober professional careers for boys and respectable suburban marriage for girls, all surrounded by repressive social institutions. For Michael Blakemore, two decades before, it had been both an individual's revolt against his father's middle-class aspirations and a professional necessity to allow a career in the theatre. Now, revolt almost seemed the norm.

Fashionably Revolting *OZ*

The compounding of these older traditions of rebellion with new possibilities was personified in the three softly spoken *OZ* editors, Richard Walsh, Richard Neville and Martin Sharp. On one of Sydney *OZ*'s more public occasions, before the New South Wales Court of Criminal Appeal in February 1966, they dressed in the English style of the day. Neville looked 'rather like a young Oscar Wilde in blue corduroy suit, blue shirt and elastic-sided boots'. Martin Sharp wore a more conservative 'grey corduroy suit, striped shirt, gaily floral tie, mid-thirties waistcoat and Ringo [Starr] hairstyle'. In contrast Richard Walsh was the Sydney professional in a 'sober suit and Sydney University tie'.[11]

OZ magazine was a product – and a shaper – of these personal and cultural changes. *OZ* was conceived in the vast inland of eastern Australia, in the hermetically sealed world of a car, in July 1962. Four student performers-cum-entrepreneurs were thrown together in a large American Ford Customline on the long 1400 kilometre journey from Sydney to a conference of student editors in the 'Athens of the South', Adelaide. At the wheel was Alex Popov, who had borrowed the car from his father. Verbally sparring were the short and well-spoken Peter Grose, arts/law student, and his co-editor of *Honi Soit*, the medical student Richard Walsh, comprising the rational and political half of the foursome. Their partner in this travelling verbal tennis match was a thin artistic longhair, Richard Neville, editor of the new University of New South Wales student rag, *Tharunka*. A few months earlier he had met Martin Sharp, the artist and co-editor of the *Arty Wild Oat* at Sydney's only bohemian campus, East Sydney Tech art school.

On April Fool's Day 1963, after a short period of gestation, the progeny of the trip came upon the world – the first issue of *OZ* magazine, a monthly magazine of satire and youthful wit. In its lineage, it was the product of two worlds. One was the burgeoning of satire of the early 1960s. An early manifestation in Australia was Barry Humphries' record *Wild Life in Suburbia* (1958) while its high point was *The Mavis Bramston Show*, on television from 1964. Mavis, the 'star' of the show, was, in the actor June Salter's words, 'an Australian lady of very little talent who had tried her luck overseas, became a megastar and returned home to regale her countrymen with her questionable talent'. One of the show's stars, Carol Raye, remembered Mavis Bramston as a different character from a colonial culture – 'an English actress' with the 'name used by Melbourne actors to describe someone not all that talented'.[12] Cameoing only briefly, with Maggie Dence as Mavis, wearing her over-large hat, the returned expatriate of song and story might be seen as a mythical beast of an Australian cultural origins myth. She mirrored the Joan Sutherland return season and anticipated the Dame Edna Everage character. She was the central symbol of the show, which also had a Sixties theme song – 'There should be more togetherness' – and roots in the popular 1950s Phillip Street revues in Sydney.

In Britain, the satire boom's expressions included the comedy of Peter Cook and Dudley Moore, the high points of the Cambridge Footlights revue, television's *That Was The Week That Was* ('TW 3') and *The Frost Report*. Its sharpest, even jagged, edge was found in the US in Lenny Bruce's mono-logues, which, to Richard Neville's deep chagrin and despite his entrepre-neurial efforts, were censored in Sydney in 1962.[13]

That other world was a Sydney one of rebellion against authoritarianism and materialism. Often the roots of such rebellion began in childhood. Richard Neville and Richard Walsh had shared similar school experiences, despite their differences of style and mien. Richard Neville recalled Knox Grammar as a place of 'barely suppressed sexual sadism' centred around the hierarchical authority of the teachers, the prefects and the compulsory Monday afternoon army cadets. Adolescence reinforced these tendencies in the all-male private school: while this late developer was still just a child, 'suddenly one's friends were hairy and masculine and flicking each other with towels and playing football'. Neville rebelled at an early age. He was amongst a group of students who organised 'a little revolution', locking the prefects up in a room and warning 'that if they didn't curb their detention-giving attitudes' blood would be spilt.[14]

Richard Walsh's Barker College experience was equally enriching. Alienated by the dominant sports ethos at this school, this unhappy boy was viewed as 'naughty' and, according to his later recall, 'caned regularly every day'. University was an escape from school, which he hated. Even there restrictions had to be fought. Under pressure from his father, who had left school early because of the Depression, Richard Walsh went to university to study law, which became arts, and then finally medicine.[15] Richard Neville had a similar experience. Having finished school, he read the positions vacant in the *Sydney Morning Herald* while his father intoned repeatedly 'You must be an accountant'. Richard's wandering eye looked further down the columns, to 'Advertising'.[16]

Both Richards sought fulfilment beyond their courses at university. Richard Walsh was soon involved in drama and debating, the Students' Representative Council (SRC) and the seizure of the co-editorship of the student paper *Honi Soit* in a coup, only to fall in another one. He would later become President of the SRC and International Vice-President of the National Union of Australian University Students. Richard Walsh recalled 'the golden era of Sydney University' where he had the company of future dramatic, literary and political leaders – the Shakespearean actor John Bell and the theatre director Ken Horler, Germaine Greer and a number of future Canberra political correspondents.[17]

The two Richards found even these pools too small and too limited. After Richard Walsh and Peter Grose had been fired by the SRC, reinstated and then resigned as editors of *Honi Soit*, they were finding student politicians to be 'particularly authoritarian', like all politicians when criticised by the press. At *Tharunka*, Richard Neville also satirised and opposed authority.[18] *OZ* gave them the chance to 'do their own thing'. They also sought other opportunities. Richard Walsh wrote scripts for *The Mavis Bramston Show*, starting with a segment called the '*OZ* Newsroom'. The young medical student was already entering the mainstream media, in the form of a column in the Sydney *Sun*. Richard Neville, who also wrote for the '*OZ* Newsroom', found occasional work in advertising at Farmers department store. There he gained skills, and the money for coffee, wine and imported and illegal Lenny Bruce records.[19]

Sydney Vitalism vs 'the Alfs'

Derivative and 'indigenous' stimuli came together in the early Sixties. The young Richard Neville was stimulated by English weeklies and by Lenny Bruce's capacity to shock. A different influence was Sydney libertarianism and its antecedents, only one of which was Andersonian 'Free Thought'. The contemporary expression of libertarianism came through a loose group known as 'The Push', even for those who weren't habitués of its pubs (particularly the Royal George). Free love as well as free thought, a youthful or bohemian desire to shock the bourgeoisie and Sydney elite distaste for the values of the masses, working-class as well as middle-class, were the Push's cup of coffee.[20] Indirectly, they all nurtured the satirical land of *OZ*.

In place, *OZ* was a bright plant thriving in the lush and wandering sub-tropical garden of Sydney vitalism. The celebration of vitality was rooted in Dionysian and often elitist traditions reaching back to earlier Sydneys. The bohemian 'pushes', the literary groups of the 1890s, had been followed by the Nietzschean poetic ideas of William Baylebridge two decades later. The ersatz eroticism of Norman Lindsay's Beardsleyish pen and ink sketches, the Lindsay Eros, was opposed to the spirit of Thanatos of his vile and violent Great War cartoons. The poems of his 'Vision' school of the 1920s found their successor in the *London Aphrodite*. Published by the Fanfrolico Press, the magazine transfused colonial aestheticism to 1920s London through its founders, Norman's son, the writer Jack Lindsay, and the Queensland Rhodes Scholar and mercurial man of letters, P. R. ('Percy') Stephensen.[21]

Sydney vitalism – whether the older traditions or the Push's 1950s/1960s libertarianism – was a bohemian pearl; it grew in reaction to the grit of the provincial shell. Sydney's art was also the product of a refugee culture. From the artists Arthur Streeton and Norman Lindsay to the writers George Johnston and Charmian Clift and the writer-performers Barry Humphries and Germaine Greer, refugees came not only from the bush or the suburbs but also from Melbourne. Contemporary vitalism reacted against the ethos of Sydney suburbia; the inner-city intellectuals of the Push were disaffected, both by the wowserism of its low church Anglican establishment and the beery ockerism of the working class of this port city. There was one quali-fication – the Push inverted these views, celebrating booze, gambling and sex (ideally accompanied by thought) as the opposite of materialism and Sydney respectability. As Germaine Greer sang the old song, 'I'll be seeing you in all the old familiar places' became 'in the pub and at the races'.[22] It also had roots in the emotional style of its philosophical mentor John Anderson's former Trotskyism. It was a conflictual and authoritarian culture, and, in a Sydney way, a male-dominated society which left an imprint on Germaine Greer forever.

The young cultural radicals of *OZ* also defined themselves against the patriotic and suburban conventionality of the day. Against the royalism of Sir Robert Menzies, who in 1964 prostrated himself worshipfully before the visiting Queen Elizabeth, invoking the poetic line of worship, 'I did but see her passing by, and yet I'll love her till I die'. Against the new loyalism of his successor: Harold Holt, happy vassal in the Vietnam War of US Presi-dent Lyndon Baines Johnson, took *his* lines from the Democrats' election slogan, pledging that Australia would also go 'All the Way with LBJ'. Against the Sacred Cows of God, Queen and Governors, Judges and the RSL (the

Returned Services League). Against the 'Alf' (or, optional plural, 'Alves') who sought 'to convert you to a clean-living, all-Australian anti-erotic, healthy, mentally retarded citizen', ready to 'crush minority groups such as blacks, atheists, Nazis, anti-fluoridationists, intellectuals and Communists'. The Alves, *OZ* believed, reflected the 'wonderfully tolerant' worldview of 'the Australian public' – the view that it would be 'a damn good idea if everyone stopped writing and talking and thinking and became DECENT AUSTRALIANS'.[23]

The *OZ* principals came from the respectable Sydney of the North Shore and the Eastern Suburbs. Richard and Jill Neville had grown up in the comfortable milieu of upper middle-class Mosman. Like the divided Mackerras family, they were stimulated by their parents' contradictions – their accountant father's suburban values and commercial, if media, background, and their mother's performing side. Another factor was their exposure to the bush when at their house in the Blue Mountains at Mount Victoria. His father's skills and his mother's power were creative forces for Richard, who found the family less constricting than had Jill. Perhaps the family's contradictions allowed, as well as provoked, his generational celebration of play, as opposed to bourgeois respectability.[24]

In the spirit of what older heads called 'the baby Push', some early *OZ* meetings were held at the Mosman parental home. Martin Sharp was even more 'comfortable'. He was a scion of the even wealthier Eastern Suburbs from which Charles Mackerras, Michael Blakemore and Jocelyn Rickards, an earlier student at East Sydney Tech, had come. Later, surrounded by icons of his own creations and collection (including 'Tiny Timia'), he would live in his parents' mansion at Victoria Road in exclusive Bellevue Hill.

OZ's secretary, Marsha Rowe was less privileged than the *OZ* quartet (soon to be a trio, when Peter Grose left in the first few months). Although she had grown up on the North Shore in Neutral Bay her 'engineer' father had a working-class job and her middle-class mother had a Victorian house which was expensive to buy and costly to renovate. At a time when the education of boys seemed more important than that of girls, Marsha Rowe left school and did a typing course at the tech college. From the family world of reading – the Packer tabloid, the *Daily Telegraph*, and the *Reader's Digest*, rather than the *Sydney Morning Herald* – she went first to a secretarial job at CSIRO in the Sydney University grounds. She then escaped to work as a secretary for this new magazine, *OZ*. Despite her father's consternation a compromise was achieved. She continued to live at home for a few months and worked for *OZ* for the next two years.

OZ, as an alternative magazine, mirrored some contemporary values. Like the Push, in which men were definitely on top, in the pub, in philosophical debates and in bed, it put women in an inferior position. Marsha Rowe later remarked on her role as a 'punctual' secretary, 'Workin' for the (underground) man', 'dutifully doing all those boring jobs like subscriptions and accounts and explaining why manuscripts had been lost'. Office everyday drama could also include male humour ('Lord Root's dead', a male joke outside her cognisance). One day Richard Neville threw tea at the mirror due to her failure to adjust the temperature of an electric kettle and then used her sanitary napkins to mop it up. Although Marsha Rowe's straight sides brought her into conflict with gay men and with dope smokers (anticipating future conflicts on the other side of the world), *OZ* was exciting. Her own work was less so, and at times involved 'boring . . . masses of paperwork'. Class snobbery and gender prejudice ensured that her role was menial; typing and sweeping the floor were higher priorities than research, a possibility forgotten not long after it was suggested.[25]

OZ on Trial

OZ soon landed itself in trouble. In the continuing Sixties' play, the courtroom drama of the rebels against censorship, respectability and war, the three editors were put on trial in 1964 for *OZ*'s free and often 'dirty' speech. At first, the *OZ* editors believed that the problem was local. It was not the dominant conventionality and respectability in Western society which they, along with Lenny Bruce, the publishers of D. H. Lawrence, the anti-censorship and civil liberties movements and Kenneth Tynan in the theatre, were challenging, but a distinctively Australian provincialism.

When *OZ* found itself in court, charged with obscenity, that view seemed confirmed. In a magazine which took on censorship and advocated sexual freedom in nearly every issue, an account of surfie gatecrashers and sex was one of many dramatic stories. However, this piece put Neville, Sharp and Walsh in the dock of the Sydney Magistrates Court. Despite their respectable suits, and the long list of distinguished artistic, intellectual and university defence witnesses who argued for the literary merit of *OZ*, the three defendants were found guilty on 23 September 1964. Neville and Walsh were sentenced to six months jail and Sharp to four months. Fortunately, on appeal Stipendiary Magistrate G. A. Locke's verdict and sentence were thrown out by Judge Levine in February 1965, and again, following a Court of Criminal Appeal hearing on matters of law, in February 1966.[26]

The *OZ* trial was a 'jarring experience' – 'horrifying', as Richard Walsh thrice repeated when looking back on the events. Not only did it take 'so much time and emotional energy' out of them, but he was worried at the 'scary prospect' of being barred from a future career in medicine. 'We all came from fairly middle-class kinds of families who were not enchanted . . . with what we were doing' and found 'seeing their kids on the front pages of the papers' even worse.[27] Positive as well as negative possibilities emerged.

The trial involved a national campaign, a large number of witnesses and the participation of prominent barristers. *OZ* had already led to other activities including the *Mavis Bramston* segment, and an *OZ* Revue created by Jim Sharman, later the innovative director and producer of rock musicals in London and Australia. In the world where visual culture met print culture, J. D. Pringle, editor of the *Sydney Morning Herald*, offered both Sharp and Neville jobs. Other new avenues emerged. The conventional media were opening up, following the creation in 1964 of the *Australian*, the first national newspaper, by Rupert Murdoch, who was spreading beyond his Adelaide base. The then adventurous broadsheet ran Sharp cartoons.[28]

The long trial experience had differing impacts for the *OZ* three. As Australia changed, Sharp and Neville chose to escape in search of other worlds, while Walsh pursued medicine and several media careers in Sydney.

OZ Reborn

Richard Neville's world in London was for him not a limitation but an opportunity, the beginning of a meteoric journey which went far beyond the known. On his first Saturday night in London, Jill, the observer and collector of literary people, threw a party at which she introduced Richard to a number of London friends and writers. A little later he was interviewed by the London *Evening Standard*, which reported that Neville and Sharp were planning a London *OZ* with the headline 'Rebel Aussie whiz-kid to publish here'.

Soon tabloid prophecy became counter-cultural reality. Gathering together several travelling Australians and some English student writers, *OZ* was reborn. *London OZ*, as it was called for the first three issues, began in the satirical spirit of its parent and was produced in a room in Jill's house. In the year in which *Sergeant Pepper's Lonely Hearts Club Band* took the Beatles and rock in psychedelic directions, *OZ*, under the banner of Martin Sharp's covers and posters, was travelling a similar route. At first though, Richard, of the 'baby Push', looked as well to his Sydney predecessors. He ran articles from Germaine Greer and Clive James, and from Lillian Roxon in New York. The then London-based art critic Robert Hughes had written for Sydney *OZ* no. 2 under the headline 'OZ Interviews God'. Now, with characteristic timing, he was at the artistic centre of things, having just returned from the 1967 Florence floods.

Always one to educate his elders, Richard claimed that he took Germaine Greer away from the Cambridge call to twinsets, tartan and a beehive. She returned from her 'respectable' persona to an older colonial role more akin to the 'damned whore' than to its opposite, 'God's police', and reflected on the subject 'In Bed with the English' for *OZ*. (At this time she transformed her visual persona, frizzed her hair and rediscovered whisky and dope.) A Peter

Porter poem offered a different link with an Australian and family past. An early contribution from Colin MacInnes – the different underground expatriate, who knew black London, and whom Jill had introduced to Richard – also reflected the miscellany of the first issues.

Over time, first at Jill's place, later in offices in Soho and Holland Park or at Martin Sharp's abode, 'The Pheasantry' on the Kings Road, *OZ* became a commune. In the rhetoric and practice of the time, it could often be a love-in as well as a bed and a hive of activity for new arrivals. Many Australians performed in this underground spectacular. Jill, in mini-skirt and bright tights, shared the eternal youth which seemed a Neville family blessing. At the beginning, she provided contacts, space and a telephone. As *OZ* developed, Louise Ferrier seemed to keep the whole ship moving while consoling its theatrical captain, Richard. Marsha Rowe had gone to London, working her way on a Greek ship, and then travelled in Greece. She returned to find herself on that familiar urban stage, *OZ*, despite her intentions to the contrary. Jim Anderson, the gay counter-culturalist, also came on board after he came back from Tunisia in 1969. Don Atyeo was a boy from rural Colac in Victoria who had been forced to stand at the Regent Picture House when 'God Save the Queen' was played, or be thrown out. After visiting his artist uncle, Sam Atyeo, in the south of France, and sleeping in a lift in Paris, he bedded down on the Embankment in London. He also travelled clutching his letters of introduction to the journalist Sam White.[29] Other Australian characters in the *OZ* cast included: Stan Demidjuk (a multicultural face from a changing Australia); Andrew Fisher, who later edited *OZ* before returning to become a Sydney barrister; the ubiquitous Irish-Chinese-Australian artist and designer, Jenny Kee, then an intimate friend of John Lennon and later partner of Michael Ramsden from Sydney *OZ*; and Alex Mitchell, *Sunday Times* researcher-cum-Healyite (Trotskyist) radical and counter-cultural fringe dweller.[30]

OZ, like the counter-culture itself, and many groups in international London, was the product of cross-fertilisation. It was more than the issue of an expatriate cultural ghetto, or the old story of expatriate, or immigrant, new blood invigorating an English institution. Amongst its English cast were the Left counter-culturalist David Widgery, the young designer Jon Goodchild and the later entrepreneur Felix Dennis. The visiting John Wilcock of the *Village Voice* took Richard Neville on the no. 31 bus to meet the black radical Michael X. In the flux of the 1960s, the *OZ* people interacted with the rock scene: Martin Sharp shared a flat with Eric Clapton, designing Cream album covers and a Dylan poster; and there was also the John Lennon connection.[31]

The Australians were, like the Sixties itself, a breath of fresh air: from Martin Sharp's 'clean and pure and dayglo' vision of psychedelia to their radical energies. Duncan Fallowell, one English participant, contrasted the generosity and colour which the Australians brought, creating *OZ*'s 'fantastic' qualities, with the English 'who go round with corks up their arses'. For David Widgery, the people around *OZ* were characterised by their self-taught qualities and enthusiasm for discovery; their expressions varied from the Push-influenced writing of Germaine Greer to visual innovation. The *OZ* combination – the escape from a 'conformist homogenous mono-culture that couldn't bear laughter that it couldn't understand' (Richard Neville), and the exciting opportunities of Sixties London – generated the flourishing new plant. Along with the other alternative papers of the day – *IT*, which was the *International Times* until the London *Times* sued over the name, and *Friends*, which was also *Frenz*, to and from which *OZ* contributors came and went – *OZ* was part of London's urban underground and nascent counter-culture. Radical history and the spirit of the age of Aquarius came together on one occasion. *OZ* joined with *IT* to promote a London Digger Love Commune, which sought to take the radical tradition of the Diggers during the English civil war of the sixteenth century to unexpected heights of ecstasy.

In the spirit of the Sixties London, *OZ* was many things. In its brief early satirical moment the first issue ran, in Richard Neville's assessment, 'a very good piss-take of *Private Eye*'. The comedian Peter Cook publicly burnt the offending issue in a Soho pub. More typically, it was part of the counter-cultural luxuriance of these international times, rather than just a 'colonial' challenge to English elites and their ghettoes. From the beginning *OZ* was efflorescent and psychedelic designs, book, rock, concert and festival reviews, radical reports from alternative press agencies, and photographs worth a thousand words. It was also: surreal layout in a transcendent era in which the medium was the message; underground stories on dope, the counter-culture and alternative lifestyles, including in Europe and the US; and the rich fruits of the diverse guest-editors Richard Neville fished up, including the too famous school kids' *OZ*. It was also advertisements for books, clothes, sex aids and alternative events. In the liberationist spirit of the era, it ran 'personals' for people desperately seeking somebody. Once, when going to Paris seemed more fun, it was the issue which failed to appear.

Martin Sharp, tall, gangly and with an elfish smile, was the most Sixties of the *OZ* principals. Painting and drawing to music, smoking dope, designing rock posters and album covers, he personified the psychedelic Sixties. However, like many newly arrived Australians, and other newcomers, he felt lonely for some time; he stayed with Jill Neville and then a friend, art critic Bob Hughes, until he finally found a place of his own. He lived in The Pheasantry in the fashionable Kings Road area, with a changing cast including various girls and Eric Clapton; there he was, eventually, at the urban centre of the counter-culture. Here he caught the waves of Sixties style, which he was soon shaping. His Australian and Sydney childhood, and more specific artistic stimuli, also influenced him. Books, cartoons and Van Gogh taught to this 'dreamer' at the gentler Eastern Suburbs private school, Cranbrook, by the artist Justin O'Brien, and the *Bulletin* cartooning tradition, which he sought to go beyond, helped shape his sense of line and artistic emotion. His sense of colour had other sources, spatial as well as temporal. Summer holidays at Port Hacking, swimming under water and watching the fish of many colours, including a large turquoise blue fish, walking in the bush with its wallabies and its deer, heightened his awareness of colour and light; the psychedelic Sixties would intensify that vision. At East Sydney Tech he found other avenues for his creative energies. With a fellow student, Garry Shead, he had published two issues of the alternative paper, the *Arty Wild Oat*. Somehow, it seemed, anticipating the Sixties performance culture which would reach its peak in London, Amsterdam and San Francisco, the art students' balls were 'the most creative things that were done' at the Tech.[32]

Conventional Sydney and an older generation had also influenced him. From Barry Humphries he learned the monologue, or storytelling, style as a way to present cartoons. Working in the summer holidays as a despatch boy at the George Patterson advertising agency, upstairs from the *Bulletin* magazine office, allowed other influences through osmosis. In the culturally exploding Sixties, the influences were diverse – from the painter Colin Lanceley to American *Vogue* and the music of Bob Dylan.[33]

By the mid-1960s, as in Australia and the US, the exciting era of liberation was bringing new hopes and new conflicts. At first, Britain seemed to be the place of hope and freedom. The appearance of swear words and buttocks on the London stage (the latter in the 1969 musical *Oh, Calcutta!*) came after the end of the licensing, that is censorship, of plays by the Lord Chamberlain. The abolition of capital punishment and the legalisation of homosexuality made liberal Britain attractive to refugees from the repressive former colonies. In 1967 in Victoria, conservative Premier Sir Henry Bolte hanged the prisoner Ronald Ryan despite a massive campaign against capital punishment. Among the many 'colonial' travellers who stayed in London were Peter Hain from South Africa and Patricia Hewitt from Australia, both of whom would play major roles in the Council for Civil Liberties, the young Oxford law student Geoffrey Robertson from Sydney, and several Sydney libertarians, including the philosopher Tony Skillen and the psychology student and 'Push' graduate Lynne Segal.

There was conflict in London, as well, however. Repression was emerging in face of anti-Vietnam demonstrations in London, at one of which Germaine Greer burned an Australian flag. Internationally, the years after 1968 saw the rise of radicalism *and* repression – from Chicago to Haight-Ashbury, from Brisbane to Hobart and from Trafalgar Square to Belfast. This was not the 1960s of 'Three Days of Peace and Love', the theme of the Woodstock rock festival in the US. Nor was it the London of visual fantasy, the dream world captured in Antonioni's 1967 film *Blow-Up* (with costumes designed by Jocelyn Rickards), or in the adolescent androgyny of Mick Jagger. It was the international world of radical splits and creeping violence, from police raids and terrorist bombs to death at the Rolling Stones' Altamont concert. By the late 1960s the 'Age of Paranoia' was threatening the underground around the world. In Britain too, the clouds of repression were gathering. Harold Wilson's 1964 rhetoric of 'technological revolution' remained unrealised, the Beatles, the mini-skirt and the Mini-850 combined had failed to solve Britain's economic problems, and the IRA (the Irish Republican Army) was becoming more active. Even the Beatles had gone from the romance of 'I Wanna Hold Your Hand' through the psychedelic experience of *Sergeant Pepper's Lonely Hearts Club Band* to deep disharmonies within the group.

OZ on Trial 2

OZ would figure twice in the drama of the transition from Sixties idealism to 1970s conflict and repression. Central was the *OZ* trial of the English summer of 1971. The radically rude, who had been called to account in the Sydney magistrates court, were now on trial before the Old Bailey. Neville was in the dock along with Jim Anderson and Felix Dennis. Among several related charges of indecency, as publishers of the sexually explicit publication *School Kids' OZ*, they were charged with having 'conspired with certain other young persons to produce a magazine' which would 'corrupt the morals of young children and other young persons', and having intended to 'arouse and implant in the minds of these young people lustful and perverted desires'.[34] At the same time as the new Tory government was prosecuting the violently radical Angry Brigade, the cultural liberationists of the Sixties were on trial. Radical dreams of liberation and Sydney vitalist and libertarian challenges to convention and repression were about to receive their comeuppance. In addition, one December day in 1970, Richard Neville had been cosily in bed with Louise Ferrier in their £7-a-week basement flat when they were rudely interrupted by police. On this occasion they came not in search of questionable literary material but seeking a different forbidden fruit, cannabis. Later, each would be fined £25.[35]

In the English summer of 1971 the forces of respectability and authority were personified by Detective Luff and Judge Argyle. The defendants mixed counter-cultural theatre and careful strategy. Richard Neville, the performer, conducted his own defence. The barrister John Mortimer, who was later better known for his literary/television creation of the eccentrically rebellious barrister 'Rumpole of the Bailey', played by Leo McKern, personified the progressive values of Sixties liberal England, and defended Anderson and Dennis. He was aided by the research of Geoffrey Robertson, the Sydney Rhodes Scholar, who would write a play about the trial and then pursue future careers as an international civil liberties barrister, author and as conductor of television discussions, *Hypotheticals*. He was supported by many *OZ* people, including Marsha Rowe and Louise Ferrier. Their considerable efforts were complemented by the work of the Friends of *OZ*, the 'Save *OZ*' meeting in Hyde Park, the support of John Lennon, and defence witnesses including the young Edward de Bono and the conservative psychology professor Hans Eysenck. In this complex replay of the Australian case, all their efforts would, however, count for little.

The revenge of respectable Britain against the subversive values of the 1960s was the real agenda. Richard Neville was taken in the Black Maria from the Old Bailey to Wandsworth Prison and later to Wormwood Scrubs: sentenced to 15 months jail for the minor charge of postal indecency. Jim Anderson was sentenced to 12 months and Felix Dennis to ten months. The British subjects, but Australian citizens, Neville and Anderson, were to be deported after completing their sentences. It seemed that the death certificate had been written for the Sixties' dreams of freedom. Despite being acquitted of conspiracy to corrupt public morals, which carried a possible sentence of life imprisonment, despite Richard Neville's high morale throughout the case, despite Marsha Rowe and Louise Ferrier working into the early morning typing the transcripts to help prepare for the next day's hearing, the trial did more than take the pleasure out of *OZ* and out of the alternative press.

The excessive penalties imposed by Argyle and the compulsory prison haircuts on sentencing seemed like real and symbolic attacks in a generational war. However, their very excessiveness would in the end return the '*OZ* Three' to freedom. They would be acquitted on appeal. However, the Sixties' alternative dream would never recover. The trial exhausted Neville. Marsha Rowe and Louise Ferrier, worn down and disconsolate, went off to recover with Germaine Greer in Italy. The steam had gone out of *OZ*, and several *OZ* principals were beginning to found a new magazine called *Ink*. Richard Neville had lost his sense of fun. His 'great fear' was that *OZ* would become, in the words of Felix Dennis, '*Punch*'; that 'it would become some dreadful boring old rag with which his name would be associated'.[36] At this point the Sixties explorers made different decisions. Richard Neville's other 'fear', of becoming a public voice of the counter-culture, was realised when he returned to the *Evening Standard* as a Thursday columnist under the title 'The Alternative Voice'. Like many travellers and some expatriates, his response to a reverse, in his case the trial, was to move on and then to return to Australia. He covered American politics and culture for the *Evening Standard* in the election year of 1972, and met the counter-cultural radicals of 1968, Abbie Hoffman and Jerry Rubin.[37]

Once again he would meet up with the other Richard, Richard Walsh, who had made his career in Australia. 'Straighter', Walsh was more of a rationalist but also a media man, an entrepreneur and a cultural nationalist. Married and with a young child, he left conventionality of one kind behind – although graduating in medicine, he never practised. He found a media career as exciting as catching the boat to the great centres of cultural activity overseas. From the early 1970s, he edited *Nation Review*, the satirically edged news magazine which ushered in, and also challenged, the Whitlam era.

The paths of the two Richards, Neville and Walsh, which had diverged in 1966 came together again. In the culturally and politically reinvigorated Australia of the 1970s, it was no longer the 'tail end of the Menzies era ... uninspired ... politics ... very dull' when 'it didn't look as though Menzies would ever go'.[38] In the new age of the jumbo jet, Richard Walsh flew Richard Neville to Australia to guest-edit an issue of *Pol*, a new and innovative glossy magazine which reflected a changing society; other guest editors included Don Dunstan, the reforming Premier of South Australia, and Germaine Greer. If in the 1960s London had been the place to be, by the 1970s it had become, for some people, the place to leave. Disillusioned by the corruption of the counter-culture, worn down by events in 'that place with no sun', 'sick of living in a basement' and 'marooned by celebrity', he eventually followed, as he had done before, Louise Ferrier, who had a house at Bondi.[39]

The alternative Aquarius Festival at Nimbin in northern New South Wales appealed. So, from December 1972, did the 'new Australia' of the reforming Whitlam Labor government. No longer did the exodus of talent mean the colonial absence of intellectual and alternative cultures in Australia. Neville would quickly find his feet – and his editorial dancing shoes – working in Melbourne, editing the alternative *Living Daylights*, an offshoot of Richard Walsh's *Nation Review*. The 'transient' had returned, at the end of a period which to many progressives, both expatriates and alienated intellectuals in Australia, had seemed like an unchanging 'ice age' since the Liberal Party's 1949 election victory. Not all expatriates endorsed this revised view. Some self-consciously issued condemnations of Australia which would recur, like Freudian gestures against the father (and the mother), over the next two decades. Different options presented themselves for others. For Jim Anderson, gay California around the Bay area provided a freedom from repressive Britain and Australia, at a time when Sydney had not yet become the second gay city of the Pacific. Don Atyeo, like Richard Neville, as much a communicator as a counter-culturalist, pursued career opportunities in the semi-commercial alternative media in London, on the critical 'what's on' magazine *Time Out*.

Free Love ... Freedom for Boys

For many of the women, who had left as an expression of a desire to spread their wings rather than to settle down in suburbia, new possibilities were emerging. The personal freedoms of the Sixties, whether in Push Sydney or basement London, had had their complications. Despite the Dylan anthem of liberation 'I Shall Be Released', Richie Havens voicing 'Freedom' at Woodstock and The Who's declaration 'We're not gonna take it', the male adventurers' goals were often simply expressed as 'Lay lady lay'. Upon reflection, the culture of play in which Marsha Rowe had believed was, in practice, men's idea of play, in work and in bed. Men not only had the pick of the more interesting work on the alternative press, they also called the shots in other ways. The Sixties, like the Push, 'gave older men a chance to sleep with younger girls', endorsed by a formal rejection of 'duogamy', the world of couples.[40] Unlike the less self-conscious do-it-yourself bohemians of Jill Neville's 1950s circle, floating relationships and communal sexual exploration came with the warrant of the counter-culture. Goals of expanded consciousness and sensual pleasure also made for other private worlds. The counterculture at play enjoyed London as a stage and put to one side the career aspirations which shaped the lives of other expatriates.

The old inequities were still there: from the woman at *OZ* down on her hands and knees cleaning the floor to Louise Ferrier keeping the magazine moving (while engaging in a world of open relationships) when Richard was out and about, the cultural entrepreneur ever busy dreaming up the next possibility. Chinks in the wall appeared, however, as they did in what they called 'straight' society. Along with the Equal Pay Act of 1970 and divorce reform came a special women's issue of *OZ*, and the prospect of a freer culture on the proposed new magazine, *Ink*. That was not realised at *OZ*, however. Decisions were still made by Ed Victor, Andrew Fisher and Richard Neville in a little room of their own.[41]

When the macho Melburnian Pete Steedman perfunctorily disposed of two of three new women typesetters, the meetings of women's groups had growing appeal for an anxious Marsha Rowe. Following the first Women's Liberation conference at Oxford and the women's march down Oxford Street, the group 'Women in the Underground' emerged. Reflecting a new orientation, it attracted Louise Ferrier, Michelene Wandor (then married to Ed Victor) and Sheila Rowbotham.[42]

OZ was the most visible part of the underground, the high-profile persona of the travelling Australians of this most travelling of all decades. Many young women, with less career opportunities or aspirations than their male contemporaries, graduates, office workers, nurses, spread their wings on the other side of the world. Working and enjoying themselves in London and travelling in Britain and Europe for several years, they had left behind the family pressure to settle down and some of their peers, who seemed to be becoming more suburban every day. While the death of the urban countercultural dream had occurred in the conflicts of the late Sixties, including the *OZ* trial, for many women new possibilities were emerging. If the end of the *OZ* period made many men return to other scenes in Britain and

Australia, several women were finding new political and personal alternatives through groups such as Women in the Underground.

As Marsha Rowe's anger grew, she became interested in new avenues. When the American Bonnie Boston suggested a new women's magazine, Marsha Rowe put up the proposal at a meeting and found the only taker was the Englishwoman, Rosie Boycott. *Spare Rib* first appeared in June 1972. This magazine of liberation for independent women was an alternative voice which also aimed at women who read the more humdrum conservative women's magazines. Situated somewhere between the 'unstraight' underground press and the more stylish glossies, such as the sexually liberated *Nova* and *Harpers & Queen*, it was genuinely innovative. It also aspired to collective rather than hierarchical organisation at a time when women's groups were, often painfully, seeking new ways of interacting. Over time the stress of 'communal editing' claimed as many or more victims than conventional media productions. However, in the early 1970s the radical enterprise offered political and social choices different to the usual individualist careers of most expatriates in other cultural professions.[43]

The early *Spare Rib* had a strong Australian input, with Marsha Rowe's initial role, the contribution of her former *Vogue Australia* contemporary Sally Doust to the early artwork, and sporadic pieces by other writers such as Margaret Walters on images (Marilyn Monroe/Janis Joplin) or later Lynne Segal on politics. Despite these contributions, and those of other expatriates from several countries, *Spare Rib* was more English than Australian. It was part of the English city garden of 1970s feminism. Its harmonies and divisions, its competing bushes and flowers, and alleged weeds, all arose in the 1970s era of emerging social and economic conflict in Britain.

From this beginning a dozen Australian women helped shape the women's movement, and then the several women's movements, and feminist publishing in Britain. Meanwhile in Australia, similar women, including some who had come from elsewhere, built the equally determined Australian women's liberation movement and its legacies. Some feminist women chose more individual paths. Germaine Greer, deploying her pen and her theatrical abilities, found new outlets in the different media of publishing and television. This was the beginning of the contribution of Australasian women to English feminism. The New Zealander Stephanie Dowrick at the Women's Press, Carmen Callil at Virago, Dale Spender as a prolific author, Gillian Hanscombe as a contributor to feminist debate and lesbian literature, Carole Spedding convening the international feminist bookfair (and later working as a Literature Board publicist for Australian books in Britain), and Lynne Segal as a participant in socialist–feminist debate, were amongst the more prominent. Most fused feminist and literary/publishing interests. For Marsha Rowe and several other 1960s travellers, feminism, career and expatriation went together.[44]

Chapter 10

Journalists' Journeys[1]

Australian journalists have often defined their work in terms of the dramatic events they cover – from wars, politics and disasters to the ups and downs of the rich and famous. This reflects the connection of the word 'journalism' to 'journal', a record of the events of the day or a measure of a day's work. But, as the Sixties would show, journalism is about more than 'big stories'. Like all careers and lives, it is also about 'journeys', a word which is itself etymologically linked to the French *journée* (the day) and *journal* (a diary of events as well as a newspaper). For the Australian journalists discussed in this chapter (and those, discussed in Chapter 3, who left during the postwar decade), travel for work took them on journeys through time as well as life. In their journeying these journalists (or 'hacks' as many ironically termed themselves) sought meaning and significance as much as income, interesting jobs and success. Sometimes that meaning was found in big stories and prominent by-lines. Sometimes it was more complex as it built on different stages of the journey: people and places in Australia and London and beyond; 'making it' as a name in one field or city; working in different capacities – as writer or editor, employed by a large newspaper or freelancing; and writing in different styles – reporting and feature articles to reviews and books. At times journalism was itself a creative profession.

The odysseys of expatriate journalists varied according to their gender and generation, luck and skill, and their aims and aspirations. The journey, along with the idea of expulsion, is one of the mythic themes of Western civilisation. Australians had grown up with these myths and their several specific variations. One was the return to the 'Home' country or civilisation. Another was expulsion and exile, either from an Australian home in which limitations of cultural and professional opportunities denied talented young people their birthright, or banishment from the original European source. It would involve both forms of expulsion and discovery as some wanderers dispersed themselves around the world, becoming double expatriates if not nomads. Or it could involve, sooner or later, the return of the expelled to an antipodean Eden. Although most journalists did not often reflect publicly on the search for self, expatriation, like their careers, had elements of that personal odyssey as well.

This study pursues only a few people, a handful of the Australian journalists who worked in London. Those included here are the cluster of journalists at the 1960s–70s *Sunday Times* such as Murray Sayle, Bruce Page and Phillip Knightley; several women, including Sandra Jobson and Barbara Toner, who became authors as well as journalists; and the prominent *Daily Mirror* and international television journalist, John Pilger. Their stories of expatriation are varied. Some simply stayed in London, some went further afield. Some became 'serial commuters' between London and Australia and some returned to build new careers. Those who went to Australian bureaus in London to work for a year or two, and those who merged into British society, are outside the scope of the story. Michael Charlton, for example, already had a BBC accent at ABC TV's *Four Corners* in Sydney. He moved effortlessly into *Panorama* and the BBC, showing little evidence of his colonial Antipodean origins.

Phillip Knightley's departure from Australia, noted earlier, had come after being embroiled in controversy during the 1954 Royal Tour. He had un-patriotically reported that the Queen had varicose veins; he also made public that the royal bodyguards were not armed as 'Anglo-Saxons are not natural assassins'.[2] His interest in detail, in the assumptions of the elite, and in security matters, was already strong. When he departed for Britain, the old order was changing. The old certainties of Empire, and of ANZAC in Australia, were no more. British Prime Minister Sir Anthony Eden and his loyal colonial assistant Prime Minister Robert Menzies had been humiliated by President Nasser in the Suez crisis of 1956. In culture and politics, the 'Angry Young Man' playwrights and the Campaign for Nuclear Disarmament led a chorus which queried Prime Minister Harold Macmillan's 1950s slogan – 'You've never had it so good'.

Phillip Knightley's story says much about the role of luck. His return to Australia in 1962 was a couple of years too early for the resurgence of Australian print journalism and the rise of ABC radio and television current affairs. After six months in Sydney, Dame Fortune smiled on him in the form of a £6000 Sydney lottery win (nearly £50 000 or over A$100 000 in today's money) which he shared with his mother.[3] With the win he shouted the bar at the *Daily Mirror* pub, funded his return to London, and had time to play tennis and to think about other forms of writing than daily newspaper reporting. One such piece was the television playscript, *Cosy in a Basement*. The six months in Sydney with ABC news also allowed him to think about the possibility of media work in which 'you didn't have to compromise your ethics about making up stories'.

He was no longer just 'cosy in a basement'; his winnings allowed him to buy a house in Northumberland Place, W2, just off Westbourne Grove. (This bombed area around Notting Hill Gate, to which the 1950s immigrants had gravitated, was not far from Palace Gardens Terrace, where Murray Sayle and Jill Neville had lived, and Kensington Palace, both to the south. Walking north, it was near to Paddington Station and international Bayswater, an area already becoming desirable.)

In this era the satire boom and popular music were giving birth to the 'Swinging Sixties', in which 'neophilia', the love of the new, challenged the certitudes of British tradition. Newspapers referred to a 'New Aristocracy' or a 'New Class' comprising popular singers (the Beatles and Mick Jagger), designers and models (Mary Quant and Jean Shrimpton), upwardly mobile working-class actors (Michael Caine and Terence Stamp), photographers (Lord Snowdon), artists (David Hockney) and editors (Mark Boxer of *Queen* magazine). Although, in a very English way, the 'new' aristocracy had links with the old, London was becoming 'the most exciting city', 'the most swinging city in the world'.[4] These youthful celebrities revolted against the 'stuffy', 'old-fashioned' values of ruling elites. As in the name of Peter Cook's new club, 'the Establishment', the new was challenging the old.

An Open Door on Grays Inn Road: the 'New' *Sunday Times*

After a decade in which Phillip Knightley had languished, and the mercurial Murray Sayle had risen and fallen with equal expediency, the Sixties provided a new opening. Several Australians left the peninsulas of Australian bureaus, subbing at Reuters, the 'life of Riley' of parties and new arrivals in sleeping bags on the floor, for a career of kinds. At the *Sunday Times* on the Grays Inn Road, now owned by the dynamic but non-interventionist Canadian Roy Thomson, editor Denis Hamilton was ringing the changes. New sections and supplements and a clear-out of the 'dead wood', a soon to be 'eclipsed generation', provided new opportunities at 'the new *Sunday Times*'. 'New' would be a recurring adjective in Hamilton's recollections of the paper that soon began to live up to the slogan invented over lunch – 'one of the world's great newspapers'.[5]

In Phillip Knightley's words, 'the doors of the *Sunday Times* were open to anyone with talent and in many cases the formalities of recruitment went out the window'. He himself had 'walked into' the newspaper on 30 June 1964 with a story on a loophole in British agriculture regulations which allowed tinned corn beef from uninspected foreign abattoirs to be routed 'through a Commonwealth country – in this case Gibraltar'. The connections of Mohammed Babu (Sayle's London post office friend, mentioned earlier, and now a minister in the Tanzanian government) led to another story, and full-time work followed. Knightley opened the door for Murray Sayle who came in to join the additional Saturday staff and also write church notices. He then, literally, bicycled ahead of the other newspapers, by following Goldie, an eagle which had decamped from London Zoo. A little bit of tactical hanging around led to regular work with the Insight team and on special assignments.[6]

Working with the Insight team of 'investigative' research changed the lives of Sayle and Knightley, while its 'investigative journalism' redefined quality journalism for a time. First formed in 1964, its group research, pursuing a story in detail over months rather than days or weeks, exposed the slum landlord Peter Rachman and explored the Profumo case. Insight features also utilised a form new in London, a *New Yorker*-style narrative of retelling a story over 6000 words.[7]

At the *Sunday Times* the geographical and social mobility of the expatriate coincided with the search for significance, and seemed to confirm the colonial–provincial Australian notions that 'overseas', in the 'real world', were found bigger events and larger complexities. Except that, aided by the colonial-cum-international perspective of expatriates (not all Australian), it looked beyond the Thames, Europe and Britain's former empire to the wars of the post-colonial, but not post-Cold War, 1960s. The experience opened windows on the world. It took Murray Sayle to wars, conflicts and adventures on four continents. It gave Phillip Knightley a chance to pursue subjects which fascinated him, from the deceptions of spies to those of pharmaceutical and beef companies.

Insight's glory days came after 1967. Reborn under the generalship of the Melbourne-trained journalist Bruce Page, and encouraged by the newspaper's new editor Harold Evans, Insight promised 'scoops of interpretation' as well as 'scoops of fact'. Of central importance was its genuine openness to talent. 'Harry' Evans, a northerner and the son of an engine driver, was on first name terms with his journalists, an unusual situation in respectable Fleet Street. His social and intellectual openness came together in the 'two Britains' at Insight: the elites who by virtue of their birth or brains came to the newspaper as Oxbridge graduates, and the new talent (including the 'unorthodox talent' of Murray Sayle), who came from the provinces, the former colonies and from around the English-speaking world.

Phillip Knightley believed that someone like Harry Evans, who had graduated in economics from a redbrick university after doing his national service, had more in common with the Australians on his newspaper, the South Africans, the Americans ... the Canadians ... than he did with the Oxbridge types he also employed. He certainly got on better with us ... and that was the reason there were so many Australians there. At one stage, there must have been six, seven Australians working with him, maybe more, and they dominated the Insight team.

In contrast to the social gap between Evans and the older English elite, the Australians' 'classless' relationships with Evans were free of the tense social pecking orders of English society. Yet, as Nelson Mews reflected, some Australians looked up to aristocrats such as William Shawcross.

Mews himself, a Perth boy of English parentage, had married an English-woman of higher station, and returned to England with her in 1967. He joined the newspaper after ringing Bruce Page, and was put on a story straightaway, as many of the reporters were in the Middle East in the lead-up to the Six Day War. At a time when it seemed like 'there were hundreds of Australians' around Fleet Street, being Australian didn't do him any harm, particularly at the *Sunday Times*. There, Mews met his old Canberra press gallery friend Alex Mitchell. He worked as a researcher on the Kim Philby spy story with Phil Knightley and the Englishman David Leitch (the husband of Jill Neville), under the direction of Bruce Page.

London and the newspaper were both revelations to Mews. Having a flat in the Kings Road, Chelsea, the centre of fashionable Sixties London, was 'terrifically exciting for a young chap from Perth' who could look out the window and see 'very exotic girls and people walking leopards on leashes'. Exciting in a different way was Mews' new workplace. He had 'never imagined anywhere in the world there was a paper as good as the *Sunday Times*. It was just the most wonderful thing working for it. The level of intelligence and intelligent debate ... on the paper was far higher than ... in Australia'. It was also far higher than that of most English newspapers, including the pre-Murdoch *Sun*, where he had also applied for a job. Intelligent scepticism replaced the corrosive cynicism which featured at so many newspapers. The 'playing fields' of Grays Inn Road were not only up the hill from Fleet Street, like a kind of Mt Olympus, they also provided pro-fessional and personal links, which he later maintained, when political editor of another serious 'Sunday', the Sunday morning current affairs TV program, *Weekend World*.[8]

Page, Sayle and Knightley were central players in Insight's main achieve-ments – exploring dramatic events, exposing secrets, and fusing original reporting and good writing. The *Sunday Times* and Insight challenged various establishments and the 'stories' which they told the world. Importantly,

Insight's work opened up the possibility of entrepreneurial links between newspaper journalism and book publishing.

The *Sunday Times* pursued adventures, intellectual and physical. Murray Sayle, wearing his troubleshooter hat, flew in a one-engined plane (the other engine had stopped) to take photos of Francis Chichester rounding the Horn on the first ever single-handed voyage around the globe. Insight and Sayle pursued other intellectual adventures. In December 1967, as resident 'whiz-kid' and elucidator of complex scientific ideas, he researched the immunology of resistance to foreign tissue, which was even more important than the complex surgery in Dr Christian Barnard's first-ever heart transplant. This inquisitive Aussie polymath asked more questions than a schoolboy with a strong raised arm. A pub expert able to lecture or interrogate, an amateur scientist, a lover of physical as well as intellectual adventure, and finally a performer, he was capable of many roles, from the dominator of party conversation to the ersatz English gent. He was always interested in going beyond the immediate and the obvious. This fellow traveller with John Anderson (he often denied the association) was always looking for the 'unintended consequences' of actions, and even more for 'unlikely causes'. In the tradition of the Greek philosopher Heraclitus, the contradictions were more interesting than the apparent or professed causes of particular actions. Sayle sought to understand the mind of the Reverend Ian Paisley, the Unionist political leader in the Northern Ireland conflict, through reading his PhD thesis at Bob Jones University.

The social hybrid of the Australians and the scions of the English elites was mirrored by an intellectual fusion. The Australian street-oriented stress on practical research ('getting a story') coalesced with the more desk-bound English concern with good writing. In practice, this was expressed in the two stages of the Insight team's work. 'Stage one', as Mews reflected, 'was proper hard reporting, endlessly . . . going out and interviewing people, trying to find out what was going on'. In stage two this material went 'through the type-writer', or more importantly the mind, of Bruce Page, or of other writers such as the 'Brit', Lewis Chester, or Phillip Knightley. They were charged with 'making something literary' out of the research. Long pieces of over 3000 words needed dramatic shape and literary finish, unlike shorter feature articles. Insight pieces could not 'just be knocked off' in an inspired hour or two.

Not that there was an intellectual division of labour between Antipodean fire-engine chasers and gentlemanly Englishmen sitting at their desks. Bruce Page, the Melbourne University economics graduate, had a (colonial perhaps) hunger for knowledge. This 'Australian of voracious intellect . . . called on Machiavelli, Marx, Coleridge and Keynes with all the vehemence of the autodidact'. Sayle and Knightley also pushed their pens with skill and wit. Nor were the *Sunday Times* war correspondents, such as Nicholas Tomalin who was killed in the Middle East, all adventurous colonials.[9]

Central to the *Sunday Times* experience was the challenge by outsiders to ruling elites, their ideologies and their secrets. Such an attitude came more easily to expatriate Australians. Like their very different compatriot, Rupert Murdoch, they were not in awe of or beholden to British institutions. Knightley reflected that these 'sort of outsiders . . . [who had a] reputation for riding rough-shod over objections' about the harm a story might do to the 'national interest', and who had the freedoms and resources of the *Sunday Times*, could get to 'the heart of the matter'.

The *Sunday Times* took on various organisations, from the Distillers company (which had made thalidomide), to the British intelligence establishment (in stories like that of Kim Philby, who became a spy for the Russians). Some years later, in 1987, a writ was handed to Knightley, just before he was to talk at a Sydney literary lunch about his new co-authored book on the Profumo affair, *An Affair of State – The Profumo Case and the Framing of Stephen Ward*. Prevented from discussing the book, Phillip Knightley instead extemporised on the theme of the Establishment. It was an appropriate subject for this well-dressed gadfly of the British secret service, journalistic, manufacturing and trade elites (MI5, MI6, foreign correspondents, Distillers, the Vestey family and its tax-avoiding companies):

> I imagine it is a loose, flexible, ever-changing conspiracy to protect
> the common interest of the conspirators . . . Its basis, I think, in the
> UK . . . is one of birth, and relationships; it's one of schools; it's one
> of regiments, one of clubs; and in Australia, I don't know, but I
> suppose mateship must come into it somewhere.

In the Insight team Knightley had learned to question an establishment in business, in politics and in gentlemanly society which turned a blind eye to unsavoury behaviour by members of the better classes and their organisations. Sydney journalism and the experience of research into English elites had made him sceptical about groups in power. Later he explored the limitations of his own profession in his account of war correspondents, *The First Casualty*, its title a reference to the old saying 'the first casualty when war comes is truth'.[10]

The Establishment, both in Britain and Australia, was 'essentially a male thing . . . dominated by male values and by male bondages', Knightley argued. This liberal believer in the fourth estate's role in ensuring accountability and the social democrat critic of the self-interest of the rich and powerful, believed that the Establishment in each country often contradicted the public interest. Conversely, Knightley recognised the temptation facing the journalist who dealt with power and corruption, and mused to himself that his next book might be on 'How to become a member of the Establishment', or 'how to persuade the Establishment to accept you'. 'They might perhaps buy me off by making me a member as well', he concluded. The scent of power, particularly illicit power, had an often contradictory appeal for journalists who sought to expose its misuse.[11]

The 'Third Man' of Russian counter-espionage, Kim Philby, was pursued by this new elite of Grays Inn Road – a group of outsiders, dissidents, Australians and renegades from the Establishment. Murray Sayle, this 'deceptively convivial hard reporter', met Philby over vodka (Philby had his pistol and the back-up of armed guards in the corridor) in Room 436 of the Minsk Hotel in Moscow. Sayle had successfully tracked down his man at the general post office, where he picked up his mail and the *Times*, for the latest Test cricket scores. Philby, a 1930s Cambridge graduate, denied that he was a traitor, declaring: 'To betray you must first belong. I never belonged'. He had always fought against 'fascism' and against 'imperialism ... fundamentally the same fight'. As Harold Evans observed about Bruce Page, the leader of the Insight team, perhaps only an outsider could know that English society was even more complex than it seemed.[12] To Evans, Page had:

> [an] Aussie contempt for the British establishment, a contempt that the Philby story perfectly supported: 'We're dealing', he would say, 'with a lot of unemployable twerps selling off the old country to any old bidder'.[13]

Phillip Knightley reflected on the gravity of this long-suppressed spy story. Kim Philby was not some minor defector, but the former head of the anti-Soviet section of SIS (MI6) and the chief liaison officer with the CIA and the FBI. Or, as Knightley put it, in a journalistic tone of astonished revelation: 'The man running our operations against the Russians was a Russian agent himself!'[14]

The Philby case reflected the *Sunday Times* Insight's quantitative, as well as qualitative, approach to journalism. Eighteen reporters worked on the case in Britain, North America and the Middle East, in addition to Sayle's meeting in Moscow. The book based on the Insight articles sold well in North America as well as in Britain and the traditional Commonwealth markets, and was published in ten languages. Earning £40 000 in royalties, it suggested new possibilities.[15] As Phillip Knightley reflected, 'long-term projects' kept journalists happy, even when there was no possibility of a weekly by-line. Evans also allowed the journalists to keep a percentage of book royalties, although they were already on salary, an approach which shocked the accountants. Even more creatively, he encouraged 'sabbaticals' in which a couple of months leave without pay might be added to accumulated annual leave. Compared to the daily grind of journalism, four months to work on a book was a luxury. The *Sunday Times* also gained, as it often serialised the new work.

Looking beyond Grays Inn Road – Phillip Knightley and the coming of Rupert Murdoch

Possible outcomes of the Insight experience might have been the consolidation of Fleet Street careers, the principals becoming part of the institutional establishment of the Street. Or, to the expatriates returning. Nelson Mews moved into television; the son of an English immigrant with an English wife settled in Britain while maintaining continuous links with expatriate Australians, including the publisher Peter Grose and his journalist wife, Ros Grose. Alex Mitchell went off to various Trotskyist newspapers, leaving them later, and eventually returning to Australia and a column in the Sydney *Sun-Herald* in the 1980s. Bruce Page became the 'moderate' (that is conservative) editor of the *New Statesman*; he then left journalism and turned to other ventures integrating computers and publishing.

In different ways Sayle, Knightley and Harold Evans looked to American and media connections which opened up wider horizons for them over the next two decades. Evans eventually left the employ of Rupert Murdoch and moved to a career in American magazine publishing. Sayle and Knightley would each develop more indirect American connections. Even in the early 1970s, after only a few years at the *Sunday Times*, Knightley and Sayle were looking beyond Grays Inn Road, entertaining other possibilities. Sayle was a congenital freelancer. He had always been paid commission and expenses, even when others enjoyed security and good salaries. For a time it worked very well. In 1972 he obtained, as he remarked, 'Money for old rope' – the newspaper paid him £20 to allow him to buy 50 yards of old line for the *Sunday Times* yacht he was about to sail in the single-handed trans-Atlantic race.[16]

While Sayle had many mountains to climb (including Everest and Fujiyama), Knightley's independent bent was more entrepreneurial than physical. This talent would develop, despite earlier failures – a failed restaurant and a very short career as a non-selling vacuum cleaner salesman. Utilising the 'sabbaticals' at the *Sunday Times*, he wrote *The First Casualty*, published in London and in New York in 1975, which he accurately described as 'a sort of world book'. The *Sunday Times* had allowed Knightley a chance to exercise his mind, and opened the door to publishing beyond journalism.

In the 1980s British journalism was in decline. Robert Maxwell's *Mirror* led the other tabloids downhill in the wake of Murdoch's *Sun*. In the era of Thatcherism, Murdoch took over the *Sunday Times* and the *Times* in 1981. The old freedoms of Grays Inn Road were now under pressure. In the Thomson era, Knightley could have his journalistic cake and eat it too. As he later reflected, 'I can honestly say that I never wrote a story that I was not interested in or did not believe in'. Thomson gave his editors and journalists complete freedom to publish, although some stories, such as the

CIA involvement in Guyana or thalidomide (which saw the newspaper's single largest advertiser, Distillers, withdraw its advertising entirely), harmed his business interests.[17] Murdoch's war on the print unions made Knightley feel increasingly uncomfortable. At the *Sunday Times*, new editor Andrew Neil measured productivity in more short-term ways. By the 1980s Knightley had growing reservations about his profession. By then he considered journalism 'fairly ephemeral and not as important as people like to think it is'. Even in those 'ten great years on the *Sunday Times*' he could 'count on the fingers of one hand ... the stories that had any real social effect'.

Harry Evans had gone, briefly, to edit the *Times*, and Sayle and Bruce Page had long gone: Sayle to Hong Kong and adventures in the Far East. When Britain had become drunk with the jingoism and racism of the Falklands conflict of 1982 ('this crazy war', this 'major aberration of history'), and there was no place for articles on the origins of the war, it was time for Knightley to go (although he did not make a clean break from Grays Inn Road until 1985). He would later publish an article in the *Journalism Review* on the war as 'a textbook example ... of how a government can manage news during wartime and how the newspapers just lay down and asked to be raped'.

Harold Evans' account of his 'Good Times, Bad Times' at the *Sunday Times* and the *Times* captured the change: 'The truth is that passing from Thomson to Murdoch was a transition from light to dark; and all of us involved were diminished by the shadows'.[18] It was also a transition in Britain more generally. In one of the ironies of time, place and liberty, Knightley had fled from Australia partly because of Cold War political and cultural repression. Now, Rupert Murdoch, a scion of the Australian Establishment who was dubbed the 'Dirty Digger' in Britain, was bringing a new repression to Fleet Street and then Wapping. He found a fertile soil for his values in Mrs Thatcher's 1980s Britain. As Murray Sayle had written in 'As Far As You Can Go' (published in *Alienation*, 1960), Australia's rulers conducted themselves 'half-bullyingly, half-paternalistically, like an isolated garrison watching a mutinous population'. In Britain, where the working classes still looked up to the 'Guv'nor', the governors now included Margaret Thatcher and her chief apostle, Rupert Murdoch. Except, unlike in Australia, the population did not 'mistrust' the 'governors', their 'illiberal rulers'. It seemed to Sayle in 1960 that the British working class would sometimes 'swallow anything'. Now, it was arguably even more so. In the 1980s, as a result, estranged liberal intellectuals were even more in evidence in a troubled Britain than in a changing Australia.[19]

At first, after leaving the *Sunday Times*, Knightley anxiously threw himself into freelance journalism and reviewing, accepting anything he could get, taking every commission, however badly paid.[20] Then he realised that the second advance of the book contract for his unfinished book on intelligence services was more than he had earned in six months of freelancing. Soon the pattern of his income from the later *Sunday Times* days – 60% from journalism and 40% from books – was reversed. His books included *The Vestey Affair* (1981), a story that was Australian and international as well as British, on how the Vestey meat millionaire family empire paid no tax. *The Second Oldest Profession: The Spy as Bureaucrat, Patriot, Fantasist and Whore* (1986) was followed by a volume which drew on his interviews and correspondence with Kim Philby, *Philby KGB Masterspy* (1988), while another book punctured the British myth of Lawrence of Arabia. Knightley still had something to contribute to debate. His findings were too valuable to be relegated to the inside pages of an unrecognisable Murdoch *Sunday Times*.[21] He successfully acquired an international reputation and sales for his writing. He was not attracted to television, despite doing some work in the medium. Colonial scepticism, metropolitan experience, an international perspective and a freelancer's resources (including 'the London Library, an author's dream'[22]), all reinforced by hard work, led to tangible results.

Double Expatriate – Murray Sayle Looks East

Murray Sayle took a very different route. Less conventional than Knightley and further from his social democrat views and his critique of Empire, Sayle was a creative sceptic, influenced by Anderson. Was the intellectual anarchist a de facto conservative? Critical scepticism about illusion and reality was his major theme. The 1960s had also made this natural freelancer and traveller not 'want to settle down' – 'bourgeois life in London was as unattractive to me as bourgeois life in Sydney'. Sayle also had an almost existentialist sense of life's transience, drawn from his journalistic and especially his war experience.

War was an Australian and a journalistic theme, the key to 'seeing the world' for hundreds of thousands of young Australians in the twentieth century. In their wake, as noted earlier, came a battalion of war correspondents – Chester Wilmot, Alan Moorehead and Sam White in Europe and the Mediterranean during World War II, George Johnston and the filmmaker Damien Parer in New Guinea, and Wilfred Burchett at Hiroshima. The Changi prison camp experience shaped the writer Russell Braddon, while several generations of correspondents included Tony Clifton and Diane Wilman in Beirut, and a Vietnam generation which included Sayle, John Pilger and the cameraman Neil Davis.[23]

In a sense war was also the great Australian adventure: 'it's overseas, you're out of the suburbs. That's the first great attraction'. Sayle believed he shared the 'hunger for the rest of the world [which] is a universal Australian attribute'. Actually going away contrasted with the imaginary world created by 'the bottle of plonk' (wine), as in the expression 'round the world for half a crown'. He believed 'that people in bars in this country [Australia] are in many cases just drowning their longings to get on a bloody plane or boat or so on and go out and see the big world'.

Sayle argued that 'anybody who really knows something about war is not anti-war'. In this he was expressing sentiments similar to those of *Her Privates We* (1930), the book by the earlier Australian expatriate Frederic Manning, and in Joseph Heller's *Catch 22* (1960). In Sayle's terms, 'war is, in a speeded up form, life'. Like life, it was orchestrated by chance:

> Who dies and who doesn't die is a matter of wholly purely chance,
> that the soldier learns to respect the enemy and despise anyone who
> is not running the risk he is running because at least the enemy is
> up there with him, except he's just over the line.

Sayle's almost physical, existentialist sense of the experience of war was linked to a larger understanding of its frequency and its futility. The former is apt in a century of 'endless wars' in which over 100 million people have been killed. The latter recognised each war's contribution – 'in the sense of its arbitrariness, its futility, the fact that what seems desperately important one minute is utterly unimportant':

> Great deeds on the battlefield were like great deeds in journalism.
> Neither mattered when there were other positions to be defended
> or when yesterday's newspaper was being used to wrap the fish.

He agreed with the Canadian novelist, and for a time London expatriate, Mordecai Richler, that all novels are about death – the 'great human predicament', that we know we will all die. War was also about death as a fate which comes to all of us. Love and war both put off that eventuality. A new war or a new woman generated excitement. 'In both cases you are abolishing death, the enemy', thus experiencing 'the intensity of here and now'. He recalled the experience of being under fire in a midnight attack in Vietnam – 'of mortars, rockets and deaths over the next four hours ... and then suddenly it was morning and the VC had departed and those of us who were alive were alive. We weren't just alive, we were super alive'.

In love and war though, Sayle found the world unjust. Reflecting on actions based on passion, he remarked that 'the emotions of that kind are like the battlefield, they are monstrously unjust, things never work to plan, nobody ever lives happily ever after'. Perhaps it was his experience, bad and good, which had brought him closer to 'the Oriental view of the passions as destructive of order and life'. Perhaps Sayle's voyaging and his eventual choice of a port (a landlocked village in Japan) were both products of his Australianness. After all 'alienation, exile' was *the* Australian story, from

Marcus Clarke's convict tale, *For the Term of His Natural Life* (1874) to Henry Handel Richardson's trilogy, *The Fortunes of Richard Mahony* (1930) and the 1950s Greek island odyssey of George Johnston.

Sayle, International Reporter of the Year in the IPC Awards, and 1970 Reporter of the Year (awarded by Granada's *What The Papers Say*), recognised the limitations of journalists. The journalist, he later remarked, was mainly a reporter. 'Most journalists are not very interesting people to talk to because they don't have any ideas of their own. They are experts at reporting other people's stories.'

By the end of the Vietnam War Sayle needed a change. In London, his base for most of the last 20 years, he had accumulated emotional baggage. Despite Sayle and Knightley later being dubbed 'the executives of the Australian Mafia in Fleet Street, honour-bound to care for other Australian refugees',[24] he had no aspirations towards climbing the institutional ladder.

Perhaps it was a retreat from these different stages – the interiors of pubs and parties and the physical world of the foreign correspondent. Perhaps it was time for the raconteur, wit, adult educator and watcher to keep his own counsel, to only occasionally tread the boards in London and Sydney society. After all he had been 'on the tear' in pursuit of booze, conversation, the fair sex and life's education for most of the last few decades, longer than the normal years of freedom and excitement. War and adventure were becoming dangerous. He was 'lucky to be alive'. He had lost friends in journalism (Nicholas Tomalin), in mountain climbing (Mike McMullen) and yachting – 'half the people I started out with are dead'.

He embarked on a new adventure and a new passion, the former *Sunday Times* researcher Jenny Phillips, beginning with a *Newsweek* job in Hong Kong. Coming up to his fiftieth birthday he decided that

> if I keep on going the way I'm going I'm going to have my head blown off to no great purpose, and I set out for something more like an intellectual adventure. This coincided with the end to the war in Vietnam in 1975 and with some reluctance, I will tell you, I thought, I'm getting a bit old to be a glamorous figure in a flak jacket.

Further, the job of a war correspondent wasn't exactly desirable for someone who now had 'family responsibilities'.

Hong Kong proved only to be a port of arrival. His time with the respected but formulaic and editorially restrictive *Newsweek* was short – 'they didn't like me and I didn't like them'. Then it was Japan, first the great metropolis of Tokyo. Then, eventually, with his children, to a quieter life in Hanbara, a rural village in the hills of Kanagawa just behind the great Tokyo-Yokohama conurbation. Now he was combining the domestic and the private with a new adventure – 'the East'. He was near the new centre of international economics, a short trans-Pacific flight to the US and 'a sort of half way house to Australia'. Despite his London flat and media contacts, and his parents and sister in Sydney, Sayle was now a double or even an international expatriate, a restless wanderer who had found a new place to camp.

At first, he was more closely tied to Tokyo, a couple of hours away by train or freeway, through the Foreign Correspondents Club. In those days before fax and e-mail, journalists also needed to find 'pigeons' (volunteer couriers) at Haneda and then Narita airports to carry stories to London or New York. His connections to the world also included several Japanese English-language newspapers delivered daily.

Japan was opened up for him by his family. The children studied in local schools and Jenny Sayle improved her Japanese, working as a teacher in schools and in adult classes. They would bring Murray Sayle into that local orbit. While he was becoming a 'double expatriate' with an international intellectual, rather than political, beat, his family were in a sense immigrants. They were welcomed as 'honorary Japanese' by the people of Hanbara. However, unwelcoming Japanese citizenship laws (based on descent rather than place of birth) made it most unlikely that these longtime sojourners would settle forever in the land of cherry blossom and pachinko parlours.

At times the Sayles were running in many directions – Japan, England, North America and increasingly Australia. Murray Sayle still had the London flat, in Tennyson Mansions near the Queen's Club, whose members, including Phillip Knightley and Shirley Abicair, still took to the grass courts. Sayle's stories covered subjects of an international kind, some specifically Japanese, others British or American. Two stories involved other Asian connections: the Russian shooting down of the Korean jetliner KAL 007 (for the *New York Review of Books*), and the decision to bomb Hiroshima (for the *New Yorker*).[25] Travel would take him not just to Hong Kong or elsewhere in the region, but, by the late 1980s, around the world. In the new era of cable TV channels and international co-productions, he narrated TV documentaries on Japan and Canada, and on lighter subjects (sex and food) for his friend Elliott Erwitt for the American Home Box Office and PBS channels.[26] These assignments paid well. Sayle's international career would develop through a new London chapter – a regular article in the *Spectator*, which soon had American monthlies interested in his work. He would later write for the *New Yorker*, placing its shingle on his corrugated iron office adjacent to a children's clothes and stationery shop in the hills of Hanbara. But, like all hungry free-lancers, he would do jobs he was asked to do – reviews for his conservative friend Auberon Waugh's *Literary Review*, articles for the Fairfax papers in Australia, and later travel stories for the Conde Nast *Traveler*. After all, he had five mouths to feed, and several animal mouths as well.

Sayle had his international triumphs, but paid a cost in a world of specialisation and more settled careers. Neither was advanced by his need for time to think and a restless search for new stimuli. Nor did television prove to be his metier, in part because it took forever to do, in part because of his appearance – a tall thin frame, barrel chest and an unduly prominent proboscis. Yet in his cruising socio-documentaries he transcended the clever narrator role of laughing at the foreigners, a common persona in English television. Sayle's rather odd narratorial style is a counterpoint to other depictions of the silliness of foreigners and their foreign ways. The persona differs greatly from that in some Clive James TV shows, in which the studio and home audiences laugh at the 'silly Italians' and their variety shows, or at the game shows and advertisements of the 'stupid Japs'. Sayle is part of the joke, rather than outside it.

Sayle's work as a journalistic distance runner in the American periodicals, writing essays and investigative reports of up to 8000 words (his study of the Hiroshima decision ran to 22 000 words), was an anomaly in modern journalism. When newspaper opinion and feature articles were becoming shorter and shorter, sometimes under 1000 words, Sayle was a dinosaur, an endangered species, a *Sunday Times* larger-than-life beast from another era. He was an essayist, as well as a journalist, in an era of 'grabs' and 'cameos'.

Although Sayle left Australia by ship, in the 1960s, he joined the aeroplane generation. The jet plane, and occasionally the yacht, would take him to all parts of the world. Now, his family had multiple orbits: the call of Jenny Sayle's family, friends and work in England; work and friends in the US; the Japanese village in which, especially through the children and Jenny Sayle's role as an English teacher in the schools, they were accepted as part of the community; and to Australia, to friends and family in Sydney, and occasionally to work. As the children got older, Australia, or to be exact Sydney, called more and more. In the absence of citizenship, it made sense to return to the English-speaking world even though it required a reverse transition. After all these years, might the three children bring the expatriate 'home'?

Serial Commuters and Converts: The Different Voyages of Women Journalists

In the 'Sixties' four young women separately left Australia for Fleet Street. Sandra Jobson and her journalist husband Rob Darroch headed off in the early 1960s. Going in the same direction were the Chatswood girl Barbara Toner and her British journalist husband, Chris Greenwood, whom she had married at the age of 19. Later, Ros Owen (originally from Sydney) left Perth for London 'with ballet shoes in one hand, typewriter in the other'. In 1970, near the end of the great wave of Australians travelling to London, Judy Wade, who had grown up in the Western Suburbs of Sydney, made her romantic journey to the London she had so often read about as a child.

Their individual searches for freedom and fulfilment, and sometimes for fame ('making it'), were partly the product of the times, of the dreams they had grown up with and the then limited working possibilities for women in Australian journalism. The authoritarian culture which then pervaded many newspapers could also be found in the women's sections. Women were also usually denied general reporting opportunities, paid in the lower 'C' and 'D' grades, and could be dismissed when they became engaged to marry. Sandra Jobson was fortunate that her first job was at the *Daily Telegraph*, where women were not confined to the women's pages. But when she tried to join the *Sydney Morning Herald* she found that it refused to employ women on general news. While the women's section offered opportunities for occasional feature articles and pieces on social issues, it was a constricting little world. Sandra Jobson escaped to *Woman's Day*, which then gave excellent opportunities for feature writing.

Circumscribed by the journalistic conditions of their times, these women had, like most Australians, grown up with a romantic vision of England, Europe and Empire. A dream world of princes and princesses, pomp and pageantry reflected the fabled garments of history and its colourful pages. Sandra Jobson had a more 'Dickensian' view, but found London 'less dark', rather cleaner and more pleasant, than she had assumed.

For these four journalists – and for a larger number of other known and unknown names – expatriation to Fleet Street was more than the journalistic response to contemporary circumstances and childhood socialisation. It was also a choice on the part of brave and determined individuals, made in search of adventure and experience as well as opportunity. Underlying these stories are similar patterns, usually beginning with either rebelliousness or an independent streak from childhood. Their 'voyages' over time and place would also seek to achieve forms of freedom and independence in their working lives. They sought as well to work at their relationships to Britain, particularly London, and to Australia, particularly Sydney. Sandra Jobson and Barbara Toner would be 'serial commuters' living and working in both cities for extended periods. All four would also seek to work out an employment situation which combined personal satisfaction, an income and a degree of freedom. The journalists would be influenced by the events and people they wrote about, but also seek to find their own ideal role and persona. All four aspired to go beyond the daily grind of newspaper or magazine writing.

Drawn to London, Ambivalent about Australia

A young Sandra Jobson had reacted against North Shore Roseville with its 'red brick two-storey houses with immaculate lawns'. She escaped to the

Julian Ashton art school, with its diversity of students and its harbourside location. Like Michael Blakemore and John Pilger, she had a Sydney water and beach fantasy. However, as well as surfing and sailing, for her it extended to the rocks and rockpools of Long Reef where her father, an anaesthetist, had taught her to look under rocks and find 'the most amazing things'.

The escape from the newspapers to magazines was made in different ways. Barbara Toner went from the *Sun* to *Pix* magazine. Sandra Jobson wrote book reviews for the *Sydney Morning Herald*, before she moved into women's magazines. Both married young in the way of the times. Soon after both took the overseas trip which was – as much as marriage – a rite of passage, a separation from the original family and a movement towards adulthood and independence. As Barbara Toner said to a colleague who had married and was about to go – 'you're going to get out of here'. The modes of departure varied. In 1965 Sandra Jobson and Robert Darroch paid an extra £10 on the *Patris* to be on the exclusive boat deck, suggesting an aspiration for a degree of comfort.

London was less than swinging for both Sandra Jobson and Barbara Toner. Barbara Toner and her husband found themselves in the heart of North London suburbia at Palmer's Green, staying with relatives in a 'world without excitement'. 'It was nothing that I'd wanted it to be.' She also faced rebuffs at work. The 19-year-old from the colonies was seen as unduly pushy when she demanded a suitable salary at a London magazine.

Sandra Jobson and Robert Darroch found life even more frustrating. On the positive side, Sandra Jobson displayed normal expatriate fast footwork in conning her way into a sub-editor's job at *Women's Own* magazine, despite having no experience at subbing. She soon discovered that in the English class system 'you have to keep your place', and felt the wrath of a repressive chief sub-editor. When colleagues bitched about her being Australian, she responded by telling stories about being told as a child to eat all her food as the poor little children in England were starving. Fortunately Rob Darroch's sub-editing on *Weekend* magazine paid well. Later he enjoyed excellent Saturday rates for Sunday's papers. Their living environment was not welcoming. They felt out of place in the sedate environs of Swiss Cottage, and their landlady read their mail. They also reacted against English inefficiencies, particularly post office queues, and found London a lonely city.

London would become more fulfilling for them, as it would for Barbara Toner, when she escaped 'the appalling kippers and curtains' suburbia of North London. They had come to break free from suburbia, to find other milieux. Sandra Jobson discovered the more 'internal' life of the English winter – 'a life of the mind rather than the body all the time' – of reading, writing, theatre and films, which contrasted with the external culture of sunny Sydney.

Barbara Toner had long had a desire to escape Australia, one which went back to her hatred of school. Even then she had escaped through writing. The desire to escape, as she later reflected, was 'vaguely associated with fame and fortune ... to be recognised in the world sphere'. This was both general and particular. It stemmed from an early 'loss [of] faith' in Australia as 'the centre of one's universe'. It was also partly an escape from the demands of the group. Later the author of the novel *The Need to be Famous* (1988), she had herself, at first, wanted to be 'famous amongst [her] peers'.[27]

In this escape she found that it was exciting to be on the outside, something she begrudged giving up when she returned:

> the attraction of being expatriate ... is to be away from judgment. The thing about being in Sydney is that you are judged in whatever is considered to be your proper context.

Not only did the world of peers crowd in on you, 'They do judge you. It's very harshly, and they want you to be the same as them. And if you're not the same as them, they think you're a wanker'. In contrast the expatriate in London could 'maintain this individuality', and always be 'the court jester'. The 'performer' could be 'forgiven for being absolutely cracked' because they were Australian. Australia, however, offered her English husband Chris Greenwood freedom from the pecking orders and internalised angsts of English class society.

Links – London and Australians

Sandra Jobson and Barbara Toner both kept up their Australian links – with expatriate society in London and with Australia itself. Jobson and Darroch returned to Sydney in the late 1960s, leaving suburbia behind for a terrace house in Glebe. Barbara Toner returned in 1972 with a six-month-old daughter and Chris Greenwood worked as a TV producer on the new *Mike Walsh Show*.

Sandra Jobson's London life mixed different social worlds. As a hostess her London dinner parties included Australian journalists and other friends, and her English, literary, tennis and later horse-riding friends. She knew that sometimes they didn't mix well, given the difference, after a bottle or two, between the directness of Australian communication and the indirect and 'mannered' English mode. Her London environments also varied. One was popular journalism, another was writing a biography of the pre-World War I Bloomsbury hostess Lady Ottoline Morrell. She researched her papers, including love letters from Bertrand Russell, at the University of Texas at Austin. Working in London and Cambridge, she met 'the most amazing eccentric and fabulous people . . . weird and wonderful people. I really almost forgot I was an Australian'. The expatriate desire for transcendence, in part a colonial dream, ran into the journalist-writer's desire to enter into the lives of her famous and wealthy subjects by telling their stories.[28]

Barbara Toner's climb towards significance was different. Her ladder was grounded in the suburban life of the working mother, which she explored in the column 'Tales from Tessa Wood' in *Woman* magazine, and in the non-fiction book *Double Shift* (1975). Barbara Toner acquired a kind of 'fame', which allowed her to transcend her other life as 'Mrs Greenwood', who picked the kids up from school. Eventually, she worried that she was lapsing into a kind of middle-class suburban life herself, 'getting older' and 'settling down'. Choices had to be made. One was to spend more time in Australia, appealing because of the physical and sensual beauty of the country, and the fact that Chris could work there. However, she was conscious of restrictions – losing the luxury of being an expatriate, losing her larger status as a well-known columnist, enduring dinner parties dominated by fatuous conversations about real estate prices, the anti-intellectualism of Australian media executives (many of whom had no time for universities and their 'load of bullshit'), and a journalistic culture in which she feared that the ruling view was that 'the minute you're burnt out at 30, you either go into PR or you become a drunk or whatever'. Media Australia seemed a land of 'provincial mediocrity', in which talented people became 'jaded' because they were 'not allowed to explore their talents to the full'. She saw it as a society 'in which you're encouraged to be mediocre'.

After working for the *Sydney Morning Herald* in London, where women were permitted to cover general news, Sandra Jobson returned to Australia again in the mid-1970s, and reported on general news for the *Herald* in Sydney. Disappointed at having missed the Whitlam years, she faced several frustrations. First she had to adjust to Australian accents on the phone. Working then at the *Australian*, she was also given a very unpleasant job when, after a major train disaster, she was 'told to go out and re-interview the grieving widows in the dead of night'. Was this par for the course? Or was it a special treat for the returned expatriate, like Sam White's 1940s experience, discussed in Chapter 3? Her Morrell biography was questioned by her colleagues. 'Why had she written a biography of someone called "Lady" Morrell?', demanded one sceptic. Her husband Robert Darroch had a similar but different experience, as his pioneering work on D. H. Lawrence's novel *Kangaroo* and his account of Lawrence's contacts with secret armies in Australia was critically scrutinised by some academic reviewers.[29] Like all first-time authors, they did not enjoy the chill winds of criticism.

For both Toner and Jobson, life's choices were about careers and places to live. Barbara Toner knew that her other choices included a country cottage and a London flat, or a larger London suburban house, or living in Sydney.

The Jobson-Darrochs moved even closer to the city, from Glebe to Victoria Street, Potts Point, on the edge of the Cross. In London they gravitated to Notting Hill, buying a flat above a shop in Kensington Park Road and, much later, buying a four-storey house in Westbourne Park Road, near Paddington and Bayswater. Inner-city property ownership and income would have costs as well as benefits. Having returned to London later in the 1970s, they discovered that an erratic tenant, whose business turned out to be pornographic photography, had damaged their Potts Point place, costing them a sudden trip to Australia and over a thousand dollars for repainting. Nor was property always the best way of escaping from the penal conditions of the wage slave, as they found in the early 1990s when both Sydney and London prices had crashed.

Sandra Jobson made her escape into freelance work through various routes. Her serious articles were accepted, along with women's magazine stories about the royals, the rich and popular stars, for example Prince Andrew's actress friend, Koo Stark (which also found an additional market in the Swedish tabloid newspapers). She wrote two Australian-oriented books, one a popular biography of the rising actor, *Paul Hogan* (1988), and the other a book of interviews with Australian men – *Blokes* (1984). But even popular books wouldn't make you rich. Robert Darroch continued as a correspondent for the *Bulletin*, and they found other sources of income running the Australian Consolidated Press office in London, and their own business, a syndication agency, from their Westbourne Park Road house.

Barbara Toner's dash for freedom was slightly more dramatic. Some years after the brash colonial had 'stuck out like a sore thumb at *Petticoat* magazine', she was working mostly as a columnist. The column offered the ideal solution for a freelancer – regular work at a distance. It required neither the burden of daily institutional employment nor the freelancer's nightmare of having to work as hard at selling stories as writing them.

To be independent was the ideal situation, she reflected in the early 1980s. As a writer, as an expatriate and as a middle-class working mother, she valued it. Her parents, like many expatriates' parents, had different backgrounds – her grandfather was an Orangeman, her mother was descended from Catholic Dubliners. Her parents had given her independence from the beginning – 'they've always let us do precisely what we wanted to do'. Having maintained her career while bringing up a young family, she had reservations about being labelled a feminist. She had 'always been a feminist. Just by nature that's what I am, in temperament – to me it's instinctive'. This made her sceptical of dogma and movements and 'all the crap they laid on top of that instinctive feeling'. (Her economic success helped, too: a nanny made it possible for her to have the two careers of writer and mother.) For her, feminism and personal independence were natural. While endorsing the feminists' opposition to American missile bases at Greenham Common, she rejected their confrontationist methods.

Expatriation was often about that search for personal freedom. It was particularly important for women of her generation, when women's working opportunities were often confined, restricted and poorly paid. Yet, as Barbara Toner reflected, sexism was in some ways worse in London. She had been patronised on the grounds of age and sex, and perhaps nationality when she arrived in the UK, by 'all those dreary English middle-class men who wouldn't consider your opinion'. In Australia they at least listened, unless that had been a privilege won by youthful charms. Later, while doing some work for the ABC, she found that the bureaucratic doors of the institution closed rapidly in the face of a woman perceived as being overly pushy, probably more than they would in the face of an equally pushy man.

Rising with the *Sun*: English Dreams, Expatriate Nightmares

Ros Grose and Judy Wade, two single journalists who travelled to London in the 1960s, also experienced the complexities of journalistic expatriation. Ironically, they won their freedom and financial rewards by writing clever stories for a tabloid newspaper which their educated friends looked down on. If they had escaped limited creative opportunities in Australia, they had discovered a London world which was more interesting, and more crude, however clever the language of *Sun*-speak.

In the 1960s, romance and reality seemed closer and the choices seemed simpler than they would become later to Judy Wade and Ros Grose. London offered romance. Judy Wade, a sixth generation Australian from the Western Suburbs of Sydney, had always wanted to travel and found Australia 'very limiting'. Since childhood, inspired by reading about the royal family, in novels, stories and English history books, she had wanted to go to Britain. Two short visits to Britain during the 1960s were preludes to the longer, permanent journey. Her work in radio brought her to the edge of the footlights of showbiz and the famous. When she finally left in 1970 with £600 to support her, in her heart she knew that she was 'coming for ever', although she didn't say that to those around her.

'Writing for entertainment' would provide a natural career path. The romantic Wade eventually found work as editor of the Murdoch magazine *Romance*, and then work on the very well-paid Murdoch *Sun*. For a woman journalist interested in the world's romantic dramas as well as its big events, London offered opportunities. 'The best stories are here', 'the best people to interview are here – the number of people you would get in a year in Sydney you can get here in a week', she observed in the early 1980s.

Eventually the romantic dream took two forms. One was living in a 500-year-old village, 'small but lovely and cosy', among the charms of rural Hertfordshire. The other was becoming a 'Royals' writer on the *Sun*, covering the big weddings: Charles and Diana in 1981, Andrew and Fergie in 1986.

Royal-watching would become a particularly lucrative journalistic trade, demonstrated by her book, *Charles and Diana: Inside a Royal Marriage*, published by the Australian (and also Murdoch-owned) publisher, Angus & Robertson.[30] Personal romance was more elusive, but her marriage to an Irishman provided her with the blessings of a daughter and working rights in Europe.

When she gave up her Australian passport for an Irish passport, it meant that she needed a visa for Australia. Perhaps that symbolic estrangement mirrored a more fundamental divorce. Whereas once she had felt that she could 'go back any day and take up her place in Australian society', by the 1980s she felt 'estranged', not 'belonging anywhere', not English as her accent indicated, not Australian. Yet, if pressed, her 'allegiance' (using language to which royal correspondents are attached) was to Britain rather than to Australia. Paradoxically, a royal tour with the rat pack following Fergie caused her to see the Red Centre and Great Barrier Reef with 'new eyes'. It was more interesting than the image of a grim interior, hostile and threatening, and the story of the explorer Sturt dying in the desert, which she had learned about at school.

Australian women often merged more easily into the 'English country garden' and its suburban equivalents than did Australian men. Defining their world a little more widely, knowing the neighbours, taking kids to school, buying furniture, fashion and everyday things more often than the more work-oriented men, they became more Anglicised. Sometimes this began with accents, for private school girls were encouraged to speak in a pseudo-English manner. (However, this could transcend gender. Peter Grose, who went from journalist to publisher with Secker and Warburg, had an English mien. Although descended from one of Australia's earliest settler families, Grose had a gentlemanly manner of speech which seemed to some people more English than Australian. This was not completely uncommon amongst the 'university men' of early 1960s Sydney University and was something he shared with the Epping Boys High graduate, Geoffrey Robertson.)

Sometimes the transition had its origins in family and childhood. Ros Grose, formerly Ros Owen, had an English father with relatives in Surrey. She also had connections intensified by fantasy; it was partly the strangeness which appealed. Like many other girls who lived in Sydney bungalows, she read children's stories which told of 'going upstairs to bed', of squirrels and historic buildings. Her parents had always known, she later reflected, that she would go. She had travelled first to Perth. Then, her two loves, dance and journalism, both nocturnal pursuits, drew her to London 'with ballet shoes in one hand, typewriter in the other'.

At the *Sun* the two women journalists found a mix of romance and reality, pleasure and sometimes less than pleasant practices. Here Ros Grose and Judy Wade found their metier as performers in words. Stories of frivolity for the *Sun* became one of Ros Grose's staples. The *Sun's* readers liked stories such as: 'How to spot a Wally'; 'You can tell a man by his underpants', a story based on six photos of men with trousers around their ankles; and '100 ways to say "No" to a man'.

Despite the opportunities for meeting the rich and famous, despite the pay and expenses, despite the satisfaction derived from clever coinages of words in this enter-info-tainment paper, there were costs. It was hard for someone who did not share Mrs Thatcher's values to approve of the 'Bingo/Jingo' politics of the *Sun* during the 1980s, and its Falklands War headlines: 'Gotcha', showing the sinking of the warship *General Belgrano*, or the *Sun's* encapsulation of the British view of the Argentinians, 'Stick It up Your Junta'. Not only could it be socially embarrassing to work for the *Sun*, but with sales of over four million its influence helped shape the divided Britain of the 1980s. When Rupert Murdoch took the paper to Wapping, creating a violent industrial confrontation with the unions, the *Sun's* politics were not the only difficulty. Outer Docklands was a long way from the employees' preferred haunts and watering holes in the city and the West End. It also took forever to get there.

This raised other questions about the costs and benefits of full-time employment. Reacting against the two-hour trip from Hertfordshire, even when working a four-day week at the office, Judy Wade went freelance in 1988. One of the first users of the modem, she sent off stories from her 1718 house in the country. Fortnightly trips to London were more satisfying than a daily trek to work and back. Ros and Peter Grose, who had a holiday cottage in Wales (to which their journalist friend Nelson Mews went on occasions), would make a similar break from the city. It was a clear decision about work and freedom for Judy Wade, and about the less than romantic aspects of work and commuting. 'I no longer want to be available for 24 hours a day with this monster called a newspaper which always wants more', she declared. The critic of Australia as a land of lotus-eaters became a convert to working for herself – 'everyone with any go wants to work for themselves'.

Ros Grose and Judy Wade defined their freedom in many ways, in creative opportunities, in being well-paid and in redefining working conditions. Freedom was also London, the local city and the international city, despite the traffic and the tube. To them, whatever the everyday problems, it went without saying that the capital of a country of 60 million people would always be more interesting than Australia, however much it had changed. In London in the 1980s, Ros Grose 'felt at home here' and never thought about going back. So settled was she that she was 'almost amazed' at the question.

Yet Australia had a kind of pull. For Barbara Toner, the desire for Australia was 'almost entirely physical'. A common theme linked the beach, the water and the sun. This was not a unanimous infatuation. Ros Grose had once found living by the beach at Cottesloe in Perth could be 'true heaven'. She had then discovered that 'eventually the beach bores you to death'. She had come upon 'Paradise and found it lacking'. In London, Ros Grose and Judy Wade shared a recurring nightmare. It was the other side of their childhood dreams. That nightmare was 'to wake up and find we're in Australia'.

John Pilger: The Romantic as Radical

Expatriation was often an individual journey. Judy Wade and Ros Grose had embarked on a romantic as well as professional journey. Phillip Knightley was conscious that he had chosen flight rather than fight; like many of his generation he had gone off, rather than staying to oppose the evils of Menzies' Cold War Australia. Murray Sayle focused more on the events than on the cause. His friends were those who had gone through the experience of 'going out to see the world together', ones with 'a strong territorial imperative and a strong acquisitive instinct', not for 'material things ... [but for] adventure, experience and knowledge'.

John Pilger was of a later generation of young travellers, some of whom would become expatriates. In 1962, when the 22-year-old Sydney journalist left for Europe he was one of many young Australians heading off overseas. 'My leaving had more to do with following a moving crowd rather than [with] any bold expression of individualism', he later reflected.[31] The *Daily Telegraph*-trained journalist had previously not shown any deep political commitments, despite his left-wing family background. Adventure and competition for him had been the Bondi surf and rowing. Danger meant speeding his new Volkswagen up the Pacific Highway through Sydney suburbs in a late night car race, as his competitor Bernie Giuliano recalled.

A few months enjoying Italian life and sun, running INTEREP, a 'newsagency', which Pilger, Giuliano and their third partner Peter O'Loughlin had invented, visiting relatives in Germany and having a good time seemed like a good start to the overseas trip. Pilger might have been one of many journalists who stayed only briefly in Fleet Street. In this chameleon profession where journalists took on roles, he could have followed in the footsteps of Anthony Delano, who added an Italianate touch to the Street in his dress style. (Delano would later write a book, with another ex-Mirror Group employee and fellow Australian Peter Thompson, on the Robert Maxwell phenomenon, and then successfully reinvent himself as a journalism academic, in Toowoomba, Brisbane and London.) Other examples were the international correspondents who became 'Archbishops' of their media dioceses and of their bars, such as Sam White at Le Crillon in Paris or Richard Hughes at the Foreign Correspondents Club and in his corner at the Hilton Hotel Grill in Hong Kong.[32] Or Peter Thompson, who later became the editor of the *Sunday Mirror*, and enjoyed the life of the walking, as well as the wealthy gentleman's, suburb of Mayfair. Or he might have identified with the cultured expatriates who had 'dismissed Australia as a second-hand Europe … and longed for visions of England as only the truly colonised can'.[33]

Journalism itself encouraged different emotions. Ideals of influence and significance, personal and social, were one side. It was also a trade in which the employees often voted Labor and the employers supported the conservative parties. Journalists sometimes were 'writing one thing and believing another', an 'apparent contradiction' which, for Pilger, 'helped to explain why so many journalists assumed a fake cynicism towards their craft, their readers and themselves'. Older journalists 'outfitted [themselves] in the armoury of the instant "hack"'.[34] At best, such cynicism encouraged a sceptical approach and an analytical questioning of various authorities and ruling opinions; at worst it became a corrosive cynicism. It led many journalists to the bottle, or to simply climbing the ladder of institutional careerism, or to an early escape into PR.

John Pilger was different. Something was driving him. Was it his family's politics or its past experiences of discrimination? His German grandfather Richard had lost a job in 1914 and his mother had fallen out of favour when she married down, to the 'Bolshie' carpenter Claude Pilger. Or was he amongst the last rebels against the Menzies experience? Perhaps he had been shaped by a romantic idealism. Bernie Giuliano remembered first hearing him make an unexpected political statement in November 1963. At Pilger's place in London they heard the news of the assassination of President John F. Kennedy. A visibly upset Pilger 'said something like "the bastards have got Kennedy"'.

Pilger the engaged, the political, even Pilger the driven, pursued by the furies which later daily runs on the Clapham Common couldn't shake off, would emerge over the next three decades. His 1960s progressive tabloid journalism would be supplemented by television documentaries in the 1970s. Through print journalism and the TV documentaries which became more central in the 1980s in the era of Margaret Thatcher, Rupert Murdoch and Robert Maxwell, Pilger would make his mark. As a print journalist, an independent writer and documentary maker, John Pilger, rower and surfer, would become known as 'John Pilger, crusading journalist'.

As mentioned, the doors were open to Australians in the early 1960s. One disgruntled British job applicant, hearing an Australian accent in a newspaper foyer while waiting for an interview, remarked 'you've got to be a kangaroo to get a job around here'. Pilger went from subbing at Reuters, where he was 'scolded for poor time keeping', to a great Fleet Street institution, the labour-oriented tabloid, the *Daily Mirror*. The newcomer's agility helped keep the door open. The assistant editor Michael Christiansen was delighted at the prospect of another Australian journalist, just a week before an important cricket match against the *Daily Express*. When asked what he did, Pilger declared himself a spin-bowler. He started almost immediately. The next day he sent a memo admitting that he knew nothing about cricket and asking if this meant 'a record short innings on the *Mirror*?'[35] It didn't.

The 1960s offered Pilger significant opportunities. The *Daily Mirror* under Hugh Cudlipp was an unusual tabloid newspaper with unparalleled resources and an innovative approach to blending words and images in larger stories. It even had special 'shock issues' devoted to particular political and social problems. Pilger covered the 'The North' for two years, a 'north of Watford' assignment which some London colleagues saw as 'the equal of banishment to Pitcairn Island'. His approach of knocking on doors, an Australian accent unplaceable in the class system and his sympathy for the underdog gave him an unusual understanding of working-class Britain.[36]

In a year-long journalistic tour of the Third World, he saw a poverty even more shocking than in Newcastle or Manchester. The young reporter was already making his mark. He would become 'Chief International Correspondent' of the *Daily Mirror*, with a negotiated freedom to come and go. Like an in-house freelancer, he turned his hand to the new documentary medium of television from 1969, first with Granada, based in Manchester, and then with Associated (later Central) TV in Birmingham. Significantly, his first director, David Munro, had a background in drama rather than documentaries.

In over 40 television documentaries and several books, as well as in articles in the *Mirror*, and later in the *Guardian* and the *New Statesman*, Pilger wrote of the victims of war and repression. Pilger and Phillip Knightley were the only journalists to ever win the British Press Awards' UK Journalist of the Year twice, an unparalleled achievement. Pilger's 1977 campaign for compensation for the victims of thalidomide (taking up the earlier *Sunday Times* campaign) and his 1980 documentary *Year Zero* had powerful public impacts. The award citation for the Cambodia film read:

> John Pilger, in his documentary work, virtually saved, single handed, large numbers of the Cambodian people from extinction. *Year Zero* directly and indirectly raised 40 million dollars for relief work in Cambodia and was the main force of persuasion to the British Government's decision to abandon recognition of Pol Pot.[37]

Pilger's strong words and clear images, first cultivated under Hugh Cudlipp, and his use of dramatic human examples made possible the transition from print journalism to television. His accounts of human savagery attracted television audiences usually only won by the ravages of other animals, the preying lions and hungry crocodiles of nature documentaries. They rated. Pilger, and his producer-directors (including the expatriate Australian Alan Lowery), recognised television's preference for the straightforward story emphasising the view from one side; the medium has little place for qualifications or footnotes. Pilger's gripping documentaries fused human horror with '*J'accuse!*' advocacy. His programs would become 'news events' themselves, rather than just news and current affairs reports. Critical comments in newspapers and subsequent letters to the editor from 57 Hambalt Road, SW4, as Pilger jousted with his critics, challenged the 'hidden agendas', whether the subject was Cambodia or East Timor or the Australia of Prime Minister Bob Hawke.

In the interests of 'balance', television stations 'placarded' some documentaries with the disclaimer 'A personal view', while his critics, as well as his allies, labelled him a 'campaigning journalist', suggesting that there was something 'odd' or 'peculiar' about the Pilger view. They also questioned his veracity, taking particular delight in a 1982 case when he was hoaxed into presenting a Thai girl, Sunee, as a child slave for sale.[38] To the critics, some politically conservative, some just professional journalists, Pilger was in a different business to them. He was more concerned with appealing to the heartstrings than with the facts. His conservative enemies coined the term 'to Pilger', to distort the realities, to describe a certain kind of journalism of advocacy. His tabloid television was in the tradition of the Sydney afternoon (or Fleet Street morning) tabloid newspapers, which presented exaggerated reports as analysis and fact. His journalism, his motives and the expatriate perspective were all debated regarding his accounts of Australia. A July 1969 article in the English women's magazine *Nova*, the 1982 and 1988 documentaries, *Island of Dreams* and *The Last Dream*, and the 1989 book *A Secret Country* present Pilger's changing and unchanging vision of Australia.[39]

In 1969, when the British media celebrated 'sunny Australia' as a destination for £10 assisted migrants, Pilger declared in *Nova* that he wanted to present 'the culpably neglected other side to the Land of Wondrous Opportunity', to balance the ideal of the 'great' 'Australian way of life'. He declared that his motives were of the purest kind – 'I happen to love Australia', a statement he reiterated in 1986.[40] Placarded with the subtitle, 'Diatribe on his native land by a disenchanted Australian', it was accompanied by a Barry McKenzie-ish cartoon by the New Zealand expatriate Nicholas Garland. A behatted Aussie drinker lamented this 'load of bullsh!' from a 'poor old galah with a chip'. The critic had knocked his mates with cries of 'stinkin' fish' in an article published in 'Pom land' in 'a sheila-type publication'. Pilger's article took up a Sixties critique made by Australian intellectuals. He assailed suburban materialism and mediocrity, men with lawnmowers and superficial 'mateship', and imprisoned housewives in their 'gloria soame' (glorious home), the prison and the palace of married women. Pilger accurately condemned both media and government for trying to keep bad news off the front pages and the TV news bulletins. A familiar critique was also emerging:

the Press, television and the politicians of Australia operate a mag-
nificent conspiracy at maintaining the people in their everything-is-
just-beaut-so-let's-crack-another-frostie mood.[41]

He reported a society in which the 'Fair Go' did not extend to the poor or
Aboriginal Australians 'kennelled in "reserves" and "missions" in the Out-
back', and in city slums, where prejudice against 'Wogs' was also the norm.
Such accounts were accurate. However, in the year of the 1969 Moratorium,
after three years of angry protests against the Vietnam War, his view that in
this 'nation still without a mind' 'there has been negligible questioning' of the
war was itself questionable.[42] Or was it cultural lag, an essentialist vision
formed in an earlier time, and, like many expatriate views, fixed in that
period?

Like Phillip Knightley in *Cosy in a Basement*, he differentiated himself from
the Earls Court Aussie ghetto. In 1969, he distanced his alternative view from
those of the 'duffel-coated bores at the bar of the Overseas Visitors Club, Earls
Court'. That self-separation from what he took to be mainstream views would
be manifested again in the 1980s. Then, he sought to explore the continuing
Aboriginal situation and the 'Order of Mates' of Prime Minister Bob Hawke
and such millionaires as Rupert Murdoch, Alan Bond and Kerry Packer.[43] The
'secret country' had realities hidden from the people by its conservative and
timid media. He attacked 'the provincialism of these keepers of the received
wisdom' who 'wish to deny that expatriate ingredient from those who have
seen Australia in a different way'. He pulled no punches. The *Guardian*'s
Sarah Bosley described *The Last Dream* as a series that 'disembowels his
fellow Australians for their racism towards the indigenous Aborigines and the
venality of the establishment'.[44] Bob Hawke dismissed him as a foreigner:
'You bloody Poms come out here and think you know exactly how things are
done in Australia'. 'I'm an Australian', Pilger replied.[45]

Pilger would soon become a populist hero and villain. One letter writer to
ABC TV's *Backchat* suggested that Pilger, who 'appears to be a Pom ... should
be sent back to England as soon as possible, preferably shipped back upside
down in a crate'. A British reviewer condemned this 'miserable bludger who
has come along to pee in the [Bicentennial] soup'. In contrast, the audience of
Andrew Denton's ABC radio program (2BL Sydney) voted Pilger 1989 'Person
of the Year', while *A Secret Country* joined the best-seller lists.[46]

Pilger saw himself as an 'outsider'. In a 1981 series of TV interviews for
Channel Four, and a subsequent book, he defined the term. Outsiders were
often individuals, freelancers rather than institutional people and political
leaders, 'People who for significant periods during distinguished lives
have been outside the establishment, and whose talent places them beyond
labels and institutions'. Yet the successful could not be disqualified by
'wealth, power, success or privilege'. These outsiders included Jessica Mitford,

Helen Suzman and Salman Rushdie. Perhaps, despite their different politics, Wilfred Burchett provided a role model for the radical journalist as outsider:

> Wilfred Burchett epitomised the integrity and courage of the outsider. He could easily have slipped into the role of successful and respected media worker, but chose a life which brought him much pain and anguish. He was threatened, abused and at one period even made stateless. As a man on the Left, he would often identify with a cause, but disillusionment prevented him from staying 'inside' any regime or country for too long.[47]

Pilger saw himself as an outsider even as he became a London and international media star and a *New Statesman* and *Guardian* insider. That was also the paradox of the television radical who won personal fame as the individual face of his crusades. Simultaneously, Pilger was the stirrer and ally of the underdogs and, as such, a populist 'hero'. This status disturbed some members of the chattering classes in Britain and Australia, although others approved.

Pilger also believed that Australia had a strong outsider condition, even arguing that 'in one sense, to be an Australian is to be an outsider'.[48] Pilger's outsiders, contrasting with those controllers of opinion who rejected all criticism, traced their roots back to Irish forebears and other Australians who had arrived in chains. Australian traditions had their roots in this time and in Australian space – in nature.

Here lay the underlying contradiction which shaped Pilger's expatriate vision. His first wife Scarth Flett, the Australian journalist he had met in London in 1964, believed that John Pilger was 'not really political as a person', more 'liberal, a humanitarian' than 'left wing'. What underpinned Pilger's vision was an idealist commitment to justice and sympathy for the underdog. It was perhaps this fundamental romanticism, with its commitment to oppose injustice, which made Pilger maintain his rage when others on the Left had become disillusioned. Pilger stayed at the documentary barricades while Communism crashed and Thatcherite capitalism reigned.

This romantic ideal took specific form in his dualistic conception of Australia. One was natural, the other artificial. One was egalitarian and democratic, the other colonial and class-ridden. One was characterised by the grace, 'friendship, warmth and diamond light of my homeland'; the other was stultifyingly provincial. At best, Australian society had struck 'a fine balance between the needs of the community and the individual'.[49]

In *A Secret Country*, with its two cover photos – Max Dupain's 'Sun Bather' and Peter Rae's 'Aboriginal behind Bars' – Pilger argued that 'Australia's true democracy' was found on the beach, in the natural self immersed in the Bondi surf. For most Australians it was the 'one link with our ancient continent about which we know little, and whose surface we have grievously disrupted and whose original people we have banished and killed'. It was from the beach rather than the 'bewigged Georgian founding fathers' or some 'antipodean Gettysburg', that Australians derived their freedom.[50]

Against this noble savage ideal of unclad, bronzed democracy he put a stuffier, provincial Australia, one in which families denied the convict 'Stain' and admired 'English reserve' which was 'equated with respectability and therefore cultivated'. Menzies, who 'spoke like an English Home Counties Tory, an affectation he would top up during his pilgrimages "home"', was said to have this quality. 'Prim houses with red tiled roofs' and 'double-breasted serge suits' denied Australian nature. They were complemented by 'the repression of feelings': respectable Australians avoided discussing 'religion, race, "domestic matters", sex or politics'.[51]

Pilger had no time for these social and cultural lies, or what he saw as the era of 'Menzies' comic sycophancy to the upper reaches of the English class system'. He also differentiated himself from the would-be-cultured expatriates, those who found their homeland wanting and travelled to fawn more fully to Britain.[52] Had expatriation forged Pilger's polarised vision of Australia? Had it influenced his approach to the world, his capacity to see dramatic political events in terms of *Heroes*, the title of another major book, and villains, whether the Pol Pots or on a lesser scale, Australian cabinet ministers?

Tony Clifton, the co-author of the tale of the horrors of Beirut, *God Cried*, suspected that Australian war correspondents

> may get a little more emotional than a lot of other journalists . . . we come from a little country which has always been dominated by, or been in danger of being kicked around by much bigger countries, and so we tend to sympathise more readily with the underdogs in any given confrontation – it is easier with our colonial past and our twentieth-century 'independence' ('All the way with LBJ' as our late great leader H. Holt put it), to identify with some small country or racial group getting the shit kicked out of it.[53]

Clifton's analysis helps explain the forensic analyses of intelligence of Phillip Knightley, and the committed documentaries of John Pilger and the filmmaker David Bradbury, as well as some of his own work. Clifton's own experience of trying to explain why wars were happening, and his identification and sympathy 'with the people you are with', and his 'great admiration for civilians and most soldiers who endure fire, and genuine contempt for virtually all politicians', were in an older Australian Digger and populist tradition. Such an understanding also had points of agreement with the very different Pilger and Sayle philosophies of the role of a war correspondent.

The Pilger case supported Clifton's argument about how 'the most adventurous, most daring and probably the most rootless journalists Australia produced' headed for London, following in the tracks of the great Australian correspondents of World War II. In this semi-imperial phase, the lack of overseas opportunities working for the Australian newspapers, friendly immigration laws and recent history opened doors in Fleet Street; as a result the numbers were many. It would retreat as Australian opportunities grew, British immigration rules were tightened and Fleet Street newspapers suffered from declining resources and fading vision.[54]

Was there something else about Pilger? Was there more to the Pilger narrator role than the demands of television for a personal view with an individual presenter and living, breathing (or dead) examples of the human impact of events? Pilger's personal vision of Australia featured Bondi and the Alice Springs of Aboriginal painter Albert Namatjira, but had no Melbourne or Adelaide. It was also rooted in the expatriate experience. Evelyn Waugh believed that all English expatriates in the outposts of Empire suffered from a 'fatal deficiency', 'a deficiency in that whole cycle of experience which lies outside personal peculiarities and individual emotion'.[55] Did Pilger also share this overly focused vision? Did he, like some other Australian expatriates, see only an 'essential' Australia, which he had grown up with, both that which he affirmed and that which he rejected?

Did this idealist 'photographer, using words instead of a camera' (Salman Rushdie), see only the noble and ignoble within his lens' dualistic frames? His shocking revelations of what was known to many, not to others, made him a kind of hero and a villain. He was a populist hero of the oppressed, as well as a villain who distorted the shot for effect, according to those with either greater knowledge or greater conservatism. Or is John Pilger as much a painter as a photographer? In the expressionist manner, his strong brush-lines bring out social and political conflicts. Like any figurative expressionist, he paints a 'distorted' reality as he sees it, to bring out what he perceives to be its underlying character.

Pilger cites T. S. Eliot's argument that the whole point of a journey is to come back to the place you left and see it for the first time.[56] His own work, almost simultaneously, deepened public knowledge about Australia's dreams, illusions and nightmares while returning resolutely to an unchanging expatriate picture. That is why John Pilger, the expatriate journalist, sees in his Australian skies both the beach sunlight of optimism at 'Bondi, my beach', and the dark clouds of black despair. Different journalists' visions, like the disparate events which they covered, varied greatly.

Chapter 11

Crucible to Firmament: Barry Humphries, Germaine Greer and Clive James and the Expatriate Search for Fame[1]

Over the last quarter of the twentieth century, five Australians made it onto the television viewers' and newspaper readers' list of 'well-known Aussies' in Britain. One is the television and press journalist discussed in the last chapter, John Pilger. A second, with a broader Australian accent, is the popular entertainer, former competition swimmer and exhibiting artist known for his children's television shows and Christmas 'pantos' – Rolf Harris. This popular entertainer made his name with two 'signatures': his illustration of songs with rapid strokes of a house painting brush, and his image as a stereotypical though exotic 'Aussie' of the type featured in his original hit, 'Tie Me Kangaroo Down Sport' (1960). (A later song, his melodic version of Led Zeppelin's rock anthem 'Stairway to Heaven', attracted a cult following.) The other three are similar and different but are often bracketed together. All are very successful multimedia personalities with a talent for controversy as well as entertainment, stars of television and print and in one case, stage. All are known in Britain as outrageous and dramatic Australians, and are almost as well-known in Australia. They are the writer, social critic and television chat show/newspaper column performer, Germaine Greer; the television reviewer-cum-performer, literary critic and travelling observer and writer, Clive James; and the star of one-man stage shows about Australian characters, the television performer, writer and collector, Barry Humphries.

Often these three multimedia performers are seen as the image of the expatriate Australian. To some people they represent the high-profile, larger-than-life image of talented and successful Australians who have made it on a larger stage. To others, they are the often disgruntled expatriates who have found Australia wanting. Along with the very different New York expatriate,

Robert Hughes, who also left Australia for London in the 1960s, they are welcomed back to Australia to headline arts festivals' literary forums, despite these reservations. *Once an Australian*, by Ian Britain, takes the threesome and Hughes as the subjects of a close-up study of the creative and expatriate experiences of these distinctive characters.[2] Whether by choice or by chance, the three have made multimedia careers in the role of the 'professional expatriate' – the talented or ugly Australian, the Antipodean abroad.

What made them leave? Why have they been so successful? In one view, they are particularly talented, if otherwise typical examples of the Australian expatriates who departed in the late 1950s/early 1960s. In another view they are atypical – in their ambitions, in their abilities, in their fame and in their feelings about Australia.

Does their experience say something about Australian attitudes to 'tall poppies', to successful and/or 'different' individuals? Or, does it say something about expatriates' views of the country from which they departed and vice versa? In 1962, a Barry Humphries caricature depicted a bitter Australian journalist whose open letter to the returning Joan Sutherland told her and her 'ex-Australian mates', 'SORRY JOAN, YOU'VE LOST YOUR TOUCH!'. They had 'turned [their] back on Australia and [gone] after the bright lights and the facile acclamation of a bunch of snobs' in England.[3]

Like the other expatriates in this study, Barry Humphries, Germaine Greer and Clive James were products of their times, their class and their gender. Their personalities and stories were shaped by the lower middle and middle-class Australia of the 1930s to the 1960s, by familial and childhood experiences of World War II and suburbia. Their later lives would also be influenced by the changes in the cultural and media life of London of the late 1960s/early 1970s, and those of Australia from the late 1960s onwards.

The truism 'the child is father to the man' is particularly apt for Barry Humphries, Germaine Greer and Clive James, locating their families as the crucible in which the desire for expatriation was formed. Individual aspirations and family psychology were as important as the persistently colonial social, cultural and institutional relationships of some parts of Australian society to the British 'parent'. These three distinctive individuals came from a small in-between generation which came after the great postwar exodus and before (in some ways at least) the great late Sixties waves of baby boomers and international travellers who had lived through the very different Australia of anti-Vietnam War protests.

Camberwell to Shaftesbury Avenue and Return (via Moonee Ponds): The Journeys of Barry Humphries

All three experienced forms of childhood separation and loss on the one hand and a feeling of being enclosed on the other. Barry Humphries, born in 1934, was a child of newly suburban Camberwell, where his father's company built houses on the Golf Links Estate. He felt enshrouded by his immediate family and his aunts in a world from which he had to escape. He would later remark that 'if England is the Motherland and Germany is the Fatherland, Australia is certainly Auntieland'.[4] It was a world he never really left. As 'Edna Everage', and as a lover of old Melbourne, this time dwelt with him forever.

From a young age, Humphries was a square peg very ready to demonstrate that fact to the round holes which surrounded him. At Melbourne Grammar, at Melbourne University and around Melbourne theatrical circles (the Union Theatre Repertory Company), and later even in the wilder satirical environs of the Phillip Street revues in Sydney, he was the joker in the pack. Bizarre practical jokes, which coupled Daliesque inversions of reality with everyday shock and discomfiture, became his way of making people notice him, even if unfavourably. They would remember the provocation if not the perfection of the performance, the annoyance if not the implied challenges to the everyday.

Humphries was interested in power as well as culture. Earlier, at South Camberwell State School he was put in a corner with a sign around his neck – 'I am a bully'. He believed he was innocent. He would long remember the name of the teacher, Miss Jensen, giving her due credit in his autobiography *More Please*, over 50 years later.[5] A gulf between him and his parents, and his creation of an eccentric persona at Camberwell Grammar and then Melbourne Grammar, would ensure an unusual relationship between him and the world. Humphries reacted against Melbourne Grammar, the authoritarian and conformist school which his fellow student Chester Eagle remembered as combining repression and sadistic humiliation, 'hidden reserves of cruelty', 'Jew-baiting' and 'sadism'. The boys' violence was 'emotional'; and offered ways of ridiculing the weak, the lower orders and the different ('pooftahs', i.e. gays), as well as the idiosyncrasies of the masters.[6] Barry Humphries learned his lessons well at one of Melbourne's 'best' schools. Humphries 'escaped' from what he later dubbed the Junior School of the Melbourne Chamber of Commerce into his own Dada art on the stage of everyday theatre, and into female roles in the school plays, the English farces which the school put on. Yet he remembered all too well the bullies and their ways.[7]

The Humphries who played out the inter-war suburban and female values of his Camberwell would find his theatrical 'shtick' in the wider domestic world of 1950s suburban Australia. At the suggestion of Ray Lawler, Humphries first put Edna Everage on stage in the UTRC Christmas revue, *Return Fare*, on the propitious 13th of December 1955, as a 1956 'Olympic Hostess'.[8] All the familiar characteristics were anticipated then, from Edna's xenophobia to her 'hubby' Norm and the 'burgundy Axminster' carpet.

Having been dismissed by the UTRC, Humphries went to Sydney to the Phillip Street theatre. 'Sinny', including this lazy pronunciation, was not quite his cup of tea. Although impressed by the talent of Max Oldaker, he found Sydney revue culture too cosily close to the 'society' it satirised.[9] He felt uncomfortable amidst the alternative bonhomie of the Sydney pub and, reciprocally, his sick-to-surrealist sketches were too strong for the Sydney public. He would, however, find material for his great creation, Sandy Stone, and later more 'ocker' characters, in the Returned Services League's clubs. Sandy would be heard on the record *Wild Life in Suburbia*, released in 1959. While Sydney counterpointed Melbourne, it was, in its larrikin style and superficial materialism, both a liberation and a limitation. His essentially Melbourne-centred, if quirky, view of the world found little there.[10]

Like many an elite boy in the 1950s with an artistic bent, he looked overseas. Having felt an exile in uncouth Sydney, the Melburnian refugee headed for London. In Rome, he met the distinguished Australian writer Martin Boyd, uncle of the Melbourne artist Arthur Boyd. He would later see something of the artists around Highgate, including Arthur Boyd, Charles Blackman and Francis Lymburner. On one occasion Colin MacInnes introduced him to Malcolm Williamson at the Colony Room in Soho. London called as the place of superior status and, perhaps, of higher standards of elocution and sartorial splendour, and drew the nascent art connoisseur in Humphries. It was a city in which this student of the Victorian and Edwardian dandy and the performer could find a stage – on the streets, in soirées and salons and even in theatres. Commanding the room to practise his routines at parties in London, as he had in Sydney, he did not always captivate those present. Murray Sayle recalled his 'tendency to "shoosh" everyone at parties' so that he could do his act.[11]

Barry Humphries would emphatically define himself as an expatriate. Most other expatriate performers in the arts and entertainment left Australian subject matter behind as they worked at their professions, while maintaining links with family and friends. Sometimes, they felt strongly about their separation from their native land, but their professions demanded it. Humphries' subject *was* Australia. Edna and Norm Everage and Sandy Stone came from 1950s suburbia. Later constructs included Craig Steppenwolf, the Monash University radical, Neil Singleton, Left intellectual, and Lance Boyle, self-serving ugly trade unionist. Less directly 'political' were two 'stone the crows' ordinary Aussie males – the innocent abroad Barry ('Bazza') McKenzie and the salivating Les Patterson. These creatures, only partly based on real-life Australian models, were sharpened by the increasingly acidic ink of caricature. Establishment figures became rare. Instead a litany of dubious Lefties and Ocker Australians reflected Humphries' underlying political conservatism.[12]

Like many recently arrived expatriates, Humphries at first struggled to make a living in London. In 1959, when he was working at night in Walls Ice Cream factory in Acton and auditioning by day, Australian 'friends' sent him unfavourable notices of his record *Wild Life in Suburbia*. One posed the 'open question' of 'how long Barry Humphries would last'.[13] His reactions were understandably intense. His anger and ambition were now being forged in another crucible, one not unrelated to the family and peer group 'vessel' from which he had escaped.

The expatriate who had reacted against – and sought to exorcise if not destroy – the demons of childhood now had new motives for taking aim at Australia and its suburban life. Humphries entitled his autobiography *More Please* not in recognition of his role in *Oliver!*, but of his desires: 'I ALWAYS WANTED MORE. I never had enough milk or money or socks or sex or holidays or first editions or solitude or gramophone records'. He would realise his desires, as his later life and career gave him things aplenty, including success, fame, wealth, travel, works of arts and wives.[14]

Humphries' deep and bitter antipathies regarding Australia, towards his childhood and the critics and towards expatriate-haters, were a constant in his performance. Like some other expatriates, his original bitterness towards family, school and society would be enlarged and transformed into a wider denunciation of Australian society. The sympathetic writer John Lahr quotes Humphries on his absent parents – his 'very, very busy' father of whom he 'didn't see a great deal'. His mother, he recalled, was 'a distant figure as well', partly due to being absent during a period of illness. Humphries caricatured his father as Colin Cartwright on the record *Sandy Agonistes* (1960), parodying his complaint that despite all a father does 'for his kids . . . what does he get for it?' Things had been an inadequate substitute for time and affection. Humphries acknowledged the origins of Edna as a symbol of his separation from the everyday world and from his parents.

> I invented Edna because I hated her. I suppose one grows up with a desire to murder one's parents, but you can't go and really do that. So I suppose I tried to murder them symbolically on stage. I poured out my hatred of the standards of the little people of their generation.[15]

On one occasion, he and his third wife Diane Millstead had returned home with a new baby. His mother seemed to be more worried about a discussion on radio about what people thought of her son, and the harm he was doing to Australia's image overseas, rather than just pleased to see them. An enraged Humphries rang the radio station in his Edna persona to report that 'Barry Humphries' own mother', who was in the next room, 'thinks *exactly* the same' regarding the unpatriotic Humphries.[16]

Beyond Godzone – London Views

Humphries performed on several stages in the early 1960s. He played Mr Sowerberry, and understudied and later played the role of Fagin in *Oliver!* in

London and then New York. His own show at Peter Cook's Establishment club failed with audiences and critics. Neither was amused by images of food parcels being received from Australia, or remarks about the English lack of interest in taking regular baths.[17]

During this decade his life continued to be troubled, including his anxieties as a performer, his relationship with his parents, with drink, with Australia and with the critics. He remained in a strained relationship with Australia, with the conventional Australia which had left its mark on him. It was not just a personal reaction, however bitter he sometimes felt. It was also the sharp point of a generational reaction which he shared with a number of intellectuals, most of a redder political hue than Humphries' native Camberwell Tory blue. Also alienated from suburban Australia, and perhaps from the values of ordinary men and women, these cultural dissidents identified with Humphries' caricatures of suburbia. They preferred original oils to blue ducks on the walls. They too believed that they could transcend the world of 'Godzone' ('God's Own') country, of suburban vacuity – the everyday life of television, Holden cars, Sunday roasts and diligent lawn-mowing. They lamented a chauvinistic self-satisfaction about the achievements of sub-urban Australia and the 'Australian Way of Life'. Despite this, many of them also lived in the suburbs and watched television … but that was another story.[18]

Had Humphries been a young adult in the wilder wartime era, he might have found himself not so out of place in wartime cities which allowed and expected eccentricity. However, this anti-suburban pearl, generated by the values of middle to lower middle-class Camberwell, was the perfect counterpoint to the mono-cultural values of the suburban, family-oriented 1950s. He was able to present its only bi-cultural aspect, the potent smothering female world of Edna and his aunts and the powerless male world of Sandy Stone and Norm Everage. As unlikely as it might have seemed a decade before, Humphries the Melbourne-to-London aesthete became one of the leading 'surfers' of the new waves in popular culture, a variant on the feelings which led to the satire boom in Britain and Australia, from *That Was The Week That Was* to *The Mavis Bramston Show*. Barry Humphries offered a theatrical expression of that rejection of suburban materialism and conformist conventionality by the new middle class and the 'arty' dissidents of the old middle class. His career was also leaving the underground behind for mainstream success. His first one-man show *A Nice Night's Entertainment* (1962) had been a surprising success in Melbourne, where the season had been extended, and then in Sydney.[19]

London also had much to offer. By the mid-1960s, the Humphries had moved up in the world – from attic and basement flats in Ladbroke Grove and Notting Hill Gate to the greater comfort of Highgate, 'inheriting' a rented flat from the artist Leonard French. An even more decorous environment in Little Venice, a flat in a Georgian house at 25 Maida Avenue, W2, followed.[20]

Humphries had already begun work on that very London and Paris in the Sixties, and very Humphries book, *Bizarre* (1965), with its collected exotica. Meanwhile his new one-man show, *Excuse I*, opened in Australia in 1965. Success on the stage was complemented by the appearance of his Barry 'Bazza' McKenzie comic story in *Private Eye*, which introduced a character who coupled Kangaroo Valley beer-swilling with a provincial and unworldly innocence. As Bazza wandered ingenuously amongst the world of 1960s 'pseuds', Humphries fired volleys off in all directions.

The Barry McKenzie cartoons in *Private Eye* from 1964 to 1974 showed Humphries at his most creative. With Nick Garland, the New Zealand cartoonist, he captured the boozy ingenue, the innocent Aussie male abroad. This gauche denizen of Earls Court was counterpointed, however, not just by the London of Cockney cabbies and city stockbrokers with bowler hats reflecting the spirit of Surbiton and the city. Also sent up was the demi-monde, the London of alternative pretension, which Humphries knew too well – the underground media capital with its trendy arty types, into television, dope and sexual exotica. Jewish psychiatrists and other gurus guided them through the dense thicket of alternative-to-ulterior London in the 1960s.[21]

Bazza's alcohol-loving creator's story of the innocent's search for sexual experience mainly ended up with the scatological pleasures of a 'piss-artist'; however, his 'one-eyed trouser snake' took him to different worlds of imagery and experience. At a time when the nuances of Australian English were attracting scholarly and popular attention (from S. J. Baker and academic linguists and Afferbeck Lauder in *Let's Talk Strine*, 1965), Humphries added to the Australian vernacular with his – collected and invented – down-under metaphors surrounding the fly: 'siphon the python', 'slaying the dragon', 'shake hands with the unemployed'.[22]

Bazza was also Humphries' first character to win over an English audience. In 1972, he won a new mass appeal through one of the take-off vehicles of the emerging Australian film industry, *The Adventures of Barry McKenzie*. It was created by a triumvirate of the film director Bruce Beresford (back from several years apprenticeship in London and Nigeria), the Melbourne advertising genius-cum-columnist-cum-secular prophet and orchestrator of government support for film, Phillip Adams, and Humphries himself. The 1968 banning of a 'Bazza' McKenzie comic book by the Australian Customs Department and the subsequent publicity had already given Humphries a symbolic importance in Australia's transition from 1960s repression to the liberation of the early 1970s Whitlam era.[23] The film was innovative and new. While celebrating the past Australia of 1950s–60s Earls Court and Australian male excess, it brought everyday Australian voices and Australian imagery to a screen which had for so long lacked those authentic sounds. 'Bazza' caught the new wave of 1970s Australia – the era of the film renaissance, the opening in 1973 of the Sydney Opera House and Whitlam's new nationalism. Declarations of a degree of independence in foreign policy (withdrawal from Vietnam, recognition of China) were coupled with declarations of cultural independence – support for the arts, a points-system for Australian content in television drama and a minimum quota for local music on radio.

Paradoxically, the performance culture of 'Ockerism' – the 'old' male Australia of beer rather than the 'new' Australia of riesling and claret – was humorously recognised in this era of national self-amusement. Whitlam, the Prime Minister who introduced the Order of Australia in 1975 (beginning the process which abolished imperial honours), welcomed 'Mrs Everage' off the plane from England with a peck on the cheek, and then made her a 'Dame'. It seemed that Australian politics had a sense of humour as well as an enthusiasm for culture. It seemed, too, that expatriate critics and dissidents were being welcomed home. At the same time Humphries was moving in a conservative political direction, joining the board of Peter Coleman's conservative review, *Quadrant*. Perhaps his cultural and political conservatism contained an implicit protest about the disappearance of an Australia which he once knew.

Stairways to 'Heaven'

Humphries' appearance on the big screen would prove to be the next step on his red-carpeted escalator to the top – towards the brightest lights of the West End theatres and the media, to television in Britain, Australia and beyond. In 'one man' shows (and at times, as Edna, 'one woman' shows), he and Edna created their own theatre, audience and critique. The shows included *At Least You Can Say You've Seen It*, 1974, *Housewife-Superstar*, 1976, *A Night with Dame Edna*, 1979, and *Tears before Bedtime*, 1985. By the 1970s, the phalanxes of gladioli-waving fans would form the chorus for his melodies of cultural dissonance. Humphries had created his own Dada, his own alternative theatrical mode.

Underlying his critique were bitterness and bile, however. A fine line between love, manifested as affection, and hatred permeated his work. This would become apparent when he perfected his – by then explicitly politically conservative – attack on the cultural nationalism of the Whitlam Labor 1970s, through the persona of Les Patterson, Cultural Attaché to the Court of St James. The elements of caricature, which had sharpened the edge of his earlier characters such as Edna, had by now taken over. Lance Boyle was the progeny of polemical bitterness and Right politics, rather than of a deeper imagination.

Humphries the fop, Humphries the dandy, Humphries the gentleman, Humphries the Melbourne Grammar boy, Humphries the conservative was having his revenge on Australia. Not just on suburban Australia but on working-class Australia and even on those intellectuals who had once clasped his viperous wit, then directed at others, to their bosom. Despite endorsement by cultural progressives from the historian Manning Clark to Patrick White and Gough Whitlam, Humphries was on another wave-length and had other agendas, political as well as personal.[24]

Humphries actually came out of an Australian tradition, both old and new. The put-down of members of the audience – the 'canaries' in the 'ash-trays' (as he termed the theatre's boxes), and those who came late – was almost as old as Ned Kelly. It had its roots in music hall and vaudeville variety (at the Tivoli), and was practised by the great radio compere, Jack Davey, in his 'amateur shows' and public quizzes. His successor, Humphries, had also come from a land down under where 'stirring', and 'shit-stirring', were a popular art form. Humphries had mastered another old Australian comic tradition – overstepping the line of good taste. The 'blue' joke had been the staple of the Tivoli as exemplified by 'Mo McCaughey' and later comedians such as the television host Graham Kennedy (who once he gave a crow's call, or 'Faaark!!') maintained it. Both traditions continued in the vox pop interviews and blue humour of Sam Newman on the *Footy Show* in the 1990s.[25] Richard Ingrams had banned the Barry McKenzie cartoons from *Private Eye* in 1974, after tiring of depictions of lechery and perversity in several locales including Australia House and the Queen's bathroom.[26]

By the late 1970s, Humphries' characters had found new stages and new dimensions. Television beckoned. Now, Humphries discovered the chat show. In an era when the media was increasingly feeding on itself, the chat show became to television what the interview portrait was to feature and personality journalism. Cheap to produce and celebrity-oriented, it had supplanted the more expensive variety show. In a mass media era which focused on celebrities, with their television and magazine image haloes, 'Dame' Edna Everage made her entrance onto the set. Dame Edna's chat shows were less arduous than the one-person show on stage and took the Dame to new audiences, not only in Britain and Australia, but also in Germany and on US pay-TV. Humphries used another Australian ploy, that of the simple provincial innocent catching the famous unawares, which was perfected by 'Norman Gunston' (Garry McDonald) in his 1970s interviews (he had, for example, asked Warren Beatty 'Did someone write a song about you?'). Humphries also toyed with the famous. The quick wit which could shoot down targets in the audience found stars used to living in a lather of fame and applause even easier to have fun with. Of their petty vices this God (or Goddess – Dame Edna Megastar) made sport.[27]

Humphries had lost touch with Australian society, despite regular visits to Australia and the fact that he had 'never wished to live permanently in

England, much as [he] loved it'.[28] Dame Edna Everage Megastar (no longer just 'Housewife-Superstar') who, like her creator, was in touch with contemporary media reality, contrasted with Edna Everage housewife, 'born' 1955, who was out of touch with the everyday Australia of 1975, 1985 or 1995. Humphries had invented a fresh character who (or was it 'which'?) captured the mass media culture of celebrity which he had now joined through becoming a TV star. This matinee monster role, characterised by the energies of an increasingly glittering Edna, was a commercial success. As John Lahr has noted, *Back with a Vengeance!*, Humphries' 1989 stage show at the Theatre Royal, was taking £160 000 a week. and *The Dame Edna Experience* drew 48 per cent of the television audience in Britain.[29]

Most controversial, especially with the critics, was his 1976 'fabrication', Sir Les Patterson. At this time British opinion about Australia varied. A traditional elite view of Australia as the uncultured colony of convicts, peopled by 'the poor who got away', contrasted with a more positive view of Australia as a sunny place to migrate to.[30] Les, larger than life, protruding teeth and spraying saliva, was in part a 'panto' monster like Edna. An 'exuberant clown, and revolting drunk, folk anti-hero' in Peter Coleman's summary, his role inevitably 'contributed' to the debate about the character of the 'Antipodes'. Les Patterson was a cardboard character, right down to his liking for casks of Chateau Chunder. The sick side of this regurgitator monster spewed forth with vitality, often spreading his salivary excess to the front rows of the theatre.[31]

In the early 1980s in London newspapers most Australian stories were still subbed with the words 'Sport', 'Mate', 'Sheila' and 'Bonzer' and embellished with an image of a hat with corks (this was still happening a decade later). In this context, Les represented a certain image of a provincial Ocker Australia. Humphries had 'Sir Leslie Colin Patterson, Cultural Attaché to the Court of St James', formally opening 'the Australian Research and Studies Establishment' or 'ARSE') in Bloomsbury in 1982, the same year that the Australian Studies Centre at the University of London opened in Russell Square, also in Bloomsbury. Humphries used Sir Les as his vehicle for assailing his critics and the new nationalism. In opening ARSE, Sir Les Patterson quoted his Prime Minister:

> Australia's international image needs a bit of spit and polish and you're just the man to put his mouth where Australia's money is. Let's face it, Les, our lanky leader, went on to infer, London's chock-a-bloc with expat knockers making a fat quid selling Australia's credibility short. Smart-alec galahs like Germaine Greer, Clive James and that old sheila, Dame Edna, who dresses up as a man and tips the bucket on our incomparable cultural attainments in front of the crowned heads of Europe.[32]

Humphries had a reply to such expatriate bashing. In 1977, after reflecting on his Melbourne Grammar schooldays more than two decades before, he argued that:

> Modern Australian society, vitiated by the worst excesses of egalitarianism, desperately needs all the 'elitist' talent it can muster, all the exceptional, eccentric brilliance it can summon up to defeat the kill-joy puritanical pinkos and the dismal forces of Ockerocracy.[33]

Criticism of Humphries was not new, however, as shown by English and Australian responses to *Just a Show* in 1969. Sheridan Morley termed it 'a sustained hymn of hatred of his native Australia'. Irving Wardle suggested that Humphries came 'pretty close' to 'the unlovable type of Commonwealth entertainer who specialises in flattering the metropolitan public by sneering at the habits of his own country'. In the later summary of his biographer, Peter Coleman, 'Humphries' Australia, the critics agreed, was a land of louts, drunks, philistines, bigots, bores and bums'.[34]

In Australia there were fierce differences of opinion between Humphries' supporters and critics. Coleman, Humphries' first biographer, was an intellectual conservative, and a leading New South Wales Liberal. He sympathetically summarises Humphries' response to the late 1960s critiques in London and Australia, ones which would ramify in subsequent years. In what was touted as the era of a new and sophisticated Australia, Humphries ridiculed the suggestion that he was '*living in the past*'. This assertion, he said, revealed

> the critics' deepest fear – the fear that the expatriates working in the metropolitan centres of the world are living *in the future* and that it is their critics in the world's provinces who are really living in the past.[35]

The answer to that question regarding the future was complex, but would become clearer over time. Was Humphries an Australia-hater, or someone who suffered from a cultural-psychological condition which confused past and present? He denied the former accusation in a series of interviews in the early 1990s. He suggested that he had left behind what had been a staple of his work, his distaste for Australia. 'I've never thought of myself as an Australia-hater ... I've thought of myself as a patriot', he told ABC Radio's Terry Lane. In other interviews he declared that he shouldn't get 'upset when a journalist or an academic with no sense of humour accuses me of being unpatriotic or misanthropic'. He had 'no scores to settle ... that's all long past'.[36]

His critics were unmoved. They saw his denials as like those of a politician, except that Humphries was selling his shows rather than his party. The

Australian critics were unrelenting. They disliked him both because of his expatriate venom and because of his dated notions of 'class'. He was seen as a snob regarding both class and the colonial relationship with Britain. In 1983 Dan O'Neill, literature scholar and radical academic at the University of Queensland, asked

> How much longer can this curious ritual last, a Londoner with quick uptake, retentive memory and verbal flair coming over here on a regular basis, to tear the living fang out of us for being 'Australian'? It is hard to imagine an Argentinian, or Angolan, or Indian or a Vietnamese who elected to live in the former colonialist capital returning now and again to the ex-colony to bore it up everyone for the various ridiculous ways in which they were Argentinian, Angolan, Indian or Vietnamese.[37]

Craig McGregor, who had earlier questioned the private school origins of the *OZ* crowd's view of the 'Alf', condemned Humphries as a critic of political minorities and radical opinion:

> So Barry Humphries is back with us again, waving his gladdies, cracking his racist jokes, pillorying pinkos, Abos, unionists and of course women (whom he seems to loathe), presenting his show *An Evening's Intercourse* ...

McGregor had always admired Humphries. However, he now argued that 'instead of satirising the great and powerful and famous, the traditional and deserving subjects for satire, Humphries turns the full bilious force of his contempt upon the losers and the defenceless in society ... the great mass of common people ... are mere subjects for scorn'. The 'Madge Allsop' character seemed to confirm that critique. Madge Allsop, whose name rhymes with mop, Edna's Kiwi bridesmaid, is a drudge-like creature and Edna's 'punching bag'. Her protean presence increasingly graced Dame Edna's 'glittering' chat shows.[38] The playwright David Williamson discerned in Humphries 'almost a total hatred of Australia'. Williamson described him as 'a satirist who loathes Australia and everything about it'.[39]

Another critic was Malcolm Turnbull, the Republican leader and legal thorn in the side of the Thatcher government in the 1980s 'SpyCatcher' case, regarding British intelligence secrets. In 1998 Turnbull dismissed Humphries as 'basically making a quid out of denigrating Australia'. 'He caricatures Australia in the way they [the Brits] want to see Australia.' Turnbull believed that the way Humphries '[sent] up Moonee Ponds 1950' was as pointless as sending up Moonee Ponds of 1850.[40] In a fine piece of Melbourne Grammar superiority, he had transferred his Edna Everage character across town and down-market, from Camberwell to lower middle-class Moonee Ponds. In the best tradition of Grammar he directed his barbs at those below him. Even the more sympathetic and rounded character of Sandy Stone, a unique creation in the Humphries repertoire, came from further down the social scale.

The other consistent feature was the bile which seemed to inform some of Humphries' characters. Sir Les and Lance Boyle were the offspring of that expatriate hatred for family, society and country. Affectionate moments could be found in Humphries' *A Book of Innocent Austral Verse* (1968). Sandy Stone was an Everyman whose pathos suggested that the ordinary human could be a noble and even tragic figure. However, these were exceptions. Humphries' stock in trade was a fusion between pantomime and Dada, manifested in ugly figures with repeated rituals, who, aided by his quick wit, picked out victims in the audience. Humphries, like other Melbourne Grammar boys, had learned to humiliate his fellow students and, even more, the lower orders. A vital Humphries stage persona was the Queen of Prejudice and Cruelty. This was evident in the foyer sign jokes about ethnicity (directed at Greeks and Turks in Melbourne shows, and Australians in London shows) and disability ('Paraplegic Toilets 8th Floor. Please Use the Stairs').

The dated nature of Humphries' characters had been recognised by some critics as early as 1968. However in 1998, when Humphries put Dame Edna on stage again in London (nearly half a century after the middle-aged matron's creation in 1955), even British reviewers declared that the game was up. In Australia in the early 1990s, the scholar Jim Davidson, a longtime admirer, had discerned an out-of-touch Humphries whose characters 'no longer particularly engaged with the Australian present'.[41] Yet it could at least be said that Humphries, in the words of the old Chinese curse, lived in interesting times. Marriages and divorces, stardom and wealth, bouquets and battles all marked his years in London, and, to a much greater extent than most expatriates, in Australia. Yet the performer who had formaldehyded 1950s Melbourne in his shows also contributed to the rediscovery of Australian English when middle-class society was trying to forget it. And if, in the 1970s, Australia had a cult of Ockerism (as well as new nationalism and a cultural 'renaissance'), Humphries and the Barry McKenzie films were amongst its progenitors. Perhaps the creator, earlier, of Dada's 'Pus in Boots' (Germaine Greer had helped make the custard) had now generated more spew than he had consciously intended.

The personal and the public were intimately related for Humphries, whose private life of excesses and jagged edges mirrored his public life. He would get out some demons on stage, while still fighting an endless battle with another demon, drink. Geoffrey Dutton recalled Humphries at supper in Adelaide after *Just a Show*. Humphries approached the piano with the approval of the pianist, but when he sat down his head fell on the keys. Dutton and his other friends helped remove him from the room after what some other guests thought was 'a brilliant performance'.[42]

There were many sides to Humphries, including the decent dull suburbanite, living with perfect dustless London interiors. The expatriate photographer John Garrett found Humphries' 1980s house to be

> like the site of a posh hotel ... so tidy and immaculate ... so cold ... even with his collection of erotic art. Some children's toys were banished to the background as if all evidence of life had to be removed.

The London gent, the dandy, was also an art collector, who coveted the 'decadent' impressionist art of Charles Conder. Earlier, he had also found it possible to live in a cosmic haze, one more of inebriation than decadent elegance. His battle with alcohol was accompanied by a wandering eye, the clubs of Soho furnishing him with new bottles and interesting new women as well as new ideas and images.[43]

Expatriation allowed Humphries the opportunity to live part of his life through a series of invented characters. At best perhaps it allowed him to discern an essential Australia – or at least a certain middle-class suburban Melbourne of the postwar years. But was this essence fundamental and immutable? Humphries declared that 'Melbourne is really an English suburb ... However much Australians might like to think they're Americanised, it's really the Home Counties in the South seas – with a fair bit of Irish thrown in around Sydney'.[44] To Humphries this was forever the Australian ethos. Or had it changed – for better or worse? His fascination with Melbourne's past – he often campaigned to save historic buildings – allowed him to discover some essential truths from the 1950s while missing others, after his original 1959 departure. According to his critics, after the moment of his first departure Australia was frozen forever. How similar and how different were the experiences of his fellow Melburnian, Germaine Greer, and the kid from Sydney's southern suburb of Kogarah, Clive James?

Germaine Greer: Odysseys for Changing Times

Germaine Greer's journey was no less dramatic. It took her from the crucible of family life in the bayside suburb of Mentone and the Star of the Sea Convent in nearby Gardenvale in Melbourne to life as an internationally known writer and performer. In a larger firmament she would become author and controversialist, portrayed as both haloed saint and martyr in the mass media, the target of many attacks.

In that transition, she would both project herself onto larger stages and play to the image that her critics and fans relished: the 'untamed shrew', the description Christine Wallace used for the title of her often hostile biography.[45] From Sydney, Melbourne, Cambridge, Warwick and Tulsa universities to the feature pages of the newspapers, television chat shows and public auditoriums, her larger-than-life personality would stimulate and shock.

While Barry Humphries was formed by his suburban childhood, Germaine Greer was shaped by the disruptions to everyday life of World War II. Born in 1939, the same year as Clive James, who lost his father in the war, she was a beneficiary and a victim of her early experiences. She grew up with a father away at the war (and later unable to demonstrate affection), and a powerful mother who did not believe in 'sparing the rod'. She would never forget that stick of childhood.[46]

Fundamental distances between her and both parents were evident even then. Later they would be explored and acknowledged with venom. From the moment her father Reg arrived at Spencer Street Station on his return from the war, it was clear he was a psychological wreck, a situation more common than the popular legend of the Digger allowed.[47] Greer's book, *Daddy, We Hardly Knew You* (1989), tells of her discovery of the disturbing fact that her father had changed his identity early in his life, and of her low estimation of her mother. The views Greer expresses of her parents in this book seem to reach deeper than the relatively common problem of working out a relationship with an idealised father and a critically regarded mother. In this book she does not abide by the convention of public respect towards parents, whatever the private truth.

She describes her mother as 'an almost completely worthless human being'. The book similarly portrays a distance from her doubly or triply absent father, Reg. His initial absence at the war and his return as a shell of his former self later seemed confirmed by the gulf between fiction and reality – that 'Reg Greer' was actually Eric Greeney, and had lied about his past. It was as if the rude awakening of her discovery explained and confirmed the psychological distance between daughter and father, even 40 years later. When she discovered that her father was not what she had hoped but the 'office philanderer ... a bully ...', she lamented that she 'just took after him. I turned from being a clod into a harpy! I was going to f– get him!'[48] Perhaps this was her delayed vengeance against this weak and shadowy figure.

Like many an Australian child of the 1940s and 1950s, she was shaped by the strange combination of a weaker father and a stronger mother. It was not just her family. In part it was the impact of the war which had made many returned men more brittle than it was acceptable to admit at the time. In part it was their postwar transition, either to what the artist John Brack pictured in *Five o'clock Collins Street* as a dull conventional nine-to-five working life, or to the female domain of the suburban home, with or without Edna Everage. It was also the power over the family of strong women who had been denied larger career opportunities in this era of idealised suburban family values. Women who had put their energies into the roles of mother and wife, dominant roles which they also accepted, expected and even chose.

Although her discovery of the truth about her father came when she was nearly 50, her insecurities as well as her talents had been on display at a much younger age. Even as a convent girl her tendency to make a strong impact, and her intelligence and ability with language, were apparent. Later she would attribute her confidence to the convent, in which the girls were fostered by the love and care of the nuns. She believed that her standards and her orderliness on the one hand, and her wilder side on the other, came from this education. She had never been 'properly domesticated ... because I was actually socialised by a gang of mad women in flapping black habits'.[49]

The Catholic convent provoked and stimulated, as well as giving an occasional sense of deep seriousness, to this tall, theatrical and incessantly talkative young talent. Another force which gave rise to the pearl was a different sort of grit: what she later called her 'very boring childhood in Australian suburbia where books were few and far between and conversation didn't exist ... [an era of] stupor, the deep suburban sleep'.[50] Yet, she was a girl who could not help but be noticed. In the words of her former English teacher, Sister Raymonde, she 'made an impact on anyone she was with'.[51]

Searching for a Stage

Around Melbourne University and at the Swanston Family Hotel (also frequented by Arthur Boyd, the Blackmans and the ubiquitous Barry Humphries), and around the Melbourne push (known as 'the Drift'), she had an increasingly theatrical presence. She knew many people. They included the actor Richard Pratt, with whom she starred in the revue *Up and Atom*; and the photographer Athol Shmith, with whom she had an affair.[52] She was remembered as a 'larger than life star of student theatre', sitting in deep armchairs when wearing no underwear (preferably when opposite a priest), and either 'fornicating more than the rest' or, in the qualification of her longstanding critic Beatrice Faust, merely talking about it more.[53]

In contrast to Humphries, she preferred the Sydney alternative scene to the 'second rate' world of 'the Drift'. In Melbourne, and then around the wilder shores of the Sydney Push, two or three Germaines were already apparent: the solid, serious student; the wild performer and seeker after free thought, free speech and sometimes free sex; and the very different 'Auntie Germs' character, the compassionate tutor of young students in English at Sydney University. Perhaps there were even more. Her own reply to a TV talk-show host's question of whether there were two Germaine Greers was 'At least!'.[54] A student of Greer's at Sydney University, the journalist Bruce Elder, recalled her going through her 'Am I a good Catholic girl or am I a free spirit?' phase, as 'she castigated the Catholic priests and nuns one week and played Verdi's *Requiem* the next'.[55]

Push libertarian ideology and parties had already anticipated aspects of Sixties culture and gave her – and many others – a rationale for independence of thought and action which left the repressive Australia of the church, the respectable home and suburban materialism behind. The transition from libertarian values, like the 'Do your own thing!' culture of the Sixties, into consumer capitalist ideology expressed in the cult of the self and material consumption was still to come. Indirectly, unwittingly and unintentionally, liberationist and libertarian values also paved the way for the 'Greed is good' values of the 1980s and the 'Just do it!' self-gratification ideology of the 1990s. How important would the material wealth, lavish payment and fame of the new culture be for the dislocated freelancers when they came to strut their hour upon the celebrity stage?

Germaine Greer's second breakout was one made by many other Catholic girls. When the dam of Catholic repression had burst, she developed a sense of fleshly delights, echoing some medieval and renaissance meetings of sensuality and spirituality. In the culture of the Push, where bed had almost the same iconic status as philosophy and the pub, she was at home. Except for her, sexual freedom had come earlier, when other girls were still decently imprisoned in twinset and pearls – and, perhaps, more often. Despite an horrific experience of rape and later being the victim of gynaecological explorations, she was often in control. As in so many things, her powerful personality and redoubtable intelligence meant that she was dictating the terms – of both 'roots' and relationships. Yet not quite. In Sydney Push culture, sexual freedom had initially meant the freedom for the men who dominated the Push to score more often with more women. Like the earlier larrikin pushes, the gangs, of the old inner suburbs, Push culture was shaped by dominant males, by its 'king roos' and top dogs. Libertarian and social anarchist ideologies were arguably added on. They included the local version of bohemian challenge to respectability – a preference for gambling on the horses and for parties and philosophical play over conventional careers. However, beery and fleshly pleasures often took precedence. In Christine Wallace's argument, the Push gave Greer 'the life philosophy to justify the way she was living. That was the core philosophy she took to feminism'.[56]

Shaped in part by Sydney Push iconoclasm and anarchist ideas of personal freedom, she also had a deep seriousness, rooted in Melbourne, in Catholicism and in the quasi-religious moralism of Leavisite literary earnestness. The Leavisite search for moral significance and greatness in literature was elitist and earnestly serious in tone; in both respects it was 'heavier' than Push scepticism. Carrying those contradictions, she departed for Britain in late 1964.

She again found herself in different worlds in those early years in Cambridge and London. The more sedate culture of the ancient and Establishment university contrasted with the Sixties London underground. At Cambridge she was the serious student and the Footlights revue performer, mature by comparison with most students. In London she was a writer, a performer and an alternative scene groupie, researching her *OZ* story 'In Bed with the English'. She shared the 'groupie' role with the other *OZ* habitué and later Sydney fashion designer, Jenny Kee.

Performing in Footlights was also an introduction to English sexism. The Footlights club did not admit women as members until this 'revolutionary' policy was introduced in October 1964 (Greer was one of the first four women elected). Committee membership was also barred until November 1965, when she became 'Registrice'. (The first woman president would not be elected until 13 years later.) The change also undermined a very old Footlights tradition. As Eric Idle remarked 'there was no need for drag – Germaine did all that'.[57]

Her bawdy side and her Push connections would find later expression in her 1968 marriage to the builders labourer and arts graduate, Paul du Feu. In some ways it was a breakout for the newly free graduate student who had just submitted her doctoral thesis on Shakespeare. In other ways it was a retrograde step, as suggested by the domestic story of her desire for an early morning post-coital cup of tea. As du Feu tells it, he was about to bring her tea but 'got sidetracked from executing the order'. Propped up on her elbow, she 'glared at me with her tough-guy expression and said, "Listen, sport, I've asked twice for a cup of tea and all that happened was I got fucked. D'you reckon if I asked for a fuck I'd get a cup of tea?"' Despite her brilliant use of the politics of wit, the marriage lasted only a few weeks. Du Feu later published an account of his relationship with the world-famous feminist author, *Let's Hear It for the Long-legged Women*.[58]

A Book and a Media Halo

The transition which took Germaine Greer from underground writer and performer to contemporary media megastar had two components. One was *The Female Eunuch* (1970), a book which caught – and then enlarged – a rising wave of popular feminism, itself grounded in the liberationist spirit of the times. Her original proposal for the book, for her fellow Cambridge expatriate student and publisher, the Indian-born Sonny Mehta, began with the contemporary theme of the liberation of the American Negro, which Greer would extend to women. The appeal for the book came in part from her method of projecting and extrapolating from her own experience and psychology to the general constrictions on women realising their full selves. She believed that this book, to be comprised of a series of organically linked essays rather than developed as a formal study, had to be empowered by her own intense feelings. It also had to be about her. As in New Journalism, the reporter was the subject and, in this case, the 'heroine' of the book.[59] As Christine Wallace points out, Greer's conceptions of female freedom owed much to the Sixties' ideas of liberation – particularly sexual liberation – to the Push libertarians of Sydney. They would be reinforced and added to by the culture around *OZ* and *Suck* and other London underground magazines with which she was long involved.

Germaine Greer, wit, performer and thinker as well as writer, had appeared on television (in a Kenny Everett comedy show) before the publication of *The Female Eunuch*. However, it was the selling of this book in the media, in Britain, the US and Australia, which transformed her into a 'superstar', or 'megastar', as her friend and later Labor Cabinet Minister, Susan Ryan, later described her.[60] Already a striking – and bawdy – Chaucerian woman, she became larger than life under TV lights. Male journalists and producers were unusually sympathetic to her, partly because she was the attractive feminist who liked men. They also appreciated her as a great media talent. She was everywhere – on TV chat shows, at the National Press Clubs in Canberra and Washington, in a 'feminists and the beast' debate against Norman Mailer in New York, interviewed at length in *Playboy* (a magazine of which she was severely critical), in feature articles and as a guest editor of Richard Walsh's innovative magazine, *Pol*. Neutral observers, journalists and feminists noted the many labels she had already acquired – 'media freak' (her own term, which recognised the process), 'media-darling', 'high priestess of women's liberation'. Then, and later, some critics suggested that her great skill was self-propaganda, that she sold her story and her self as much as the book.[61]

Feminists were stimulated and frustrated by *The Female Eunuch*. Many women felt passionately and personally that it gave them a sense of what they could achieve, of how they could transcend traditional suburban assumptions on the part of men and women about the primacy of female domestic roles. It tuned into feelings which were very much 'about' in the early 1970s. Academic and political feminists would also become increasingly frustrated by Germaine Greer as maverick, her moral to psycho-cultural analyses, powerful images projected from a powerful mind and based in part on personal experiences, but hardly in any relationship to the developments in feminism and the women's movements since the late 1960s. Often she was provocative. In the early 1980s, she ridiculed the English view that she had become a feminist 'because Australian men are so dreadful. They've got to be kidding. I'd rather fuck an Australian than an Englishman any time. Any time'.[62]

The Female Eunuch had appeared at a time of innovation in non-fiction writing. Analysis and emotion were often joined in the literary performance of radical critiques. *Oz* fused words and images, and in the US the 'New Journalists, Hunter S. Thompson and Tom Wolfe, interwove their own consciousness with the events around them. Several books had an emotional edge and a unity located in polemic. In the UK, from a different point of view, the 1950s–60s radical and artist Jeff Nuttall generated *Bomb Culture* (1968). In Australia, Humphrey McQueen's radical critique of nationalism and labour, *A New Britannia* (1970), and Anne Summers' later feminist classic, *Damned Whores and God's Police* (1975), fused powerful emotions with a polemical edge.[63] To some accustomed to more sober, analytical modes of thought, this new writing could be unduly subjective, excessively polemical or just 'over the top'. In these often neo-romantic modes, authors, particularly Greer, privileged emotion and self. To the critics, she expressed a kind of Sixties feminism – in which she saw sexual liberation for women, a kind of 'cunt-power', as a form of emancipation from monogamy – which still owed too much to male heterosexual definitions of women's role and to the bawdy pub language of sexual liberation of the Push.[64] To more sympathetic eyes, her sexually outrageous side was in a proud proto-feminist and Australian tradition of self-assertiveness which had a long history. Like domestic feistiness, it went back to the strong convict women, and would be restated over a decade later in the TV comedian 'Elle McFeast's' role as the 'Power Pussy'.

To The Green Room!

The Sixties change in the media opened the doors of the 'green room' to Germaine Greer. By the late Sixties, even as conflicts grew, 'radical chic' had TV appeal in those new forms, the chat show and the interview. In New York, Leonard Bernstein entertained the Black Panthers. In the UK, the Irish radical Bernadette Devlin, the Pakistani-born student radical Tariq Ali and Germaine Greer herself were a late Sixties triumvirate of intense performers and small screen stirrers, as well as playing other political and intellectual roles.

It was the performer in Greer that appealed to the media – the beautifully shaped phrases, the rapier-like repartee, the often formal sentences leavened with frank (or 'vulgar') sexual remarks, the confessions and even the skill with accents. Harold Evans gave her writing opportunities in the *Sunday Times* (1971–73), as Richard Neville had become an *Evening Standard* contributor. The underground, or at least its brightest stars, had gone overground. The radicals had demonstrated that they were as much in the business of media – writing, communicating, performing – as they were in the business of cultural and sexual politics. She would continue to write columns and articles for English papers and American reviews.

Soon Germaine Greer would become one of the three talented Australians (the only ones, according to some British media elites and audiences) 'across' the media. The ubiquitous 'high priestess of feminism' had made her mark, along with Clive James, who wrote his first columns on television in 1972, and Barry Humphries. They drew on Australian directness but left behind the bush hats, broader accents and bush references of Bill Kerr and Rolf Harris. They presented themselves to British audiences as that strange phenomenon – 'cultured Australians'.

War and Peace?

Over time Germaine Greer changed. She would make a kind of peace with the Catholic Church, celebrating her convent school years and also developing conservative (and romanticised) views regarding the traditional rural, peasant societies and their methods of contraception in *Sex and Destiny* (1984). She would confront her childhood in *Daddy, We Hardly Knew You* (1989), then and later making critical remarks about her dead father and her still alive mother.

She did not, however, make her peace with contemporary feminism or with Australia. In the first case, her influential early role, her profile as a feminist hero due to *The Female Eunuch* and her complex later views led to a mutual self-denying ordinance, whereby she and the several feminist movements agreed not to cross swords in the media or to debate ideological water under the bridge. While feminist radicals in academe suggested that her links with the women's movement had always been tenuous (one of the few major feminist publications which published her was *Spare Rib*, the location of her old *OZ* mates, Marsha Rowe and Rosie Boycott), this was rarely a subject of public debate.[65]

Her rejection of Australia remained a *leitmotif*, however. One thing stayed constant, whatever she was doing. Whether visiting her country of origin, escaping the UK taxman and entertaining Federico Fellini in Tuscany, in dispute with squatters in her London property or (having gone full circle and more) as an English eccentric wearing Wellies and pearls on her farm, Australia remained her *bête noire*. It was almost as if she and the Australian media had a different mutual agreement – to retain their adversarial relationship.

On visits in 1972, in 1975, 1982, and in 1997, and *in absentia* in 1988, she maintained her expatriate rage. While selling *The Female Eunuch* in 1972, however, she had played a politically valuable role. Applying for full membership of the Journalists Club in Sydney and being refused, she then refused to address it, and supported women journalists' protests outside the all-male club, helping end its gender bar. Women won full rather than just associate membership. She declared then that she could never live in Australia, a country 'without a decent newspaper', and with 'the present [McMahon Liberal] Government'. She was 'fed up with the Australian institutions' which had not changed, and were 'so complacent, so inefficiently run it is unbelievable'.[66] She did return, as promised, after the election of the Whitlam government with its aspiration to be a new broom, but her critical stance and unwillingness to contemplate permanent return continued. Strangely, the inefficiency of Britain was one of the most common expatriate plaints in their first years in London, often put ahead of the weather and the alleged controlled coolness of the English.

Greer's adamantly critical stance reappeared in 1982 in two major feature articles for the *Observer*. (A related, and recurring point concerned how poorly Australian newspapers paid, although, as former *Age* editor Michael Davie reflected, they paid her more than they did other contributors.) In one article, on the Aborigines of the Northern Territory, she wore her romantic hat, celebrating the Aboriginal Australians and developing a fantasy of decline and fall, in the style of Oswald Spengler, of a coming Antipodean Armageddon which would see the whites driven back into the sea. Returning to her native Melbourne, she came out against city and nation with all guns blazing:

> Australia is a huge rest home, where no unwelcome news is ever wafted on to the pages of the worst newspapers in the world. The vast mass of the population snoozes away roused only for a football match or a free beer ... Australia is a land of lotus-eaters.

This was the Germaine Greer who had not been reading the Fleet Street tabloids or talking to Australia's unemployed. Her picture of Melbourne offered pure expatriate stereotype, frozen in the jar of a bitter remembered past. 'Nothing has changed' she intoned before going on to describe Brunswick Street, Fitzroy, echoing Ray Mathew's 1962 general lament about their native country. Unfortunately her description of part of the street as 'little more than a string of "opportunity" shops ... a horde of "derros" ... and "winos" ', unchanged since her student days, was simply short-sighted.[67] Had she walked, or even looked, a little further down the street she would have seen a different streetscape: a centre of alternative fashionable Melbourne, with a string of cafes, galleries, ethnic restaurants in a city of great multi-cultural food and art, bookshops and craft shops. Brunswick Street *had* changed, but those changes were outside her vision.

In 1988, she took aim against the Bicentennial celebration of white settlement (or invasion) 200 years earlier. She rightly recognised that the underlying problem of Aboriginal culture was dispossession and subsequent paternalism (and therefore white solutions didn't always help all that much). She postured, as well as protested, over the events of 1988. Many Aboriginal protest groups and white supporters successfully used the occasion to highlight the costs to indigenous Australians of the invasion of their land. That the melodramatic observations of a rich expatriate who jetted in occasionally from London didn't necessarily help the cause may not have been apparent to her, whether she was wearing her megastar halo or her everywoman coat of identification with the suffering ordinary people.

This solidarity, whether with Fourth World Australian Aborigines or Third World peasants, could take perverse forms. When asked to speak at a January 1989 conference at the University of Florence on the subject of Australian artists in Tuscany, she rejected the offer. She was neither novelist nor painter and had not had any dealings with Tuscan intellectuals. She wasn't particularly interested in Australian literature, and had boycotted anything connected with the Bicentennial. Nor did she approve of a conference in Italy being held in English. Not usually resident in her small, unheated Tuscan house at that time of the year, she declined the request.

Her refusal disappointed the conveners – and their students – who were looking forward to meeting her as well as the artist Jeffrey Smart and the novelist David Malouf and other guests. Jeffrey Smart, a friend, and a fan of her talent, was not able to talk her round as he had hoped.[68] Her expressions of refusal would become a minor domestic art form over the next few years. Using much more strident language, she warned off interviewers, prospective biographers and other unsavoury characters from her private -- yet already public – Queendom.

In the 1980s, when approaching 50, Germaine Greer was perhaps attempting to come to terms with her theatrical self, her contexts and her personal aspirations. The media loved images of a 'mellowed' Germaine.[69] Some accounts pictured a lonely spinster now living on a farm outside Cambridge, as much to be pitied as envied. Even aside from these images and the 'good life' clichés, the opposite of the outrageous, powerful performer strutting the media stage, she was adjusting to change. By the end of the decade she had retreated from the Mediterranean dream of living eventually in Tuscany (she sold her house to a banker), and was also reflecting on where home was. In 1985, she said of the UK:

> I only live here because it's easier for me to work here. England certainly isn't home. Actually nowhere is home for me any more, not even Australia. I don't really think there's any such thing. I think the idea of a home is a fantasy, something we create in our minds. I don't think it exists in reality.[70]

While admitting that she had kept her Australian passport and nationality, Australia was declared unwanted as well as unwelcoming. Sometimes,

succumbing either to the selfishness of the age or to the exigencies of the freelancer-cum-media star, she performed for her supper. In the same 1985 interview quoted above, she bucketed British Prime Minister Margaret Thatcher for, by her own account, mercenary and material reasons. 'I have a new farmhouse and I need a new dishwasher, don't I.'[71] In this 'frankness' she was, as in her books, maintaining another side – the presentation to public audiences of her foibles, follies and sufferings. If reviewers and biographers occasionally depicted her as insufferably arrogant or a foolish victim of success, she had provided them with the ammunition to fire their salvoes, often right down to intimate details of weakness or anxiety.

In 1997, after many years of an absence of invitations, Australia called. The Melbourne International Festival, under the stewardship of the former advertising guru Leo Schofield, and the then Melbourne Writers Festival invited a series of expatriate tall poppies as 'star attractions'. In 1995 it was Robert Hughes, Clive James came in 1996, and in 1997 it was Germaine Greer's turn to address the Writers Festival. Whether with an eye for talent and a respect for Australia's overseas stars or with a related cultural cringe focus on the box office principle that the great come from overseas, the 'old firm' were invited back. Germaine Greer packed the Melbourne Town Hall (with some tickets resold by scalpers!) and offered the audience a thrill-a-minute ride. She had already played a familiar tune, describing Melbourne as a 'tiny, little town; with run-down inner suburbs', and imaginatively, or fantastically, anticipating an 'Aborigine Republic' and an Aboriginal House of Lords.[72]

On this occasion, she returned to an older combative feminist theme. The author, who had once had her most intimate orifice photographed for *Suck* magazine, declared war on 'penetrative sex' and on the unfortunate influences of magazines for adolescent girls. Speaking of the 'blood sport' of sex and of how 'people get hurt', her subjects included sadomasochistic sex, drug-induced sexual excitement, anal sex, surgical gender-reassignment, formula baby food, the Barbie doll and the abuse of children. In broadcaster Ramona Koval's account of 'this piece of performance art', she was 'doing funny voices, taking cheap shots, entertaining her audience with well-worn turns of phrase'. This pacy show was 'a hit with the audience', who responded with 'tumultuous applause', yet Koval wondered when its members would get a chance to 'stop feeling and start thinking'.[73] She was one of several reviewers who asked of this 'entertainment' whether the game was worth the candle. Under the heading 'Definitely not germane', the *Herald Sun*'s editorialist expressed a larger Antipodean discontent:

> HO HUM. Another expatriate has just landed, brimful of gratuitous advice for the country on which she turned her back 20 years ago. Perhaps the faded rebel Germaine Greer thought the best way of commanding attention after so long in the English shade was to be outrageous.

The editorial went on to condemn the other 'ill-informed' expatriates such as Barry Humphries who 'bagged the plans for Federation Square' from England, Robert Hughes who had 'delivered a homily on immigration [and] multiculturalism' and 'monarchist Clive James [who had] bought into the republican debate'.[74]

More sedately, an *Age* editorial headed 'Greer and the second sex' differentiated the 'feminist' revolution of the 1970s (concerned with the position of women in Australia in the workplace, education, and marriage) from the 'sexual revolution', on which her lecture had focused. In these spheres, Australia had been a leader in the empowerment of women (in many areas of anti-discrimination legislation it was ahead of Britain), and was influenced by an active and practical political women's movement, to which, Christine Wallace lamented, Germaine's 'isolated' role and her more recent rhetorical performances contributed little.[75]

Perhaps Germaine Greer was the product of fundamental divisions – paradoxes, contradictions and antagonisms which strengthened and weakened her as a writer and performer and as a human being. At the Star of the Sea Convent she had been torn between two selves, between 'the orderliness … [and] the calm' of the school and its wilder sides – 'All girls' schools are fairly hysterical institutions', she had remarked. The 'freedom' from institutional socialisation engendered by expatriate isolation had powerful consequences. Catholicism and hedonism, Leavisite moralism and Push libertarianism conspired to pull her in opposing directions.[76]

The Apollonian pole of order had as its opposite the Dionysian phallus of vitalism which she found at university and in the Push in Sydney. The divide between the moral orientation of the Leavisites (a dominant force in English at Melbourne University, a doubly dedicated minority at Sydney University) and the alternative values of the Push had further encouraged her fluctuation between different orientations. Both groups however, certain of their own superiority, differentiated themselves from the mainstream. These self-styled elites also moved from pessimism about ordinary people to a sense of their own self-importance. The Leavisite literary critics sought to civilise and moralise the masses while the 'anarchistic pessimists' of the Push drank, screwed, gambled and talked – and sometimes thought – as they played out their iconoclastic theatre of opposition to the seeming ordinariness of social convention.[77] Reinforced by the dualism of the 1960s, a denizen of the London underground and an older Cambridge doctoral student, Germaine remained divided between very different selves.

That duality would continue and it would be expressed in her variety of roles. In the media, she was a 'Queen' of media feminism, who would say astonishing things. Her range ran from piously moralistic to 'shockingly frank', with moments of both egotism and self-laceration thrown in. She had a similar range in speech and dress. Australian observers noted – with regret

or the pleasure of cultural *Schadenfreude* – how the beautiful hippie and striking woman had been supplanted by a creeping middle-class Englishness of hairstyle, and a very different, even dull, dignity in dress. Yet she did not give up the 'untamed shrew' tongue. This ranged from bawdy humour to atomic put-downs of those who gave the 'Queen' displeasure. Her biggest target in the 1990s was her uninvited biographer, Christine Wallace. She publicly barred her friends from talking to this intruder in her life, this 'dung beetle', 'amoeba', 'intestinal flora' and 'brain-dead hack'. The journalist, and former biographer of Liberal Party Opposition Leader John Hewson, was also warned that Greer would have her 'kneecapped' if she talked to her mother. She had already interviewed this other fearsome character, however. In September 1997, Germaine Greer threatened to walk out of any Writers Festival media conference if either the book or its author were mentioned.[78]

Paradoxically, like the admixture of self-appreciation and the social pessimism which personified the Push, Germaine Greer alternated between supreme arrogance and self-confidence and a deep inconfidence and un-certainty. Perhaps her lack of positive feelings about her parents, or the inferior role to which society relegated women, were mirrored in self-doubt. While her book *The Obstacle Race* (1979) looked at the difficulties facing women artists, a negative assessment about female talent emerged in her later study of women's poetry, *Slip-Shod Sibyls: Recognition, Rejection and the Woman Poet* (1995). The Leavisite-trained critic concluded that not only women's poetry had been ignored, but that, by the standards of the ruling male canon, the women's oeuvre wasn't up to scratch.

Did the very experience of being driven by her inner demons, expatriated from the society in which she had grown up and then catapulted into the firmament of fame, the megamonde of publicity, have costs as well as benefits? In a 1988 interview, 'A prophet in her own land', she declared that *The Female Eunuch* had 'ruined my life'.[79] The wealth, the talent and the temperament that had allowed her to choose to live and work as a freelancer had negative consequences as well as conferring an unusual degree of freedom. The experience of being an expatriate, an uprooted freelancer who had sold her emotional story as part of the private–public performance for the crowds arguably separated her fundamentally from the everyday hinges which held most people's lives in place. London allowed the independent writer to flourish, providing publishers, Sunday newspapers and the London Library. But the demands, and skills, of popular authorship led to an un-certain relationship with the academy. Often the question of academic standing preyed on the minds of those who had once been destined for humbler, but more socially approved academic careers, such as herself and her fellow Sydney University and Cambridge University student, Clive James.

Was this why she sought and found new and less individual consolations? She established an intermittently communal world at Mill Farm and sought a welcoming congregation in Newnham College at Cambridge (even as an 'unofficial Fellow') and the confirmation of her status as 'Dr Greer'.[80] The 'Dr Greer' hat was also useful when writing on such medical/sociological subjects as birth control in the Third World and menopause.

The doubly uprooting experience of living and working as a successful expatriate freelancer freed her from the rigidities of conventional thought and allowed her to develop original ideas. Her multiplicity of skills allowed her to educate and entertain in an era of infotainment and the rise of celebrity performers. Perhaps one cost of this was the need to occasionally adopt certain recurring positions as part of her script. One was the Australia-hater recycling outdated clichés which she knew the media would 'love' – perhaps for different reasons in Britain and Australia.

The projection of private demons onto a larger stage, or screen, was an expatriate experience which transcended several Anglo-Saxon traditions of restraint about one's private life. In a sense her media status as an Australian and a feminist licensed her to act in public in ways the English found interestingly eccentric. It would become less strange in an era of celebrity tittle-tattle which dominated the media later in the century. This all came at a great cost. In her writing she exposed herself. The 'heroine' put her problems as well as her talent 'up front'. As such she also presented her weaknesses, and was almost as much a victim as an all-conquering Valkyrie of the small screen and the Sunday papers. Her many stories of herself as heroine and as victim provided her critics, and the biographer Christine Wallace, with material that allowed them to both appreciate and condemn her.

The Rise and Rise of Clive James

The third of the Antipodean musketeers who made the stages, studios and broadsheets of London their own was Clive James. Born in 1939, the same year as Germaine Greer, Clive Vivian Leonard James grew up in suburban Kogarah before becoming part of that most exciting generation which enlivened Sydney University from the late 1950s. This was the Sydney University of James and his confrères (in this male era women, with notable exceptions such as Greer, tended to be offstage, rather than centrestage): the filmmaker Bruce Beresford, the scriptwriter and performer-at-large Bob Ellis, the art critic and 'performer' Robert Hughes, the *Honi Soit* editor and later book and magazine publisher Richard Walsh (who ranged from *OZ* to *Nation Review* to the *Australian Women's Weekly*), the poet Les Murray, the Shakespearean actor John Bell and a disparate trio of future political journalists, Mungo MacCallum, Laurie Oakes and David Solomon.[81]

Sydney University in the early 1960s reflected some of the different sides of Sydney. In an environment in which Andersonianism and Cold War

Imperial elephant and home away from home (Australia House on the Strand).
(Stephen Alomes)

Rolf Harris, painter and performer, with 'didge' and wobble-board.
(Rolf Harris Productions Pty Ltd)

Germaine Greer, militant at the National Press Club. (National Press Club)

Barry Humphries brings sartorial elegance to the National Press Club.
(Heide Smith)

Left Jill Neville, writer, at home in Belsize Park Gardens, London. (Stephen Alomes) *Right* Richard Neville, writer and perpetual Sixties media performer, at home in Woollahra. (Stephen Alomes)

Left Geoffrey Chard, singer, in Melbourne. (Stephen Alomes)
Right Geoffrey Parsons, travelling accompanist. (Douglas Copeland)

Going north, going south. Julia Blake and Leo McKern in Far North
Queensland, starring in the film of David Williamson's play, *Travelling North*.
(View Films)

Sydney calls – flying into the Harbour City. (Stephen Alomes)

caution meant that there were few jobs for Leftists, it lacked the political left-liberalism of Melbourne University. Robert Hughes described his own generation as 'a politically unconcerned bunch of aesthetes and artists'.[82] The institution reflected the traditional Sydney elite attitude in looking to England and Europe, offering solid courses on English and European history and English literature and the classics. In the manner of colonialism, their own country, Australia, was of less interest, despite the new Chair in Australian Literature, created in 1962 after a public fund-raising campaign. The low church evangelicalism and wowserism of the former convict colony and the working-class vitality against which the establishment reacted were usually distant, as were the lower orders themselves, bar a few scholarship boys and fewer girls.

In the late 1950s, Sydney University offered several forums for late adolescent egos and precocious talents. Clive James, the 'virgin sophisticate', lived a double life in Presbyterian Kogarah and in the arty world of university suede and corduroy, and was both 'a petty bourgeois student' and 'a libertarian bohemian'. Soon writing, in his own modest words, almost half of the revue and 'a good half of *honi soit* [sic] every week' he acquired 'a certain kind of cheap fame ... in which I pretended not to wallow'. Reading H. L. Mencken and wearing cord, he was ready to follow Robert Hughes, who was writing on art for *Nation*, into the public sphere. Having learned of the libertarians' view of 'sexual guilt as a repressive social mechanism', a recipe for sexual freedom which anticipated the Sixties, he lost his virginity to the auburn-haired beauty, 'Lilith Talbot'.[83]

The 'cultural' university was paralleled by a social one, populated by the Bellevue Hill and Rose Bay set, with their sports coats and matching MG TC sports cars. They went to Sydney University to do medicine or law, played rugby union as they had done at their private schools and looked for a suitable match. This was nearly two decades after Michael Blakemore and Russell Braddon had begun their studies in medicine and law.[84]

On New Year's Eve 1961, Clive James sailed away on the Greek ship *Bretagne*. A Push contingent was on the shore and some of the Bellevue Hill rugby players were on the boat with James, also going to the source of elite society. En route, James visited Changi (where his father's weight had been reduced to that of a ten-year-old) and had a Singapore suit made, which personified upward mobility. Later, as he worked his way up, he would use a simply cut blue suit as the trademark of his TV persona.[85] Many of his generation travelled, including Robert Hughes, the filmmaker Bruce Beresford and Mungo MacCallum, not the distinguished classical scholar but his grandson, later the doyen of political commentators-as-wits, who did for the 1970s Australian parliamentary circus what James would do for British TV.

In the 1980s James sought to put an expatriate metaphysical gloss on his flight across the world. 'Passing between the Heads was like being born again.' Yet his early progress would be more formulaic than spiritual. Leaving the boat at Southampton in the English winter of 1962, he got onto an Overseas Visitors Club bus, 'full of Australians' and bound for Earls Court. Later generations of travellers would be picked up by mini-buses of the Walkabout Club and the Colonial Club at Heathrow. Although he escaped after a week at the OVC hostel – to B&B landladies, flats and bedsits in Earls Court, Swiss Cottage, and Tufnell Park Road in not yet trendy Kentish Town – he would be drawn back to the Holland Park/Kensington colonies, to parties in the Melbury Road house which had long been a Sydney expatriate landing pad and settlement. As Peter Grose recalled of that experience, it was as if 'the last party you'd had in Double Bay [had] folded up and moved to Melbury Road where it resumed'. James would venture out. He was, however, sexually rebuffed as a mere colonial, put down with an educated 'Really?' by an Englishwoman whose attentions he courted ('it was like being flicked in the face with a wet, sandy towel'), before again pursuing 'Lilith' in her London setting, a bedsit in Maida Vale.[86]

Having missed the *de rigueur* Anderson lectures at university, he caught up by reading the only book he had brought from Australia, John Anderson's *Studies in Empirical Philosophy*, picking up the 'critical scepticism' which would later offer a form of philosophical underpinning for his point-scoring wit as well as a rationale for conservatism. The nearest James would ever come to political involvement was participating in a Campaign for Nuclear Disarmament Aldermaston march, as did several unlikely and disparate contemporaries including Charles Osborne, Barry Humphries and Murray Sayle. However, the 'realist' conservative later believed that participating in the march was 'a colossal mistake, a real lulu'. The protestors were 'acting out a fantasy because it was more fun than what I knew to be truth'.[87] Work in feature journalism was hard to get – despite an introduction to J. D. Pringle at the *Observer*. On one occasion, he met an old drinking mate who was now in a three-piece suit and sounded 'like the Queen broadcasting to the Commonwealth'.[88] In Westminster, even more than on Pitt Street or Collins Street, some expatriates loudly exhibited the marks of their social mobility.

James shared several experiences with Barry Humphries and Germaine Greer. Like Greer, he had an absent father. A POW in Changi, James senior had been killed in a plane crash on his way home from the war. Like Humphries, Clive had experienced the school culture of bullying.[89] One legacy of this was a desire to project himself onto larger stages. Another, shared by the former Changi and Burma Railway POW Russell Braddon (whose book, *The Naked Island*, would jolt James), was a profound ambivalence towards the Japanese which ranged from fascination to deep distaste.

In part playing to his English audience – or to popular prejudice at large – his repertoire of verbal and visual jokes often involved the mocking of silly foreigners, particularly the wartime enemies, the Japanese and the Italians.

Although he remarked that he was not brought up in 'a vengeful spirit', he also recognised, regarding the war, that 'it's over but it's not over'.[90] On the other side of the coin, he would later develop a love affair with Japan and write a novel, *Brmm! Brmm!* (1991), with a Japanese hero.

Ian Britain's portrait of James depicts a fatherless son very close to his mother, yet seeking to go beyond that suburban nest. Quoting James, he sees in the 'fatherless child' a recognisable pattern of 'self-love and the unassuageable need to have it confirmed'. Overemphasising the fact that James lived at home (in Australian capital cities students have often lived at home), he pictures James as a 'misfit'. Ambivalent about his sexual attractiveness and his body, the later TV doco host would present himself as a voyeur, fascinated by women, women's fashion and muscular males. Britain's picture of James' flirt and ogler persona, able to step onto bigger stages as a result of these insecurities, involves Freudian imaginative leaps.[91] However, the narrative of James, the habitué of the Journalists Club (he worked for a while as a *Sydney Morning Herald* journalist), later taken up by the visiting English comedian Joyce Grenfell (James regarded her as a 'second mother'), at least confirms the picture of the self-consciously colonial boy 'falling towards England', with or without the Freudian gloss.[92]

Of equal or greater significance, James was a product not of the world of celebrities, into which he would later move, but of Menzies' Australia. This was a society which, while valuing conformity at large, had a role for the clever individual who, like Menzies himself, could rise above the pack. The conservative values underlying this individualism emphasised talent rather than larger social and cultural questions; they also influenced the ambitious Melbourne Grammarian Barry Humphries and the rising convent girl, Germaine Greer. The conception of the successful man (rarely was it a woman) dominating the stage was as big in Australia as in the 'Room at the Top' aspirations of the upwardly mobile working class in Macmillan's England. James even sought to semi-theorise the idea, linking individualism with expatriation. In a favourable review of a Robert Hughes TV series on modern art, he characterises the expatriates as different. To 'set up an individual identity, instead of being absorbed in a collective one, was the main reason they left home in the first place'.[93] James' late injection of Andersonianism was a prophylactic against radicalism. Implicitly, he invoked the Andersonian doctrine of the dangers of 'unintended consequences' in distancing himself from the 'radical certainty' of the Left.[94] Unfortunately this apolitical high ground would often lead to an abdication of understanding, or even a deficiency in analysis, when he sought to pursue social and political questions: television, fashion and Formula 1 were easier.

James' transition from clever colonial and prodigious reviewer to a TV megastar began just a fraction later than the rise of Barry Humphries and Germaine Greer to electronic popularity. He had begun graduate research studies in literature at Cambridge but did not finish his degree. Instead, he took a 'First' in Footlights. Coupling prodigious energy with a talent to amuse, he became president in 1966 and directed and wrote for every revue from 1967 to 1970. The rising political conflicts of the late 1960s were less dramatic in Britain than in Australia. They did affect Cambridge, but not Clive James, however. Although he achieved 'pace and style' in his revues, they were guilty neither of a sharp political edge nor of any hint of satirical *lèse-majesté*.[95]

After leaving Cambridge he was initially tempted by the 'Grub Street' option of being a London literary journalist and reviewer. It was one of the hats Peter Porter wore – to the benefit of his bank balance but at a cost to his time for writing poetry. James conceptualised the role in his first collection of essays, *The Metropolitan Critic* (1974). In several ways this located him as the stereotypical colonial, a literary Dick Whittington, seeking his fortune in the metropolitan capital, as well as a reviewer outside of academe. Although he kept a kind of Australian accent (later acquiring a fashionable 'mid-Pacific' or 'trans-Atlantic' American twang), he was very much the colonial Willy Loman who wanted to sell his wares and to be liked, to be approved of. It was perhaps this social climber aspect, along with a booming self-confidence, and increasing success on television, which encouraged media gossip columnists to later make play with his professional and private ups and downs.

To Paul Morley in the *New Statesman & Society*, the first in the 1989 series of *Saturday Night Clive* was 'as deliberately banal, sarcastic, superior and lost-in-waste space as all of the last series'. Morley had little time for the 'dead' 'formula' that Britain had 'the best television in the world and everybody else's is laughable to the point of insanity'. It wasn't just the laughing 'at the backward Russians' or the 'cute dog commercials', but the fact that British television mirrored the society, which Morley believed was 'crooked and crumbling'. Sometimes the criticism was more personal, more base. A column in the London *Daily Mirror*, under the headline 'Poet Clive's Cash Boast', reported that 'he has been boasting to colleagues that, for 1980 and 1981, he expects to make a total of around 250 000 pounds'. 'James', the article went on, 'is widely regarded in London as an ill-natured fellow'. It concluded by noting, however, that he was 'popular' with a wealthy socialite. Television viewers and reviewers loved or loathed Clive, the 'lightweight heavyweight'. One Australian viewer condemned the 'Contrive James' of his postcard from Berlin, and the 'jokey images' which supplanted a more serious understanding of that city of historic conflicts. James was unworried by the accusation that his 'smugness and corny, Americanised delivery gets right up people's noses'. If he got up the noses of a few journalists, critics and of some viewers it didn't matter. All that mattered was that he didn't get up the public proboscis, making them turn off.[96]

Nor was the criticism just saved for his television work, perhaps inevitable after a decade of scoring points off the medium himself. His *Charles*

Charming's Challenges on the Pathway to the Throne, 1981, was savaged as fawning to the Court of St James, a piece without bite. Some other critics espied a 'Law of Diminishing Returns' for his autobiographical novels. After the brilliance of *Unreliable Memoirs* (1980), it was downhill all the way if the next two volumes, *Falling Towards England* (1985) and *May Week Was in June* (1990), were any indication.[97]

While he differentiated himself from his less cultured compatriots left behind, and had a growing cockiness which some Australian observers thought was just 'Sydney flash', the gap between him and other expatriates grew. International TV commitments gave him less time for some old friends in London while some expatriates, including John Pilger, felt distinctly un-comfortable at what they saw as his crawling manner around London functions. As a colonial 'on the make' in Britain (his own self-definition), his strength would be to comment on the nouveau riche at play in other milieux (on their games and forms of display, from Rio to Hollywood and on fashion shows, from Paris to the Melbourne Cup). James was one of the last talented 'colonials', the expatriate who sought acceptance in London society. He would tell the story of his initial journey, but he was not predisposed to question his own trajectory or the social contradictions of the English elite societies around which he sometimes lurked.

His personal lack of interest in understanding the colonial relationship which had produced him, and its decline, limited his ability to understand Australia. In the early 1970s, he became an expatriate mocker of the assumed renaissance in the cultural desert which he had left. Thus he paraded the Australian stereotypes (the Qantas pilot, the beach, the sun, the nouveau riche at alfresco lunch) with a genial hint of London elite mocking, while claiming social, if not spiritual, fraternity with these materialist souls. Over time he appeared to mellow in his view of the land which had given birth to him, or the land he had escaped from, and his accounts became milder. Now that the ABC was showing his TV specials, praise also had its benefits. He even became a kind of literary patron, writing *Times Literary Supplement* reviews in occasional special issues on Australian books.

In Australia, James continued to be seen as out of touch, particularly in one Australian series in which the Melbourne writer Barry Dickins unsettled James and his fellow guest, Barry Humphries. 'I want to go to Yass', Dickins replied to a nonplussed James who had asked if he wanted to go to New York again. Martin Flanagan described James as belonging to 'a generation of Australian intellectuals who believed that life is elsewhere, that Oxford and Cambridge universities represented the Wimbledon of the mind, and that until you won over there, you didn't really exist'. Flanagan, inspired in part by the Aboriginal model, rejected those who sought to do the impossible – 'to deny your origins' – while also quoting, from the other pole, Auberon Waugh's view of 'this cringing man on the make'.[98]

James the individualist was, however, a loyal player ready to applaud the achievements of several members of the expatriate 'Away' team. In reviews and essays, he praised the books of his 1970s contemporaries Germaine Greer, Richard Neville and Barry Humphries ('the greatest entertainer of his age' and 'Australia's greatest commentator, the Raymond Williams of the South Pacific'), the poetic achievement of his former acquaintance Peter Porter, and the TV series on modern art created by his trans-Atlantic cobber, Robert Hughes.[99]

James' retort to the criticism of being an expatriate was that 50 per cent of any nation's culture is produced by expatriates, as Sandra Jobson reported in the *Australian Women's Weekly*.[100] (He went on to assert, interestingly, that 'I've always done whatever I've done in the media without trying to change my voice or my accent'.) However, his belief in the artistic power of relocation did not prompt him to become acquainted with the immigrant artists who were increasingly contributing to Australian culture. He was not even, as the reviewer Don Anderson lamented, aware of any Australian literature or criticism from later than his own generation. 'Whether he is other than vestigially Australian is open to debate', Anderson observed. James' assertion that 'There is still no Australian literary world ... the literary world is in London and New York' and the view that 'Europe' was 'a word which is, after all, only shorthand for the history of the world entire' were mocked by this other kid from Kogarah as evidence of James' 'monumental provincialism'. Nor was Anderson, although a critic of 'the besetting sin of Bicentennial boosterism', inspired by James' self-absorption and his self-oriented theme of the necessity of being an expatriate. The shortage of facts and of contemporary and new names in his 'generalisations' about Australian literature was also not this Sydney critic's cup of cappuccino.[101]

Notwithstanding the contradictions of colonial upward mobility, Clive James was clever, prolific and in the ways of the media, sagacious. Putting aside, temporarily, his desire to be taken seriously by the literary elites, he recognised that the best way to get into television was to write about it. In his weekly column in the *Observer* he had taken television apart or, more accurately, scored points off the silliness of TV programs' forms and pretensions. He was always at his best commenting on the superficies of life, especially on the glittering surfaces which seemed to be simultaneously his target and his own aim.

Neither studying literature nor his later reading of Andersonian philosophy had taught him about larger social and cultural patterns. Iconoclasm, from Anderson to Mencken, from the Push to a TV column, taught him to be a witty commentator on human foibles and pretensions. James had adopted, almost to the point of parody, a Sydney sensibility which combined both that city's working-class cynicism and the Andersonian philosophical position which justified it. To be sophisticated, in the Sydney way, was to be sceptical, distant, ready to mock at any sign of earnestness or morality, any social or political conviction. In Sydney, this characteristic was far from unusual. In London, it gave James a trademark.

By writing amusingly as '*Observer* Man', he entertained Britain's chattering classes when they opened their newspaper every Sunday. These were his audience, these were the people whom he wanted to accept him. The clever boy from Kogarah wanted to be wanted: by the *Times Literary Supplement* and the *London Review of Books*, by the educated middle class who read the *Observer*, by the royals (he became a media adviser to Lady Diana Spencer in her troubled times) and by popular television.

The other transition which underlay his rise to considerable fame and even greater fortune was related to television and to the Sixties. The rise of the seriopop media, offering infotainment rather than information – from television to newspapers – provided opportunities for the '*J'amuse!*' performances of Clive James and Germaine Greer as well as the '*J'accuse!*' journalism of John Pilger. Infotainment meant serious newspapers succumbing to witty sub-heads, some good, some cheap. In post-imperial Britain even the progressive, left-liberal and internationalist *Guardian* ran sub-heads ridiculing the silly colonials. Their targets ranged from post-imperial Malaysia to a cast of 'Sheilas', 'Cobbers' and the ubiquitous 'Bruce' in contemporary Australia.[102] Such out-of-date usages indicated that the clichés were pickled in jars from the past. Like national prejudices about 'silly foreigners' in Calais and beyond, or southern English prejudices about the 'North' (which 'begins at Watford'), they were the stuff of infotainment journalism. This profoundly trivialising change (in Britain and Australia) created a larger space for infotainers such as Clive.

In the 1980s James caught that upwards escalator and turned it into a stomach-rearranging, fast mid-Pacific elevator. Having broadened his print subjects in the 1970s with feature articles, often of personal travels, he pursued two television forms. One was the familiar 'celebrity-as-guide' to a foreign place ('Clive James in Jerusalem'), the travel documentary in which the idiosyncratic visitor 'meets the natives', seeing them through his slightly eccentric and egocentric eyes.[103] 'Clive James at the Melbourne Cup' was the Australian episode of this tale of the familiar (the self-deprecating but familiar and famous everyman) meets the exotic: the funny fan, the rich, the famous and the beautiful, all almost out of reach for 'our Clive'. The other vehicle was the studio show which also used videoclips and 'live' interviews. One studio segment demonstrated how the serious had met the popular. Clive's introductory comments on the silly 'Page ones' of the tabloid newspapers were often rich with 'blue' double entendres and his own version of tabloid wit. Similarly, the silly foreign television advertising segments were not merely entertaining. While they played to the British crowds, or to 'groundlings' everywhere, they may have been more deeply rooted in his personal sense of World War II and the enemy which had imprisoned his father.

Clive James' television had one amazing, perhaps astonishing characteristic. James' TV narration was not written by a factory of scriptwriters. James scripted most jokes – the good ones and the bad ones – himself. One frequent characteristic of the uprooted expatriate was a desire for fame and significance. Another expat. quality, in James' case, as in so many other cases, was a quick and inventive intelligence combined with sheer hard work.

James, the would-be 'intellectual' who praised Australian expatriates, felt uncomfortable with the Australian arts. In the 1970s and 1980s he utilised a rhetorical formula when writing about Australian culture. In the language of the popular TV magazine letters pages, every time he threw a 'bouquet' he also despatched a 'bucket'. Writing appreciatively of the density of the poetry of A. D. Hope, he contrasted Hope with the rest – the many 'Australian poets who have had bulk in the same way that a trailer-load of sponge-rubber has bulk'. The same dualistic formula he applied to Australian TV: 'Hell is in Australia and is otherwise known as Australian television', was his initial generalisation. Despite this, Britain could learn lessons from the new multicultural channel '0', later SBS. Similarly, he deployed the 'nothing has changed' reply to challenge suggestions of development in Australian culture in the 1970s. He gave the bouquet to wine and the bucket to the arts. 'Australians talk in the one breath about the giant strides made in wine and poetry, but the awkward truth is that while the advance made in Australian wine is beyond dispute, to claim an advance in Australian poetry is largely meaningless'. While Australia had changed 'in the minutiae of existence' since he left, 'in the large abstractions it seems to me to have stayed roughly as it was'.[104]

Like his other rough 'assessments' of Australian culture as provincial, he adopted the tried and tested principle of the metropolitan amateur, 'no names, no pack drill'. He lambasted the new cultural nationalism, and maintained his implicit expatriate formulation – the 'tall poppy' idea that good Australian talent went overseas and what remained was by definition inferior. Thus he asserted that Australian artists had lost touch with the rest of the world (no names, no evidence cited) and therefore had been 'forced into copying the rest of the world', and condemned 'the ideology of nationalist self-sufficiency – the Australian "renaissance" [which] has mainly acted as a licence for provincialism, not just in painting but in films, drama and literature as well'.[105]

'My Composition'

Such views and an underlying ignorance about contemporary culture often made his return visits difficult. As noted above, James returned to Australia in 1996 as the high-profile guest of the Melbourne Writers Festival, following

Robert Hughes in 1995 and preceding Germaine Greer in 1997. James' lecture was titled 'My Idea of a National Culture'. Known as a confident character, happily acknowledging himself as a 'show-off', he seemed quite terrified. How would the witty person known for his throwaway lines be received when giving his 'serious talk' to the punters paying $22 a head?[106] The first half of the evening was TV-style Clive, a raft of witty lines, as if he was introducing himself as a guest on his own chat show. After the interval he read his 'composition'. The name was big and the title sounded good, but unfortunately there was little evidence that he had anything deep to say about the subject he was assaying, except to trumpet the individualist and creative virtues of looking beyond the national, and to condemn cultural nationalism's extremes. He moved from knocking down the easy 'straw men' of Nazi Germany and Soviet Russia to a defence of the current Australian flag with the Union Jack in the top left hand corner. His argument, as summarised by Shane Maloney in the *Age*, was that the wish to change the flag sprang from 'a dangerous urge to repudiate our origins'. In Maloney's view, the attitude of this monarchist and traditionalist to 'national culture' was that he was 'agin it'. Under the *Age* sub-editor's heading, 'Will the real Clive James please shut up?', Maloney suggested that later generations than James had given up the cultural cringe, which assumed the inferiority of Australian talent. They 'no longer feel compressed into a crouch by a dead weight of a cultural chip on their shoulders'. Yet, in Maloney's assessment, in his enthusiasm for the international James failed to understand that 'internationalism is not as much of a two way street' as he 'would have us believe'. Publishing decisions made in London and film decisions made in Hollywood refuted this simple idea. Perhaps James was trying to justify the ways of Clive to those he felt he had left behind, to those who had stayed, unlike the famous kid from Kogarah. A considerable gap existed between the amusing, and very profitable television commentary on the displays of society's peacocks and peahens, and a deeper understanding of the ways in which contemporary society worked. Or was it just that his craft as a London humorist for courts and commoners did not allow time to keep in touch with a changing Australia? Perhaps Raymond Gill's response to a 1994 lecture hit the spot. Gill argued that even James' laudatory words about how Australia was no longer a beer-swilling backwater were glib, no more than 'superficial observations ... the thoughts of someone whose knowledge of Australia is gathered solely from satellite feed, back home in London'.[107]

Clive James' strengths and weaknesses, worldview and oeuvre were neatly characterised by Bruce Page:

> James wouldn't have too many values that were separate from the Establishment ... he's a brilliant guy and a very characteristic Syd-ney type ... [with] an Australian characteristic which is essentially

European, that is not seeing too many boundaries in academic subjects. Clive's real breakthrough was ... [that] he'd have a crack at anything.

A more ringing condemnation, by the Australian academic Christopher Lloyd, appeared in the *London Review of Books*. He argued that Humphries, James and Greer are

> essentially refugees from a despised culture, yet they cannot distance themselves from it, as most other refugees have done (e.g. Peter Porter). They proclaim their Europeanness almost as if they were the only Europeanised Australians, yet they have become professional Australians abroad – the cultured counterparts of the denizens of Kangaroo Valley who begin to act the grotesque part of 'Australians abroad' as soon as they arrive, but shed the role when they leave ... The Humphries-James-Greer image of Australia has become both partly constitutive of their own roles and a source of income for them. The real Australia has passed them by and they can only survive here in their present guise as long as they can maintain the niche they have constructed within those receptive parts of the declining English middle-class which are eager for reassurance that there is still somewhere about which they can feel superior.[108]

Lloyd, an economic historian, discerned a monetary as well as psychological imperative in their frozen roles and their 'Rolf Harris-like' Australianness, however considerable their capacity as wordsmiths.

Was there also something locally distinctive about them, about their origins or their trajectories? Barry Humphries and Germaine Greer had been formed by Melbourne moralism (though in different ways), as James had been shaped in part by Sydney hedonism. Did Humphries and Greer have something of one character in David Williamson's play of the *Emerald City* (1987) who was assailed with the charge 'you Melbournians – you're so stuffed full of moral rectitude, the only time you open your mouths is to lecture'. When Humphries lectured through Dame Edna and his other characters, and Greer expatiated in all directions while also joking as if in a Push pub, this 'city culture' explanation was valid.[109] The answer may have been post-imperial if not global, economic rather than cultural. Had the success of performance distracted Humphries from his greater literary ability? Had the media, and expatriation, first pushed up and then 'cut down' these 'tall poppies'? Talent, expatriation and fame mattered as much as being cast in a mould at a very early age for these three travellers from crucible to firmament.[110] Now, having been projected into the sky of fame, they found it impossible to come down to earth.

Chapter 12

Home and Identity

Changing Times, Changing Places ... Changing People

In 1986, Leo McKern returned again to Sydney, Melbourne and North Queensland, as he had before. This time it was not to settle, but to play the male lead in the film of the David Williamson play *Travelling North*. His co-star was the brilliant English immigrant actor, Julia Blake. She had come to Australia in 1962, on an assisted passage as a 'ten pound Pom', with her husband, the returning Australian actor Terry Norris. Her journey south had been a little less expensive than McKern's own £325 trip north, made 16 years earlier. The David Williamson story dramatises questions of age and family, city and beyond, as a couple retires from middle-class Melbourne to tropical Far North Queensland. It is a tale of changing times as well as places. On retirement, as well as on holidays, Australians now sometimes travelled around Australia, as had Leo McKern and family in a Kombi van in 1970–71. Australia appealed to young and old, often as much as the 'big trip' overseas. Many would leave the cities to settle by the coast, in the country or in the tropical North.

Would the expatriates instead travel south? Would they, as Murray Sayle predicted in 1960, return to Australia by their own routes? The prophets might return, as in the words of A. D. Hope's 1938 poem, to where, now, 'such savage and scarlet as no green hills dare/Springs in this waste'. And return to different Australias, from coastal grey-green to the red interior. An Australia in which the people felt more in touch with the land and its history than the derivative English 'cultural pattern' they had left. As age increased, and intimations of mortality dawned, the expatriates had to choose where to live

– to return to Australia or stay in London or Britain. They could choose to visit Australia regularly, for periods of work, or not at all. Would they find some entirely different solution, some idyllic place offering Mediterranean sun or modern comfort? Or did an Australia now call, one of cosmopolitan capitals, cities vibrant rather than draining, no longer places, after Hope, 'Where second-hand Europeans pullulate/Timidly on the edge of alien shores'?[1]

Several matters are central to these expatriate experiences. First, the question of return for these 'lucky' postwar generations.[2] Second, the question of expatriate identity and Australian identity raised by that experience. Expatriate identity was more subjective, the product of personal experience and professional work as well as of time and place. The question of Australian identity related to cultural history, to historic British connections and to changing populations and values in Australia and Britain. Finally, had the days of the transplanted colony in London, and of 'export-import' proposals for Australian cultural development, departed in a global world? Did the different imperatives, from the need to escape overseas to the Cringe, still matter in a world in which Australians looked to North America, Europe and Asia as well as to their own continent and to London?

The Return

The question of return exercised the minds of several long-term expatriates during the 1980s–90s. Social and political events, as well as professional and personal factors, influenced many of them. When Britain succumbed to extreme jingoism during the 1982 Falklands War, an experience then followed by the social civil war, crumbling footpaths and services of Thatcherite Britain, several expatriates found the appeal of Australia increasing. Peter Porter, Phillip Knightley and Geoffrey Robertson, all of whom had left an illiberal Australia for a liberal Britain in the 1950s and 1960s, looked home. The nationalist self-confidence of the 1980s and a newly multicultural society seemed much preferable to a strife-torn Britain in which the old conflicts of class and race were taking a newer and nastier turn.

Most expatriates were excited by a more diverse Australia, in which different ethnicities and cultural tastes made it no longer a crime to be different. At the same time the political ramifications of the social and cultural changes troubled some expatriates. Dame Joan Sutherland and Rolf Harris, who had come to Britain on the 'British Passport' (as it declared on the outside cover) Australians carried in the 1950s, felt British after all these years. Although a resident of Switzerland, Joan Sutherland had no truck with republicanism. On a 1992 family visit Dame Joan tired of journalists' questions about Australia becoming a republic. One of 24-only members of the Queen's Order of Merit, 'the Sovereign's personal gift', she replied that 'it was hardly likely that I was in agreement if I accepted such Honours from the Queen. Really!' Clive James, who carried an Australian passport, had shown little interest in Australia's past, a contrast with the New York expatriate Robert Hughes, who had written the book *The Fatal Shore* (1986). However, James had rejected the repudiation of Australia's past, which he saw as lying behind the proposal for a new Union Jack-free flag. Rolf Harris' father was Welsh and he performed regularly at Royal Variety concerts. Having made his career in both countries, he also lamented the declining British connection. He recalled being 'treated as if I belonged' when he arrived, perhaps a contrast to the occasion on which the Actors Equity critics 'told me I wasn't really Australian' during the wars over the Sydney Opera House opening. 'I did belong. I've always had this love affair with both Britain and Australia, together. And I think it would be a pity to lose that linkage.' Leo McKern reflected that 'we've been torn between the two countries for years . . . [having] tried to settle in Australia three times'. Yet, when asked if he felt Australian, the small, old bull jocularly roared: 'I've got the passport to prove it'.[3]

A number of Australian expatriates successfully returned for several years at a high point of late career, as in the 1970s–80s musical engagements of Dame Joan Sutherland, Barry Tuckwell and Sir Charles Mackerras. Others were regular visitors, writing about Australian subjects (Phillip Knightley, John Pilger) or coming back for specific projects. Michael Blakemore's film *Country Life* (1994), produced by Robin Dalton, explored family tensions over expatriation, although it was received better overseas than in Australia. He regretted not releasing it overseas first, where it had been successful. Perhaps 'international' reviews would have helped guarantee success in Australia! Henry Lawson's century-old maxim that 'Australian literature had to fight its way home to its own country by the way of England' had not completely lost its currency, it seemed.[4] Despite the pull of television's 'Horace Rumpole of the Bailey', Leo McKern also came back. He returned several times to work, usually by boat due to the aversion to flying which he shared with another expatriate, Arthur Boyd. McKern starred as 'Dad' opposite Joan Sutherland's 'Mum' in a film of Steele Rudd's Dad n' Dave stories, *On Our Selection* (1994), while Robin Dalton produced the film of Peter Carey's *Oscar and Lucinda* (1997). Clive James and Germaine Greer performed at arts festivals in the 1990s, and some stage entertainers, including Barry Humphries and Rolf Harris, would always tour. In several senses they had never left Australia, or at least their kind of Australia.

The Pull of Family . . . in Both Directions

Family ties both drew expatriates to Australia and kept them in England. Home was where the hearth was as well. Many expatriates, including

Geoffrey Parsons, Phillip Knightley, John Pilger, Jill Neville and Murray Sayle, came back to Australia to visit ageing parents. While sons rarely felt the same pressures as daughters to look after ageing relatives (Jill Neville was conscious that she was the daughter who had gone away), faster travel and the money provided by successful careers made annual returns possible. After parents had died, one 'pull' towards the country was gone. In contrast, some expatriates, such as Peter Porter, had been partly driven away by the sense, or the reality, of the traumatic experiences of childhood. Others had left concerned about their parents' possible views of their homosexuality. Both groups felt more relaxed about returning, and about their relations with Australia when ghosts had been laid with the death of the parents.

Several expatriates came, still, for Australian sun and relief from the long English winter or to work on Australian projects. Often visits in February, in the depths of the northern winter, appealed more than the traditional, but often tense, family gathering at Christmas. Others also sought sun in Spain, in Italy or at Biarritz, 'the nearest thing I can find to Sydney in Europe', as Robin Dalton put it.[5]

Home was often where your new family was. For the actor Alan White, who travelled the world with London's National Theatre but never returned to Sydney, his family was in London. It offered a continuity which the now unrecognisable city of Sydney, which he had left in 1954, could not. His son's research into the American literary expatriate Henry James was, however, a legacy of a different kind. Family rooted the expatriate as much as career and friends. Phillip Knightley's daughters were making successful careers in London, and most of Arthur Boyd's children and grandchildren were in England. Similarly, Lady Mackerras was drawn to her children and family in Britain as well as to Charles' dreams of music by Sydney Harbour.

Sometimes, though, the family pulled the expatriate home. Very often, Australia was a place of excitement for children and adolescents. Since it was a holiday visit, they often felt a great sense of freedom, as if the land in the sun fitted with an older stereotype of a lucky country of perpetual holidays. At different times in the late 1970s and early 1980s, the children of Peter Porter, Barry Tuckwell and the expatriate in France, Alister Kershaw, spent first short, and then longer periods in Australia. As for the children of Australian immigrants returning to Britain, Italy or Greece, it was a way of finding out about part of themselves. Like many overseas trips for young Australians of all ethnicities, it was a journey of youthful self-discovery. If the children settled in Australia, it often had a powerful pull. The Bonynges had spent the second half of the 1970s and early 1980s mainly in Australia, when their son Adam Bonynge was in his late teens and early twenties. He would eventually settle down into a career and marriage in Sydney. Also, Geoffrey Chard had returned in 1985, three years after his son, who had grown up with him in London, had gone to Australia.

Originally, many of the male expatriates had followed women overseas. Now, several wives and partners rejected Australia. A common theme was articulated by a resident in response to a question about the likelihood of his expatriate brother staying in Australia: 'the wife doesn't like it'. Such an emphasis may sound like a gendered rendering of human life and decision-making. It is a valid analysis, however, regarding the predominantly male expatriate stars of several fields of the postwar generations. At that time, women sacrificed their careers for their husbands. Sometimes this could have positive results for the Australian arts. Singer Glenda Raymond, who had gone to London in the 1940s and had engagements with the London Philharmonic, returned in 1950 to marry the radio and music entrepreneur, Hector Crawford, and as a result performed in Australia.[6] To theatre's loss, however, Jane Holland gave preference to her family, while Leo McKern made his distinguished way on London stages and TV screens.

Sometimes, the decision not to return to Australia was made because the children were in England, a decision made by the Boyds who visited Australia as much as ship travel would allow. Sometimes it was not children but partners who most influenced the decision not to return to Australia to live permanently. Phillip Knightley's Indian wife, Yvonne, comedian Dick Bentley's English wife, Peta, Rolf Harris' Welsh wife, Alwen, were all said to be not very enthusiastic about living in Australia. Many other Australians had married British or European women (Keith Michell's wife was Czech), thus acquiring northern hemisphere connections. For several Australian career women who felt that they had escaped, return was unthinkable – to wake up in Australia was their worst nightmare! Other expatriates, including Tony Clifton and Ros Grose, recanted. Grose began to enjoy their trips back to Australia. In another transition, the Groses ended a rural interlude in Britain and returned to London, making Ros Grose want to 'kiss Kensington High Street' when they arrived.[7]

Many wives also managed their husbands' careers and shaped both family and professional decisions. The industry of presentation as well as art that became Sir Sidney Nolan was orchestrated first by Cynthia Nolan and then by his second wife Mary Nolan, as well as by the artist himself. More subtly, Yvonne Boyd protected Arthur Boyd from a thousand interviews and requests for public involvement, so that he could get on with his work; the relative isolation of Suffolk and of Bundanon (near Nowra in New South Wales) also helped. In each case, European artistic traditions were amongst the 'pull' factors of the northern hemisphere. At the same time prolonged absence added to an artist's mystique in Australia. After his death in 1992, the Tate Gallery claimed Sir Sidney Nolan, who had spent most of the past four decades in England, as a 'British' artist and a Nolan collection in Britain was proposed. This outraged artistic opinion in Australia. Under the headline 'How the British hijacked Ned Kelly', one report told the story of how the larrikin Aussie son of a tram driver who became a knight had picked up his brushes and easel and gone away.[8]

Class, as well as gender, sometimes influenced the extent to which the expatriate 'settled' into English society or remained an outsider, whether their continuing social milieu was mainly Australian or included the many different peoples who had come to London. Research published by the linguist Arthur Delbridge in 1964 showed significant gender differences in Australian speech: boys outnumbered girls as speakers of 'Broad Australian' in a ratio of seven to three, while girls predominated over boys in a ratio of nine to one as speakers of 'Cultivated Australian' (a category which included those who spoke 'properly' and those who adopted 'high' or quasi-southern English accents). Historical research has supported the gender-based analysis of speech differences. A study of 'The Lady and the Australian Girl' shows how women in the late nineteenth century were encouraged to identify with airs and graces, with civility and Englishness, rather than with the robust 'male' culture associated with pioneering, the bush and the colonial tradition.[9] Such tendencies, linked with upper middle-class aspirations to higher social status in class and culture, would persist, as they did for Mrs Leggat in *The Piccadilly Bushman*, into the last phases of provincial Australia in the 1960s. Perhaps, as in Lawler's play, which was performed again in 1998, this class, gender, culture combination would still persist. Like a vestigial appendix, subject to inflammation, it was present in some artistic circles for several decades more. Sometimes, in Britain, the change was professional rather than social. Michael Blakemore reflected that Australian actors in Britain 'had to do a nose job on our personalities to get work'.[10] He might equally have been talking about voice.

Was Australia an excessively male society in which women felt less comfortable? Was it defined by a male boozy culture? On his short returns, Phillip Knightley reflected that his journalistic mates 'worked on him' in shifts, usually well-lubricated ones. Yet, literary and journalistic London were often awash as well. Perhaps it was that women settled more into English society because they defined themselves, at that time, in social more than career terms, or, that they were capable of both. Maybe it was simply that Australian women adapted more readily to a 'derivative' southern English style. In contrast, many men identified with the typical Australian 'indigenous' stereotypes, those expressed in the Bush and ANZAC myths and the sporting hero. (The fact Australian women did better than Australian men at Olympic sports was another story.) Whatever the explanations, those returning in the 1980s–90s were travelling to a very different Australia than the sex-segregated society which many of them had left several decades before.

Professionals Returning

Some expatriates sought to make regular returns. Phillip Knightley was a frequent 'fly-in', despite the jet lag of one of the longest long-haul, time-zone crossing flights on the earth. Sometimes, the ideal of living and working at both ends of the earth was difficult. Knightley made it a little easier by having a flat in Potts Point, setting himself up with a computer at both ends, and travelling with most of his material on disk. The Bonynges had a useful arrangement, buying at Whale Beach in northern Sydney and also having use of an Australian Opera-provided apartment in the city. Alan Seymour returned to an inner-city Darlinghurst apartment. Even he found that he was missing his *suburban* house in London and that he was often working on scripts for British productions. The only greater irony for the expatriate author was when he played Alf, the 'bloody Australian' in a reading of his play *The One Day of the Year* at the Australian Studies Centre in London in 1990. Murray Sayle, the 'double expatriate', found a kind of improvised solution for his life of many cities which owed much to the co-operative spirit of his younger days – he had friends living in the London flat, so that he could also bunk down in it when back in town.

Professional returns were often curtailed by engagements in Britain which came from a track record and regular contacts there. Returns could also be difficult for those who did not have superstar status. Geoffrey Chard was conscious of the limited opportunities in Australian opera and of the need to prepare for his return. (Only a Sutherland could just swan in, trumpeted by her grand stature.) Chard was a very successful expatriate opera singer, one of many Australians performing with Sadler's Wells, which became the English National Opera. The principal baritone of the company from 1969 to 1985 was not, however, a superstar. He had returned to Australia after 20 years to sing opposite Joan Carden in *Cosi Fan Tutte* at the time of the 1982 Commonwealth Games in Brisbane.

After a long absence, re-establishing himself in Australia required planning. Unlike a very 'tall poppy', he could not write his own ticket. His old colleague, the agent Jenifer Eddy, was 'the architect of my revival here'. This began with a pattern of coming back to do performances on a regular basis. Singing the title character role in Richard Meale's opera of the Patrick White novel *Voss* consolidated his credentials and his presence in Australia. Although he did some part-time teaching at the Sydney Conservatorium, it was not his desire 'to go into an academic post and sink without trace'. In the small world of Australian opera, paradoxically the Sydney-based Chard managed to develop a career with the Melbourne-based Victorian State Opera during the 1980s. Like most actors, the singer had no superannuation, so continuing work on the opera stage and teaching were necessary as well as desired. His wish to continue singing, and perhaps a preference for his native Sydney, led to him turning down a job running the opera school at the Victorian College of the Arts. 'They say they want a performer and then they say they want you there 48 weeks a year', he remarked of this difficult situation. Like Don Banks in Canberra in the 1970s, he was aware of the tension between earning a crust on a regular basis and getting on with his artistic work. His preference for Sydney was not, however, unequivocal. Unusually, in some ways he and his wife felt more at home in 'European' Melbourne than in familiar Sydney.

Others were luckier, returning to secure work within the comfort-zone of their old institutional-professional homes, which others saw as 'battleships' which were not open to new ideas or talents.[11] Ray Lawler came back to where he had begun at the Melbourne Theatre Company, while the plays of the other Melburnian, Richard Beynon, were taken up by the Playbox in Melbourne and the Ensemble in Sydney.

'Bloody Pommies' or 'Blunt Aussies'?

Return raised again questions of identity and acceptance at both ends of the earth. Sir Charles Mackerras felt uncomfortable both in Britain and Australia, though in different ways. The dilemmas were social and psychological despite the happy homecoming of the 1980s. In her book on Mackerras, Nancy Phelan describes her *déraciné* subject as someone who 'really did not know where he belonged'. He

> was not even quite sure what he was. In England he was constantly labelled *Australian*, in certain circles his Mackerras directness and impatience with humbug were seen as rather crudely 'colonial', yet in Australia he was often regarded as a 'bloody Pommie'. To the British his accent was almost 'ocker', yet in his own country his voice was referred to as 'plummy British'. He was too cosmopolitan now to belong completely anywhere.[12]

Barry Tuckwell felt even more deeply the problem of being an expatriate. Tuckwell reflected on the longtime expatriate's elemental but difficult relationship with his place of origin:

> I was very nostalgic. I always have been and I think the thing that saddens me is that I know now that I'm probably not enough of an Australian because I haven't lived there, but I still feel it. It is like a rat which is taken away from the pack and they clean it up, so it doesn't smell like a rat and it goes back to the pack and they attack it because it doesn't smell right, they don't recognise it. Whereas that rat smells everybody and says 'Here guys, I am home'. And I have been away long enough for people there to think of me as just somebody who is not Australian any more. In the same way that I will never ever be totally part of England because I wasn't born here; it's just a fact of life. So in a sense I have lost both.

Tuckwell found an unusual personal, professional and material solution – a compromise which was neither Australia nor England. Becoming conductor in 1982 of the new Maryland Symphony Orchestra (which he had co-founded), he met his third wife, Sue Levitan, the former *Baltimore Sun* sports reporter. His continuing engagement as conductor, and a regular season conducting the Northern Sinfonia in Newcastle-Upon-Tyne, not far from where his sister lived, would offer a kind of resolution. Maryland offered new world comfort and efficiency and a rather different, if also dramatic, climate. It was also easier to maintain links across the Atlantic than to keep up with the country he had first departed around half a century before, and which was a long haul from either North America or Europe. Barry Tuckwell placed very high demands on himself as a performer, conscious that a professional life either had to be lived at the highest level, or should be put aside. He retired from the French horn in 1997 but found a continuing role with the baton.

'I Work, Therefore I Am'

Other expatriates recognised the true realities of their profession. This had two elements – their work and London. Many lived for their work. It defined their identity rather more than did their nationality, family or any other aspect of their experience. Throughout their working lives, their professional and social networks were found mainly in London, though they had friends scattered around the world, a complex side-benefit of travel. The first reality meant that expatriation itself was not the aim – it was rather the route to continued work at one's profession. That was the path taken by Alan White in films and at the National Theatre. Other expatriates who maintained their working commitments included Charles Mackerras, who visited Australia to conduct the SSO in 1998, and Murray Sayle and Phillip Knightley. Some expatriates, including Russell Braddon in 1995, Geoffrey Parsons in 1996 and Jill Neville in 1997, would, like the warriors of ancient myth, die in harness; Neville had been working on her latest novel and writing her regular 'Literary London' letter for the *Australian* when claimed by cancer.

The continuing search for work was part of the freelancer's story. Not having a job or regular paid employment was the lot of many actors, who auditioned for roles rather than having a career. They were either performing or 'just resting' between engagements. So too were freelance musicians and other performers at large, such as Clive James, Germaine Greer, Barry Humphries and Rolf Harris. This 'freedom' had another side – the opportunity to 'not retire'. On the one hand, for example, Murray Sayle had not had a regular job since his employment by various news bureaus in the 1950s. On the other hand, when living in expensive Japan with a family and pets, he could not afford to retire, even if he had wanted to.

Professional networks, often merging into old contacts, were even more important for the freelancer than for someone with a regular job. Authors needed sympathetic publishers for books and articles, and an audience – a market in which they were perceived and valued as a 'name'. Actors and musicians needed helpful agents and managements who knew their work. While several expatriates had Australian connections, most of their networks were in London.

Londoners

Most of the postwar expatriates had forged their careers in London. They were inhabitants, habitués and even lovers of the great city and its many parts. For the Australians, London was a base, a living-place, and a theatre of performance with its newspapers, stages and concert halls. Sometimes it offered windows on the world at large. Sometimes it led to an English, or Eurocentric, vision of less and less breadth. Phillip Knightley was an Australian who lived in London, a journalist whose sense of self was strongly formed when he came there. His modestly described 'hack's progress' would bring other influences – those from India, and, from his research into international espionage, economics and politics, and 'the Establishment' and established myth in Britain and Australia.

Musicians, who caught planes even more than most journalists, would increasingly see themselves as 'London-based'. Sometimes 'based' meant having a house, perhaps family, perhaps a garden to which they got back to too rarely, to rest, recuperate and to practise. As a self-descriptor, the term helped avoid the pejorative connotations of 'expatriate'.

In distinctive ways, two younger musicians made London, or its villages (now on the scale of large towns rather than small communities), their domain. The guitarist John Williams, who had grown up in London from the age of 11, had both a London accent (as against a BBC or so-called 'standard English' accent) and a social network which ranged from literary-musical Hampstead to the semi-alternative politics and community of the adjacent inner northern suburbs. He had several marriages and a musical career which also had 'pop' and Australian dimensions, including the jazz-rock fusion band Sky, with several Australian members. In the face of this flux he would occasionally retreat, finding rural peace east of Melbourne on the Mornington Peninsula. However, his London friends offered the most fundamental form of continuity.[13]

John Williams became a Londoner of a sort, while maintaining other parts of his heritage, including the Australian. This 'Londoner' was in some ways a contrast to 'an Australian living in London' (Phillip Knightley) or the 'London-based' musician. For Knightley and for the 'complicit outsider' Peter Porter, being a Londoner was a kind of resolution. It did not require them to cease being Australian and to become English, even as each of them combined metropolitan urbanity with an ironic Australian self. Contemplating the oil painting-like view of the Thames at evening, which made him feel a Londoner, Knightley reflected on his situation:

> In truth I am both. One lesson I have learnt in this 40-year long journey is that I do not have to decide. I am an Australian who lives some of the time in London; I am a Londoner who lives some of the time in Australia.[14]

In a similar way, the sun on Sydney Harbour Bridge in the evening also enraptured the senses of this romantic journalist.

A Separate Nationality or A Colonial Lag?

Australian ambivalence about expatriates was dramatically, if accidentally, demonstrated in the summer of 1990–91. In December 1990, a Canberra media release from Federal Minister for Education John Dawkins (who had returned to Western Australia for the Christmas summer break) went wrong. Under the headline 'Govt to fund lecture tours by whingeing Aussies', media reports referred to a Donald Horne Australia Day lecture to be given by whingeing Aussies living overseas. The word 'distinguished', written in this often critical Minister's hand, had been typed as 'disgruntled'.[15] Perhaps the editors, sub-editors and readers had such famous 'ex-patriots' as Barry Humphries, Clive James and Germaine Greer, or even John Pilger in mind as they took up this Australia-bashing-cum-expatriate-bashing theme. In London a contemporary 1980s version of Gilbert and Sullivan's *Mikado* 'put Australians on the list ... they wouldn't be missed'.[16] Were Australians also joining a chorus against some expatriates? Or, instead, in an increasingly global era, did many Australians and many Britons share a pride in the London-based Australian stars of much of the English-speaking world?

Many Australian expatriates also felt ambivalent. Several were troubled, feeling outsiders in London and not always at home in Australia. Perhaps the Australian expatriate did have a separate nationality. Sometimes this identity was expressed in the role of an exaggerated Australian style, if not necessarily boozy 'Bazzaness'. At other times its manifestation was the 'professional Australian expatriate' persona – outspoken but cultured, the Australian who had departed the cultural desert.

In one view the postwar expatriate generations were the product of a time of transition. They had left an Australia which was 'absurd', an upside down land, with many of its social and cultural institutions derived from Britain.

Their destination was London, then the centre of the empire, soon to be the Sixties world city. Now, neither culture, of colony or of empire, existed. Australians had started to come to terms with their land, their history, their nature and their society, while the red and pink hues of imperial Britain had retreated as the sun set on the Union Jack. No longer did Australians ignore the fact that they had intruded on Aboriginal land. Coming to terms with their own past was giving them greater 'ownership' of their shared experience.

Perhaps the expatriates were the last colonial lags, transported back to a 'Home' which was for younger Australians no longer a second home. Were they a cultural fragment, an island frozen in times past, on an imaginary Strand by the Thames in London, reversing the original process whereby the early Australian white settlements were fragments of Georgian England?

The London cultural colony of Australians was in many ways an artificial plant, a transplant or even a fragile potplant, in the great city. Like the gum tree in Leo McKern's garden it was exotic, even if planted in a city full of 'exotics'. Several individual talents sent deeper roots into the musical and theatrical soil of London, and many others returned to Australia sooner or later, by choice or due to lack of success. The cultural colony was, however, a post-colonial aberration, engendered by the meeting of the last post-imperial waves with the emerging era of international travel and global diversity. Thus the high point of the Australian contribution to London from the 1960s to the 1980s, the moment of 'Australarts' by the Thames, was both a peak and the end of an era. Population and affluence provided greater opportunities for the arts at home. Faster national and international travel and restrictive immigration laws simultaneously made London more important as a place Australians visited, and sometimes still studied in, and less important as a long-term destination. Frank Moorhouse, writer and continuing traveller, saw the 1970s as the watershed: 'It was the decade when writers, at least, stopped going to live in other countries – the end of the expatriate tradition'. It was also, at last, the beginning of the 'de-dominionisation of Australia'.[17] The centres of gravity moved to the Australian cities (to Charles Blackman's 'one-city Australia') and even beyond the city. While Australians continued to be great travellers, no longer was the 'real world' to be found 'over there', within cooee of Trafalgar Square or Shaftesbury Avenue. Now, too, Australia's gain was often London's loss, as London's gain before had sometimes, inevitably, been Australia's loss.

This involved a fundamental transition in the self-assessment of the Australian arts. For several decades a colonial-to-provincial tradition had identified 'landmarks' in the Australian arts, events viewed as artistic Mt Koszciuskos rising from a dull, flat plain. Such a view, like the colonial idea of 'Coming of Age', often impeded Australian cultural development, because it assumed the absence of a tradition more than its presence. But no longer was Australian theatre just the *Doll*, Australian music John Antill's *Corroboree*, Australian opera Joan Sutherland's Lucia di Lammermoor, the novel just Patrick White and a Nobel Prize, and Australian cultural spaces only the Sydney Opera House. Nor was overseas affirmation of Australia's culture the compulsory measure of achievement, even if, for good and bad reasons, it was still welcomed with enthusiasm.

Britain and Europe were part of Australia's European inheritance. No longer, in an era of the democratisation of cultural activities and the internationalisation of cultural influences, were they the sole founts of cultural wisdom. In an era, in Britain as well as Australia, in which the future and the present were valued more than the past, Australia had the advantages, not the disadvantages, of youth and diversity. Younger generations, including immigrants and their children and returned travellers (expatriates and wanderers) were re-making the society. Was there truth in the flattering remarks of the expatriate art curator Patrick McCaughey, on returning to Melbourne from North America in 1998?

> Apart from New York, and I suppose, LA and Chicago, there are no cities in America that have the artistic life that Melbourne has. In fact [Australia is] a remarkably unphilistine society, the arts are now absolutely accepted as every Australian's part of life.[18]

In a romantic conception, a rediscovered national essence, a 'found' Australian identity was part of the story. Its vision of a rich, colourful garden of human endeavour, now diverse in its conceptions of culture, ethnicity, class, gender and values, contrasted with the deserts of Hope's poem. Now, unlike before, this post-colonial society had a population greater than that of London. But was this transition the reason for the rejection and the welcome of the expatriates, the explanation for Australians alternating between respecting the achievements of the 'tall poppies' and rejecting them? Were Australians still capable of applying the Colonial Cultural Cringe and the Cultural Cringe Inverted towards people from overseas, particularly towards their own?

In his memoirs the musician Jim Davidson, looking back on his experience as a returning expatriate, discerned a fundamental problem in Australian culture. He believed that an Australian performer had to make a choice between performing overseas and in Australia. The eminent bandleader, who had been passed over for the position of ABC Director of Variety in 1947, had left for London and later the BBC. When he returned to Australia in 1964, after his retirement from Assistant Head of Light Entertainment, Sound at the BBC, he became a consultant with the ABC. On both occasions he felt uncomfortable. 'When I left home in 1947 I felt like an unwanted outcast. I felt very much alone in my disillusion with the showbiz scene of postwar Australia, and in my inability to settle back comfortably into civilian life.'

While he shared this postwar sense of disorientation – 'feeling frustrated, empty, and rootless' – with performers from many countries, later experiences confirmed a sense of dislocation from Australia and Australian attitudes. Before Davidson returned to Australia in 1964, the tenor Donald Peers, who had just come back from a tour, asked him a question regarding a 'strange syndrome': 'Why don't Australians like Australians?' Davidson believed that he might have an answer:

> if you are Australian then it is permissible to be successful *inside* Australia or *outside* Australia. In either of these cases, your countrymen will applaud you. But don't ever attempt to mix the two! If you are successful overseas, you'd better stay there. The nation will still be proud of you, and everything you do is news. But if you are unwise enough to return home again, then the attitude seems to be 'Don't come back here and tell us Aussies what to do. We've been getting on very well without you!'[19]

Were the expatriates part of another romantic tradition: the creative, individual artist who, like Ulysses, had to travel to succeed? Such brilliant individuals needed the stress and stimulus of dislocations, or the stages and concert halls of London and the world, to realise their potential. For the expatriates, like the immigrants to Australia, was relocation a prerequisite for individual achievements? Did the talented and adventurous go and the provincial and conventional stay? It was a principle which might apply in either direction.

It was also a question which occupied Australian minds. Andrew Riemer had come to Australia in the 1940s as a child in a Hungarian Jewish refugee family, and later become an academic in the English Department at Sydney University. After he took early retirement from academia to pursue a fruitful career as a writer, he looked back on his chosen route. Would he have achieved more on a larger stage had he followed his Sydney and Sydney University contemporaries, Clive James, Germaine Greer and his friend Robert Hughes to London? He wondered if it 'would have been possible for Hughes to have acquired not merely international fame but also his intellectual boldness had he stayed in Sydney', 'mostly' thinking it would have been impossible. Would his own life have been more rewarding had he not been 'too cowardly' to set out on such an adventure? Was Australia still a land 'trapped within the mentality of gaolers and their prisoners'? Or, he might have asked of that last colonial era, as did the Sydney University graduate and peasant mandarin of the North Coast, Les Murray, if it was true that 'a major in English made one a minor Englishman'?[20] That could apply, as Andrew Riemer feared, to the academics who stayed, 'turning themselves into parodies of Ivy-League professors or Oxbridge dons'[21] and, perhaps more than Riemer realised, to many who went away with their 'P&O English'.

Metropolitan Exiles ... 'International' Stars

What had been the costs and the benefits for the expatriates – for Porter or Pilger or Humphries or Jill Neville – of almost becoming metropolitan exiles? Several had won fame and riches in great quantities. Others, as Jill Neville reflected, had 'carried reviews, like buckets of water, across deserts of unpaid rent'. Several had written and performed works intensified by a distracted and dislocated vision. Did the achievements in intensity, and in style, make up for the loss of a more grounded sense of life? Did expatriation encourage creative projection for good and for bad? That was a question about their art and their work.

The American critic Rob Nixon has argued that the metropolitan exile plays to their home metropolitan audience, reiterating imperial visions of colonial backwardness in the sun-struck land which they have left behind. Writing of V. S. Naipaul (later Sir Vidia Naipaul), the Caribbean Indian writer in London, Nixon assays a writer claiming to be detached, an outsider and an individual. Instead, as a metropolitan, Nixon asserts, he displays a traditional Eurocentric condescension towards the shallow, 'primitive', 'tribal', 'simple', 'irrational', 'philistine' colonial societies which the artist has left behind. Despite the differences between a settler-subject colony such as Australia and a subject colony, an expatriate few expressed a similar contempt for the culture of their compatriots. Several 'professional expatriates' looked down on their sun-tanned (rather than brown-skinned), intellectually malnourished 'tribal' brothers and sisters back home, going through the daily paces of their colonial, provincial conformist lives. Were *some* Australian expatriates prisoners of Eurocentric, or English or London, prejudice towards the former colony? Their views resembled Western prejudice, looking down on the East, which Edward Said had discerned in his study of the Western ideology of 'Orientalism'.[22]

Undoubtedly, talented writers such as Murray Sayle, Phillip Knightley and John Pilger found larger canvases in international politics, as well as the bigger markets and better remuneration of London and New York publishers. Talent, and also the colonial cultural cringe, meant that they often sold more in Australia than Australian authors. For 1950s actors, singers and musicians there was little choice. Going away was the best route to a professional career. Later musicians – including the singers Yvonne Kenny and Joan Carden, who had left in the 1960s, and the conductors Stuart Challender and Simone Young – pursued opportunities in Australia and London. Singer and director Robyn Archer performed in London in the 1980s, but remained based in Australia. Similarly, actors and directors such as Bryan Brown, Geoffrey Rush and Fred Schepisi took up opportunities in Australia and in Hollywood, followed by a 'gumnut mafia' of young television and film stars. A smaller number of women directors and actors, including the director Lindy Davies and the producer Helen Montague, went to London. Both groups would work in Australia as well as overseas. Lindy Davies would become one of the new 'to and fro' artistic generation, working in Melbourne and directing occasionally in London. The returning boomerang now flew regularly, for work and travel.[23]

The structures of both production and of prestige had improved in Australia in the half-century after 1945. Despite this, continuing limitations existed. Dispersed opportunities for employment across several capital cities limited artistic careers. The separation and isolation of the cities could also encourage a kind of parochial complacency in the larger 'flagship' organisations.

'I Still Call Sydney Home?'

This changed situation raised several questions. First, to what extent were the expatriates in fact expatriated not from Australia, their country of origin, but from their city of origin, in particular Sydney? Nearly all expatriates returned to their original city, or in the case of Alan Seymour, who returned to Sydney rather than Perth, to the city in which they had started to pursue their careers. A disproportionate number of expatriates seemed to return to Sydney. The related question is why so many expatriates had come from Sydney. One explanation was that Sydney offered more employment opportunities in broadcasting, theatre and publishing for creators and performers, attracting them from around Australia. More generally, another cause was deeply rooted in history. In the colonial way, Sydney elite culture looked even more to Britain, as in the Latin motto of Sydney University 'Sidere mens eadem mutato', translated as 'though the heavens are changed the mind remains the same', than did the elites of other Australian capitals. Or, in contrast, had the male culture of the port city driven the sensitive away? In this city more of individuals than of groups, notwithstanding the Push, did Sydney culture, which was unlike that of Melbourne or Adelaide, also encourage the talented to depart for overseas?

Whatever the cause – and this study may even be slightly skewed by chance, the author having 'come upon' several Sydney expatriate networks – Sydney was central. One returning expatriate fantasy was also a Sydney one, often Bondi Beach. In some cases it was the known beach of childhood – for John Pilger and Michael Blakemore, or for Sandra Jobson's partner Rob Darroch who had also grown up there. The Jobson-Darrochs, not wanting to remain expatriates forever, returned to Sydney where they would buy a flat within cooee of its salt spray, overlooking the beach. (Other Australians associated Bondi with parking problems and solid matter in the water, or with the Gelato Bar.) Was Bondi significant because it had become an expatriate dream and an English ideal, an icon of the new world, a bright image in the grey, gritty depths of the tube on a winter's day, as well as in migration advertising? For the cold, if not necessarily jaded expatriate, a warming prospect in a grey London winter, or the fantasy inversion for the young or old travelling 'Pom' – a Christmas Day party on the beach in 30 degree heat? Was it the body and the senses which missed the homeland most?

A larger double-barrelled question was more important. What had the expatriates given to the culture of the imperial capital-cum-world city, London, and to Britain, and what was the cost or the benefit to Australia of that gift? Tony Delamothe has argued that the contribution to Britain was tangible, but not irreplaceable. This expatriate Queenslander and theatre critic discerned a distinctive Australian characteristic – a greater physicality in performance. (A case could also be made for a great interest in artistic fusion and in colour.) Only in dance did Delamothe see a distinctive impact, through Robert Helpmann and Constance Lambert. A British actor to play Horace Rumpole or Henry VIII would have been found, he asserts, rather less convincingly regarding the first case. However, the contributions made were 'purchased at a price to Australia':

> in the case of the theatre, the large-scale emigration of Australian actors, directors, writers, and designers postponed the arrival of an Australian voice in the theatre for at least a generation. When the reaction to this lack came, it came with a particular force.[24]

A third question concerns not just expatriates, not just Australians but all inhabitants of the 'new' world. Generations of Australians had grown up in a partly derivative settler culture. They had held onto their legacy in a society which had invaded another land, one which at first seemed completely foreign. That experience of dislocation was the product of the change wrought on the world by two centuries of European colonialism and by the impact, for good and for bad, of the several industrial revolutions since 1788. The 'international' world which resulted could lead to another form of dislocation – of being an expatriate and feeling not quite 'placed' in an almost familiar Britain, but also 'displaced' in London and Australia.

Were the expatriates like canaries in a mine, both as dislocated individuals and as artists? Did they, in the romantic conception of the artist's social role, sense even more than others the anxieties affecting everyone in the modern world? Even someone who lived in one place for their whole life would find that the world they lived in was different from the world they had grown up in, a world they had lost. As the expatriates were leaving Australia in the 1940s and the 1950s, the immigrants were coming by ship or plane from the other side of the world. Other 'migrants' travelled by train, bus and car from country to city. At the same time, children were being taken from families –

the British orphan children who were sent to Australia and the Aboriginal children who were taken from their homes. For them, like the 'boat people' who came in smaller craft to the 'lucky country', or the diversity of immigrants to postwar Britain, dispossession was part of modern life. This was experienced by expatriates, more dramatically by some than others.

Displacement, deracination, or uprooting, was the way of the world. It had made Australia, but also London, Paris and New York. The expatriates were typical as well as atypical, ordinary as well as exceptional. Many immigrants also held on to parts of their own past and did not feel fully part of their new society. The paradox, though, of modern life was that the affluence of the West and the technology of the jet plane and satellite telephone communication now made it possible to return to the place of origin more often than in the era of travel by sea. Once, as in the lament of the exiles who had been transported to Australia, settling was almost the only option. Now, affluence increased the choices, engendering a different sense of discontent at the impossibility of satisfying all of those possibilities.

Global Neighbours at Home and Away

The newIMAGES campaign, aimed at presenting the changing faces of Britain and Australia in both countries, was launched in 1997. It came after more than a decade of the presentation of Australian art, literature and popular culture in Britain, in a phenomenon some saw as the Australian colonisation of the 'old country'. At Australia House, amongst the newIMAGES co-ordinators was Rebecca Hossack, who had exhibited Australian art, including immigrant-influenced and Aboriginal art, through her Soho gallery. The newIMAGES project came 15 years after the creation of the Australian Studies Centre at the University of London, which had also helped develop popular 'Literary Links' seminars at Australia House and Russell Square.[25] On a larger stage, it came after the Booker prizes to Peter Carey and Tom Keneally, the international critical acclaim of David Malouf, the emergence of Australian film, and the high profile of several Australians – Clive James, Germaine Greer, Barry Humphries and the popular entertainer Rolf Harris – in the British media. Australians were also prominent in other fields – Pilger, Knightley and Sayle in journalism, Sutherland, Tuckwell, Mackerras and Bonynge in music, and in theatre, Keith Michell, Michael Blakemore and Madge Ryan, and particularly, Leo McKern in *Rumpole of the Bailey*. The ubiquitous global citizen Rupert Murdoch remained omnipresent. Younger expatriates – the cultural essayist Peter Conrad, the civil liberties lawyer Geoffrey Robertson and his 'outrageous' partner Kathy Lette – kept up the Antipodean profile. Arguably, the published works of Conrad and Robertson had made a greater intellectual impact in Britain than those of Clive James and Germaine Greer.

In the everyday sense, Britain knew more about Australia. It had become the fashionable country of the 1980s. An Australian syndicate had done the impossible, winning the America's Cup for yachting in 1983. Australia was also the land of Paul Hogan's successful, iconic *Crocodile Dundee* movie, in which the 'innocent' Aussie bush hero went to New York, rather than London.²⁶ The 1988 bicentenary of white settlement capped these events in a celebratory, if equivocal, way. When Burnum Burnum appeared at the white cliffs of Dover to claim Britain for Aboriginal Australia, Britons also had to think twice about Australian settlement. In simpler terms, British people now travelled more to Australia, saw Australian film and television regularly, and could buy Australian wine at their local shop, rather than only through the Australian Wine Centre in Soho. On television, *Neighbours* and *Home and Away* were amongst the most popular evening soaps. A few of the chattering classes still looked down on the colonials. So did others, working-class Brits who also clung to Empire-style fantasies, even in a post-imperial and European-to-global era; after all, they needed someone to look down on. However, many other English, Scots, Welsh and Irish people saw Australia as a new America, a land of sun and opportunity. That dream was reinforced by the bright lighting and style of the suburban soap operas, and by the reality of an interesting and welcoming multicultural society. It was also quali-fied by the problems of unemployment and pollution, and by the political and economic cycles and ideologies, which affected all developed societies. Southern sun did not guarantee wealth, or equality, a diminishing ingredient in 1980s–1990s Australia.

New generations of Australian stars came to London into the media, in music and in theatre and publishing. Kylie and Dannii, the Minogue sisters, made their impacts in soaps, in television and music. Jason Donovan and Jonathan Coleman came too. In music, Yvonne Kenny, Simone Young and the opera and theatre director Elijah Moshinsky also worked at both ends of the world. These 'London-based' artists, like Sutherland before them, could sometimes be tagged as 'British'.²⁷ Identifications were also changing. Kathy Lette satirised English society in her own Australian way in several novels, including *Foetal Attraction* (1993) and *Mad Cows* (1996). So did an older generation of Australians, and other outsiders, including Jill Neville, in the Marsha Rowe collection of short pieces, *So Very English* (1991).²⁸

London continued to be important as an English-speaking city with a range of professional institutions and opportunities. However, in a global world, it was no longer *the* centre. In one interpretation, that centre of gravity had moved to New York, which attracted the Australian novelist Peter Carey, whose fictional interests included the relationship between a great imperial power and a small power, between the US and Australia. In theatre, Michael Blakemore directed in New York, 'on' and 'off' Broadway, and was nominated for five Tony awards. Germaine Greer's first publisher, Sonny Mehta, moved to New York, and Harold Evans of the *Sunday Times* left Murdoch's London embrace for Conde Nast publications in 1986, his partner Tina Brown taking over the *New Yorker* in 1992. Murray Sayle and Clive James were amongst the 'London' talent who wrote for the *New Yorker*.

Despite this tendency, electronic communication means that the world has no single centre. Even aside from a resurgent Europe and a rising Asia, challenging the traditional centres of London and New York, distance is diminished by communications. One Italian financial journalist writes his column from Australia, while travel around the world continues to become cheaper. In this sense Britain and Australia are now amongst many familiar neighbours in a global world.

In a contrasting view, however, Australia faces the same structural economic problems as in the 1950s, when imported television decimated the radio industry, and/or in the 1890s–1900s, when British publishing agencies weakened Australian publishing through their cheaper colonial editions. In the global era in the cultural industries, will the defeat of the local by imported technology and new entrepreneurial institutions worsen? One unusual expatriate was the Fleet Street and Wapping publisher, Rupert Murdoch, the 'Dirty Digger' to his British critics, now a global media magnate and an American citizen and resident. In 1998, in the same week that he bought out the Australian record company Mushroom (as he had earlier made Angus & Robertson just an imprint of Harper Collins), his company Fox began spending five million dollars advertising the *Titanic* movie video in Australia. This was part of a worldwide campaign, an advertising blitzkrieg. Will the new communications again undermine local cultural activity? Or will they, along with the new Fox studios in Sydney, and the sale of the Melbourne TV production company Artist Services to Granada of the UK, assist in disseminating Australian works to 'global' audiences? In publishing, the world book, driven more by marketing than by talent, is already threatening local production. World trade treaties, which include the cultural industries, may soon spell the end of local quotas for Australian content on television, for subsidy in film and for Public Lending Right for Australian authors.[29] Sylvia Lawson argued in her account of J. F. Archibald, creator of the *Bulletin* magazine of the 1890s, that the 'colonial paradox' was the over-valuation of the metropolis:

> Metropolis, the centre of language, of the dominant culture and its judgments, lies away in the great Elsewhere; but the tasks of living, communicating, teaching, acting-out and changing the culture must be carried on not Elsewhere but Here.[30]

In the same way that drama traditionally arises out of a community, or that music and art are often inspired by a place, 'here' is important. It is *not* that in the twenty-first century Australian cultural activity should be denied the benefits of stimulus from around the world. It is *not* that Australians should not be able to perform and to pursue careers in London, or elsewhere. It is *not* to deny David Malouf's observation, in his Boyer Lectures, that Australians have the 'complex fate' of being the 'children of two worlds' (or more, it might be added). Nor to deny his argument that when asked to make the 'false choice' between them, their answer should be 'Thank you, I'll take both'.[31] It *is* that in every society, including Australia, the structures of prestige and of production should allow artists, writers and performers to work at the highest level and to tell their own 'home-grown stories'.[32] In so doing, the 'prophets' might help to irrigate the deserts, spreading understanding, as well as growing their own artistic flowers. Then, those who understood Australia would be appreciated, instead of those who only knew the Australia that they had left. It is now important that Australia, as well as London, calls. Then, this generation of expatriates could be recognised for what they had achieved. Their odyssey, which left so many of them 'forever after torn in two', as Robin Dalton reflected, and made some see Australia through a distorting lens, would now be understood. Finally, they would have their place in the sun – at home and away.[33]

Notes

Preface

1 'The Albatross Colony' in Charmian Clift (edited by Nadia Wheatley), *Trouble in Lotus Land: Essays 1964–1967*, (Sydney: Angus & Robertson, 1990), pp. 152–5.

2 Doireann MacDermott and Susan Ballyn (eds), *A Passage to Somewhere Else*, (Barcelona: PPU, 1988), pp. 1–10, 135–42.

3 On British–Australian relations and the Australian contribution to Britain see: A. F. Madden and W. H. Morris-Jones (eds), *Australia and Britain: Studies in a Changing Relationship* (Sydney: Sydney University Press, 1980); T. B. Millar (ed.), *The Australian Contribution to Britain* (London: Australian Studies Centre, University of London, 1988). The Poetry Society, which attracts several Australians including Peter Porter and Katherine Gallagher, is in Earls Court.

4 Sir William McKie was organist of Westminster Abbey from 1946 to 1963. Amongst the numerous Australian academics working in British universities, Sir Kenneth Wheare was Vice Chancellor of Oxford University from 1964 to 1966 and president of the British Academy and Sir Brian Windeyer, of the old New South Wales family, became Vice Chancellor of the University of London from 1969 to 1972. Those stories – like those of the Australians who won Nobel Prizes while working in British laboratories (including Mark Oliphant and Howard Florey), and the successful efforts of the Australian National University to bring back Oliphant in 1950, and later, the distinguished historian Keith Hancock, and others after World War II – are cognate with this study. Other Australians in British public institutions included Rex Leeper, architect of the growth of the British Council, Kit (Sir Christopher) McMahon at the National Westminster bank. Later, Bruce Gyngell managed several commercial television stations. In politics, Russell Kerr was a Labour Party Member of Parliament for Feltham (Middlesex) from 1966, while Patricia Hewitt was secretary of the National Council for Civil Liberties from 1974 to 1983, a 1980s staffer of the Leader of the Opposition and from 1997 Labour MP

for Leicester West. Peter Tatchell, 1980s–1990s radical, unsuccessful Labour candidate for Bermondsey and gay activist, played a different political role.

1· Introduction – Going Away

1 Leo McKern, *Just Resting* (London: Methuen, 1983), pp. 65–70, 127.
2 See John M. MacKenzie (ed.), *Imperialism and Popular Culture* (Manchester: Manchester University Press, 1984) and John M. MacKenzie, *Propaganda and Empire* (Manchester: Manchester University Press, 1984).
3 Stella Bowen, *Drawn from Life* (London: Collins, 1941); Christina Stead, *For Love Alone* (London: Peter Davies, 1945); K. S. Inglis, in D. Fitzpatrick (ed.), *Home or Away? Immigrants in Colonial Australia* (Canberra: Research School of Social Sciences, Australian National University, 1992); Ros Pesman, *Duty Free: Australian Women Abroad* (Melbourne: Oxford University Press, 1996). A later expatriate novel is Patricia Rolfe, *No Love Lost* (London: Macmillan, 1965).
4 *Travellers, Journeys, Tourists*, thematic issue, *Australian Cultural History*, no. 10 (1991); R. Pesman et al., *The Oxford Book of Australian Travel Writing* (Melbourne: Oxford University Press, 1996); R. Pesman et al. (compiler T. McCormack), *Annotated Bibliography of Australian Overseas Travel Writing* (Canberra: ALIA Press, 1996); Murray Bail, *Homesickness* (Ringwood, Vic.: Penguin, 1982); Rosemary Creswell (ed.), *Home and Away: Travel Stories* (Ringwood, Vic.: Penguin, 1987).
5 Jim Davidson, *Lyrebird Rising: Louise Hanson-Dyer of Oiseau-Lyre* (Melbourne: Melbourne University Press, Miegunyah Editions, 1994); Patrick Hutchings and Julie Lewis, *Kathleen O'Connor: Artist in Exile* (Fremantle: Fremantle Arts Centre Press, 1987); Gaetano Prampolini and Christine Hubert (eds), *An Antipodean Collection: Australian Writers, Artists and Travellers in Tuscany* (Geneva: Slatkine, 1993). One specific study, Carol Mills, *Expatriate Australian Black-and-White Artists: Ruby and Will Dyson and Their Circle in London, 1909–1919* (London: Working Papers in Australian Studies, no. 33, Sir Robert Menzies Centre for Australian Studies, 1988), pursues another tradition of achievement and expatriation. Roslyn Russell, *Literary Links* (Sydney: Allen & Unwin, 1997) emerged from an exhibition on British–Australian connections.
6 Charmian Clift, *Peel Me A Lotus* (Sydney: Angus & Robertson, 1992; first edition, 1959); *Mermaid Singing* (Sydney: Angus & Robertson, 1992; first edition 1958); Alister Kershaw, *The Pleasure of Their Company* (St Lucia: University of Queensland Press, 1986), pp. 166–79; Clyde Packer, *No Return Ticket* (Sydney: Angus & Robertson, 1984); Russell Braddon (ed.), *Australia Fair?* (London: Methuen, 1984); Hannie Rayson, *Hotel Sorrento* (Sydney: Currency Press, 1990); Jack Hibberd, *Malarky Barks* (unpublished playscript, 1983).
7 Geoffrey Serle, *From Deserts the Prophets Come: The Creative Spirit in Australia 1788–1972* (Melbourne: Heinemann, 1973, revised edition, 1987, entitled *The Creative Spirit in Australia: A Cultural History*). The growing body of reference works include: William H. Wilde, Joy Hooton and Barry Andrews (eds), *The Oxford Companion to Australian Literature* (Melbourne: Oxford University Press, 1985, new edition 1994); Katharine Brisbane (ed.), *Entertaining Australia: An Illustrated History* (Sydney: Currency Press, 1991); Warren Bebbington (ed.), *The Oxford Companion to Australian Music* (Melbourne: Oxford University Press, 1997);

P. Parsons (ed.), *A Companion to Theatre in Australia* (Sydney: Currency Press/ Cambridge University Press, 1995); Ann Atkinson, Linsay Knight and Margaret McPhee (eds), *The Dictionary of the Performing Arts in Australia* (2 vols) (Sydney: Allen & Unwin, 1996). Amongst general books are Roger Covell, *Australia's Music* (Melbourne: Sun, 1967); Geoffrey Dutton (ed.), *The Literature of Australia* (Ringwood, Vic.: Penguin, 1964, revised edition, 1976); Laurie Hergenhan (ed.), *The Penguin New Literary History of Australia* (Ringwood, Vic.: Penguin, 1988); Peter Holloway (ed.), *Contemporary Australian Drama* (Sydney: Currency Press, 1981, new edition, 1987).

8 See, for example: Ernest Earnest, *Expatriates and Patriots: American Artists, Scholars and Writers in Europe* (Durham, N.C.: Duke University Press, 1968); Allison Lockwood, *Passionate Pilgrims: The American Traveller in Great Britain 1800–1914* (New York: Cornwall Books, 1981); Robert McAlmon and Kay Boyle, *Being Geniuses Together 1920–1930* (London: The Hogarth Press, 1984).

9 The Australian Broadcasting Tribunal inquiries into Australian content in the late 1980s referred to an 'Australian look'. *Sounds Australian* is the name of a major Australian music journal. In practice, diversity rather than national singularity was seen to be part of this essentialist-sounding idea. On identity politics and support for the arts, see: David Williamson, 'Subsidies seed the soil of home-grown stories', *Sunday Age*, 13.9.1998.

10 H. C. Coombs to Don Banks, 9.7.1974, Banks Papers MS 6830, National Library of Australia.

11 See the collection 'Culture and the "Tall Poppy" in Australia', *Australian Cultural History*, no. 3 (1984).

12 Serle's chapter title for the period 1935–50, with the question mark deleted, in *From Deserts the Prophets Come*.

13 J. V. Connolly, 'The Export of Talent' in J. C. G. Kevin, *Some Australians Take Stock* (London: Longmans, Green, 1939); Stephen Alomes, *A Nation at Last? The Changing Character of Australian Nationalism* (Sydney: Angus & Robertson, 1988), chapter 3. Stephen Alomes and Catherine Jones (eds), *Australian Nationalism: A Documentary History* (Sydney: Angus & Robertson, 1991), pp. 140–201. J. H. [Jim] Davidson 'The De-Dominionisation of Australia', *Meanjin*, vol. 38, no. 2 (July 1979) looks at the gradual decline of this orientation.

14 Jacques Martineau, *Letters from Australia* (London: 1869), p. 21, cited in W. S. Ramson (ed.), *The Australian National Dictionary* (Melbourne: Oxford University Press, 1988), p. 157.

15 Noted by A. A. Phillips, 'The Cultural Cringe' in his *The Australian Tradition: Studies in a Colonial Culture* (Melbourne: Cheshire, 1958), p. 92.

16 This was how I was, jocularly, received when arriving in London in 1972. I replied, belatedly, that I 'found Britain quaint'. Kathy Lette, Angela Catterns program, ABC 3LO, 23.11.1998. See also Sabine Durrant, 'Kathy Lette: A Black Belt in Tongue Fu', *Guardian*, 2.11.1998.

17 S. Hazzard, *The Transit of Venus* (Harmondsworth: Penguin, 1981), pp. 31–2.

18 Henry Lawson, quoted by W. K. Hancock, *Australia* (Brisbane: Jacaranda, 1961), p. 42.

19 F. Fanon, *Black Skin, White Masks* (London: Paladin, 1970), pp. 13–15.

20 A. A. Phillips, 'The Cultural Cringe' in his *The Australian Tradition: Studies in a Colonial Culture* (Melbourne: Cheshire, 1958).

21 Henry Lawson, 'The Sydney *Bulletin*', p. 355 and 'Letter to Earl Beauchamp', pp. 225–7, in B. Kiernan (ed.), *Henry Lawson* (St Lucia: University of Queensland Press, 1976).

22 On exile see: Edward Said, on the difference between political exile, or banishment, and usually voluntary cultural ideas of exile, 'Reflections on exile', *Granta*, no. 13 (Autumn 1984), pp. 157–72; Paul Tabori, *The Anatomy of Exile* (London: Harrap, 1972); Leon and Rebeca Grinberg, *Psychoanalytic Perspectives on Migration and Exile* (New Haven: Yale University Press, 1989).

23 Two of the physicists, who had come to Britain in the 1940s, stayed, and went on to successful academic careers, were Tom Kaiser, who became professor of space physics at Sheffield University, and John Malos, who worked in physics at Bristol University. See: 'Tom Kaiser', Obituary, *Australian*, 18.8.1998. The McCarthyism of the Cold War impacted severely on the Council for Scientific and Industrial Research (which became the CSIRO) from the 1940s; see Rohan Rivett, *David Rivett: Fighter for Australian Science* (North Blackburn: Rivett, 1972), chapters 1, 8.

24 Particularly the Langton novels, e.g. *The Cardboard Crown* (Melbourne: Lansdowne, 1972, first published 1952).

25 V. Daley, 'When London Calls' in R. Hall (ed.), *The Collins Book of Australian Poetry* (Sydney: Collins, 1981).

26 Lambert and Lindsay quoted in P. Rolfe, *The Journalistic Javelin* (Sydney: Wildcat Press, 1980), p. 219.

27 Bernard Smith with Terry Smith, *Australian Painting 1788–1990* (Melbourne: Oxford University Press, 1991), p. 152. Genesis, Exodus and Leviticus are Smith's chapter titles for these periods.

28 *Age*, Travel, 3.2.1996; W. Vamplew (ed.), *Australians: Historical Statistics* (Sydney: Fairfax, Syme and Weldon, 1987), p. 157.

29 *Report of the Select Committee on the Encouragement of Australian Productions for Television* (Vincent Report), Commonwealth of Australia, Canberra, 1963, p. 16.

30 While American film and song – from Frank Sinatra to rock n'roll – was influencing Australian popular culture, a core of popular entertainment remained British – the Ealing comedies, Tony Hancock, Sid James and the expatriate Australian Bill Kerr on radio and then television. In professional society, the forms derived from Britain – the bewigged barristers, the medical specialists who trained in London and the doctors' organisation, which was an Australian branch of the British Medical Association until 1962 when it became the Australian Medical Association.

31 Jim Davidson, *The Expatriates* (Geelong: Deakin University, 1978), p. 8.

32 See Murray Sayle, 'As far as you can go' in Timothy O'Keefe (ed.), *Alienation* (London: MacGibbon and Kee, 1960).

33 On British perceptions of Australia, see: Tony Delamothe and Carl Bridge (eds), *Interpreting Australia: British Perceptions of Australia since 1970* (London: Sir Robert Menzies Centre for Australian Studies, University of London, 1988); Stephen Alomes, 'The British Press and Australia', *Meanjin*, vol. 46 no. 2 (June 1987).

2 An Australian Theatre or A Career on the Stage?

 1 Interviews drawn on and quoted from in this chapter: Allan Ashbolt (April 1992), Richard Beynon (November 1989), Michael Blakemore (January 1987), John Bluthal (November 1982), Walter Brown (April 1990), Robin Dalton (Eakin)

(November 1989), Lloyd Lamble (January 1991), Keith Michell (November 1989), Jocelyn Rickards (November 1989), Alan White (November 1982, November 1989).

2 Geoffrey Serle, *From Deserts the Prophets Come: The Creative Spirit in Australia 1788–1972* (Melbourne: Heinemann, 1973, revised edition 1987, titled *The Creative Spirit in Australia: A Cultural History*), chapter 8.

3 Australian Archives (ACT): The Theatre Council of Western Australia; Series A571/1, Item 1944/1171 Pt 1.

4 See: S. Alomes, 'The search for a national theatre', *Voices*, 3, 3 (Spring 1993), pp. 26–7.

5 L. Rees, *A History of Australian Drama*, vol. 1 (Sydney: Angus & Robertson, 1978), pp. 178–80, 215–227; Doris Fitton, *Not Without Dust and Heat: My Life in Theatre* (Sydney: Harper & Row, 1981).

6 F. Salter, *Borovansky: The Man Who Made Australian Ballet* (Sydney: Wildcat, 1980).

7 Geoffrey Dutton, *The Innovators* (Melbourne: Macmillan, 1986), chapter 14; Garry Kinnane, *George Johnston: A Biography* (Melbourne: Nelson, 1986), chapter 5; Trader Faulkner, *Peter Finch* (London: Angus & Robertson, 1979), chapters 5–14; Elaine Dundy, *Finch Bloody Finch* (London: Magnum, 1981), chapters 4–12.

8 M. Pate, *An Entertaining War* (Sydney: Dreamweaver Books, 1986).

9 See: Dundy, *Finch Bloody Finch*, chapters 12–14 ; Faulkner, *Peter Finch*, chapters 13–14.

10 Dundy, *Finch Bloody Finch*, pp. 59–63; Faulkner, *Peter Finch*, pp. 46–52.

11 Alomes, 'The search for a national theatre', pp. 28–30.

12 *Equity News*, September 1948, p. 3; *New York Times*, 19.1.1958.

13 *Equity*, December 1949, p. 18.

14 Dundy, *Finch Bloody Finch*, chapter 13.

15 Dundy, *Finch Bloody Finch*, pp. 129–34.

16 Dundy, *Finch Bloody Finch*, Part 2, chapters 1–3; Faulkner, *Peter Finch*, pp. 132–7.

17 Leo McKern, *Just Resting* (London: Methuen, 1983), pp. 164, 75, 66–8, 144.

18 McKern, *Just Resting*, pp. 65, 69–74.

19 McKern, *Just Resting*, p. 67.

20 McKern, *Just Resting*, pp. 77–81.

21 McKern, *Just Resting*, p. 26.

22 McKern, *Just Resting*, pp. 74–5.

23 R. Eakin, *Aunts up the Cross* (Melbourne: Macmillan, 1967), pp. 24–7, 71, 102. Her longer story, including a period in Thailand, is told in R. Dalton, *An Incidental Memoir* (Ringwood, Vic.: Viking, 1998).

24 Eakin, *Aunts up the Cross*, pp. 42, 63–6, 80.

25 See M. Blakemore, 'The straight poofter' in R. Braddon (ed.), *Australia Fair?* His short film, *A Personal History of the Australian Surf* (1982), is based on this narrative.

26 Blakemore, 'The straight poofter', pp. 38, 25, 35.

27 Blakemore, 'The straight poofter', pp. 35–7, 40–1.

28 Dutton, *The Innovators*, chapter 8.

29 Dutton, *The Innovators*, chapter 8; J. Rickards, *A Painted Banquet: My Life and Loves* (London: Weidenfeld and Nicolson, 1987), pp. 21–2.

30 Rickards, *A Painted Banquet*, pp. 23–5; Dalton, *An Incidental Memoir*, pp. 73–5.

31 See: P. Coleman, *Obscenity, Blasphemy, Sedition*, revised edition (Sydney: Angus & Robertson, 1974), chapter 2; M. Heyward, *The Ern Malley Affair* (St Lucia:

University of Queensland Press, 1993), part III; R. Close, *Of Salt and Earth* (Melbourne: Nelson, 1977), chapter 6.

32 Richard Haese, *Rebels and Precursors: The Revolutionary Years of Australian Art* (Melbourne: Penguin, 1988), chapter 7; Tucker quoted, p. 256.

33 *Equity*, special 50th anniversary issue (November 1989), pp. 16–20, 34–7.

34 Australian Archives (ACT): ASIO Minute, 23.4.1953, 'Communists in Actors' Equity of Australia', Assistant Regional Director to Principal Section Officer, B1, p. 123; Series A6122 XR1, Item 186 (The 'Definite' category had 11 names, 'Very Doubtful' three and 'Doubtful' five. Finch ('Very Doubtful') and Tamara Tchinarova ('Definite') received a paragraph entry of their own.); D. McKnight and G. Pemberton, 'Seeing red', *Sydney Morning Herald* (*Good Weekend*), 21.5.1990.

35 L. Lamble to S. Alomes, 17.1.1991.

36 Australian Archives (ACT): Commonwealth Investigation Service Minute, 'Communism: Trade Unions: Actors Equity' (Section 4: Officials, p. 3), 17.2.1949, R. Williams, Deputy Director CIS, Sydney to Director, Canberra, pp. 82–9; Series A6122 XR1, Item 186.

37 Commonwealth Investigation Service Minute, 'Communism: Trade Unions: Actors Equity', pp. 82–9; L. Lamble to S. Alomes, 17.1.1991.

38 ASIO Minute, 23.4.1953, 'Communists in Actors' Equity of Australia'. These are only four of the 19 names. Finch, already overseas, had moved into the 'Doubtful' category while Tamara Tchinarova remained a 'Definite'.

3 Sydney or Fleet Street

1 Interviews drawn on and quoted in this chapter: Allan Ashbolt (April 1992), A. Mohammed Babu (January 1991), Anthony Delano (December 1985, June 1992), Virginia Edwards (January 1991), Liz Hickson (April 1990), Phillip Knightley (November 1983, January 1996), Alister Kershaw (January 1991), Bill Harcourt (April 1992), Ed Morrisby (April 1992), Ken Minogue (November 1983), Jill Neville (November 1983, January 1991), Timothy O'Keefe (November 1989), Barry Porter (July 1997), Michael Provis (February 1997), Glen Renfrew (November 1983), Murray Sayle (August 1990, January 1991, May 1997), Tessa Sayle (November 1983), Marea Terry (December 1990), Alan White (November 1982, November 1989).

2 Patrick Buckridge, *The Scandalous Penton* (St Lucia: University of Queensland Press, 1994).

3 Pat Burgess, *Warco: Australian Reporters at War* (Richmond, Vic.: Heinemann (Australia), 1986); Richard Hughes, *Barefoot Reporter* (Hong Kong: Far Eastern Economic Review, 1984); C. Pearl, *Morrison of Peking* (Sydney: Angus & Robertson, 1967).

4 G. Kinnane, *George Johnston: A Biography* (Melbourne: Nelson, 1986).

5 Three to four decades later, Peter Grose, from Sydney, came to head Secker & Warburg, and Carmen Callil, from Melbourne, who had been a principal in establishing Virago, rose to the top at Chatto & Windus.

6 Donald Read, *The Power of News: The History of Reuters 1849–1989* (Oxford: Oxford University Press, 1992), pp. 2, 293–5, 342–5.

7 Tom Pocock, *Alan Moorehead* (London: The Bodley Head, 1990); Sam White, *Sam White's Paris* (London: New English Library, 1983); Donald Horne, *Portrait of an Optimist* (Ringwood, Vic.: Penguin, 1988).

8 Kinnane, *George Johnston*, chapter VI.

9 Kinnane, *George Johnston*, chapters III–V, VII–IX.

10 Kinnane, *George Johnston*, pp. 136–40; George Johnston, *My Brother Jack* (London: Collins, 1964); Charmian Clift, *Mermaid Singing* (London: Michael Joseph, 1958); Karen Ruth Brooks, 'Odysseus Unbound and Penelope Unstable: Contemporary Australian Expatriate Women Writers', Unpublished PhD thesis, University of Wollongong, 1997, chapters 2–3.

11 See: Brian Kennedy, *A Passion to Oppose: John Anderson, Philosopher* (Melbourne: Melbourne University Press, 1995); A. J. Baker (ed.), *Anderson's Social Philosophy* (Sydney: Angus & Robertson, 1979); John Docker, *Australian Cultural Elites: Intellectual Traditions in Sydney and Melbourne* (Sydney: Angus & Robertson, 1974); Judy Ogilvie, *The Push: An Impressionist Memoir* (Sydney: Primavera, 1995).

12 Michael Heyward, *The Ern Malley Affair* (St Lucia: University of Queensland Press, 1993), p. 130.

13 Phillip Knightley, *A Hack's Progress* (London: Jonathan Cape, 1997). Sam White had left for Europe in the 1940s, but his story had a folk resonance at the *Telegraph* and its pubs for several years.

14 Knightley, *A Hack's Progress*, chapters 1–3.

15 R. Close, *Of Salt and Earth: An Autobiography* (West Melbourne: Nelson, 1977), chapters 15–17, pp. 213, 240, 248.

16 Close, *Of Salt and Earth*, pp. 248–9; P. Coleman, *Obscenity, Blasphemy and Sedition* (Sydney: Angus & Robertson, 1974 edition), pp. 38–40.

17 Sayle, 'As far as you can go', in Timothy O'Keefe (ed.), *Alienation* (London: MacGibbon and Kee, 1960), pp. 96–7.

18 Murray Sayle, 'Love and art in old South Wales', *Independent Monthly* (April 1992), pp. 20–22; M. Sayle–S. Alomes, 6.3.1991.

19 Sayle, 'As far as you can go', p. 104.

20 Sayle, 'As far as you can go', pp. 114, 115, 117.

21 P. Knightley and G. Edwards, *Cosy in a Basement*, unpublished manuscript, nd, 71 pp.

22 Sayle, 'As far as you can go', pp. 120, 123, 126.

23 This was not entirely new, as in the distinguished example of the American war correspondent, from the Spanish Civil War to Vietnam, Martha Gellhorn. See also Siobhan McHugh on women in Vietnam, *Minefields and Mini-skirts: Australian Women and the Vietnam War* (Sydney: Doubleday, 1993), pp. 29–36. Later prize-winning Australian overseas correspondents included the ABC's Monica Attard, who covered the end of Communism in Russia. See Monica Attard, *Russia: Which Way Paradise?* (Neutral Bay, NSW: Transworld, 1997).

24 Knightley, *A Hack's Progress*, pp. 73–6.

4 Musical Directions

1 Interviews drawn on and quoted in this chapter: Geoffrey Chard (August 1991), David Lumsdaine (November 1992), Charles Mackerras (December 1989), Geoffrey Parsons (December 1989), Joan Sutherland (August 1990), Barry Tuckwell (November 1989), Malcolm Williamson (November 1983).

2 Nancy Phelan, *Charles Mackerras: A Musician's Musician* (Melbourne: Oxford University Press, 1987/London: Victor Gollancz, 1987), pp. 40–1, 47–50.

3 Phillip Sametz, *Play On! 60 Years of Music-Making with the Sydney Symphony Orchestra* (Sydney: ABC Books, 1992), chapters 3–4.
4 *Sydney Morning Herald*, 17.11.1995.
5 James Murdoch, *A Handbook of Australian Music* (Melbourne: Sun, 1983), pp. 38–39. In 1948, *Canon*, vol. 2, no. 1 (August 1948), Goossens lamented his inability to find Australian orchestral scores: 'Where are the scores?'.
6 Sametz, *Play On!*, pp. 45–7.
7 Sametz, *Play On!*, pp. 66–70.
8 Phelan, *Charles Mackerras*, pp. 19–22, 27–43.
9 Phelan, *Charles Mackerras*, pp. 37–9, 49–53.
10 Brian Chatterton, 'Malcolm Williamson' in F. Callaway and D. Tunley (eds), *Australian Composition in the Twentieth Century* (Melbourne: Oxford University Press, 1978), pp. 146–58; Malcolm Williamson, 'A composer's heritage', *Composer*, no. 19 (Spring 1966), pp. 70–73; 'The music master' (interview), *Hemisphere*, vol. 27, no. 2 (1982), pp. 108–13.
11 See Thérèse Radic, 'The Australian National Theatre Movement as the catalyst for the Australian Opera: tugboat to flagship' in N. Brown et al. (eds), *One Hand on the Manuscript: Music in Australian Cultural History* (Canberra: Humanities Research Centre, Australian National University, 1995). On Goossens, see: Sametz, *Play On!*, chapters 3–4; Ava Hubble, *The Strange Case of Eugene Goossens and other tales from the Opera House* (Sydney: Collins, 1988); Eugene Goossens, *Overture and Beginners: A Musical Autobiography* (London: Methuen, 1951); E. Goossens, 'Reflections', W. Wagner, 'Five years with Goossens', in *Canon*, vol. 5, no. 12 (July 1952).
12 Neil Warren-Smith (with Frank Salter), *Twenty-five Years of Australian Opera* (Melbourne: Oxford University Press, 1983), pp. 24–28, xi.
13 Russell Braddon, *Joan Sutherland* (Sydney: Collins, 1962), pp. 19, 28–35.
14 Phelan, *Charles Mackerras*, pp. 55–63.
15 Phelan, *Charles Mackerras*, p. 55.
16 Braddon, *Joan Sutherland*, pp. 32–50, 61–65. Other biographies include: Norma Major, *Joan Sutherland* (London: Queen Anne Press/Futura, 1987); Brian Adams, *La Stupenda* (Sydney: Vintage, revised edition, 1993) and her autobiography, *A Prima Donna's Progress* (London: Orion/Sydney: Random House Australia, 1997).
17 Phelan, *Charles Mackerras*, pp. 60–67.
18 *Canberra Times*, 26.7.1981.
19 Phelan, *Charles Mackerras*, pp. 102–3.
20 Phelan, *Charles Mackerras*, pp. 69–71, 97–101, 102–13.

5 Patterns of Discovery: Artists

1 Interviews drawn on and quoted in the chapter: Barbara Blackman-Veldhoven (June 1993), Murray Sayle (January 1991).
2 Brian Adams, *Sidney Nolan: Such is Life* (Melbourne: Hutchinson, 1987), p. 136. On Nolan see also: K. Clark, C. MacInnes, and B. Robertson, *Sidney Nolan* (London: Thames and Hudson, 1961); Elwyn Lynn, *Sidney Nolan: Myth and Imagery* (Melbourne: Macmillan, 1967); Elwyn Lynn and Sidney Nolan, *Sidney Nolan: Australia* (Sydney: Bay Books, 1979).

3 Bernard Smith with Terry Smith, *Australian Painting: 1788–1990* (Melbourne: Oxford University Press, 1991), pp. 342–347.

4 G. Dutton, *The Innovators* (South Melbourne: Macmillan, 1986), pp. 98–114; Robert Hughes, *The Art of Australia* (revised ed., Ringwood, Vic.: Penguin, 1970), chapter 7.

5 Alan McCulloch, *Encyclopedia of Australian Art* (2 vols) (Melbourne: Hutchinson, 1984).

6 Murray Sayle, 'Memories of Lymburner' in H. Kolenberg and B. Pearce (eds), *Francis Lymburner 1916–1972* (Sydney: Art Gallery of NSW, 1992), p. 105.

7 Smith with Smith, *Australian Painting*, pp. 344–8.

8 Smith with Smith, *Australian Painting*, chapters 4–6.

9 Smith with Smith, *Australian Painting*, pp. 301–2, 344–7; Adams, *Sidney Nolan: Such is Life*, chapters 8, 9; Clark, MacInnes, Robertson, *Sidney Nolan* pp. 7–50; Peter Quartermaine, 'British Perceptions of Australian Arts in the Post-war Decades' in Tony Delamothe and Carl Bridge (eds), *Interpreting Australia: British Perceptions of Australia since 1770* (London: Sir Robert Menzies Centre for Australian Studies, University of London, 1988); Christopher Heathcote, *A Quiet Revolution: The Rise of Australian Art 1946–1968* (Melbourne: Text, 1995), pp. 145–150. On the AAA January 1953 exhibition, see Wendy Bradley, 'Alannah Coleman: the woman and her role in promoting Australian art and artists in the United Kingdom 1950–1990', Unpublished MA Thesis, Victoria College, 1991, pp. 52–5.

10 Sayle, 'Memories of Lymburner', p. 105.

11 Barry Humphries, 'Lost at Life' in Kolenberg and Pearce, *Francis Lymburner*, pp. 17–18.

12 Bernard Smith, 'A Personal Memoir' in Kolenberg and Pearce, *Francis Lymburner*, pp. 19–20 (Lymburner, paraphrasing Smith, in a letter to him). By 1967, the fashion had spread to Melbourne. Smith with Smith, *Australian Painting*, pp. 443–4.

13 'Chronology' in Felicity St John Moore (ed.), *Charles Blackman: Schoolgirls and Angels* (Melbourne: National Gallery of Victoria, 1993), pp. 20–21.

14 For accounts of this society, see: 'Barbara Blackman: Chronology' in Felicity St John Moore (ed.), *Charles Blackman: Schoolgirls and Angels*, and Barbara Blackman, *Glass after Glass: Autobiographical Reflections* (Ringwood, Vic.: Viking, 1997); see also Barry Humphries, *More Please: An Autobiography* (Ringwood, Vic.: Penguin, 1992), pp. 203–4.

15 'Chronology' in Moore (ed.), *Charles Blackman: Schoolgirls and Angels*, p. 22.

16 Several studies see the 1950s as a time of positive developments, for example: John Murphy and Judith Smart (eds), *The Forgotten Fifties* (Melbourne: Melbourne University Press, 1997).

17 Peter Quartermaine, 'British Perceptions of Australian Arts in the Post-war Decades', p. 86. (The term *'jardin exotique'* was used later by Robert Hughes. See Quartermaine, p. 91.)

18 Humphries, *More Please*, pp. 203–4.

19 Wendy Bradley, 'Alannah Coleman', p. 82; Philip Jones, 'Painters' muse showed our best to the world – Alannah Coleman', Obituary, *Australian*, 30.9.1998.

20 Smith with Smith, *Australian Painting*, pp. 301–2.

21 'Chronology' in *Charles Blackman: Schoolgirls and Angels*, p. 22. However, he had an exhibition at the Zwemmer Gallery in the same year, to some acclaim.

22 'Chronology' in Moore (ed.), *Charles Blackman: Schoolgirls and Angels*, pp. 22–3.

23 'Chronology' in Moore (ed.), *Charles Blackman: Schoolgirls and Angels*, pp. 23–4.

24 Bruce Bennett, *Spirit in Exile: Peter Porter and his Poetry* (Melbourne: Oxford University Press, 1991), p. 90.

25 Bennett, *Spirit in Exile*, p. 90.

26 Adams, *Sidney Nolan*, p. 147.

27 Alan McCulloch and Susan McCulloch, *Encyclopedia of Australian Art* (revised ed., St Leonards, NSW: Allen & Unwin, 1994), pp. 537–8. The Australian tendency to mainly show emerging artists at events like the Venice Biennale, rather than older distinguished artists such as John Brack, meant that Brack, for example, was almost unknown overseas.

28 Christopher Heathcote, *A Quiet Revolution: The Rise of Australian Art* (Melbourne: Text, 1995), pp. 145–7.

29 Adams, *Sidney Nolan*, pp. 11, 167, 248.

30 Adams, *Sidney Nolan*, pp. 167, 241–252, 259. The earlier commission was more mutually satisfying, with the hanging of his *Paradise Garden* images at the Victorian Arts Centre (Adams, p. 249).

31 Adams, *Sidney Nolan*, p. 12. Nolan also uses a football analogy to describe some of the 'dirtier' play between Nolan and his Melbourne adversaries. Adams, p. 252.

32 'My Defining Moment, by six prominent Australians', *Age*, 14.1.1996; Sandra McGrath, *The Artist and the River: Arthur Boyd and the Shoalhaven* (Kensington, NSW: Bay Books, 1982), p. 30. See also: Ursula Hoff, *The Art of Arthur Boyd* (London: André Deutsch, 1986); Franz Philipp, *Arthur Boyd* (London: Thames & Hudson, 1967); Lisa Bowman (ed.), *Australians on Arthur Boyd* (Melbourne: Australia Post, 1999).

33 McGrath, *The Artist and the River*, preface, pp. 16, 30. McGrath suggests in the preface that Boyd found the landscape alien, as she, an American, had also found it.

34 Adams, *Sidney Nolan*, p. 236.

35 Hannie Rayson, *Hotel Sorrento* (Sydney: Currency Press, 1990), pp. 63–73.

36 Dermot Bolger (ed.), *Ireland in Exile* (Dublin: New Island Books, 1993), editor's note, p. 7.

6 Patterns of Exploration: Writers

1 Interviews drawn on and quoted in this chapter: Russell Braddon (May 1991), Katherine Gallagher (November 1983), Alister Kershaw (January 1991), John Laffin (January 1991), David Lumsdaine (November 1992), Craig McGregor (September 1998), Jill Neville (November 1983, January 1991, September 1992), Charles Osborne (November 1983), Peter Porter (December 1982), Murray Sayle (January 1991).

2 H. M. Green, *A History of Australian Literature* (2 vols), (Sydney: Angus & Robertson, 1961); *The Macquarie Dictionary* (North Ryde: Macquarie Dictionary, Macquarie University, 1981).

3 R. Nile and D. Walker, 'Marketing the Literary Imagination: Production of Australian Literature, 1915–1965' in Laurie Hergenhan (ed.), *The Penguin New Literary History of Australia* (Ringwood, Vic.: Penguin, 1988), pp. 291–8.

4 Nile and Walker, 'Marketing the Literary Imagination', p. 292.

5 Lawson, 'Pursuing Literature in Australia' in B. Kiernan (ed.), *Henry Lawson* (St Lucia: University of Queensland Press, 1976), p. 210.

6 Morris West, interview, ABC Radio, 11.9.1987.

7 Donald Horne, *Confessions of a New Boy* (Ringwood, Vic.: Viking, 1985), p. 289.

8 Moorehead, quoted in Geoffrey Serle, *From Deserts the Prophets Come: The Creative Spirit in Australia 1788–1972* (Melbourne: Heinemann, 1973, revised edition, 1987, entitled *The Creative Spirit in Australia: A Cultural History*), p. 125. See also Drusilla Modjeska, *Exiles at Home: Australian Women Writers 1925–1945* (Sydney: Sirius/Angus & Robertson, 1981); Jack Lindsay, *Life Rarely Tells* (Ringwood, Vic.: Penguin, 1982); H. W. Chaplin (ed.), *Jack Lindsay* (Sydney: Wentworth Press, 1983); Robert Mackie (ed.), *Jack Lindsay: The Thirties and Forties* (London: Australian Studies Centre Occasional Paper, no. 4, November 1984); Bernard Smith (ed.), *History and Culture: Essays in Honour of Jack Lindsay* (Sydney: Hale and Iremonger, 1984).

9 J. V. Connolly, 'The Export of Talent', in J. C. G. Kevin (ed.), *Some Australians Take Stock* (London: Longmans, 1939).

10 Serle, *From Deserts the Prophets Come*, pp. 125–6. (This discussion closely follows Serle.)

11 Garry Kinnane, *George Johnston: A Biography* (Melbourne: Nelson, 1986), p. 94. Randwick is Sydney's major racecourse.

12 Serle, *From Deserts the Prophets Come*, p. 135. On Australian publishing see: Geoffrey Dutton, *A Rare Bird: Penguin Books in Australia 1946–96* (Ringwood, Vic.: Penguin, 1996); Geoffrey Dutton, *Snow on the Saltbush: The Australian Literary Experience* (Ringwood, Vic.: Penguin, 1984); Judith Brett, 'Publishing, Censorship and Writers' Incomes 1965–1988' in Hergenhan (ed.), *The Penguin New Literary History of Australia*, pp. 454–66; Thomas Shapcott, *Biting the Bullet: A Literary Memoir* (Brookvale, NSW: Simon and Schuster, 1990), pp. 211–22.

13 The postwar expatriate generation included the war writers Braddon and Brickhill, the novelist Dymphna Cusack, the romantic novelist Catherine Gaskin, the scriptwriters/playwrights Alan Stranks and Hugh Hastings, the novelist and short story writer Dal Stivens, the editor and art curator Harry Tatlock Miller, the writers and scriptwriters Rex and Thea Rienits and the playwright Betty Roland. Others, including the war correspondents Alan Moorehead and Chester Wilmot, two academics, the classicist Gilbert Murray and the historian of the British Empire W. K. Hancock, the writer of children's novels Mary Elwyn Patchett, the freelance non-fiction writer Jack Lindsay and Patrick White had been in Britain for longer. Some of the earlier generation returned, including White (1948) and Hancock (1957), who took up a chair in history at the new 'national university' in Canberra.

14 Wilmot became one of the great European war correspondents after he had been banned by the army from New Guinea following his representations to Canberra, suggesting that inadequate support was being given to the troops defending the Kokoda Trail against the Japanese advance on Port Moresby and Australia. On the AAA launch see *Australian Cultural News* (March 1995) published by the Australian High Commission.

15 Russell Braddon, *End of a Hate* (London: Cassell, 1958), pp. 64–5, 72.

16 Braddon, *End of a Hate*, pp. 70–71, 73–5.

17 J. Laffin, *Digger: The Story of the Australian Soldier* (London: Cassell, 1959). The author of over 100 books returned to Australia in 1989, after 30 years in Britain. In some respects disappointed, he returned to the UK. See John Laffin, 'An Expatriate's Lament', *Bulletin*, 14.3.1989.

18 Geoffrey Dutton, *Out in the Open: An Autobiography* (St Lucia: University of Queensland Press, 1994), p. 229.

19 Society of Australian Writers Papers, MS 7354.

20 Society of Australian Writers Papers, MS 7354, ts 'extract from the rules' (categories of membership).

21 Wilfrid Thomas, *Living on Air: Some of the Memories of Wilfrid Thomas* (London: Frederick Muller, 1958).

22 Ian Bevan (ed.), *The Sunburnt Country: Profile of Australia* (London/Sydney: Collins, 1953).

23 President's Report for 1954 AGM, ts, p. 3, Society of Australian Writers papers, MS 7354.

24 Society of Australian Writers papers, MS 7354. The Society shared secretarial assistance from the High Commission with the Australian Musical Association (AMA) and the Australian Artists Association.

25 The Fellowship of Australian Writers, a general writers' organisation, had existed since 1928.

26 Letter from Richard Lane of The Australian Writers' Guild to David Whittaker of The Writers Guild of Great Britain, 25.2.1968, Society of Australian Writers Papers, MS 7354.

27 Charles Osborne, *Giving it Away: The Memoirs of An Uncivil Servant* (London: Secker & Warburg, 1986), p. 41.

28 Jill Neville, *Fall-Girl* (London: Weidenfeld and Nicolson, 1966), p. 21.

29 Murray Sayle, 'Expatriate captivated literary London – Jill Adelaide Neville', Obituary, *Australian*, 17.6.1997.

30 Bruce Bennett, *Spirit in Exile: Peter Porter and his Poetry* (Melbourne: Oxford University Press, 1991), pp. 29–30; Letter, P. Porter to S. Alomes, 17.12.1998.

31 *Sydney Morning Herald*, 21.7.1989.

32 *Australian*, 25–26.2.1984.

33 Bruce Bennett, 'Peter Porter in profile' (interview), *Westerly*, vol. 1 (March 1982), p. 49.

34 Porter, quoted in Osborne, *Giving it Away*, pp. 26–7.

35 Osborne, *Giving it Away*, p. 33.

36 Osborne, *Giving it Away*, p. 31.

37 Osborne, *Giving it Away*, pp. 285–6, 272–3, 40–41, 30.

38 Osborne, *Giving it Away*, pp. 39–40, 41.

39 Osborne, *Giving it Away*, pp. 35–6.

40 Osborne, *Giving it Away*, pp. 35–6, 43, 285–6.

41 P. Conrad, *Where I Fell to Earth* (London: Chatto & Windus, 1990), p. 25; Clive James, *Unreliable Memoirs* (London: Picador, 1981 paperback edition), p. 168.

42 *Australian*, 25–26.2.1984.

43 Bennett, *Spirit in Exile*, pp. 44–5, 49–51.

44 Neville, *Fall-Girl*, pp. 35–6, 59.

45 Bennett, *Spirit in Exile*, p. 47.

46 Neville, *Fall-Girl*, pp. 60–64.

47   Bennett, *Spirit in Exile*, pp. 48–50.

48   Bennett, *Spirit in Exile*, pp. 52–9, 60–64. However, 'the most important [member of "The Group"], Martin Bell, had been at Southampton University and in the Royal Engineers in the war' and several came from 'all over the British Isles, and from Cyprus, France, the States etc'. P. Porter to S. Alomes, 17.12.1998.

49   Bennett, *Spirit in Exile*, p. 64.

50   Neville, *Fall-Girl*, pp. 48, 83.

51   Neville, *Fall-Girl*, p. 28.

52   Neville, *Fall-Girl*, p. 115.

53   David Leitch, 'Jill Neville', Obituary, *Independent*, 12.6.1997.

54   Alister Kershaw, *The Pleasure of Their Company* (St Lucia: University of Queensland Press, 1986), pp. 166–79.

55   Alister Kershaw, 'The Last Expatriate', *Australian Letters*, vol. 1, no. 3 (April 1958), pp. 35–7.

56   Patrick White, 'The Prodigal Son', *Australian Letters*, vol. 1, no. 3 (April 1958), pp. 37–40.

57   Ray Mathew, 'Uncountable within our hearts' (Interview by Kate Jennings), *Voices*, vol. 3, no. 3 (Spring 1993), p. 16.

58   Mathew, 'Uncountable within our hearts', pp. 5–20.

59   Ray Mathew, 'The Australian Tradition', *London Magazine*, vol. 2, no. 6 (September 1962), pp. 62–8.

60   Jack Lindsay, 'The Alienated Australian Intellectual', *Meanjin*, 22, 1, March 1963, p. 49.

61   Lindsay, 'The Alienated Australian Intellectual', pp. 48–58.

62   Osborne, *Giving it Away*, pp. 111–14.

63   Osborne, *Giving it Away*, p. 114; Bennett, *Spirit in Exile*, p. 61 (Bennett's paraphrase of Porter).

64   Peter Porter, *A Porter Selected* (Oxford/Melbourne: Oxford University Press, 1989), p. 88.

65   Reproduced in Osborne, *Giving it Away*, p. 114.

66   Bennett, *Spirit in Exile*, p. 24.

67   Interview, *Westerly*, vol. 1 (March 1982), p. 49.

68   Bennett, *Spirit in Exile*, pp. 146, 143.

69   Bennett, *Spirit in Exile*, pp. xvi, 136–7. Bennett remarks on Porter's sense of his 'joint inheritances as an Australian and as a Londoner with an English wife' (Bennett's words), p. 91.

70   Interview, *Westerly*, p. 56; Bennett, *Spirit in Exile*, p. 137

71   Bennett, *Spirit in Exile*, pp. 169–70

72   Bennett, *Spirit in Exile*, pp. 178–9, Dunn cited at p. 143; John Lucas, *Modern English Poetry – From Hardy to Hughes: A Critical Survey* (London: B. T. Batsford, 1986).

73   Osborne, *Giving it Away*, pp. 203–4. Brett, 'Publishing, Censorship and Writers' Incomes 1965–1988', pp. 457–61.

74   Robin Dalton, 'My Australia', in Russell Braddon (ed.), *Australia Fair?* (London: Methuen, 1984), pp. 63–4.

75   Frank Moorhouse (ed.), *Days of Wine and Rage*, (Ringwood, Vic.: Penguin, 1980), pp. 181, 183–6.

76 Christopher Koch, *Crossing the Gap: A Novelist's Essays* (London: Hogarth Press/Chatto & Windus, 1987), pp. 32–47.

77 Robert Hughes in Geoffrey De Groen, *Some Other Dream: The Artist, the Artworld and the Expatriate* (Sydney: Hale and Iremonger, 1984); Clyde Packer, *No Return Ticket* (Sydney: Angus & Robertson, 1984), pp. 4–27.

78 Brett, 'Publishing, Censorship and Writers' Incomes 1965–1988', pp. 457–461.

7 Grander Stages: New Seasons for Australian Playwrights and Actors

1 Interviews drawn on and quoted in this chapter: Richard Beynon (November 1989), Michael Blakemore (January 1987), Fenella Maguire (November 1993), Keith Michell (November 1989), Jocelyn Rickards (November 1989), David Nettheim (January 1990), Terry Norris (September 1998), Madge Ryan (January 1991), Alan Seymour (November 1983, October 1987), Alan White (November 1982, November 1989).

2 Geoffrey Hutton, 'Australia 1955–56: A year of new hopes', in P. Holloway (ed.), *Contemporary Australian Drama* (Sydney: Currency Press, 1981, new edition 1987), pp. 3-4.

3 P. Parsons (ed.), *A Companion to Theatre in Australia* (Sydney: Currency Press/Cambridge University Press, 1995), p. 366. Blakemore wrote a novel about English repertory theatre, *Next Season* (London: Weidenfeld and Nicolson, 1969/ London: Faber and Faber, 1988).

4 See H. Tatlock Miller (ed.), *Loudon Sainthill* (London: Hutchinson, 1973). The younger Luciana Arrighi worked from the 1970s as production designer on Australian films (including *My Brilliant Career*, 1979), plays and operas, often designing for performances in London and Australia directed by Elijah Moshinsky, originally from Melbourne, as well as on films by John Schlesinger and Ken Russell.

5 See Hugh Hunt, 'The making of Australian theatre' in Holloway (ed.), *Contemporary Australian Drama*, pp. 11–16.

6 *Sunday Express*, 5.5.1957; Fenella Maguire, in Paris, kindly allowed me to copy her press clippings file (a photocopy of the file is now in the National Library of Australia).

7 *Times*, 7.3.1956.

8 John Sumner, *Recollections at Play* (Melbourne: Melbourne University Press, 1993), p. 72; *New York Times*, 19.1.1958.

9 *Daily Mail*, 1.5.1957; *Scotsman*, 16.4.1957.

10 *New York Herald Tribune*, 19.1.1958.

11 'Such a shake-up for the snobs', *Sunday Express*, 5.5.1957; *New York Herald Tribune*, 19.1.1958.

12 'Playwriting' by K. Brisbane in Parsons (ed.), *A Companion to Theatre in Australia*, p. 454; see also Ray Mathew, 'Uncountable within our hearts' (Interview by Kate Jennings), *Voices*, vol. 3, no. 3 (Spring 1993).

13 *Melbourne Herald*, 23.4.1957.

14 Sumner, *Recollections at Play*, pp. 116–19; Jennifer Palmer, 'Alan Seymour', interview in J. Palmer (ed.), *Contemporary Australian Playwrights* (Adelaide: Adelaide University Press, 1979), pp. 56–68.

15 A. Seymour, 'Australian Theatre – Afterword from an Exile', *Theatre Quarterly*, vol. 7, no. 26 (Summer 1997), pp. 86-7. Ray Lawler believes that Sumner and

Hunt achieved a great deal in the face of difficult odds. R. Lawler–S. Alomes, 12.2.1999.

16 Seymour, 'Australian Theatre – Afterword from an Exile', pp. 86–7; Alex Buzo, *The Young Person's Guide to the Theatre and Almost Everything Else* (Ringwood, Vic.: Penguin, 1988), pp. 67–8.

17 'Ray Lawler', interview in Jennifer Palmer (ed.), *Contemporary Australian Playwrights*, p. 48.

18 A. A. Phillips, 'The Cultural Cringe' in his *The Australian Tradition: Studies in a Colonial Culture* (Melbourne: Cheshire, 1958), p. 92 note.

19 'Ray Lawler' in Palmer (ed.), *Contemporary Australian Playwrights*, pp. 48–50.

20 'Ray Lawler', *Contemporary Australian Playwrights*, pp. 44, 51.

21 Ray Lawler, Hazel de Berg interview, National Library of Australia, October 1971, pp. 6374–8; William H. Wilde, Joy Hooton, Barry Andrews (eds), *Oxford Companion to Australian Literature* (Melbourne: Oxford University Press, first edition, 1985), pp. 619–20, (second edition, 1994), p. 686.

22 'Ray Lawler' in Palmer (ed.), *Contemporary Australian Playwrights* pp. 47, 53.

23 Ray Lawler, *The Piccadilly Bushman* (London: Angus & Robertson, 1961), pp. 70–1, 47, 104, 48–50.

24 Lawler, *The Piccadilly Bushman*, pp. 77–8, 85–6.

25 'Alan Seymour' in Palmer (ed.), *Contemporary Australian Playwrights*, p. 67.

26 'Summer PM', ABC Radio, 16.1.1997. The Playbox Theatre in Melbourne has had several seasons in the 1990s dominated by *new* Australian plays.

27 'Alan Seymour', *Contemporary Australian Playwrights*, p. 57.

28 'Alan Seymour', p. 67.

29 *Age*, 30.7.1964.

30 'Richard Beynon', *Media Information Australia*, vol. 43 (February 1987), p. 29.

31 John Elsom and Nicholas Tomalin, *The History of the National Theatre* (London: Jonathan Cape, 1978), pp. 311–28.

32 Ray Barrett (with Peter Corris), *Ray Barrett: An Autobiography* (Sydney: Random House, 1995).

33 *Report of the Select Committee on the Encouragement of Australian Productions for Television* (Vincent Report), Commonwealth of Australia, Canberra, 1963, pp. 1–2.

34 M. MacCallum (ed.), *Ten Years of Australian Television* (Melbourne: Sun, 1968), pp. 68, 83.

35 Vincent Report, pp. 16, 18, 17.

36 He took over the *Showman* job from the scriptwriter, and later Australian TV drama maker, Rex Rienits. Charles 'Bud' Tingwell sometimes filled in for Nettheim.

37 *Australian*, 16.10.1979; *Advertiser*, 28.10.1982.

38 *Sydney Morning Herald*, 21.2.1970.

8 Long and Winding Musical Roads: The Careers of Australian Expatriates and Australian Music

1 Interviews drawn on and quoted in this chapter: Peter Andry (January 1991), Morris Barr (September 1991), Geoffrey Chard (August 1991), David Lumsdaine (November 1992), Charles Mackerras (December 1989), Yvonne Minton (November 1983), Geoffrey Parsons (December 1989), Joan Sutherland (August 1990), Barry Tuckwell (November 1989), Malcolm Williamson (November 1983).

2 See Don Banks Papers, MS 6830, National Library of Australia; *Canberra Times*, 15.1.1972, 26.7.1981; *Sydney Morning Herald*, 6.9.1980; *Times*, 1.9.1962; Philip Bracanin, 'Don Banks' in F. Callaway and D. Tunley (eds), *Australian Composition in the Twentieth Century* (Melbourne: Oxford University Press, 1978), pp. 108–9.

3 Bracanin, 'Don Banks', pp. 110–11.

4 Bracanin, 'Don Banks', p. 109.

5 See: 'David Lumsdaine, Quintessential Australian' (interview), *Sounds Australian: Journal of Australian Music*, vol. 27 (Spring 1990), pp. 18, 22. In the same issue: Malcolm Williamson, 'Black and white nomads', p. 15; and S. Alomes, 'Home and away: The expatriation of Australian performers and creators to Britain (1945–1990)', pp. 12–14.

6 Brian Chatterton, 'Malcolm Williamson' in F. Callaway and D. Tunley (eds), *Australian Composition in the Twentieth Century* (Melbourne: Oxford University Press, 1978), p. 146.

7 *West Australian*, 11.11.1969.

8 Chatterton, 'Malcolm Williamson', pp. 146–55; 'The music master', pp. 108–13.

9 ANU Creative Arts Fellowships files, Chancelry, Australian National University; 'Notes on the History of the Australian Musical Association', ts; Annual General Meetings file; 'Notes on meeting to discuss formation of Australian Musical Association', Australia House, 16.2.1952 (5 pp.), 1973, p. 1; Australian Musical Association Papers, MS 7996, National Library of Australia.

10 'Notes on the History of the Australian Musical Association', ts pp. 1–2.

11 'Notes on the History of the Australian Musical Association', ts p. 3.

12 'Notes on the History of the Australian Musical Association', ts p. 4.

13 Sydney *Sun*, 22.11.1969.

14 Chard was secretary for five years, until he resigned due to 'the pressure of commitments' in 1975, and an enduring general committee member. (At times he was treasurer.) Australian Musical Association, committee minutes, 15.9.1975.

15 Australian Musical Association, committee minutes, 17.1.1972, p. 2, Australian Musical Association Papers, MS 7996, National Library of Australia. The AMA received a $3000 grant for 1971.

16 Phillip Sametz, *Play On! 60 Years of Music-Making with the Sydney Symphony Orchestra* (Sydney: ABC Books, 1992), p. 218; A. L. McLeod, 'Music' in A. L. McLeod (ed.), *The Pattern of Australian Culture* (Ithaca, N.Y.: Cornell University Press, 1963), p. 405.

17 Dame Joan Hammond, who had first studied in Europe, went to Britain at the time of the war. She made a continuing contribution over 30 years in Victoria, following her return to Australia in 1965. So did Florence Austral (nee Wilson), who returned to Australia at the end of World War II when in her 50s, having finished performing in London. She later taught at the Newcastle Conservatorium from 1954 to 1959. (Ann Atkinson, Linsay Knight and Margaret McPhee (eds), *Dictionary of the Performing Arts*, Sydney: Allen & Unwin, 1996, vol. 2, pp. 102, 14).

18 Quoted in Stephen Murray-Smith (ed.), *The Dictionary of Australian Quotations* (Melbourne: Heinemann, 1984), p. 183.

19 See Brian Adams, *La Stupenda* (Sydney: Vintage, revised edition, 1993), chapter 9.

20 Helen Bainton, *Facing the Music: An Orchestral Player's Notebook* (Sydney: Currawong, 1967), pp. 117–29.

21 Joan Sutherland, 'Tall Poppies' in Russell Braddon (ed.), *Australia Fair?* (London: Methuen, 1984), pp. 148–150.

22 *Australarts*, no. 1 (1966), p. 21.

23 C. Buttrose, *Playing for Australia: A Story about the ABC Orchestras and Music in Australia* (Melbourne: ABC/Macmillan, 1982), p. 70. Hopkins cited in same publication, p. 70.

24 In a society which had just begun to modify its traditional 'White Australia Policy', the SSO did however make an appointment which was ahead of its time in other ways – of the European-based Afro-American Dean Dixon as chief conductor. On the frustrating experience of one staff conductor, and composer, see Jennifer Hill 'Clive Douglas and the ABC: not a favourite aunt' in N. Brown et al., *One Hand on the Manuscript: Music in Australian Cultural History* (Canberra: Humanities Research Centre, Australian National University, 1995).

25 Nancy Phelan, *Charles Mackerras: A Musician's Musician* (Melbourne: Oxford University Press, 1987 and London: Victor Gollancz, 1987), pp. 122–3, 131–5.

26 Phelan, *Charles Mackerras*, p. 136.

27 Material quoted is cited in Sametz, *Play On!*, pp. 220–3.

28 Sydney *Daily Mirror*, 13.7.1967.

29 Bracanin, 'Don Banks', p. 113.

30 Doug Aiton, 'Stairway to Stardom', *Sunday Age*, 7.3.1993.

31 'Notes on the History of the Australian Musical Association', p. 5, Australian Musical Association Papers, MS 7996, National Library of Australia.

32 This was the $10 000 Britannica Australia Award. Its denial on these grounds disgusted Patrick White, who remarked that such small-mindedness explained why he had, 'for some time past, felt a foreigner in this pathetically chauvinist parish'. See H. Rowley, *Christina Stead* (Port Melbourne: Heinemann, 1993), pp. 462–5.

33 Don Banks–Antony Jeffrey, Director, Music Board, Australia Council, 18.7.1975, Don Banks Papers, MS 6830, National Library of Australia; ANU Creative Arts Fellowships files, Chancellery, Australian National University.

34 'Don Banks must not escape again', *Sunday Australian*, 28.5.1972.

35 Don Banks, ABC 'Guest of Honour', ts, 5.4.1970, National Library of Australia, p. 1.

36 Speech by Dr H. C. Coombs, 23.10.1973, Don Banks Papers, MS 6830, National Library of Australia.

37 *Herald*, 18.3.1970.

38 Bracanin, 'Don Banks', pp. 97–116.

39 *Herald*, 24.7.1972.

40 Don Banks–Antony Jeffrey, Director, Music Board, Australia Council, 18.7.1975, Don Banks Papers, MS6830, National Library of Australia.

41 Report, Sydney *Sun*, 28.2.1970; headline, Melbourne *Age*, 28.2.1970.

42 The singer-composer, Chook, in the Tim Gooding play, *King of Country* (Sydney: Currency Press, 1992), p. 25.

43 W. L. Hoffman, *Canberra Times* review, undated clipping (1967?), Australian High Commission library files; Stephanie Bunbury, 'Williamson faces the music', *Herald*, 5.12.1990.

44 Sydney *Sunday Telegraph*, 20.7.1967.

45 S. F. Pearce, *24 Hours* (June 1987), pp. 10–11.

46 Pearce, June 1987, p. 10.

47 On the several Acts tightening entry (1962, 1968, 1971 and 1981) see: S. S. Juss, *Immigration, Nationality and Citizenship* (London: Mansell (Cassell), 1993), pp. 40–55.

48 Don Banks–Patrick Thomas, 26.4.1973, Don Banks Papers, MS 6830, National Library of Australia, Folder 23.

49 Australian Musical Association, committee minutes, 15.9.1975, Australian Musical Association Papers, MS 7996, National Library of Australia (on meeting with Mr Ken Tribe of the Australia Council). In 1975, the Association also faced reduced Australian High Commission assistance and the disappearance of the *Australian News*, a useful vehicle for publicising concerts. Chairman's Report, 1974/5, p. 2. The Australian Musical Foundation in London – notes provided by Peter Andry, 16.1.1990. By then the Foundation had 'bestowed more than £60 000 on nearly 30 young Australians'.

50 Geoff Fiddian, ABC staffer and Assistant Concert Manager, Victoria, 1957–1987, who often travelled with Parsons. Communication to S. Alomes, 7.9.1998.

51 Fiddian, communication to S. Alomes.

52 Sametz, *Play On!*, pp. 289–96; Phelan, *Charles Mackerras*, pp. 223–4.

53 Sametz, *Play On!*, pp. 335, 323, 336–8.

54 Norma Major, *Joan Sutherland* (London: Queen Anne Press/Futura, 1987), p. 157.

9 The Yellow Brick Road to the Land of *OZ* . . . and beyond

1 Interviews drawn on and quoted in this chapter: Don Atyeo (December 1989), Richard Neville (May 1991), Craig McGregor (September 1998), Jill Neville (November 1983), Geoffrey Robertson (December 1989), Marsha Rowe (November 1989), Martin Sharp (November 1983).

2 R. Neville, *Hippie Hippie Shake* (Melbourne: Heinemann, 1995), pp. 56, 58–67; R. Neville, *Playpower* (London: Paladin, 1971).

3 Richard Neville, interview by Hazel de Berg, March 1975; Martin Sharp, interview by Hazel de Berg, June 1970; de Berg interviews, Oral History Collection, National Library of Australia. Neville, *Hippie Hippie Shake*, chapter 5.

4 Neville, *Hippie Hippie Shake*, pp. 58–67.

5 *Official Yearbook of the Commonwealth of Australia no. 38 – 1951*, Canberra, 1951, p. 561; *Official Yearbook of the Commonwealth of Australia, no. 5 – 1969*, Canberra, 1969, pp. 138–41; *Yearbook Australia no. 65 – 1981*, Canberra, 1981, p. 108. Ex-settlers were excluded from the 10 000 permanent departees in 1975.

6 P. Plowman, *Emigrant Ships to Luxury Liners* (Sydney: University of New South Wales Press, 1992).

7 L. Turner and J. Ash, *The Golden Hordes: International Tourism and the Pleasure Periphery* (London: Constable, 1975), chapter 6; Neville, *Hippie Hippie Shake*, chapter 5.

8 On Britain, see: A. Marwick, *British Society since 1945* (Harmondsworth: Penguin, 1982). On Australia, see: Neville, *Hippie Hippie Shake*, chapter 3; C. McGregor, *People, Politics and Pop: Australians in the Sixties* (Sydney: Ure Smith, 1968), 'Alfs and Anti-Alfs'; S. Alomes, *A Nation at Last? The Changing Character of Australian Nationalism 1880–1988* (Sydney: Angus & Robertson, 1988), chapter 6; D. Horne, *Time of Hope, Australia 1966–72* (Sydney: Angus & Robertson, 1980); Richard

Neville, de Berg interview; Richard Walsh, de Berg interview, National Library of Australia, December 1974; Sharp, de Berg interview, 1970.

9   Neville, *Hippie Hippie Shake*, pp. 66–7.

10 On the Sixties and the counter-culture in Britain see: J. Green (ed.), *Days in the Life: Voices from the English Underground 1961–71* (London: Minerva, 1989); E. Nelson, *The British Counter-Culture 1966–73* (London: Macmillan, 1989); N. Fountain, *Underground: the London Alternative Press 1966–74* (London: Comedia, 1988).

11 McGregor, *People, Politics and Pop*, pp. 86–8.

12 J. Salter, *A Pinch of Salt* (Sydney: Angus and Robertson, 1995), p. 108; C. Raye, 'Memories of Mavis', *Sydney Morning Herald Good Weekend*, 5.11.1994.

13 Neville, *Hippie Hippie Shake*, pp. 21–2; Neville later published Lenny Bruce in *OZ* (Neville, *Hippie Hippie Shake*, p. 34).

14 Neville, de Berg interview, pp. 10843–5.

15 Walsh, de Berg interview, pp. 10514–5.

16 Neville, de Berg interview, p. 10845.

17 Walsh, de Berg interview, p. 10516; see also B. Ellis, *Letters to the Future* (North Ryde: Methuen Haynes, 1987), chapter 2.

18 Walsh, de Berg interview, p. 10517.

19 Walsh, de Berg interview, pp. 10520–1; Neville, de Berg interview, pp. 10845–51.

20 See: J. Ogilvie, *The Push: An Impressionist Memoir* (Sydney: Primavera, 1995); B. Harcourt, 'The Push', *National Times*, 3–8.2.1975, pp. 28–31; Anne Coombs, *Sex and Anarchy* (Ringwood, Vic.: Viking, 1996). On Professor John Anderson, the Sydney libertarian philosopher of more conventional mien, from whom the Push's ideas of an oppositional, questioning attitude in part derived, see: A. J. Baker, *Anderson's Social Philosophy* (Sydney: Angus & Robertson, 1979); Brian Kennedy, *A Passion to Oppose: John Anderson, Philosopher* (Melbourne: Melbourne University Press, 1995); for the continuing nostalgic/critical debates and memoirs of Andersonianism from the 1970s onwards, see the newsletters *Broadsheet* ('Published by Sydney Libertarians') and the later *Heraclitus*.

21 See: John Docker, *Australian Cultural Elites: Intellectual Traditions in Sydney and Melbourne* (Sydney: Angus & Robertson, 1974); J. Lindsay, *Fanfrolico and After* (London: The Bodley Head, 1962); C. Munro, *Wild Man of Letters: The Story of P. R. Stephensen* (Melbourne: Melbourne University Press, 1984); J. F. Williams, *The Quarantined Culture: Australian Reactions to Modernism* (Cambridge: Cambridge University Press, 1995).

22 Harcourt, 'The Push', p. 31.

23 *OZ*: 11 (July 1964) p. 9; 10 (June 1964), p. 5; 9 (May 1964) p. 7; 8 (April 1964), pp. 3, 9.

24 Neville, de Berg interview, pp. 10841–3.

25 Neville, *Hippie Hippie Shake*, pp. 50, 54–5.

26 McGregor, *People, Politics and Pop*, pp. 85–90; K. Buckley, *Offensive and Obscene: A Civil Liberties Casebook* (Sydney: Ure Smith, 1970), chapter 2.

27 Walsh, de Berg interview, p. 10519.

28 Neville, de Berg interview, pp. 10848–52; Sharp, de Berg interview, p. 51919.

29 Don Atyeo, interviewed by Jonathan Green, June 1989, transcript provided by the interviewer.

30 Neville, *Hippie Hippie Shake*, passim.

31 Neville, *Hippie Hippie Shake*, passim; J. Green, *Days in the Life*, passim.

32 Sharp, de Berg interview, pp. 51914, 51911–13.

33 Sharp, de Berg interview, pp. 51918, 51921–2.

34 T. Palmer, *The Trials of OZ* (London: Blond & Briggs, 1971), pp. 25–6.

35 Neville, *Hippie Hippie Shake*, pp. 248–54, 258, 351; Palmer, *The Trials of OZ*, pp. 14–17.

36 Quoted in Green, *Days in the Life*, p. 398.

37 Neville, *Hippie Hippie Shake*, p. 349; Neville, de Berg interview, pp. 10868–70.

38 Walsh, de Berg interview, 1974.

39 Neville, de Berg interview, 1991.

40 M. Rowe, interview by Jonathan Green, transcript provided by the interviewer; M. Rowe, 'Workin' for the (underground) man', *Inside Story*, n.d. (ca 1971–72).

41 Rowe interview, Jonathan Green.

42 Rowe interview, Jonathan Green.

43 M. Rowe (ed.), *Spare Rib Reader*, 'Introduction' (Harmondsworth: Penguin, 1982).

44 Several kept up Australian connections and interests: Carole Spedding was the London publicist of the Literature Board of the Australia Council in 1988–89; Marsha Rowe, as editor, published pieces by Jill Neville and Kathy Lette; Stephanie Dowrick and Dale Spender both returned to Australia with their partners, Dale Spender becoming an active advocate, through the Australian Society of Authors, for authors' rights in the electronic era.

10 Journalists' Journeys

1 Interviews drawn on and quoted in this chapter: Lewis Chester (November 1983), Tony Clifton (November 1983, January 1986), Anthony Delano (December 1985, June 1992), Michael Davie (March 1992), Scarth Flett (November 1989), John Garrett (December 1989), Bernie Giuliano (July 1997), Roslyn Grose (November 1983), Godfrey Hodgson, Sandra Jobson (November 1982), Phillip Knightley (November 1983; Sydney, January 1986), Alan Lowery (December 1982), Nelson Mews (November 1989), Alex Mitchell (December 1989), David Munro (December 1989), Bruce Page (November 1983), John Pilger (November 1983, November 1989), Barry Porter (July 1997), Michael Provis (February 1997), Murray Sayle (August 1990, January 1991, May 1997), Tessa Sayle (November 1983), William Shawcross (June 1991), Peter Thompson (December 1985, December 1989), Barbara Toner (November 1982), Judy Wade (November 1983).

2 Valerie Lawson, *Connie Sweetheart: The Story of Connie Robertson* (Port Melbourne: Heinemann Australia, 1990), p. 298.

3 Phillip Knightley, *A Hack's Progress* (London: Jonathan Cape, 1997), p. 98.

4 Christopher Booker, *The Neophiliacs* (London: Fontana, 1970), pp. 46–8, 79–80.

5 Denis Hamilton, *Editor-in-Chief* (London: Hamish Hamilton, 1989), pp. 108–11; Harold Hobson, Phillip Knightley, Leonard Russell, *The Pearl of Days: An Intimate Memoir of the Sunday Times 1822–1972* (London: Hamish Hamilton, 1972), pp. 407–9; Harold Evans, *Good Times, Bad Times* (London: Weidenfeld and Nicolson, 1983).

6 Hobson, *The Pearl of Days*, pp. 407–9. Sayle, ever the freelancer, was not formally a member of the Insight team, although he worked on many of its stories.

7 Hobson, *The Pearl of Days*, pp. 422–7; Evans, *Good Times, Bad Times*, pp. 16–17.

8 Michael Tracey, *In the Culture of the Eye: Ten Years of Weekend World* (London: Hutchinson, 1983), pp. 35–7.

9 Evans, *Good Times, Bad Times*, pp. 13, 16–17.

10 P. Knightley, *The First Casualty: The War Correspondent as Hero, Propagandist and Myth Maker* (London: André Deutsch, 1975).

11 Jeff Waters, 'Watching the flexible conspiracy', *Canberra Times*, 5.7.1987, reports Knightley's subsequent Canberra talk, delivered under the same constrictions as the Sydney literary lunch.

12 Evans, *Good Times, Bad Times*, pp. 55–6.

13 Evans, *Good Times, Bad Times*, pp. 42–3.

14 Evans, *Good Times, Bad Times*, p. 48.

15 Hobson, *The Pearl of Days*, p. 474.

16 Knightley, *A Hack's Progress*, p. 103.

17 Knightley, *A Hack's Progress*, p. 249; Evans, *Good Times, Bad Times*, pp. 6–7, 64.

18 Evans, *Good Times, Bad Times*, pp. 7–8.

19 Sayle, 'As far as you can go', pp. 103, 121, 114.

20 Knightley, *A Hack's Progress*, pp. 253–4.

21 Knightley, *A Hack's Progress*, pp. 249–51.

22 P. Knightley, *The Second Oldest Profession: The Spy as Bureaucrat, Patriot, Fantasist and Whore* (London: André Deutsch, 1986), p. ix.

23 Pat Burgess, *Warco: Australian Reporters at War* (Richmond, Vic.: Heinemann Australia, 1986); W. Burchett, *Passport* (Melbourne: Nelson, 1969); W. Burchett, *At the Barricades* (Melbourne: Macmillan, 1981); W. Burchett, *Shadows of Hiroshima* (London: Verso, 1983); Tim Bowden, *One Crowded Hour* (Sydney: William Collins, 1987).

24 Burgess, *Warco*, p. 224.

25 Murray Sayle, 'A reporter at large: closing the file on Flight 007', *New Yorker*, 13.12.1993. 'Letter from Hiroshima: Did the Bomb End the War?', *New Yorker*, 31. 7.1995, pp. 40–64.

26 *Canada Train: Last Train to Medicine Hat* (video in possession of Murray Sayle).

27 Barbara Toner's books include: (Non-fiction) *Double Shift: A Practical Guide for Working Mothers* (London: Arrow, 1975); *The Facts of Rape* (London: Hutchinson, 1977). (Fiction) *Brain Street* (London: Macdonald, 1986); *Married Secrets: Tales from Tessa Wood* (London: Futura, 1984); *The Need to be Famous* (London: Macdonald, 1988); *An Organised Woman* (London: Hutchinson, 1996) and the 'handbook', *A Mother's Guide to Life* (London: Hodder & Stoughton, 1997).

28 Sandra Jobson Darroch, *Ottoline: the Life of Lady Ottoline Morrell* (London: Chatto & Windus, 1976); Sandra Jobson, *Blokes: An Endangered Species* (Sydney: Pan, 1984); Sandra Jobson, *Paul Hogan: The Real Life Crocodile Dundee* (London: W. H. Allen, 1988).

29 Robert Darroch, *D. H. Lawrence in Australia* (South Melbourne: Macmillan, 1981).

30 Judy Wade, *Charles and Diana: Inside a Royal Marriage* (London: Angus & Robertson, 1987).

31 John Pilger, *Heroes* (London: Pan, 1987, paperback/London: Jonathan Cape, 1986, hardback), p. 45.

32 Peter Thompson and Anthony Delano, *Maxwell: A Portrait of Power* (London: Corgi, 1988), Sam White, *Sam White's Paris* (London: New English Library, 1983), Richard Hughes, *Barefoot Reporter* (Hong Kong: Far Eastern Economic Review, 1984) (Foreword by Derek Davies).

33 Pilger, *Heroes*, p. 545.

34 Pilger, *Heroes*, p. 41.

35 Pilger, *Heroes*, pp. 49–50.

36 Pilger, *Heroes*, pp. 54–9.

37 'John Pilger', biographical ts, 1982, p. 3. (Typescript in possession of the author.)

38 Pilger, *Heroes*, pp. 579–81.

39 J. Pilger, 'The world's greatest suburb', *Nova*, July 1969, 56–9; J. Pilger, *A Secret Country* (London: Jonathan Cape, 1989; London: Vintage, updated edition, 1992).

40 Pilger, 'The world's greatest suburb', p. 56; John Pilger, 'Why I love Australia', *Sydney Morning Herald Good Weekend*, 22.11.1986, pp. 42–6.

41 Pilger, 'The world's greatest suburb', p. 58.

42 Pilger, 'The world's greatest suburb', pp. 56–8.

43 Pilger, 'The world's greatest suburb', p. 56; Pilger, *A Secret Country*, pp. 3–5, chapter 6.

44 Sarah Bosley, 'A tabloid hero in black and white', *Guardian*, 16.10.1989, p. 19.

45 Cited in David Langsam, 'Not controversial, not campaigning . . . just a journalist', *TNT Magazine*, no. 387, 28.1.1991, pp. 14–15.

46 *Backchat*, ABC TV, 25.3.1987; 'John Pilger unleashes his Bicentenary tirade', *Age Green Guide* 28.1.1988; Sydney *Sun-Herald*, Radio, 31.12.1989.

47 J. Pilger and M. Coren, *The Outsiders* (London: Quartet, 1985), pp. 9–10.

48 Pilger, *A Secret Country*, p. 5.

49 Pilger, *A Secret Country*, pp. 4–6. Pilger's critique of several regimes would be developed in *Hidden Agendas* (London: Vintage, 1998). His role in the unsuccessful attempt to create an alternative newspaper is discussed in Peter Chippindale and Chris Horrie, *Disaster! The Rise and Fall of News on Sunday* (London: Sphere, 1988).

50 Pilger, *A Secret Country*, pp. 10–11, 19.

51 Pilger, *Heroes*, pp. 28–9.

52 Pilger, *A Secret Country*, p. 161; Pilger, *Heroes*, p. 545.

53 Tony Clifton, quoted in Burgess, *Warco*, pp. 166–8; Tony Clifton and Catherine Leroy, *God Cried* (London: Quartet, 1983).

54 Burgess, *Warco*, pp. 166–8.

55 Quoted in Rob Nixon, *London Calling: V. S. Naipaul, Postcolonial Mandarin* (New York: Oxford University Press, 1992), p. 20.

56 Pilger, *Heroes*, back cover quotation from Rushdie [Pan edition]; *Heroes*, p. 543 (Eliot paraphrased).

11 Crucible to Firmament: Barry Humphries, Germaine Greer and Clive James and the Expatriate Search for Fame

1 Interviews drawn on and quoted in this chapter: Michael Davie (March 1992), Nigel Dempster (December 1989), John Garrett (December 1989), Germaine Greer (November 1983), Peter Grose (November 1982), Bruce Page (November 1983), John Pilger (November 1983, November 1989), Peter Porter (December 1982), Murray Sayle (January 1991).

2 Ian Britain, *Once an Australian* (Melbourne: Oxford University Press, 1997). They received few awards and fewer honorary degrees, unlike expatriates in music. Humphries was made an Officer of the Order of Australia in 1982, and also received an honorary doctorate from Griffith University in Brisbane. James was made a Member of the Order of Australia in 1992.

3 B. Humphries, *A Nice Night's Entertainment* (Sydney: Currency Press, 1981), pp. 71–4.

4 B. Humphries, *More Please: An Autobiography* (Ringwood, Vic.: Penguin, 1992), chapter 1; John Lahr, *Dame Edna Everage and the Rise of Western Civilisation: Backstage with Barry Humphries* (London: Flamingo/Harper Collins, 1992), p. 66.

5 Humphries, *More Please*, pp. 20–3.

6 Chester Eagle, *Play Together, Dark Blue Twenty* (Melbourne: McPhee Gribble, 1986), pp. 12, 18, 22, 25.

7 Humphries, *More Please*, pp. 83–94.

8 Humphries, *A Nice Night's Entertainment*, pp. 3–9.

9 Humphries, *More Please*, p. 163.

10 Humphries, *More Please*, pp. 155–71.

11 Humphries, *More Please*, pp. 187, 193, 203–6, 219–27, 225; Murray Sayle–S. Alomes, 15.7.1998.

12 Peter Coleman, *The Real Barry Humphries* (London: Robson Books, 1990), pp. 98–103. The private school skier who was always doing 'a bit of business for the old man' became less prominent.

13 Barry Humphries, 'Detrimental Blokes', Foreword to Keith Dunstan, *Knockers* (North Melbourne: Cassell, 1972), p. xi.

14 Humphries, *More Please*, pp. xiii–xiv.

15 Lahr, *Dame Edna Everage*, pp. 59–66.

16 Lahr, *Dame Edna Everage*, pp. 64–5.

17 Coleman, *The Real Barry Humphries*, pp. 72, 82–3; Humphries, *More Please*, pp. 194–8, 210–18.

18 On conservatism and conflict in the Sixties see S. Alomes, *A Nation at Last?* (Sydney: Angus & Robertson, 1988), chapter 6.

19 Humphries, *More Please*, pp. 208–9.

20 Humphries, *More Please*, pp. 188–9, 203, 219, 246–7.

21 Humphries, *More Please*, pp. 228–35.

22 In 1966, Sidney J. Baker published a revised edition of his 1945 classic, *The Australian Language* (Sydney: Currawong, 1966), while popular interest was evinced by 'Afferbeck Lauder', *Let's Talk Strine* (Sydney: Ure Smith, 1965) by Alistair Morrison.

23 The successful *The Adventures of Barry McKenzie* (1972), starring Barry Crocker, was followed by the sequel *Barry McKenzie Holds His Own* (1974), an artistic and popular flop. The first moves to reduce censorship had been taken by the small 'l' Liberal, Don Chipp, Minister for Customs and Excise in the Gorton and McMahon governments of the late 1960s/early 1970s. The Australian film revival began with romantic 'feminine' films on the one hand (*Picnic at Hanging Rock, My Brilliant Career*) and urban and 'Ocker' comedies basking in the broad richness of Australian English on the other.

24 Patrick White believed that his 1974 Australian of the Year award should have been shared with the historian Manning Clark, the Builders' Labourers Federation secretary and creator of 'Green Bans' to save buildings and parks, Jack Mundey, and Barry Humphries. D. Marr, *Patrick White: A Life* (Sydney: Random House, 1991), p. 544.

25 See S. Alomes, 'Class, beauty and goodness: beauties and beasts on the football shows' in S. Alomes and B. Stewart (eds), *High Mark: Australian Football and Australian Culture* (Hawthorn, Vic.: Maribyrnong Press, 1998), pp. 54–8.

26 Coleman, *The Real Barry Humphries*, p. 90 (Coleman's summary).

27 Some people suggested that Gunston was thinking of Carly Simon's 'You're so vain'.

28 Humphries, *More Please*, p. 219.

29 Lahr, *Dame Edna Everage*, pp. 1–2. It was a repeat of his 1987–8 revue.

30 Les A. Murray, quoted in S. Alomes, 'The British press and Australia', *Meanjin*, vol. 46, no. 2 (June 1987), p. 177.

31 Coleman, *The Real Barry Humphries*, pp. 138–42.

32 Coleman, *The Real Barry Humphries*, p. 142.

33 Barry Humphries, 'The Getting of Ignorance: Melbourne Schooldays', *Bulletin*, 20.8.1977, pp. 40–42.

34 Coleman, *The Real Barry Humphries*, pp. 115–17.

35 Coleman, *The Real Barry Humphries*, p. 117.

36 Terry Lane, ABC Radio 3LO, 8.10.1992; *Face the Press*, SBS TV, 14.10.1992; *Review*, ABC TV, 13.10.1992.

37 *National Times*, 27.2.1983.

38 Coleman, *The Real Barry Humphries*, p. 163.

39 Craig McGregor, 'What's wrong with Barry Humphries', *National Times*, 3.10.1982, pp. 12–13.

40 Interviewed on 'Roy and H. G. – The Channel Nine Show', ABC TV, 18.4.1998.

41 Jim Davidson, 'The demons that drive Humphries', *Australian Society* (January–February 1992), pp. 24–7. As early as 1985, Brian Hoad, *Bulletin* arts critic, depicted an unchanged Humphries unaware of a changed Australia, under the heading, 'Barry Humphries' connecting link is wearing thin', *Bulletin*, 8.10.1985.

42 G. Dutton, *Out in the Open: An Autobiography* (St Lucia: University of Queensland Press, 1994), pp. 326–7.

43 Humphries, *More Please*, pp. 225, 240–1, 245–7; Britain, *Once an Australian*, p. 81. A member of Alcoholics Anonymous, Humphries won the battle, giving up the drink.

44 Mark Lawson, 'A man with four lives', *Age*, 10.1.1992.

45 C. Wallace, *Greer, Untamed Shrew* (Melbourne: Macmillan, 1997).

46 Wallace, *Greer*, pp. 9–11.

47 Wallace, *Greer*, pp. 1–13.

48 Paul Mansfield interview, *Age*, 8.4.1989.

49 'Germaine Greer' in Jackie Bennett and Rosemary Forgan (eds), *There's Something About a Convent Girl* (London: Virago, 1991), pp. 88–9.

50 *Sunday*, Channel 9, cover story, 21.9.1997.

51 Sister Raymonde, *Sunday*, Channel 9.

52 Wallace, *Greer*, p. 37; Clyde Packer, *No Return Ticket* (Sydney: Angus & Robertson, 1988), pp. 91, 93.

53 *Sunday*, Channel 9, 21.9.1997.

54 Packer, *No Return Ticket*, p. 94; *Mike Walsh Show*, Channel 9, 1.6.1984.

55 Interviewed by Margaret Throsby, ABC FM, 20.11.1996.

56 *Sunday*, Channel 9, 21.9.1997. On the Push see: Anne Coombs, *Sex and Anarchy* (Ringwood, Vic.: Viking, 1996); Judy Ogilvie, *The Push: An Impressionist Memoir* (Sydney: Primavera, 1995).

57 Robert Hewison, *Footlights! A Hundred Years of Cambridge Comedy* (London: Methuen, 1983), pp. 150–1.

58 Paul du Feu, *Let's Hear It for the Long-legged Women* (New York: Putnam, 1973, London: Angus & Robertson, 1974), p. 118.

59 Sonny Mehta, personal communication; Germaine Greer, *The Female Eunuch* (London: MacGibbon and Kee, 1970).

60 Britain, *Once an Australian*, p. 133; Wallace, *Greer*, p. 251

61 Wallace, *Greer*, chapter 9; Mary Spongberg, 'If She's So Great, How Come So Many Pigs Dig Her? Germaine Greer and the mainstream press', *Women's History Review*, vol. 2, no. 3 (1993), pp. 407–10, 415.

62 Wallace, *Greer*, chapter 12; Packer, *No Return Ticket*, p. 98.

63 Jeff Nuttall, *Bomb Culture* (London: MacGibbon and Kee, 1968, London: Granada, 1970); Humphrey McQueen, *A New Britannia* (Ringwood, Vic.: Penguin, 1970); Anne Summers, *Damned Whores and God's Police* (Ringwood, Vic.: Penguin, 1975). Faust's continuing critique is summarised in her *Apprenticeship in Liberty* (Sydney: Angus & Robertson, 1991), pp. 339–45.

64 Wallace, *Greer*; chapter 8, pp. 184–90, 194–6, 203–5. Amongst her critics in Britain (pp. 203–4) were the Australian socialist feminist Lynne Segal and the New Zealand expatriate and psychoanalytical feminist, Juliet Mitchell.

65 In the view of Spongberg, 'If She's So Great . . .', p. 414.

66 Keith Dunstan, *Ratbags* (Melbourne: Sun, 1980), pp. 233–7; Elisabeth Wynhausen, *Manly Girls* (Ringwood, Vic.: Penguin, 1989), pp. 149–50.

67 *Observer*, 8.8.1982.

68 Communication from Dr Christine Hubert, University of Florence, Poggi Bonsi, 1993.

69 Germaine Greer, literary lunch, Regent Hotel, Melbourne, 15.11.1991; Bunty Avieson, 'Germaine Greer down on the farm', *Australian Women's Weekly*, 22.2.1986, pp. 8–9.

70 'A bucket for Boadicea, PM', *Sunday Tasmanian*, 18.8.1985.

71 'A bucket for Boadicea, PM', *Sunday Tasmanian*, 18.8.1985.

72 *Herald Sun*, editorial, 15.10.1997, p. 18; Ramona Koval, 'Germaine thoughts', *Australian*, 18–19.10.1997 (Koval's summary).

73 Koval, 'Germaine thoughts', *Australian*, 18–19.10.1997.

74 *Herald Sun*, editorial, 15.10.1997.

75 *Age*, editorial, 'Greer and the second sex', 17.10.1997; Wallace, *Greer*, pp. 327–8.

76 Bennett and Forgan, *There's Something About a Convent Girl*, p. 89.

77 Wallace, *Greer*, chapters 3–5.

78 Sally Loane, 'Germaine and I: The Obstacle Race', *Sydney Morning Herald*, Spectrum, 27.9.1997.

79 Duncan Graham, 'A prophet in her own land', *Age*, 15.1.1988.

80 Term used in her 1998 *Who's Who* (Britain) entry.

81 B. Ellis, *Letters to the Future* (North Ryde: Methuen Haynes, 1987) pp. 7–26. See P. Coleman, *Bruce Beresford: Instincts of the Heart* (Sydney: Angus & Robertson, 1992).

82 Britain, *Once an Australian*, p. 205.

83 Clive James, *Unreliable Memoirs* (London: Picador, 1981), pp. 140–2, 150–1, 155, 160.

84 James, *Unreliable Memoirs*, pp. 135, 167.

85 Clive James, *Falling Towards England* (London: Jonathan Cape, 1985), pp. 15, 39–40.

86 James, *Unreliable Memoirs*, p. 168; James, *Falling Towards England*, pp. 15, 17, 24–31, 43, 49, 72, 82, 86–95.

87 James, *Unreliable Memoirs*, p. 134; *Falling Towards England*, pp. 44–5, 37–8; 'Clive James' in Craig McGregor, *Headliners: Craig McGregor's Social Portraits* (St Lucia: University of Queensland Press, 1990), pp. 13–14.

88 James, *Falling Towards England*, pp. 27–8, 64.

89 James, *Unreliable Memoirs*, pp. 26–37; Andrea Jones, 'A one night stand with Clive James', *Sunday Age*, 22.5.1994.

90 Ramona Koval, 'An Interview with Clive James', *Australian Book Review* (December 1996/January 1997), pp. 15–17.

91 Britain, *Once an Australian*, pp. 90–3.

92 Quoted by Britain, *Once an Australian*, p. 109.

93 *Observer*, 5.10.1980.

94 James, quoted by Lee Shrubb, 'Phallus in Chunderland', *Quadrant* (March 1986), pp. 84–5.

95 Hewison, *Footlights!*, pp. 155–61.

96 *New Statesman & Society*, 20.10.1989, pp. 50–1; *Daily Mirror*, 11.6.1981; *Age*, 17.10.1996; Andrea Jones, *Sunday Age*, 22.5.1994.

97 Shrubb, 'Phallus in Chunderland', p. 84.

98 M. Flanagan, 'Behind the Gift of the Gab', *Age*, 28.12.1991.

99 C. James, *The Metropolitan Critic* (London: Faber and Faber, 1974), on Germaine Greer, pp. 211–16, on Richard Neville, pp. 195–9, on Peter Porter, pp. 66–74; Clive James, *Flying Visits: Postcards from the Observer* (London: Jonathan Cape, 1984, London: Pan, 1985), on Barry Humphries, p. 20. On Humphries, Porter and the Australian poet Les Murray, see also Clive James, *Snakecharmers in Texas: Essays 1980–87* (London: Jonathan Cape, 1988), Part One: Australia's Sons; *Observer*, 5.10.1980, on Hughes.

100 Sandra Jobson, 'Clive James, on fame, peanut butter and Australians', *Australian Women's Weekly* (August 1983), p. 59.

101 Don Anderson, 'Clive's whingeing ways', *Sydney Morning Herald*, 22.10.1988.

102 See Alomes, 'The British press and Australia'.

103 In TV reports and in his print 'postcards' such as *Flying Visits*, 1984.

104 On A. D. Hope, see: 'Augustan Wattle' in James, *The Metropolitan Critic*, p. 203; *Observer*, 4.1.1981; James, *Flying Visits*, p. 20.

105 James, *Flying Visits*, p. 29.

106 Quoted by the contemporary novelist Shane Maloney, in a piece under the editor's confrontational headline – 'Will the real Clive James please shut up?', *Age*, Metro, 18.10.1996; observations on a nervous speaker from Melbourne Writers Festival director, Simon Clews, by telephone, 22.7.1998. (Hughes spoke at the then parallel Melbourne International Festival, both James and Greer at the separate Writers Festival.)

107 *Age*, 16.6.1994.

108 Letter, *London Review of Books*, 17–30.11.1983.

109 David Williamson, *Emerald City* (Sydney: Currency Press, 1987), p. 66.

110 Some things did not change. Germaine Greer and Barry Humphries would see out the last decade of the old century in their preferred way. In March 1999 Germaine Greer's book *The Whole Woman* (London/Sydney: Doubleday, 1999) was published simultaneously in Britain and Australia. In the new book, and even more in the thunderstorms of publicity surrounding it, Germaine Greer offered a mixture of residual feminist good sense and outrageous statements such as the linguistically

innovative 'Like all women of taste, I am a pederast. Boys rather than men' (*Age*, 22.2.1999). A timely doomism gave the book an appropriately millennialist character as she asserted, almost uniquely, that the oppression of women was worsening.

In early 1999 Barry Humphries returned to Australia with a new stage show with Edna in the lead, and a television series, *Barry Humphries Flashbacks*. While the film footage was fascinating, Humphries' narration left something to be desired. His remark about a film clip featuring the architect of the Sydney Opera House, that it was hard to create 'an interesting interview with a man called Joern' [Utzon] suggested that the 'yawn' was actually on Humphries. The social observer offered what the TV critic Shane Danielson (Radio National Breakfast, 23.2.99) described as a 'very jaundiced' view of the country he had left behind. Understandably many Australians were not enthralled by what Danielson termed Humphries 'rubbing our noses in it', once again.

12 Home and Identity

1 A. D. Hope, 'Australia', in A. D. Hope, *Collected Poems 1930–1965* (Sydney: Angus & Robertson, 1966).

2 Alan Freeman, rock n'roll music DJ, from 1960s to 1990s, thought himself 'the luckiest person in the world'. Perhaps, like Kylie Minogue, soap star and singer in London, who sang a similar song during the Australian invasion of the late 1980s, many of the postwar generation had been lucky.

3 Joan Sutherland, *A Prima Donna's Progress* (London: Orion and Sydney: Random House Australia, 1997), pp. 419–20; *Age*, 18.10.1996; *Sunday Age*, 7.3.1993; *Herald Sun*, 2.2.1991.

4 Henry Lawson, 'The Sydney *Bulletin*' in B. Kiernan (ed.), *Henry Lawson* (St Lucia: Queensland University Press, 1976), p. 355.

5 Geoffrey Robertson and Kathy Lette were regular southern summer visitors. Keith Michell had a place in Spain. Robin Dalton and Michael Blakemore, who both surfed regularly, retreated to Biarritz ('Royal Dalton', *Australian*, 26–27.9.1998); Anthony Delano went to the south of France, Ros and Peter Grose bought a holiday house in Brittany, and John Pilger also went to Italy.

6 Ann Atkinson Linsay Knight and Margaret McPhee (eds), *Dictionary of the Performing Arts in Australia* (Sydney: Allen & Unwin, 1996), vol. 2, pp. 194–5.

7 Bruce Wilson, 'Far from that old Oz cringe', *Mercury*, 14.2.1998. The old Australian dream of 'Wake up in Europe', the 'fabled realm', was sometimes now qualified. See A. Riemer, *The Habsburg Café* (Sydney: Angus & Robertson, 1993), p. 8. Ros Grose made another transition in the stressful 1990s, leaving journalism to conduct a practice using hypnotherapy to reduce stress. Events turned full circle for Peter Grose, distributing *Australian Women's Weekly* cookbooks in the UK for his former *Honi Soit* and *OZ* co-editor, Richard Walsh, now of Kerry Packer's Australian Consolidated Press.

8 *Age*, 12.12.1998

9 Delbridge's research was reported in Sidney J. Baker, *The Australian Language* (Melbourne: Sun: 1966), p. 455. Beverley Kingston, 'The lady and the Australian girl: some thoughts on nationalism and class', in A. Burns and N. Grieve (eds), *Australian Women: New Feminist Perspectives* (Melbourne: Oxford University Press, 1986).

10 A. Delamothe, 'Theatre, Film and Ballet', in T. B. Millar (ed.), *The Australian Contribution to Britain* (London: Australian Studies Centre, University of London, 1988), p. 71.

11 The 'independent' Melbourne cellist Alfred Hornung was reported as arguing that in Australia 'the artist is validated only through institutions'. *Age*, 21.3.1996.

12 Nancy Phelan, *Charles Mackerras: A Musician's Musician* (Melbourne: Oxford University Press, 1987), p. 223.

13 Anna King Murdoch, 'John Williams, anarchist, reigns on', *Age*, 14.6.1996.

14 Phillip Knightley, *A Hack's Progress* (London: Jonathan Cape, 1997), pp. 266–7.

15 *Sydney Morning Herald*, 26.12.1990, Melbourne *Herald Sun*, 19.2.1991.

16 See Tom Millar, 'Steps to change the image of the ugly Aussie abroad', *Age*, 7.2.1987.

17 Frank Moorhouse (ed.), *Days of Wine and Rage* (Ringwood, Vic.: Penguin, 1980), pp. 181–2. Moorhouse would later live for a time in France and become embroiled in national/international controversies in Australia over his book *Grand Days* (1993). Scholarships to study in Britain continued, including the *Sun* Aria (which had become the McDonald's Aria) and the Tait Memorial Trust scholarships, established from 1992. (*Sunday Age*, 13.12.1998)

18 *Age*, 15.9.1998. McCaughey's old job, curator of the National Gallery of Victoria, was available at the time. His views contrasted with the negative remarks about contemporary Australia made by three visiting North American expatriates, Jill Ker Conway, Shirley Hazzard and Ross Terrill. The 'roving patriate', the novelist and 'commuter' between Canada, the US and Australia, Janet Turner Hospital, did not share such views.

19 Jim Davidson (with John Reid), *A Showman's Story: The Memoirs of Jim Davidson* (Adelaide: Rigby, 1983), pp. 198–9. He felt ignored despite ABC General Manager Talbot Duckmanton's enthusiasm to bring him back. At the BBC, he was the 'blunt tough Australian' bandleader who had risen in this most British organisation and was farewelled with a 'Jim Davidson Christmas Day Special' broadcast, after nearly two decades (1948–1964) at the Beeb. Davidson, pp. 191, 195–6, 200.

20 Les Murray, 'Sidere mens eadem mutato' (the title of Murray's poem, and the Latin motto of Sydney University), *Collected Poems* (Port Melbourne: Heinemann, 1994).

21 Andrew Riemer, *Sandstone Gothic: Confessions of an Accidental Academic* (Sydney: Allen & Unwin, 1998), pp. 213–19.

22 Rob Nixon, *London Calling: V. S. Naipaul, Postcolonial Mandarin* (New York/Oxford: Oxford University Press, 1992), pp. 6, 37–43; Edward Said, *Orientalism* (New York: Vintage, 1979). See also: Paul Theroux, *Sir Vidia's Shadow* (London: Hamish Hamilton, 1998).

23 Lindy Davies has been head of drama at the Victorian College of the Arts since 1996, usually returning to London at least once a year to direct. See: 'In search of virtuosity', *Age*, 27.5.1997. See also 'Gale force', regarding the director Gale Edwards, *Age*, 2.8.1997, and 'Coming home for hot fudge and ice cream', regarding the director Jules Wright, *Age*, 28.7.1990.

24 A. Delamothe, 'Theatre, Film and Ballet', pp. 74–6.

25 It became the Sir Robert Menzies Centre for Australian Studies in 1988 after the government grant was withdrawn and the Menzies Foundation offered essential support.

26 Hogan had, however, done a TV program on 'Hoges' in London and some amusing beer advertisements for Fosters, which 'took the piss' out of the stuffier 'Brit' types, including wine connoisseurs.

27 Elijah Moshinsky, a guest on the Margaret Throsby ABC FM interview program, was promoted as the 'British director'. This 'citizen of the world' refuted the claim, describing himself as 'an Australian who lives in England'. ABC FM, 13.8.1998.

28 Marsha Rowe (ed.), *So Very English* (London: Serpents Tail, 1991).

29 Australian Society of Authors *Newsletter* (September 1998).

30 Sylvia Lawson, *The Archibald Paradox: A Strange Case of Authorship* (Ringwood, Vic.: Penguin, 1987), p. ix.

31 David Malouf, *A Spirit of Play: The Making of Australian Consciousness* (1998 Boyer Lectures) (Sydney: ABC Books, 1998), Lecture Four: 'Monuments to Time'.

32 David Williamson, 'Subsidies seed the soil of home-grown stories', *Sunday Age*, 13.9.1998.

33 'Royal Dalton', *Australian*, 26–27.9.1998.

Select Bibliography

Adams, Brian, *La Stupenda* (Sydney: Vintage, revised edition, 1993).

Adams, Brian, *Sidney Nolan: Such is Life* (Melbourne: Hutchinson, 1987).

Alomes, Stephen, 'The British Press and Australia', *Meanjin*, vol. 46, no. 2 (June 1987).

Alomes, Stephen and Jones, Catherine (eds), *Australian Nationalism: A Documentary History* (Sydney: Angus & Robertson, 1991).

Bebbington, Warren (ed.), *The Oxford Companion to Australian Music* (Melbourne: Oxford University Press, 1997).

Bennett, Bruce, *Spirit in Exile: Peter Porter and His Poetry* (Melbourne: Oxford University Press, 1991).

Braddon, Russell (ed.), *Australia Fair?* (London: Methuen, 1984).

Braddon, Russell, *End of a Hate* (London: Cassell, 1958).

Braddon, Russell, *Joan Sutherland* (Sydney: Collins, 1962).

Brisbane, Katharine (ed.), *Entertaining Australia: An Illustrated History* (Sydney: Currency Press, 1991).

Britain, Ian, *Once an Australian* (Melbourne: Oxford University Press, 1997).

Clark, Kenneth, MacInnes, Colin and Robertson, Bryan, *Sidney Nolan* (London: Thames and Hudson, 1961).

Coleman, Peter, *The Real Barry Humphries* (London: Robson Books, 1990).

Dalton, Robin, *An Incidental Memoir* (Ringwood, Vic.: Viking, 1998).

Davidson, Jim, *The Expatriates* (Geelong: Deakin University, 1978).

Delamothe, Tony and Bridge, Carl (eds), *Interpreting Australia: British Perceptions of Australia since 1970* (London: Sir Robert Menzies Centre for Australian Studies, University of London, 1988).

Dundy, Elaine, *Finch Bloody Finch* (London: Magnum, 1981).

Eakin, Robin, *Aunts up the Cross* (Melbourne: Macmillan, 1967).

Earnest, Ernest, *Expatriates and Patriots: American Artists, Scholars and Writers in Europe* (Durham, N.C.: Duke University Press, 1968).

Fanon, Frantz, *Black Skin, White Masks* (London: Paladin, 1970).

Faulkner, Trader, *Peter Finch* (London: Angus & Robertson, 1979).

Grinberg, Leon and Rebeca, *Psychoanalytic Perspectives on Migration and Exile* (New Haven: Yale University Press, 1989).

Hergenhan, L. T. (ed.), *The Penguin New Literary History of Australia* (Ringwood, Vic.: Penguin, 1988).

Hoff, Ursula, *The Art of Arthur Boyd* (London: André Deutsch, 1986).

Holloway, Peter (ed.), *Contemporary Australian Drama* (Sydney: Currency Press, 1981, new edition, 1987).

Humphries, Barry, *More Please: An Autobiography* (Ringwood, Vic.: Penguin, 1992).

Inglis, K. S., 'Going Home: Australians in England, 1870-1900' in D. Fitzpatrick (ed.), *Home or Away? Immigrants in Colonial Australia* (Canberra: Research School of Social Sciences, Australian National University, 1992).

James, Clive, *Unreliable Memoirs* (London: Jonathan Cape, 1980).

Kinnane, Garry, *George Johnston: A Biography* (Melbourne: Nelson, 1986).

Knightley, Phillip, *A Hack's Progress* (London: Jonathan Cape, 1997).

Lawler, Ray, *The Piccadilly Bushman* (London: Angus & Robertson, 1961).

Lynn, Elwyn, *Sidney Nolan: Myth and Imagery* (Melbourne: Macmillan, 1967).

Madden, A. F. and Morris-Jones, W. H. (eds), *Australia and Britain: Studies in a Changing Relationship* (Sydney: Sydney University Press, 1980).

Major, Norma, *Joan Sutherland* (London: Queen Anne Press/Futura, 1987).

McKern, Leo, *Just Resting* (London: Methuen, 1983).

Millar, T. B. (ed.), *The Australian Contribution to Britain* (London: Australian Studies Centre, University of London, 1988).

Nixon, Rob, *London Calling: V. S. Naipaul, Postcolonial Mandarin* (New York: Oxford University Press, 1992).

Parsons, P. (ed.), *A Companion to Theatre in Australia* (Sydney: Currency Press/ Cambridge University Press, 1995).

Pesman, Ros, *Duty Free: Australian Women Abroad* (Melbourne: Oxford University Press, 1996).

Phelan, Nancy, *Charles Mackerras: A Musician's Musician* (Melbourne: Oxford University Press, 1987 and London: Victor Gollancz, 1987).

Phillips, A. A. 'The Cultural Cringe' in his *The Australian Tradition: Studies in a Colonial Culture* (Melbourne: Cheshire, 1958).

Pilger, John, *Heroes* (London: Pan, 1987).

Pilger, John, *A Secret Country* (London: Jonathan Cape, 1989).

Prampolini, Gaetano and Hubert, Marie-Christine (eds), *An Antipodean Collection: Australian Writers, Artists and Travellers in Tuscany* (Geneva: Slatkine, 1993).

Rickards, Jocelyn, *A Painted Banquet: My Life and Loves* (London: Weidenfeld and Nicolson, 1987).

Said, Edward, 'Reflections on exile', *Granta*, no. 13 (Autumn 1984), pp. 157-72.

Sayle, Murray, 'As far as you can go', in Timothy O'Keefe (ed.), *Alienation* (London: MacGibbon and Kee, 1960).

Serle, Geoffrey, *From Deserts the Prophets Come: The Creative Spirit in Australia 1788-1972* (Melbourne: Heinemann, 1973, revised edition, 1987, entitled *The Creative Spirit in Australia: A Cultural History*).

Smith, Bernard with Smith, Terry, *Australian Painting 1788–1990* (Melbourne: Oxford University Press, 1991).

Sutherland, Joan, *A Prima Donna's Progress* (London: Orion/Sydney: Random House Australia, 1997).

Tabori, Paul *The Anatomy of Exile* (London: Harrap, 1972).

Travellers, Journeys, Tourists, Australian Cultural History, no. 10 (1991).

Wallace, Christine, *Greer: Untamed Shrew* (Melbourne: Macmillan, 1997).

Wilde, William H., Hooton, Joy and Andrews, Barry (eds), *The Oxford Companion to Australian Literature* (Melbourne: Oxford University Press, 1985, second edition, 1994).

Index

306